BRIAN GLANVILLE covered the 1958, 1962, 1966 and 1970 World Cup tournaments for *The Sunday Times*. His speciality has always been world soccer and he lived for several years in Italy covering football for *Corriere Dello Sport* of Rome, etc. He scripted and part-edited the well-known film on the 1966 World Cup, *Goal!*, which won the British Film Academy's Award as Best Documentary of the Year. His books *Goalkeepers are Crazy* and *The Rise of Gerry Logan* represent the first serious fiction written about professional soccer. *The Footballer's Companion* (1962) is an exhaustive anthology of the best writing on the game, both here and in Europe, while in *People in Sport* (1967) he has produced a selection of the best from his own writings. *Soccer: A Panorama* (1969) is, as its name suggests, a full and compact world history of the game.

Cover photograph shows Rimmer of Manchester United saving a header from Geoff Hurst of West Ham United in the match played on 17 *January*, 1970. *Picture courtesy of Football Monthly.*

In the same series
in Mayflower Books

WORLD FOOTBALL HANDBOOK 1969
WORLD FOOTBALL HANDBOOK 1970

World Football Handbook 1971

Compiled by
Brian Glanville

A Mayflower Paperback

WORLD FOOTBALL HANDBOOK 1971

Compiled by
Brian Glanville

Published as a Mayflower Original 1970

Mayflower Paperbacks are published by Mayflower Books,
3 Upper James Street, London, W.1.
Made and printed in Great Britain by
C. Nicholls & Company Ltd.,
The Philips Park Press, Manchester

Table of Contents

Chapter One
World Cup 1970 7

Chapter Two
World Cup Qualifying Competition 22

Chapter Three
European Cup 1969–70 42

Chapter Four
European Cupwinners' Cup 1969–70 55

Chapter Five
European Inter Cities Fairs Cup, 1969–70 66

Chapter Six
South American Liberators' Cup 1970 87

Chapter Seven
World Club Championship 1969 89

Chapter Eight
British International Tournament 1970 92

Chapter Nine
Friendly Internationals against Foreign Opposition 1969–70 98

Chapter Ten
Friendly Internationals involving Foreign Teams 1969–70 104

Chapter Eleven
FA Cup, Scottish Cup and Football League Cup 1969–70 107

Chapter Twelve
Football League and Scottish League 1969–70 112

Chapter Thirteen
African Nations Cup 1970 116

Chapter Fourteen
World Stars 118

Chapter Fifteen
World Cup History 129

Chapter Sixteen
World Cup Championship History 197

Chapter Seventeen
European Nations Cup History 203

Chapter Eighteen
European Cup History 210

Chapter Nineteen
European Cupwinners' Cup History 238

Chapter Twenty
European Inter Cities Fairs Cup History 255

Chapter Twenty-one
South American Championship History 272

Chapter Twenty-two
South American Cup History 273

Chapter Twenty-three
Olympic Football 274

Chapter Twenty-four
England and Great Britain versus The Rest 277

Chapter One

World Cup 1970

For the third time in four years, Brazil won the World Cup, and very properly retained the Jules Rimet trophy in consequence. There was no doubt at all of the merits of their success, even if the Italian team they crushed 4–1 in the Final could scarcely claim to be the competition's second best. Brazil won every one of their matches, including a narrow and slightly fortunate win against England – thus condemned to play their quarter final in Leon, against West Germany.

Most teams seemed to solve the problem of altitude, but that of heat was simply insoluble. Goodness knows how much the temperatures in Guadalajara, which sometimes rose as high as 98° in a match, affected the England players. In the circumstances, they acquitted themselves with honour, especially Bobby Moore, rising superbly above the dingy and unfounded charges of theft brought against him in Columbia.

From an objective point of view, the success of a Brazilian team so wholeheartedly committed to attack – and definitely porous in defence – was a splendid sign in a grey footballing world. For the next four years, one was entitled to hope, the future might at long last lie with creative rather than negative football.

Brazil's triumph was the more remarkable in that they had changed horses, or managers, rather further than mid-stream, Zagalo, a hero of their 1958 and 1962 teams, succeeding the controversial Joao Saldanha.

The tournament opened, as it did in 1966, with a dull 0–0 draw; this time in the torrid heat of the Azteca Stadium, between Mexico and Russia. The Mexicans, who had lost one of their best young players, Onofre, with a broken leg, a few days earlier, and unwisely left out their most thrustful forward, Enrique Borja, who had very nearly been omitted from the 22 for "political reasons", had rather the better of things. At least they obliged the sound Russian goalkeeper, Kavazashvili, to make saves from the lively Horacio Lopez and Guzman, in the first and second halves respectively. Lopez, in the second half, received the ball in a surprisingly unmarked position, but was too slow to score.

Evriuzhikin was lively on Russia's left wing in the opening stages, but by the last twenty minutes, their cautious side had manifestly run out of steam. Asatiani made ocasional promising breaks from midfield, and Bychevetz had his moments, but all in all it was a dull Russian display.

On Tuesday, in Guadalajara, England deservedly beat Rumania 1–0, playing an efficient, disciplined game, in which they were given no protection by a Belgian referee, M. Loraux, who did not even caution Mocanu, Rumania's left-back, after three dreadful fouls on Newton (whom he put out of the game), Lee and Wright, Newton's substitute. The only goal came after twenty minutes of the second half when Ball crossed from the right, and the ball reached Geoff Hurst, via the head of Francis Lee. Very calmly, Hurst controlled the ball, beat his man, and pivoted to hit a low, left-footed cross shot into the far corner of goal.

The Rumanians attacked briskly in the opening minutes, but later settled down to what Alan Ball termed scornfully "keep ball". They did have two powerful long range shots in the second half, by Dembrowski and Nunweiller VI, but Banks got to them both. Moore had an excellent game in the England defence, Terry Cooper was superbly adventurous, and Bobby Charlton showed more fire and drive than for many an international.

In Leon, on the same day, in Group IV, an extraordinary and fascinating game between Peru and Bulgaria saw the Bulgarians go two ahead, cleverly exploiting free kicks, only for the Peruvians to recover superbly and score three times, to win.

There was a minute's silence at the start for victims of the appalling Peruvian earthquake, and it was small wonder that the Peruvians started badly. Dermendijev scored the first goal after 13 minutes, when he ran over the ball and on, to convert a cleverly taken free kick. Perhaps the Peruvians expected the same tactic in the second half when, after 4 minutes, Bulgaria were awarded another free kick on the edge of the box. But Bonvev drove the ball straight past a goalkeeper who might have had it.

The Peruvians had changed their right-back Campos for Javier Gonzalez, thus tightening a porous defence. But it was the substitution of the young centre-forward, Hugo Sotil, for the fast coloured winger, Baylon, just after Gallardo had scored with a cross shot just after Bonev's goal, which was decisive. The Peruvian 4–2–4 formation really began to move, and when Sotil was fouled, it was Chumpitaz's turn to surprise a goalkeeper directly from a free kick. With 65 minutes played, Cubillas ran on to a long ball from Mifflin and beat Chalamanov to shoot home again; the winning goal.

At Puebla, in Group II, Uruguay won unimpressively, 2–0, against a stalwart Israeli team. The Uruguayans' poor performance was not unconnected with the fact that they lost their key midfield player, Pedro Rocha, with a serious injury, after only 12 minutes.

The following day, in Guadalajara, Brazil took the field and charmed everybody with an effervescent 4–1 win over the Czechs. The Mexicans, who had long since decided to cheer Brazil and jeer England, were particularly pleased, but there was a touch of unreality about it all. Having shown up the obvious holes in the Brazilian defence and taken an early lead through Petras, the Czechs conceded an equaliser directly from Rivelino's ferocious left-footed free kick; and fell to pieces.

They conceded a second goal, early in the second half when Pelé, in splendid form, was allowed to catch Gerson's long left footed pass on his chest, control it and score. Kvasniak, who had come on as substitute after the interval, to play at a snail's pace, missed the easiest of equalising chances from a corner; and away went Brazil immediately to make it 3–1. The powerful Jairzinho looked offside when he strode on to Gerson's pass, lobbed the goalkeeper, and ran the ball in, but the goal stood.

Desperate now to score, the Czechs left larger gaps than ever, and Jairzinho forced his way admirably past three men to get a fourth. He, Gerson, Pelé and Rivelino had looked formidable; but the England players were unperturbed. After all, the Czech marking had been scandalously slack.

In Group I, Belgium had no great trouble in beating El Salvador 3–0 at the Azteca in an undistinguished game. Magana, the Salvador goalkeeper, kept the score down, but Belgium, who went ahead though a long shot by Van Moer after only two minutes, were anything but effective in attack. Their third goal came from the tournament's first penalty, converted by Lambert.

The great surprise of the day, and of the tournament so far, came at Leon in Group IV, where Morocco gave West Germany the fright of their lives. Playing with skill and spirit, Morocco deservedly led after 20 minutes when Hottges headed weakly back to Maier, in goal, and the ball dropped at the feet of Houmane – who coolly scored.

Morocco stayed ahead till the 56th minute, when Uwe Seeler converted Muller's pass with a strong ground shot. 12 minutes from time, Grabowski got away on the right wing, Loehr headed against the bar, and Muller put it in. It had been an awfully close call and a splendid riposte by the Moroccans to their many detractors.

In Group II, at Toluca, Italy squeezed through against Sweden with a goal scored from long range after 11 minutes by Domenghini, after Giacinto Facchetti had played the ball back to him from his corner. Thereafter, an Italian team which had been shaken by a contretemps between Rivera and its officials, was content to hold on to its lead. It may be said in passing that England and Bobby Moore had shown no adverse reactions at all to his misadventures in Bogota, where he'd been held in custody for several days on a manifestly absurd charge of stealing a bracelet.

The next round of matches, the following Saturday, saw Russia come most powerfully and unexpectedly out of their shells. Before a huge crowd in Mexico City, they showed the other, offensive side of their Jekyll and Hyde personality, demolishing Belgium with superb attacking football, in which Asatiani, Muntijan, Bychevetz and Evriuzhikin were outstanding, while Albert Chesternijev, that ever faithful bird dog, was massive in defence, and excellent in distribution.

Belgium might have led after 14 minutes, when Kavazashvili made a fine save from Van Moer's header, but from that point, Russia took over the game. A minute later, Bychevetz went through to open the score. Piot's saves kept Russia at bay till 12 minutes into the second half, then Asatiani, tall and strong, broke through to beat Piot with a ground shot. Two minutes more, and Bychevetz scored again, this time a right footed shot, and Khmelnitzki headed the fourth from an exchange with Evriuzhikin. Belgium's consolatory goal was scored by Lambert, after Kavazashvili had blocked Van Himst's drive.

In Puebla, Italy, interested only in survival, played a dreary draw against Uruguay without Pedro Rocha. Italy's plan to put all their eggs in the basket of Gigi Riva had certainly not borne fruit so far.

In Group III, at Guadalajara, the Czechs again took an early lead through the blond Petras, this time heading in Bohumil Vesely's right wing centre, but again were betrayed by their lack of condition. In the second half, Neagu wriggled through on the left to equalise, and when, 31 minutes into the second half, Neagu was brought down by Zlocha, Dumitrache converted the penalty to keep Rumanian hopes alive, and end those of the Czechs. The win was just about deserved.

In Leon, the Peruvians were held by the brave Moroccans till the 65th minute, but then the storm broke, and Sotil, Challe and Cubillas scored goals in a comfortable win.

Next day came the clash all Mexico, and the football world, awaited; England against Brazil. Till three o'clock in the morning, Brazilians and Mexicans deliberately laid siege to the Hilton Hotel where England were staying, with chants and motor horns, doing their best – and not without success – to keep the players awake. The police played an ominously passive role. Despite this, and the fact that the match was played at high noon, in 98 degrees of heat, England put up a magnificent performance, against splendid opponents. Had the World Cup committee not prostituted the tournament to European television, fixing all kick off times in the afternoon, who knows what might have happened? As it was, the rain broke in the afternoon, so that a 4 p.m. kick off might have made all the difference to England. But as Bobby Moore, who played another superlative game, said, "We couldn't have come any nearer. They made one chance, and took it."

This was after 14 minutes of the second half, when brilliant control by Tostao, on the left, took out three England players. Pelé, well policed by Mullery but always dangerous, rolled the ball across goal to Jairzinho, who scored at leisure.

England, however, missed chances aplenty. In the first half, Geoff Hurst stopped, believing himself in an offside position, then shot feebly, when he might have run on. Late in the second half, when Jeff Astle and Colin Bell had replaced Bobby Charlton and Francis Lee, Astle nodded down a chance which Ball should have exploited, while Astle himself missed parlously, when a defender played the ball to his feet. Later, Alan Ball clipped the bar with Felix, Brazil's uncertain goalkeeper, beaten.

But the finest save of the match was made after 10 minutes by Gordon Banks, when Jairzinho eluded Terry Cooper, crossed, and Pelé headed ferociously to the left-hand corner. Somehow Banks got across his goal to turn the ball over the top with one hand. In the second half, he made other fine saves from Paulo Cesar, twice, Rivelino and Jairzinho. Brazil clearly and badly missed their injured general, Gerson.

In Group I, Mexico made an easy meal of El Salvador, while in Leon, West Germany suddenly and devastatingly came to life, ripping apart what had once been considered a tough Bulgarian defence, to score five.

Libuda, the gifted but inconsistent right winger, had one of his most devastatingly effective games. After slack marking had allowed Nikodimov to give Bulgaria the lead from Bonev's free kick, he rounded Gaganelov and shot past Simeonov to equalise. He then beat the left-back again to make a furiously volleyed goal for Muller; then, when Nikodimov brought him down early in the second half, Muller converted the penalty. Seeler got the fourth, but Libuda was again involved in the fifth. Fouled on the edge of the box, he placed his free kick expertly for Muller to head a fine goal.

In Toluca, Israel surprised the disappointing Swedes in a very tough game, watched by only 3,000. Turesson put Sweden ahead after 54 minutes, but three minutes later, Spiegler shot the equaliser.

Brazil won their third and final qualifying game in Guadalajara in intense afternoon heat, the next Wednesday, though the Rumanians, after a bad beginning, gave them quite a game of it. Pelé, who once more had some jewelled moments, scored the first goal from a sizzling right footed after 19 minutes, Tostao jumping over the ball, and also scored the third Brazilian goal, 21 minutes into the second half, stretching out an elastic leg to push in Tostao's square pass – from Jairzinho's centre. The winger himself scored the second, the 22nd minute, after Paulo Cesar had beaten his back and gone to the line.

But Dumitrache exploited Brazil's central defensive weaknesses to get back a goal, and Dembrowski, heading in Satmareanu's cross, scored a second, seven minutes from the end. Weak goalkeeping was again a clear Brazilian failing, though it's true that the lack of Rivelino and Gerson deprived the team of strength in attack.

In Leon, Gerd Muller scored a hat trick, bringing his total to seven, and West Germany beat Peru 3–1, to lead their group. Playing with Schnellinger as sweeper, Uwe Seeler in midfield, two wingers lying wide and sending in high crosses, Germany riddled Peru's weak defence in the first half. Muller seldom moved out of the middle, but he exploited those chances he had splendidly; one of his goals was a superb header. In the second half, Germany seemed to run out of steam in the heat and altitude, and the Peruvians got one goal back and might have had more, were it not for the fine goalkeeping of Maier.

In Group II, there was a small scandal. The Uruguay v Sweden game should have been refereed by the Brazilian, Moraes, but he was replaced owing to rumours that there had been attempts to "buy" him. The Uruguayans denied them violently, played under protest – and lost to an 89th minute goal headed from a right wing cross by Grahn. Nevertheless, they squeezed through to the quarter-finals on goal difference.

In Mexico City, El Salvador defended to the death against Russia, but couldn't hold out in the second half, when the Russians scored twice through Bychevetz, exploiting a fine pass by Muntijan, and repeated the combination after 73 minutes.

Mexico then proceeded to qualify on the Thursday, beating the disappointing Belgians 1–0, thanks to a strongly disputed penalty, converted by Pena.

In Toluca, Italy disgraced themselves again in Group II, easily the poorest and most disappointing of the four, by allowing themselves to be held to a goalless draw by Israel, despite the presence of millions of lire worth of stars.

England, in Group III, were scarcely much better. They qualified thanks to their meagre 1–0 victory over Czechoslovakia, but their performance was wretched in the extreme. The changes made by Ramsey may have rested star players, but they decisively weakened the side. Jackie Charlton looked clumsily unhappy against the quick Petras, while Jeff Astle, till he was replaced in the second half by Peter Osgood, was totally inept. Bobby Charlton, equalling Billy Wright's record by playing in his 105th international, was also replaced; by Alan Ball – and things did improve a little. The one goal came early in the second half, when Kuna tackled Colin Bell, then fell on the ball and handled it. The handling may or may not have been intentional; afterwards, the French referee, M. Machin, indicated that he'd given it for a trip. Be that as it may, Allan Clarke coolly converted it – and England were sonorously whistled till the end of play. Three balls went into the crowd, and were not thrown back.

Cooper, the superb Moore, Newton and Mullery could look back on the game with satisfaction, but the Czechs were the smoother, more intelligent team, and were several times unlucky not to score – not least when Dobias' fine shot tore through Banks' hands and struck the crossbar, late in the second half – not long after Alan Ball had struck the bar for England. This apart, Banks had another excellent game.

In Leon, the Moroccans again distinguished themselves, and the Bulgarians once more disappointed gloomily, in a drawn match. Though Bulgaria took the lead with a soft goal from Jetchev's long range ground shot, Morocco fought back well, to equalise through Chazouani.

The eight quarter finalists were thus Mexico, Russia, Italy, Uruguay, Brazil, England, West Germany and Peru, with Brazil and West Germany looking much the best propositions, on form.

England went out in the quarter-finals, in Leon, to West Germany; in a match they seemed to have well won, and virtually in their pockets. It may well have been that the vicissitudes, the physical strain, of Group III took its toll in the end, it may well have been that to substitute Bobby Charlton and Martin Peters with Colin Bell and Norman Hunter was a mistake. Be that as it may, they would probably have kept their 2–0 lead had Gordon Banks not been taken ill the day before the match and forced to withdraw. His place went to Peter Bonetti, who played well enough till he was beaten by a long, diagonal shot from the edge of the area by Franz Beckenbauer. Banks, one felt, would have had that shot, and at least one of the other German goals.

For more than an hour, England played superbly, and they well deserved their two, excellent goals. The first – his own first goal in international football – was brilliantly engineered and scored by Alan Mullery. Midway through the first half, he exchanged passes with Lee, hit a fine crossfield pass to Keith Newton, then raced to the far post to smash in the responding centre.

Five minutes after half-time, Newton crossed for another fine goal, after receiving from the excellent Geoff Hurst. This time, it was Peters, much sharper in this game, who ran the ball in.

The substitution of Grabowski for Libuda on Germany's right wing was of decisive value. Where Libuda had been mastered, Grabowski was irresistible, and the balance tipped in the hot sunshine. Beckenbauer scored his goal, Hurst almost made it 3–1 with a glorious low header which beat Maier but skimmed the far post – then Schnellinger's high centre caused chaos in the tired England defence and Uwe Seeler back-headed the equaliser.

So the game, like the 1966 Final, went to extra time. Lee wriggled past Schnellinger on the line and pushed the ball across for Hurst to score; but the goal was mysteriously disallowed. Lee wasn't offside, nor had he fouled Schnellinger. So, in the second period of extra time, Grabowski beat Cooper again and crossed, Loehr returned the ball, and Muller, who had been kept quiet for most of the game, banged it home, in the goalmouth. The holders were out; in a game they should have won.

Bobby Moore had another superlative game, while Bobby Charlton, also in impressive form, beat Billy Wright's record by winning his 106th England cap.

Perhaps the largest surprise of the quarter finals was that both Group II teams, Italy and Uruguay, should get through, despite their previous drab form. The Italians played Mexico in Toluca and crushed them with a splendid second half, in which Luigi Riva, with two goals, finally justified the Messianic campaign there had been in his favour throughout Italy, while Gianni Rivera substituted Mazzola at half time and splendidly organised the Italian forward line. This was deeply satisfying to a player who had been dropped from the first match, and very nearly sent home after outspokenly criticising the team's officials. Mexico opened the score after only 12 minutes when Munguia and Fragoso set up a goal for Gonzalez, but once Italy had equalised through a deflected shot by Domenghini, they lost their grip on the game. Italy's vastly superior skills asserted themselves; as they should have done in previous games.

In Mexico City, the Uruguayans, still without Rocha, most unexpectedly beat Russia with a disputed goal in the last moments of extra time, thus justifying their astonishing record in the World Cup. Esparrago got it, after Cubilla, a very active striker, had beaten

Chesternijev and crossed from the goal line. The Russians bitterly protested that the ball had gone out of play; but though they had some near misses, they'd only themselves to blame for a lack of flair and punch in attack.

In Guadalajara, Brazil beat Peru 4–2 in an expectedly high scoring game, full of goal scoring errors. With Gerson and Rivelino back in the six, Brazil took the lead through the latter and increased it through Tostao. Gallardo made it 1–2 after 27 minutes, Tostao restored the two goal margin after 52, Gallardo scored again after a rebound from Brito, but a splendid individual goal by Jairzinho made the game safe for Brazil.

The semi-finals were won, respectively, by Italy in Mexico City and Brazil in Guadalajara. Italy's victory over West Germany was achieved in a match of extraordinary ups and downs, which will long be the source of argument. Should West Germany have had one, or even two, penalty kicks? Would they have won if Franz Beckenbauer had not been injured, and forced to play extra time with his arm strapped to his chest? Would the Germans have been favoured by a stronger, better referee than the ineptly permissive Yamasaki?

On the other hand, it must be confessed that in the second half, when they dominated an over-cautious Italy, they missed chances in superabundance. It was in the third minute of injury time that Grabowski, from the left, crossed the ball, and Karl Heinz Schnellinger banged it home for Germany's belated equaliser.

Italy had taken the lead with a good left-footed goal by Boninsegna, hit from the edge of the box after a lucky rebound from two German defenders. Only seven and a half minutes had gone, and with Italy's *catenaccio* subduing the German attack, the Italians seemed firmly entrenched.

In the second half, they brought on Gianni Rivera for Mazzola, as they'd so successfully done against Mexico. But now they lost control of midfield, went back too cautiously into defence, and surrendered their initiative to a German team which proceeded to bombard them. Seeler missed a fine chance when Cera allowed the ball to pass him, then Grabowski and Overath missed fine opportunities. Beckenbauer raced through with marvellous fluency, only to be ruthlessly chopped down on the edge of the box; an incident which cost Germany not only a probable goal but the later services of Beckenbauer.

Desperate, they took off Patzke, brought on Siggi Held – full of fire and running – and abandoned their own *catenaccio*. Held's tremendous shot was stopped on the line, Albertosi made a fine save from Seeler's header; and at last came the equaliser.

Extra time brought a flurry of goals. Germany went ahead after five minutes when Poletti ran the ball almost over his own line, and Gerd Muller provided the finishing touch. Burgnich materialised to score after Rivera's free kick, Riva pivoted to beat Schnellinger and score with a splendid left foot cross shot, and the first period ended. In the second, Seeler had another header saved by Albertosi. From the corner, however, he nodded across goal for Muller to fling himself to head an equaliser. The winner came after six minutes, Boninsegna breaking on the left, then pulling the ball back for Gianni Rivera to score.

In Guadalajara, Uruguay, still without Rocha, embarrassed Brazil by taking the lead with a somewhat ludicrous goal. Coming in from the right, along the goal line, Cubilla was confronted by Wilson Piazza. His shot, if that is what it was, went by Piazza, bounced past Felix, and ended in the goal.

It was only late in the first half that Brazil equalised through a fine goal by Clodoaldo, running through on the blind side. From that point, their superiority manifested itself. This, though Felix was obliged to make one glorious save from a header by Cubilla.

Despite the various ingenuities of Pelé, however, the second Brazilian goal did not arrive till 14 minutes from time, after a marvellous run down the right wing and shot into the far corner, by Jairzinho. A left-footed shot by Rivelino, in the very last minute, made it 3–1. Uruguay had resisted nobly against the highly gifted Brazilian team.

The third place match, which lacked Rocha, Beckenbauer and Grabowski, was a curious, paradoxical, entertaining affair, won 1–0 by a West German team which, manifestly weary, could have given away four or five goals. Twice, in the closing stages of first half, Schnellinger made remarkable saves from Montero-Castillo.

The only goal, scored after 27 minutes, was a splendid one. Libuda, always the master of Mujica, beat him once again and crossed. Seeler, astonishing as always in the air, headed back across goal to Muller, who played the ball backwards to Overath. Overath, who had been spreading some glorious passes around, now produced an equally glorious shot, which flew wide of Mazurkiewicz's left hand.

From that point, most of the pressure was Uruguay's, but Mazurkiewicz, in the second half, still had to make a couple of thrilling saves from sharp German attacks. In the event, however, it was Horst Wolter, who had been scrambling sadly for high crosses throughout the game, who saved it for Germany, brilliantly saving Ancheta's header.

Brazil, overwhelming favourites to win the Final against Italy, won it . . . overwhelmingly. This, though they did let Italy back into the game late in the first half, with a silly defensive mistake. Their football, almost throughout, was wonderfully assured, technically adroit, calm and deadly. For Italy, only the stout-hearted, incisive Sandro Mazzola and the lively Boninsegna – who was mysteriously substituted – reached the same high plateau attained by so many of the Brazilians. Gerson, who was given a bewildering amount of room by Italy, was once more his team's chief orchestrator, and restored their lead in the second half with a marvellous left-footed shot on the turn from outside the penalty box.

Pelé may have had more spectacular games, but what can one say about a player who heads one goal and makes two others? Tostao bravely laid off fine balls throughout the match, under formidable pressure, Jairzinho ran with his usual insistent power, Clodoaldo recovered from his mistake to play with high skill and resilience in midfield.

Brazil took the lead after 18 minutes when Pelé leaped gymnastically to Rivelino's high cross from the left and headed it in. Bertini, who had let him slip, was promptly banished to right-back, Burgnich taking his place in the middle. With Carlos Alberto finding infinite space on the right – his ultimate goal was a long time a-looming – Brazil seemed to have the game well in hand. But with seven minutes left till half-time, Clodoaldo's foolish backheel threw his defence into tatters, Felix rushed hastily out of goal, and Boninsegna had only to kick the ball into an empty net.

Italy, with Mazzola running and dribbling and passing beautifully, seemed to be back in the game. But Gerson's goal stunned them after 21 minutes, and from that point, Brazil took charge again. Five minutes later, they scored a third when Gerson took a free kick, Pelé touched the ball on to Jairzinho and the outside-right ran it in, on the left hand post.

Italy substituted Juliano for Bertini, Rivera inexplicably for Boninsegna, but it made no difference, other than to diminish their thrust up front. Three minutes from time, another finely articulated Brazilian movement concluded with Jairzinho finding Pelé, who laid the ball off perfectly for Carlos Alberto to come thundering in to score his captain's goal. It was, all in all, a fine day for football.

WORLD CUP 1970

GROUP I Mexico City

Mexico (0) 0 *Russia* (0) 0
Mexico: Calderon; Vantolra, Pena, Guzman, Perez; Hernandez, Pulido, Velarde (Munguia); Valdivia, Fragoso, Horacio Lopez.
Russia: Kavazashvili; Lovchev, Chesternijev, Kaplichni, Logofet, Serebrianikov (Pusacs), Muntijan, Asatiani; Nodia (Porjujan), Bychevetz, Evriuzhikin.

Belgium (1) 3 *El Salvador* (0) 0
Belgium: Piot; Heylens, Thissen; Dewalque, Dockx, Semmeling, Van Moer, Devrindt, Van Himst, Lambert, Puis.
El Salvador: Magaña, Rivas, Mariona, Osorio, Manzano; Quintanilla, Vazquez, Cabezas; Rodriguez, Martinez, Aparicio.
Scorers: Van Moer (2), Lambert, penalty for Belgium.

Russia (1) 4 *Belgium* (0) 1
Russia: Kavazashvili; Dzodzuashvili (Kiselev), Chesternijev, Khurtsilava, Afonin, Kaplichni (Lovchev); Asatiani, Muntijan; Bychevetz, Evriuzhikin, Khmelnitzki.
Belgium: Piot; Heylens, Thissen, Dewalque, Jeck, Dockx, Semmeling, Van Moer, Van Himst, Puis, Lambert.
Scorers: Bychevetz 2, Asatiani, Khmelnitzki.

Mexico (1) 4 *El Salvador* (0) 0
Mexico: Calderon; Vantolra, Pena, Guzman, Perez; Gonzalez, Munguia; Valdivia (Basaguren, then Lopez), Fragoso, Padilla.
El Salvador: Magana; Rivas, Mariona, Osorio, Cortes (Monge); Quintanilla, Vazquez, Cabezas; Rodriguez, Martinez, Aparicio (Mendez.)
Scorers: Valdivia 2, Fragoso, Basaguren, for Mexico.

Russia (0) 2 *El Salvador* (0) 0
Russia: Kavazashvili; Dzodzuashvili, Khurtsilava, Chesternijev, Afonin; Kiselev (Asatiani), Serebrianikov, Muntijan; Pusacs, (Evriuzhikin), Bychevetz, Khmelnitzki.
El Salvador: Magana; Rivas, Mariona, Castro, Osorio, Vazquez; Portillo, Cabezas (Aparicio), Rodriguez (Sermeno), Mendez, Monge.
Scorers: Bychevetz 2 for Russia.

Mexico (1) 1 *Belgium* (0) 0
Mexico: Claderon; Vantolra, Guzman, Pena, Perez; Gonzalez, Munguia, Pulido; Padilla, Fragoso, Valdivia (Basaguren).
Belgium: Piot; Heylens, Jeck, Dockx, Thissen, Dewalque, Polleunis (Devrindt), Semmeling, Van Moer, Van Himst, Puis.
Scorer: Pena (penalty) for Mexico.

Placings

	P	W	D	L	F	A	Pts
Mexico	3	2	1	0	5	0	5
Russia	3	2	1	0	6	1	5
Belgium	3	1	0	2	4	5	2
El Salvador	3	0	0	3	0	9	0

GROUP II Puebla, Toluca.

Uruguay (1) 2 *Israel* (0) 0
Uruguay: Mazurkiewicz; Ubinas, Mujica; Montero Castillo, Ancheta, Matosas; Cubilla, Esparrago, Maneiro, Rocha (Cortes), Lozado.
Israel: Vissoker; Bello, Rosen, Daniel, Talbi (Bar), Schwager (Vollach), Rosenthal, Shum, Spiegler, Spiegel, Faygenbaum.
Scorers: Maneiro, Mujica for Uruguay.
Italy (1) 1 *Sweden* (0) 0
Italy: Albertosi; Burgnich, Facchetti; Cera, Niccolai, Bertini; Domenghini, Mazzola, Boninsegna, De Sisti, Riva.
Sweden: Hellstrom; Nordqvist, Grip, Svensson, Axelsson, Larsson; Grahn, Eriksson, Kindvall, Kronqvist, Olsson.

Uruguay (0) 0 *Italy* (0)0
Uruguay: Mazurkiewicz; Ubinas, Ancheta, Matosas, Mujica; Cortes, Montero Castillo, Maniziro; Cubilla, Esparrago, Bareno (Zubia).
Italy: Albertosi; Burgnich, Cera, Rosato, Facchetti; De Sisti, Bertini, Mazzola, Domenghini (Furino), Boninsegna, Riva.

Sweden (0) 1 *Israel* (0) 1
Sweden: Larsson, Selander, Axelsson, Grip, Svensson, Bo Larsson, Nordahl, Turesson, Kindvall, Persson, Olsson.
Israel: Vissoker; Primo, Rosen, Bar, Rosenthal, Shum, Schwager, Spiegel, Vollach, Spiegler, Faygenbaum.
Scorers: Turesson for Sweden, Spiegler for Israel.

Sweden (0) 1 *Uruguay* (0) 0
Sweden: Selander; Nordqvist, Axelsson, Grip, Svensson, Larsson, B., Eriksson, Larsson S-G., Kindvall, Nicklasson (Grahn), Persson (Turesson).
Uruguay: Mazurkiewicz; Ubinas, Ancheta, Matosas, Mujica; Montero Castillo, Maneiro, Cortes; Esparrago, Zubia, Losada.
Scorer: Grahn for Sweden.

Italy (0) 0 *Israel* (0) 0
Italy: Albertosi; Burgnich, Facchetti; Cera, Rosato, Bertini; Domenghini (Rivera), Mazzola, Boninsegna, De Sisti, Riva.
Israel: Vissoker; Primo, Bello, Bar, Rosenthal, Rosen, Shum, Spiegel, Faygenbaum (Daniel), Spiegler, Schwager.

Placings

	P	W	D	L	F	A	Pts
Italy	3	1	2	0	1	0	4
Uruguay	3	1	1	1	2	1	3
Sweden	3	1	1	1	2	2	3
Israel	3	0	2	1	1	3	2

GROUP III. Guadalajara

England (0) 1 *Rumania* (0) 0
England: Banks (Stoke City); Newton (Everton), (sub. Wright (Everton)), Cooper (Leeds United); Mullery (Spurs), Labone (Everton), Moore (West Ham United); Lee (Manchester City) (sub. Osgood (Chelsea)), Charlton (Manchester United), Hurst (West Ham United), Peters (Spurs).
Rumania: Adamache; Satmareanu, Lupescu, Dinu, Mocanu; Dumitru, Nunweiller VI; Dembrowski, Tataru, Dumitrache, Lucescu.
Scorer: Hurst for England.

Brazil (1) 4 *Czechoslovakia* (1) 1
Brazil: Felix; Carlos Alberto, Piazza, Brito, Everaldo; Clodoaldo, Gerson (Paulo Cesar), Jairzinho, Tostao, Pelé, Rivelino.
Czechoslovakia: Viktor; Dobias, Migas, Horvath, Hagara; Hrdlicka (Kvasniak), Kuna; Frantisek Vesely (Bohumil Vesely), Petras, Adamec, Jokl.
Scorers: Petras for Czechoslovakia, Rivelino, Pelé, Jairzinho 2, for Brazil.

Rumania (0) 2 *Czechoslovakia* (1) 1
Rumania: Adamache; Satmareanu, Lupescu, Dinu, Mocanu; Dumitru (Tataru), Nunweiller VI; Dembrowski, Neagu, Dumitrache, Lucescu (Ghergheli).
Czechoslovakia: Vencel; Dobias, Migas, Horvath, Zlocha; Kuna, Kvasniak; Vesely, B., Petras, Jurkanin (Adamec), Jokl (Vesely, F.).
Scorers: Petras for Czechoslovakia, Neagu, Dumitrache (penalty) for Rumania.

Brazil (0) 1 *England* (0) 0
Brazil: Felix; Carlos Alberto, Brito, Piazza, Everaldo; Clodoaldo, Rivelino, Paulo Cesar; Jairzinho, Tostao (Roberto), Pelé.
England: Banks (Stoke City); Wright (Everton), Cooper (Leeds United) Mullery (Spurs), Labone (Everton), Moore (West Ham United); Lee (Manchester City), (Astle (West Bromwich Albion)), Ball (Everton), Charlton (Manchester United), (Bell (Manchester City)), Hurst (West Ham United), Peters, (Spurs.).
Scorer: Jairzinho for Brazil.

Brazil (2) 3 *Rumania* (1) 2
Brazil: Felix; Carlos Alberto, Brito, Fontana, Everaldo (Marco Antonio); Clodoaldo, Piazza; Jairzinho, Tostao, Pelé, Paulo Cesar.
Rumania: Adamache (Raducanu); Satmareanu, Lupescu, Dumitru, Mocanu; Neagu, Dinu, Nunweiller VI; Dembrowski, Dumitrache (Tataru), Lucescu.

England (0) 1 *Czechoslovakia* (0) 0
England: Banks (Stoke City); Newton (Everton), Cooper (Leeds United); Mullery (Spurs), Charlton, J. (Leeds United), Moore (West Ham United); Bell (Manchester City), Clarke (Leeds United), Astle (West Bromwich Albion), (Osgood (Chelsea)), Charlton, R. (Manchester United) (Ball (Everton)), Peters (Spurs).
Czechoslovakia: Viktor; Dobias, Migas, Hrivnak, Hagara; Pollak, Kuna; F. Vesely (Jokl), Petras, Adamec, Jan Capkovic.
Scorer: Clarke (penalty) for England.

Placings

	P	W	D	L	F	A	Pts
Brazil	3	3	0	0	8	3	6
England	3	2	0	1	2	1	4
Rumania	3	1	0	2	4	5	2
Czechoslovakia	3	0	0	3	2	7	0

GROUP IV. Leon

Peru (0) 3 *Bulgaria* (1) 2
Peru: Rubiños; Campos (J. Gonzalez), De La Torre, Chumpitaz, Fuentes; Cubillas, Mifflin, Challe, Baylon (Sotil), Perico Leon, Gallardo.
Bulgaria: Simeonov; Chalamanov, Dimitrov, Davidov, Aladjiev, Bonev (Asparoukhov), Penev, Yakimov, Popov (Maraschliev), Jekov, Dermendjiev.

Scorers: Dermendjiev, Bonev for Bulgaria; Chumpitaz, Gallardo, Cubillas for Peru.

West Germany (0) 2 *Morocco* (1) 1

West Germany: Maier; Vogts, Schulz, Fichtel, Hottges (Loehr); Haller (Grabowski), Beckenbauer, Overath; Seeler, Muller, Held.

Morocco: Allal; Abdallah, Lamrani, Moulay, Slimani; Boujema, Bamous (Faras), Maaroufi, Filali; Said, Houmane, Ghazouani (Abdelkader.)

Peru (0) 3 *Morocco* (0) 0

Peru: Rubiños; P. Gonzalez, De La Torre, Chumpitaz, Fuentes; Challe, Mifflin (Cruzado), Cubillas; Sotil, Perico Leon, Gallardo (Ramirez).

Morocco: Allal; Abdallah Lamrani, Khanoussi, Slimani, Boujema (Fadili); Maaroufi, Bamous, Filali; Ghandi (Allaqui), Houmane, Ghazouani.

Scorers: Sotil, Challe, Cubillas for Peru.

West Germany (2) 5 *Bulgaria* (1) 2

West Germany: Maier; Vogts, Schnellinger, Fichtel, Hottges; Beckenbauer, Overath; Libuda, Seeler, Muller, Loehr (Grabowski). (sub. Weber).

Bulgaria: Simeonov; Gaydarski, Penev, Jetchev, Gaganelov; Kolev, Bonev, Nikodimov; Dermendjiev, Asparoukhov, Maraschliev.

Scorers: Libuda, Muller 3 (1 penalty), Seeler for West Germany, Nikodimov, Kolev for Bulgaria.

West Germany (3) 3 *Peru* (1) 1

West Germany: Maier; Vogts, Fichtel, Schnellinger, Hottges (Patzke), Beckenbauer, Seeler, Overath; Libuda (Grabowski), Muller, Loehr.

Peru: Rubiños; P. Gonzalez, De La Torre, Chumpitaz, Fuentes; Mifflin, Challe (Cruzado); Sotil, Perico Leon (Ramirez), Gallardo.

Scorers: Muller (3) for West Germany; Perico Leon for Peru

Bulgaria (1) 1 *Morocco* (0) 1

Bulgaria: Yordanov; Chalamanov, Gaydarski, Jetchev, Penev (Dimitrov), Popov, Kolev, T., Yakimov (Bonev), Mitkov, Asparoukhov, Nikodimov.

Morocco: Hazzaaz; Khanoussi, Slimani, Benkrif, Fadili; Maaroufi, Bamous (Choukhri), Filali; Ghandi, Allaqui (Faras), Ghazouani.

Scorers: Jetchev for Bulgaria; Ghazouani for Morocco.

Placings

	P	W	D	L	F	A	Pts
West Germany	3	3	0	0	10	4	6
Peru	3	2	0	1	7	5	4
Bulgaria	3	0	1	2	5	9	1
Morocco	3	0	1	2	2	6	1

QUARTER-FINALS

Leon *West Germany* (0) 3 *England* (1) 2
after extra time

West Germany: Maier; Schnellinger, Vogts, Hottges (Schulz); Beckenbauer, Overath, Seeler; Libuda (Grabowski), Muller, Loehr.
England: Bonetti (Chelsea); Newton (Everton); Cooper (Leeds United); Mullery (Spurs), Labone (Everton), Moore (West Ham United); Lee (Manchester City), Ball (Everton), Hurst (West Ham United), Charlton (Manchester United) (Bell (Manchester City)), Peters (Spurs) (Hunter (Leeds United)).
Scorers: Mullery, Peters for England; Beckenbauer, Seeler, Muller for West Germany.

Guadalajara *Brazil* (2) 4 *Peru* (1) 2

Brazil: Felix; Carlos Alberto, Brito, Piazza, Marco Antonio; Clodoaldo, Gerson (Paulo Cesar); Jairzinho (Roberto), Tostao, Pele, Rivelino.
Peru: Rubiños; Campos, Fernandez, Chumpitaz, Fuentes; Mifflin, Challe; Baylon (Sotil), Perico Leon (Eladio Reyes), Cubillas, Gallardo.
Scorers: Rivelino, Tostao 2, Jairzinho for Brazil; Gallardo 2 for Peru.

Toluca *Italy* (1) 4 *Mexico* (1) 1

Italy: Albertosi; Burgnich, Cera, Rossato, Facchetti; Bertini, Mazzola (Rivera), De Sisti; Domenghini (Gori), Boninsegna, Riva.
Mexico: Calderon; Vantolra, Pena, Guzman, Perez; Gonzales (Borja), Pulido, Munguia (Diaz); Valdivia, Fragoso, Padilla.
Scorers: Domenghini, Riva 2, Rivera for Italy; Gonzalez for Mexico

Mexico *Uruguay* (0) 1 *Russia* (0) 0
after extra time

Uruguay: Mazurkiewicz; Ubinas, Ancheta, Matosas, Mujica; Maneiro, Cortes, Montero Castillo; Cubilla, Fontes (Gomez), Morales (Esparrago).
Russia: Kavazashvili; Dzodzuashvili, Afonin, Khurtsilava (Logofet), Chesternijev; Muntijan, Asatiani (Kiselev), Kaplichni; Evriuzhkinzin, Bychevetz, Khmelnitzki.
Scorer: Esparrago for Uruguay

SEMI-FINALS

Mexico City

Italy (1) 4 *West Germany* (0) 3
after extra time

Italy: Albertosi; Cera; Burgnich, Bertini, Rosato, (Poletti) Facchetti; Domenghini, Mazzola (Rivera), De Sisti; Boninsegna, Riva.
West Germany: Maier; Schnellinger; Vogts, Schulz, Beckenbauer, Patzke; Seeler, Overath; Grabowski, Muller, Loehr (Libuda.)
Scorers: Boninsegna, Burgnich, Riva, Rivera, for Italy; Schnellinger, Muller 2 for West Germany.

Guadalajara

Brazil (1) 3 *Uruguay* (1) 1

Brazil: Felix; Carlos Alberto, Brito, Piazza, Everaldo; Clodoaldo, Gerson; Jairzinho, Tostao, Pelé, Rivelino.
Uruguay: Mazurkiewicz; Ubinas, Ancheta, Matosas, Mujica; Montero Castillo, Cortes, Fontes; Cubilla, Maneiro (Esparrago), Morales.
Scorers: Cubilla for Uruguay; Clodoaldo, Jairzinho, Rivelino for Brazil.

Third Place Match: Mexico City

West Germany (1) 1 *Uruguay* (0) 0

West Germany: Wolter, Schnellinger (Lorenz); Patzke, Fichtel, Weber, Vogts; Seeler, Overath; Libuda (Loehr), Muller, Held.
Uruguay: Mazurkiewicz; Ubinas, Ancheta, Matosas, Mujica; Montero Castillo, Cortes, Fontes; (Sandoval); Cubilla, Maneiro (Esparrago), Morales.
Scorer: Overath for West Germany.

FINAL

Mexico City

Brazil (1) 4 *Italy* (1) 1

Brazil: Felix; Carlos Alberto, Brito, Piazza, Everaldo; Clodoaldo, Gerson; Jairzinho, Tostao, Pelé, Rivelino.
Italy: Albertosi; Cera; Burgnich, Bertini, (Juliano), Rosato, Facchetti; Domenghini, Mazzola, De Sisti; Boninsegna (Rivera), Riva.
Scorers: Pelé, Gerson, Jairzinho, Carlos Alberto for Brazil. Boninsegna for Italy.

Chapter Two

World Cup, Qualifying Competition

GROUP 1

RUMANIA deservedly qualified, even though they faltered at the last stride. Portugal, whose challenge had already faded away before the season began, failed to revive, the Swiss were no more than modest competitors, and it was left to the Greeks to engender some excitement, and a little uncertainty. They proved that Yugoslav coaches have worked their wonders among them; their team, always hard and combative, is now tactically and technically skilful, besides.

The Rumanians maintained their surprising form when they defeated Portugal by the only goal of the game, in Bucharest – thus putting out the team which finished third in the 1966 World Cup, after eliminating Brazil. Rumania, with Dobrin in superb form, deserved to win a sometimes hard game. After 30 minutes, Dumitrache beat three men, and made Dobrin the goal.

The Greeks stayed in the race by comprehensively beating Switzerland 4–1, at Salonika. The Swiss began well enough, and for half-an-hour played elegant but academic football. In the last quarter of the first half, the more direct Greeks, well supported from midfield by Haitas and Domazos, scored three goals; and the game was lost and won.

This left Greece with a nominal chance of qualification, though to take it they needed to beat Rumania in Bucharest, a task which looked beyond their powers. Meanwhile, Switzerland and Portugal, both out of the running, drew in Berne.

The Greeks, in the concluding and decisive match, did in fact spring a final surprise, holding Rumania to a draw in Bucharest. The Rumanians looked nervous, with several key players out of form, though Nunweiler, in midfield, was fortunately splendid, linking a ponderous defence to an uncertain attack. Dembrovski, outside-right and much the best forward, headed in Lucescu's corner, after 36 minutes. The equaliser came five minutes after half-time, a long shot from the excellent little Greek half-back, Domazos.

October 8	Rumania (1) 1 Dobrin	Portugal (0) 0
October 15	Greece (3) 4 Koudas Botinos 2, Sideris	Switzerland (0) 0
November 2	Switzerland (0) 1 Eusebio	Portugal (1) 1 Kunzli
November 16	Rumania (1) 1 Dembrovski	Greece (0) 1 Domazos

FINAL PLACINGS

	P	W	D	L	F	A	Pts.
Rumania	6	3	2	1	7	6	8
Greece	6	2	3	1	13	9	7
Switzerland	6	2	1	3	5	8	5
Portugal	6	1	2	3	8	10	4

GROUP 2

A closely fought group, in which the Hungarians and the Czechs finished level on points, had a most surprising climax when Czechoslovakia thrashed Hungary 4–1 in the play-off in Marseilles. Even the absence of stars such as Albert, Szucs and Pancsics couldn't explain Hungary's palpable inferiority on the day. The Czechs were far shrewder, tougher and more effective.

The atmosphere at the important match between Czechs and Hungarians in Prague was as tense as might have been expected, the crowd using the visiting team as an excuse for venting their bitterness at Hungary's part in the 1969 invasion of Czechoslovakia.

Hungary, banking largely on the Ujpest team, whose attack was chosen *en plein*, galloped away with the game in the first half, then ran out of steam, allowing the Czechs to retrieve it. Bene and Dunai combined superbly while Hungary were on top, Dunai making the first goal for Bene, then scoring a magnificent individual goal, himself, after the Czech full-back, Hagara, had equalised.

Four minutes after half-time, Hrivnak's error allowed Hungary to make it 3–1, but within a couple of minutes Kvasniak headed in Kuna's centre; and Kuna himself equalised, 12 minutes from time. Szucs, and the Hungarian midfield, dazzling at first, lost their grip on the game, as they tired. An ultimate play-off in Vienna thus became likely.

Eire, whose players expressed strong dissatisfaction with their selectors, demanding a free hand for the team manager, then lost 3–0 in Prague to the Czechs, all three goals going, in the first half, to the prolific Adamec, a veteran of the 1962 World Cup. Hungary then proceeded to defeat Denmark by the same score, Ferenc Bene scoring twice. The much altered Hungarian team had an average age of only 24. It proceeded to dispose of Eire 4–0, a match in which the familiar, if surrogate, names of Puskas and Kocsis appeared among the Hungarian goal scorers, and in which a player from each side – Dempsey and Szucs – was sent off. Halmosi, playing his second international, scored the first Hungarian goal and had an excellent match. The stage was now clear for a play-off between the Czechs and the Hungarians.

So to the play-off and its surprising result. Inspired in midfield by the loping Kvasniak, who played in the 1962 World Cup Final, the Czechs dominated the game. Not till the 89th minute did Hungary score their penalty goal; and then the Czechs teasingly substituted their goalkeeper. Their performance was somewhat marred by rough play, Petras being sent off five minutes from time, but their 4–2–4 – with wingers – was finely effective.

September 14 1968	Czechoslovakia (1) 3 Hagara, Kvasniak, Kuna	Hungary (2) 3 Bene, Dunai, Fazekas
October 8	Czechoslovakia (3) 3 Adamec 3	Eire (0) 0
October 15	Eire (1) 1 Givens	Denmark (0) 1 Jensen (pen.)
October 24	Hungary (2) 3 Bene 2, Szucs	Denmark (0) 0
November 5	Hungary (1) 4 Halmosi, Bene, Puskas, Kocsis	Eire (0) 0

PLAY-OFF

Marseilles December 3

Czechoslovakia (1) 4	Hungary (0) 1
Kvasniak (penalty)	Kocsis (penalty)
Vesely, Adamec, Jokl	

FINAL TABLE

	P	W	D	L	F	A	Pts.
Czechoslovakia	6	4	1	1	12	6	9
Hungary	6	4	1	1	16	7	9
Denmark	6	2	1	3	6	10	5
Eire	6	0	1	5	3	14	1

GROUP 3

Italy, as expected, won this group, though to make sure of it they were obliged to beat the East Germans in Naples, in the final match. This they did with some style, despite the absence of several key forwards, among them Rivera and Anastasi.

Wales, who in any case were virtually eliminated, collapsed surprisingly at home to East Germany, after dominating a first half in which they failed to score. The absence of Ron Davies affected but hardly excused them.

This lack of goals in the first half probably caused the over-eagerness which left gaps – and conceded goals – in the second. The first arrived when after 53 minutes a shot by Irmscher was deflected on to a post, and Vogel scored. Loewe got the second, made for him by the clever Vogel, key player in the match, and it was Vogel, too, who back heeled the ball for Frenzel to get a third. Wales, who had deserved a first half goal when Toshack beat Croy with a header against the crossbar, had late and faint consolation when a fine, long drive by Powell found its billet.

Injuries in the previous Saturday's League games and the absence of Ron Davies, needed by Southampton for a Fairs Cup game, still more drastically afflicted Wales for their final match, in Rome – against an Italian team whose championship had been suspended for the previous Sunday. Their mosaic team lost 4–1, Luigi Riva, insufficiently marked, scoring a devastating three goals, Mike England getting the only one for Wales. Sandrino Mazzola, who came on as a substitute, scored the other one for Italy.

So the Italians, level on points with the East Germans, had to beat them in Naples to avoid a play-off. Awarding first caps to Cera, in midfield, and Chiarugi, on the right wing, they were impressive winners against a German team which kept the ball far too close and over-indulged in the one-two move. Mazzola scored the first after seven minutes, following Chiarugi's menacing centre. A 60-yard run by the formidable Riva, through the middle, eventually gave Domenghini the second. Riva himself headed in Domenghini's cross for the third, but lost a fine chance to improve his already prolific record by missing a penalty.

Cardiff, October 22

Wales (0) 1	*East Germany* (0) 3
Powell	Vogel, Loewe, Frenzel

Wales: Sprake (Leeds United); Rodrigues (Leicester City), Thomas (Swindon Town); Hennessy (Nottingham Forest), England (Spurs), Powell (Sheffield United); Durban (Derby County), Krzywicki (West Bromwich Albion), Toshack (Cardiff City), Davies, W. (Newcastle United), Rees (Nottingham Forest.)
East Germany: Croy; Fraessdorf, Urbanczyk, Seehaus, Bransch, Koerner, Stein, Loewe, Frenzel, Irmscher, Vogel.

Rome, November 4

Italy (1) 4	*Wales* (0) 1
Riva 3	England
Mazzola	

Italy: Albertosi; Burgnich, Facchetti; Bertini (Juliano), Puia, Salvadore; Domenghini, Rivera, Anastasi (Mazzola), De Sisti, Riva.
Wales: Sprake (Leeds United), Thomas (Swindon Town), Derrett (Cardiff City), Durban (Derby County), England (Tottenham Hotspur), Moore (Charlton Athletic); Yorath (Leeds United), Toshack (Cardiff City), Hole (Aston Villa), Krzywicki (West Bromwich Albion), Rees (Nottingham Forest) sub: Reece (Sheffield United.)

Naples, November 22

Italy (3) 3	*East Germany* (0) 0
Mazzola, Domenghini, Riva	

FINAL TABLE

	P	W	D	L	F	A	Pts.
Italy	4	3	1	0	10	3	7
East Germany	4	2	1	1	7	7	5
Wales	4	0	0	4	3	10	0

GROUP 4

Ireland's promising beginning, with two wins over Turkey, availed them nothing. Dropping a point to Russia in Belfast, they already faced a mountainous enough task in Moscow. The absence of Best and McMordie made it insuperable. Russia won the match – and the group.

The vital meeting between Northern Ireland and Russia, in a Belfast then so violently divided, was an anticlimax. The Irish, with four points already under their belts, could not break through a massed Russian defence, even Best and Dougan being reduced eventually to impotence. McMordie and Best had, and missed, chances. If McMordie had scored in the first half, with only the tall, resourceful Rudakov to beat, things might have been different. But the Irish policy of high centres to Dougan's head was unproductive.

There is little doubt that the Irish team, as their captain, Terry Neill, admitted, allowed the disturbed, threatening atmosphere of the city, divided by violent riots, to affect them.

The Russians, restoring Anatoli Bychevetz to the attack and pursuing a much more enterprising policy, then easily despatched the Turks in Kiev. Muntijan, the Kiev midfield player, was in especially good form, and scored twice.

Ireland's task in Moscow was clearly to be a hard one, and it was made insuperable when Manchester United insisted on using George Best in a Football League Cup tie against Burnley, two days before the game. Best was kicked on the shin and incapacitated. With McMordie also unable to play, Ireland had to take the field without two of their key players; above all, without the man the Russians so feared and respected.

Almost inevitably, they lost, though the first goal was most unfortunate, a shot by Gerschkovitsch striking Clements and changing course to put Jennings on the wrong foot, so that Nodia scored easily. Harkin shot against Rudakov's chest just before half-time, but ten minutes from the end, Ireland's desperate attacks allowed Serebrianikov to run from halfway to make a goal for Bychevetz.

Russia then disposed of Turkey 3–1, to qualify comfortably.

Belfast, September 10

Northern Ireland (0) 0 *Russia* (0) 0

Ireland: Jennings (Spurs); Rice (Arsenal), Elder (Stoke City); Todd (Burnley), Neill (Arsenal), Nicholson (Huddersfield Town); Campbell (Dundee), McMordie (Middlesbrough), Dougan (Wolves), Clements (Coventry City), Best (Manchester United) sub: Jackson (Everton) for Clements.

Russia: Rudakov; Chesternijev, Kaplichny, Dzodzuashvili, Lovchev, Afonin; Muntian, Kiselyov, Khmelnitzki, Pusach, Khusainov.

Kiev, October 15

Russia (1) 3 *Turkey* (0) 0
Muntian 2, Nodia

Moscow, October 22

Russia (1) 2 *Northern Ireland* (0) 0
Nodia, Bychevetz

Russia: Rudakov; Dzodzuashvili, Chesternijev, Lovchev, Kaplichny; Serebrianikov, Muntian, Asatiani, Gerschkovitsch, Bychevetz, Nodia.
Ireland: Jennings (Spurs); Craig (Newcastle United), Harvey (Sunderland); Hunter (Blackburn Rovers), Neill (Arsenal), Nicholson (Huddersfield Town); Hegan (West Bromwich Albion), Jackson (Everton), Dougan (Wolves), Harkin (Shrewsbury Town), Clements (Coventry City.)

November 16	Turkey (1) 1	Russia (2) 3
	Ender	Asatiani, Nodia 2

FINAL TABLE

	P	W	D	L	F	A	Pts.
Russia	4	3	1	0	8	1	7
Northern Ireland	4	2	1	1	7	3	5
Turkey	4	0	0	4	2	13	0

GROUP 5

Sweden duly won this group, though they were thoroughly beaten by France, in Paris, at a time when the die was cast. Nor did they have an easy time of it in the key match against France at Stockholm. After an awkward first half, a somewhat disputable penalty, gained and exploited by Ove Kindvall, changed the pattern of play.

The French kept their hopes flickering by winning 3–1 away to Norway, thus avenging their 1–0 defeat at Strasbourg, the previous season. A rather less cautious approach to the game might have led to a still clearer victory. As it was, Norway's only goal came as a very late afterthought. All the French goals were scored by their St. Etienne striker, Herve Revelli.

Revelli and France, however, could manage no goals when the "summit" match took place in Stockholm. Both went to Sweden and their Feyenoord centre-forward, Ove Kindvall. The first, after 33 minutes, was a penalty, when he was obstructed by Novi's arm, and fell rather dramatically; technically a penalty, but rather a severe one. The second of his and Sweden's goals came in the 65th minute.

With Revelli still showing the effects of a knee injury and the clever, inexperienced little Chiesa somewhat outmatched physically – and indifferently supported behind – France faded after a good beginning; when Bereta might perhaps have had a penalty himself, had he fallen dramatically, instead of recovering his balance.

France took a little comfort from the last match, when a lively five minutes enabled them to defeat a Swedish team short of five of its first choice players; among them Kindvall. Bras of Liège, a late choice on the right wing, scored twice.

September 10, 1969

Norway (0) 1	*France* (1) 3
Olsen	Revelli 3

October 15

Sweden (1) 2	*France* (0) 0
Kindvall 2	

November 1

France (3) 3	*Sweden* (0) 0
Bras 2, Djorkaeff (penalty)	

FINAL TABLE

	P	W	D	L	F	A	Pts.
Sweden	4	3	0	1	12	5	6
France	4	2	0	2	6	4	4
Norway	4	1	0	3	4	13	2

GROUP 6

Belgium had already qualified, so the rest was mere academy. But Yugoslavia's spanking 4–0 home win over the Belgians made one wonder just how far Belgium's splendid, winning form a year earlier had been a flash in the pan. Joao Saldanha, the Brazilian team manager, who attended the game, said he felt the score could have been 7–0, and lamented the fact that so good a team as Yugoslavia would not be playing in Mexico. Thus, too late, the Yugoslavs confirmed the high promise that they showed in the 1968 European Nations Cup finals.

Spain, meanwhile. consoled themselves with a meaningless 6–0 home victory against the Finnish team which had beaten them, earlier in the year.

October 15, 1969

Spain (5) 6	*Finland* (0) 0
Pirri, Garate 2, Velazquez, Amancio, Quino	

October 19

Yugoslavia (3) 4	*Belgium* (0) 0
Belin, Spasovski 2, Dzajic	

FINAL TABLE

	P	W	D	L	F	A	Pts.
Belgium	6	4	1	1	14	8	9
Yugoslavia	6	3	1	2	19	7	7
Spain	6	2	2	2	10	6	6
Finland	6	1	0	5	6	28	2

GROUP 7

Scotland failed for the third consecutive time to qualify for the World Cup Finals when West Germany defeated them 3–2 in Hamburg. The match was a close one in which the Scots could probably have forced, and would have deserved, a draw, had they not thrown caution aside after making it 2–2. Thus their defence was exposed to a breakaway and a dazzling individual run by the West German right winger, Libuda, who beat Gemmell then Herriot to score. Late in the game, Gemmell, chasing Haller to take a swinging kick at him, was sent off by the referee; but the damage had already been done.

The Scots took the lead after only three minutes when Gray burst through the German defence, Maier punched out his shot, and Johnstone volleyed home. The tackling became cruelly hard, fouls proliferated, and after 35 minutes, Germany equalised. Fichtel shot in after the Scottish defence had fallen into confusion, at a throw-in.

Scotland attacked vigorously in the second half, Gemmell's shot rolling along the bar, Bremner hitting it. But Germany scored again when Seeler headed Beckenbauer's free kick across to Muller, whose magnificent left-foot volley beat Herriot. Gilzean quickly headed Bremner's cross down and in – but then came Libuda's winner. A bitterly hard but exciting game.

The final match, in Vienna, was considerably less exciting and memorable. Scotland's somewhat experimental team – Austria's, too, was weakened by absences – lost 2–0, both goals being scored by Redl. After 16 minutes, he headed in a cross by Parits; after 53, when McCann failed to gather Schmidtradner's centre, Redl headed another. Scotland brought Lorimer and Colin Stein into their attack during the second half, but it still could not manage to score a goal.

It was a sad and anti-climactic ending to Scotland's endeavours.

Hamburg, October 22, 1969

West Germany (1) 3	*Scotland* (1) 2
Fichtel, Muller, Libuda	Johnstone, Gilzean

West Germany: Maier; Hottges, Vogts; Beckenbauer, Schulz, Fichtel; Libuda, Seeler, Muller, Overath, Haller.
Scotland: Herriot (Birmingham City); Grieg (Rangers), Gemmell (Celtic); Bremner (Leeds United), McKinnon (Rangers), McNeill (Celtic), Johnstone (Celtic), Cormack (Hibernian), Stein (Rangers), Gilzean (Spurs), Gray (Leeds United).

Vienna, November 5, 1969

Austria (1) 2	*Scotland* (0) 0
Redl 2	

Austria: Harreither; Wallner, Sturmberger, Schmidtradner, Fak, Geyer, Hof, Ettmeyer, Parits, Kaiser, Redl.
Scotland: McGarr (Aberdeen); Greig (Rangers), McKinnon (Rangers),

Stanton (Hibernian), Burns (Manchester United); Murdoch (Celtic), Cooke (Chelsea), Bremner (Leeds United); Gilzean (Spurs), Curran (Wolves), Gray (Leeds United). subs.: Stein (Rangers), Lorimer (Leeds United).

FINAL TABLE

	P	W	D	L	F	A	Pts.
West Germany	6	5	1	0	20	3	11
Scotland	6	3	1	2	18	7	7
Austria	6	3	0	3	12	7	6
Cyprus	6	0	0	6	2	35	0

GROUP 8

After a brief stumble in Poland, the Bulgarians comfortably got over their final hurdle, in Luxemburg, to qualify in a difficult group. The Dutch were the disappointment, especially given the parallel form of their club teams; the Poles came on to their game just too late to keep the Bulgarians out. Yakimov played admirably for them in the last, decisive game.

Holland's chances virtually disappeared when they lost 2–1 in Poland, having led at half-time, and squandered a penalty.

Poland improved with the use of substitutes, in the second half. Jarosik, who was one of them, equalised from the left wing, and the inevitable Lubanski scored the winner. Bulgaria were thus left in a very strong position.

The Poles then went to Luxemburg and won 5–1, after a surprisingly even first half in which Luxemburg, missing several of their best players – all of them with foreign clubs – surpassed themselves. After the interval, however, the home team fell away and Poland won with some ease. At half-time, splendid goalkeeping by René Hoffmann and a goal scored, even if against the play, by Kirchens, made by Dublin, enabled Luxemburg to lead. Then a penalty, after Kuffer fouled Gadocha, gave Poland an equaliser and tipped the balance.

In a vital match played at Rotterdam, Holland allowed themselves the luxury of playing without Johan Cryuyff – suspended by their Federation, then pardoned too late for a team which had already been chosen without him – against a weakened Bulgarian side. The 1–1 draw put Bulgaria in an excellent position. It was a good, hard but thoroughly fair game in which the splendidly organized Bulgarian defence held firm against the best efforts of the Dutch.

The Poles, however, cracked it well and truly in Warsaw, where a splendid team performance brought a 3–0 win and a nominal possibility of qualification – should Bulgaria fail to win in Luxemburg. Poland attacked from the first, took the lead in 19 minutes through Jarosik, scored twice more in the second half, and might have had other goals.

September 7, 1969

Poland (0) 2 Jarosik, Lubanski	*Holland* (1) 1 Wery

October 12

Luxemburg (1) 1 Kirchens	*Poland* (0) 5 Dejna 2, Zarawezyk (penalty), Bula, Lubanski

October 24

Holland (1) 1 Veenstra	*Bulgaria* (0) 1 Bonev

November 9

Poland (1) 3 Jarosik 2, Deyna	*Bulgaria* (0) 0

December 7

Luxemburg (0) 1 Philipp (pen.)	*Bulgaria* (2) 3 Leszczynski (own goal), Yakimov, Bonev

FINAL PLACINGS

	P	W	D	L	F	A	Pts.
Bulgaria	6	4	1	1	12	7	9
Poland	6	4	0	2	19	8	8
Holland	6	3	1	2	9	5	7
Luxemburg	6	0	0	6	4	24	0

GROUP 9

England qualify as holders.

SOUTH AMERICAN SECTION

GROUP 10

The three qualifiers were Brazil, Uruguay and, most unexpectedly, Peru, at the expense of Argentina. Rivalry and confusion in the governing body, which led to the replacing of Humberto Maschio as team manager on the eve of the competition, together with the uncooperative attitude of the great clubs, weakened Argentina seriously. As a consequence of Adolfo Pedernera, a great centre-forward of the 1940s, succeeding Maschio as coach, five vital days of acclimatisation at La Paz were thrown away; though previously great care had been taken to test a party of players, there.

Many, however, felt that the Argentinians had at last paid the penalty for their ruthless, provocative approach to the game, manifested both in the 1966 World Cup, especially in the notorious match against England, at Wembley, and by such clubs as Racing and Estudiantes, in the world championship. This concentration on violence, always a well-known but previously a secondary feature of Argentinian football, at the expense of its traditional artistry, led to a severe dearth of talented forwards; whether constructive or striking.

So the Argentinians traumatisingly lost their opening match on the heights of La Paz, their players indulging in extremes of violence. The consequence of this was that the country's dictator, General Ongania, warned the team against its future behaviour. The warning was heeded; which may well have been a vital inhibiting factor on the performance of the Argentinians in their remaining matches.

The Bolivians played really well to beat them. A goal up when Albrecht mistimed a pass back to the goalkeeper, they rode Argentina's brief recovery in the last quarter-hour of the first half, and when Tarabini equalised, deservedly regained the lead from Blacut's penalty, withstood Argentina's violence, and made it 3–1 with a header by Alvarez.

Away to Peru – managed by Brazil's World Cup double-medallist, Didì, for nothing – Argentina lost again. This time the Argentinians largely behaved themselves, though Racing's notorious Basile foolishly got himself sent off in the second half. Peru, playing 4–2–4, had most of the play, but fell into sins of over-elaboration, ignoring their quick wingers, Baylon and Gallardo. It was Périco Léon, the centre-forward, who coolly and eventually lobbed the one goal of the game.

Peru, however, after taking the lead, lost away to Bolivia in their turn, the team going disgracefully berserk when an 85th minute equaliser by Gallardo was disallowed for offside. The referee was attacked, two Peruvian players were sent off and the police, who'd already had to intervene, were obliged to protect the referee from the Peruvians at the final whistle. Argentina then scraped through at home to Bolivia by a mere penalty, and stood to survive if they could defeat Peru in Buenos Aires.

This would have necessitated a triple play-off; but in the event, the Peruvians held Argentina to a 2–2 draw, and went through to Mexico; their first World Cup finals for 40 years. Bold enough to play an attacking, 4–2–4 formation, although they needed only that one point to go through, they were deservedly rewarded. It was inevitably a very rough game. With Marcos, Argentina's right winger, mastering his back, Peru using too many high balls, Argentina had the better of the first half. For the second, they changed Rulli for the clever Rendo, and their rhythm improved. So, however, did Peru, making use of the speed of Ramirez and Baylon, on the wings.

With Argentina's full-backs in difficulty, it was only the brilliantly timed rushes of Cejas, in goal, which saved his team. Then Ramirez scored. Albrecht equalised from a penalty given after a somewhat doubtful decision in favour of Marcos, who was brought down; but Ramirez got away on the left to score again. The Peruvians were playing out time when La Torre was sent off in the 88th minute – for wasting it. So Tarabini was able to equalise, but although the referee added eight minutes for stoppages and Marcos put the ball in the net from an offside position, Peru deservedly held out – for a draw which sent them to Mexico.

July 27, 1969

Bolivia (1) 3	*Argentina* (0) 1
Diaz, Blacut (penalty), Alvarez	Tarabini

August 3

Peru (0) 1	*Argentina* (0) 0
Périco Léon	

August 10

Bolivia (0) 2	*Peru* (0) 1
Alvarez, Diaz	Challen

August 17

Peru (2) 3	*Bolivia* (0) 0
Cubilla, Cruzado, Gallardo	

August 24

Argentina (0) 1	*Bolivia* (0) 0
Albrecht (penalty)	

August 31

Argentina (0) 2	*Peru* (0) 2
Albrecht (penalty), Marcos	Ramirez 2

FINAL PLACINGS

	P	W	D	L	F	A	Pts.
Peru	4	2	1	1	7	4	5
Bolivia	4	2	0	2	5	6	4
Argentina	4	1	1	2	4	6	3

GROUP 11

Brazil won this group in fine style, winning every match and scoring a flood of goals. Only in the last, and decisive, game, played at the Maracanà Stadium in Rio against Paraguay, and won by a single goal from Pelé, was their attack contained.

With Tostao a dashing and prolific striker, the defence far more secure than it had looked against England in Rio, the previous June, João Saldanha's team, based firmly on Santos, established itself as a favourite for Mexico.

It was known that Paraguay would provide the only major opposition and the door to Mexico was clearly open when they were beaten 3–0 in Asuncion, despite a ferociously hostile atmosphere both on and off the field. A Brazilian official was assaulted in the street, before the match took place, while Brito, the centre-half, had to disarm an over-zealous Paraguayan fan who penetrated the Brazilians' hotel. No training ground, moreover, was afforded to the Brazilians.

But with their experience, they gradually wore down the Paraguayan team and, in the concluding stages, despite Pelé being struck by a stone – which drew blood – they took control. The violent Paraguayans, their stamina spent, conceded an own goal to put Brazil ahead. The visiting wingers, Jairzinho and Edu, added two more. Paraguay badly felt the absence of Sosa, their best midfield player, sent off a week earlier in Bogotà, during their 1–0 win over Colombia.

July 27 1969

Colombia (2) 3	*Venezuela* (0) 0
Gonzalez 2, Segrera (penalty)	

August 3

Venezuela (0) 1	*Colombia* (0) 1
Mendoza	Tamayo

August 6

Venezuela (0) 0	*Paraguay* (1) 2
	Rojas, P. 2

August 7

Colombia (0) 0	*Brazil* (2) 2
	Tostao 2

August 10

Colombia (0) 0	*Paraguay* (0) 1
	Martinez

August 10

Venezuela (0) 0	*Brazil* (0) 5
	Tostao 3, Pelé 2

August 17

Paraguay (0) 0	*Brazil* (0) 3
	Mendoza, Jairzinho, Edu (own goal)

August 21

Brazil (2) 6	*Colombia* (1) 2
Pelé, Tostao, Edu, Jairzinho 2, Rivelino	Gallego 2

August 21

Paraguay (1) 1	*Venezuela* (0) 0
Jimenez	

August 23

Brazil (5) 6	*Venezuela* (0) 0
Tostao 3, Pelé 2 Jairzinho	

August 23

Paraguay (1) 2	*Colombia* (0) 1
Arrua 2	Segrera

August 31

Brazil (0) 1	*Paraguay* (0) 0
Pelé	

FINAL PLACINGS

	P	W	D	L	F	A	Pts.
Brazil	6	6	0	0	23	2	12
Paraguay	6	4	0	2	6	5	8
Colombia	6	1	1	4	7	12	3
Venezuela	6	0	1	5	1	16	1

GROUP 12

Uruguay, employing ruthless methods to gain a draw in Santiago, and winning 2–0 on the heights of Guayaquil, Ecuador, qualified for their sixth World Cup finals. In their two, ensuing, home matches, they made surprisingly heavy weather of defeating Ecuador, a goal by their centre-back, the promising 22-year-old Carlos Anchetta, proving the only one of the game. The 2–0 victory against Chile, however, was a very clear one, Pedro Rocha was in splendid form in midfield, besides scoring a goal in the last minute.

The opening Uruguayan game, in Ecuador, was on the brink of getting out of hand, though it never quite did. The Chile-Uruguay game, however, contained some disgraceful incidents. Brutal tackles by the Uruguayan half-back, Montero-Castillo, virtually eliminated two Chilean forwards, Arraya and Fouilloux, from taking further, effective part in the match. At the end of it, the Uruguayans had to stand in the centre of the field, taking cover from the shower of missiles hurled by the crowd.

Zubia, the Uruguayan forward, was sent off late in the game by an Argentinian referee who should long since have taken such action. In Montevideo, Nocetti of Chile was expelled.

July 6 1969

Ecuador (0) 0 — *Uruguay* (1) 2
Bareno, Subia

July 13

Chile (0) 0 — *Uruguay* (0) 0

July 20

Uruguay (0) 1 — *Ecuador* (0) 0
Anchetta

July 27

Chile (0) 4 — *Ecuador* (0) 1
Olivares 2, Valdez 2 — Macias

August 3

Ecuador (1) 1 — *Chile* (0) 1
Rodriguez — Olivares

August 10

Uruguay (1) 2 — *Chile* (0) 0
Cortes, Rocha

FINAL PLACINGS

	P	W	D	L	F	A	Pts.
Uruguay	4	3	1	0	5	0	7
Chile	4	1	2	1	5	4	4
Ecuador	4	0	1	3	2	8	1

CENTRAL, NORTH AMERICAN AND CARIBBEAN SECTION

GROUP 13

To the general astonishment, El Salvador, surviving their "football war" against Honduras, their previous victims, knocked out Haiti, the favourites, to qualify. It was the first time they had ever taken part in a World Cup.

The series between Salvador and Haiti was curiously topsy-turvy. Having surprisingly won 2–1 in Port-au-Prince, Salvador proceeded to lose 3–0 at home; then to recover to win the play-off, in Jamaica.

September 21, 1969

Haiti (0) 1	*El Salvador* (1) 2
Obas	Acevedo, Rodriguez

September 28

El Salvador (0) 0	*Haiti* (3) 3
	Desir, Francois, Barthelemy

October 8

Play-off *Jamaica*

El Salvador (0) 1	*Haiti* (0) 0
Juan Martinez	
after extra time	

GROUP 14

Mexico qualify as hosts.

ASIAN SECTION GROUP 15

The logical favourites for this group were naturally North Korea, giant-killers extraordinary of the 1966 World Cup. Alas, they withdrew on political grounds, refusing to play their eliminating matches in Israel. There was trouble, too, in the other section of the draw, none of the other participants being willing to receive or play in Rhodesia – a most dubious addition to an Asian group, in any case. The question was tortuously resolved by exempting the Rhodesians – who did,unlike South Africa, at least include black players – from the initial rounds, designating them to play a "Final" against the country which emerged on top.

This, after the brave but unfortunate Australians had been obliged to perform a modern Odyssey, turned out to be Israel. Having been obliged to travel to Seoul, Mozambique and Tel Aviv – before at last playing their ultimate game in Sydney – the Australians had good cause to be aggrieved. Moreover, though they were thoroughly out-played in Tel Aviv, the final margin of Israel's qualification was but a solitary goal.

There should, in fact, have been several more Israeli goals in Tel Aviv, and would have been, but for a marvellous exhibition of goalkeeping by Australia's Ron Corry. The only shot which beat him spun off a defender's, Dave Zeman, shoulder, after 18 minutes. Corry even saved a penalty taken by Spiegel – and saved Spiegel's following-up shot, into the bargain. But the Australian defence couldn't hold the brilliant Mordecai Spiegler, on the left, whose shot fittingly brought the only goal. It came from a free kick.

The Australians faced the return game with great confidence, sure they could win and thus force a play-off in . . . Hong Kong. But their hopes were virtually destroyed when Israel took the lead eleven minutes from time, Spiegler again being the scorer. Watkiss equalised nine minutes later; but the die was cast.

GROUP A

Israel were presented with the none too taxing job merely of eliminating New Zealand; who put up a good deal harder fight than was expected of them. Both matches were played, by-arrangement, in Tel Aviv.

September 21, 1969

Israel (0) 4	*New Zealand* (0) 0
unavailable	

October 1, 1969

Israel (2) 2	*New Zealand* (0) 0
Spiegler, Spiegel	

GROUP B

Australia most convincingly and commendably won the three-sided play-off in Seoul, at the expense of South Korea and of a Japanese team which was diminished and demoralised by the absence of its fine centre-forward, Kamamoto, a victim of jaundice. The Australians, who had improved greatly since North Korea eliminated them from the 1966 World Cup, played with force, speed and high morale. Moreover, the great majority of their players were Australian-born.

In their first match, they surprised Japan, deservedly beating them, 3–1. Tom McColl, one of the midfield trio, scored after five minutes. Watanabe equalised after eleven, exploiting Corry's goalkeeping error, but two goals in eight minutes, in the second half, settled matters. First, a strong run by Warren, again from midfield, ended with Ogi's own goal, then Abonyi's splendid run made a goal for Ray Baartz.

Japan then drew 2–2 with South Korea. The Japanese, twice behind, played with much more confidence than in their first match, completely tipping the balance of play after Kuwahara had forced his way through for a second equaliser, six minutes after half-time. The Australians then proceeded to beat South Korea 2–1, much to the displeasure of a hugely partisan crowd who encouraged their own team with orchestras, and pelted the Australians off the field.

Australia dominated the first half, scoring once when Watkiss shot home from 25 yards. Lee Lee Woo equalised from a corner, and the game grew rough and combative. Australia won it eight minutes from time, McColl heading in after a corner.

The Japanese then held Australia to a draw, giving an improved display, opening the score after only five minutes, and holding their lead till McColl equalised, 34 minutes later. In their final match, however, Japan declined again, losing 2–0 to the South Koreans, and thus finishing last in the group. Thus encouraged – and indulgently abetted by the linesmen – South Korea somewhat fortunately held a hard-done-by Australia to 1–1, in the concluding game.

This left the Australians to play-off against Rhodesia in, of all places, Lourenço Marques, Mozambique, one country after another having refused to harbour the Rhodesian team. The Rhodesians, who did, to their credit, at least field a "multi-racial" side, made up in almost equal proportions of black and white players, surprised the Australians by holding them to a 1–1 draw in the opening game on November 23, 1969.

Thompson, indeed, put Rhodesia ahead, on the hour, against an Australian team without its captain, John Warren, who fell ill before the game. After 65 minutes, however, McColl equalised.

SEOUL TOURNAMENT

October 8, 1969

Australia (1) 3	*Japan* (1) 1
McColl, Ogi (own goal), Baartz	Watanabe

October 12

South Korea (2) 2	*Japan* (1) 2
Jung Suk Kim, So Il Parr	Miyamoto, Kuwahara

October 14

South Korea (1) 1	*Australia* (1) 2
Lee Lee Woo	Watkiss, McColl

October 16

Australia (1) 1	*Japan* (1) 1
McColl	Miyamoto

October 18

South Korea (2) 2	*Japan* (0) 0
Chung Kang Chi 2	

October 20

South Korea (1) 1	*Australia* (0) 1
Park Soo Il	Baartz

FINAL TABLE

	P	W	D	L	F	A	Pts.
Australia	4	2	2	0	7	4	6
South Korea	4	1	2	1	6	5	4
Japan	4	0	2	2	4	8	2

Play-Off: *Lourenço Marques, Mozambique.*

Poor Australia now had to set off on another distant journey to play the Rhodesians, in Mozambique, in the next stage of the snakes-and-ladders tournament FIFA had so tortuously devised. They eventually prevailed, but it took them three matches to do so, after their forwards had hammered in the first two against a packed Rhodesian defence.

In the first game, played after heavy rain on a muddy ground, the Rhodesians fielded seven Negroes, four whites, of whom Jordan, a huge goalkeeper, and the Scottish centre-forward, Chalmers, were the stars. It was Chalmers who gave the generally defensive Rhodesians the lead with a tremendous shot from over 30 yards, after 73 minutes. Australia, clearly missing their captain, John Warren, who was ill, equalised three minutes later through a header by McColl.

The second match, six days later, was played in heavy, humid weather. Australia missed several early chances to score, generally played poorly in attack, and tired noticeably in the second half. In a determined Rhodesian defence, Jordan was again a star, well abetted by his centre-half, Hatton.

So it went to a play-off, the following day; and on this occasion, Australia obtained a vital early goal, Baartz beating two men, before crossing, for Rutherford to volley home. Thus Rhodesia had to emerge from defence, giving the Australians, and especially the fast Willie Rutherford, extra space to use. After 22 minutes, Tigere headed Rutherford's free kick past his own goalkeeper, but early in the second half, a brave individual run by Chalmers made it 1–2. Ten minutes later, Rutherford diverted in a shot by Warren, to make the game safe for Australia. Only 1,500 watched the game; they were, after all, once used to Eusebio....

Results

November 23, 1969

Australia (0) 1	*Rhodesia* (0) 1
McColl	Chalmers

November 29

Australia (0) 0	*Rhodesia* (0) 0

November 30

Australia (2) 3	*Rhodesia* (0) 1
Rutherford 2,	Chalmers
Tigere (own goal)	

Final Play-Off

Tel Aviv, December 11, 1969

Israel (0) 1	*Australia* (0) 0
Spiegler	

Sydney, December 14

Australia (0) 1	*Israel* (0) 1
Watkiss	Spiegler

Israel qualify.

GROUP 16: African Section

It was the Moroccans who finally prevailed in this African section, the palm thus going to (relative) international experience, rather than to the young lions from Ethiopia . . . or the Sudan. The Sudanese, in fact, crumpled at last before the Moroccans when they lost 3–0 in Casablanca on October 26, 1969, a result which tied up the group, although one game, in Lagos, remained for the Moroccans to play.

Sudan, remarkably improved, began at a fine clip in their opening match of the final group, in Ibadan, away to Nigeria. Kowartu lobbed a goal after seven minutes, scored again from 18 yards after half-an-hour, to make it 2–0; and Sudan looked as good as home. But the Nigerians then brought on two substitutes, rallied, and two goals by Okeye wiped out the lead before half-time. Afterwards, rain turned the pitch into a swamp – and Nigeria continued to make the more chances, though without exploiting them.

In Casablanca, the Nigerians demonstrated the immense improvement they have made by running the far more experienced Moroccans to the odd goal of three.

Throughout the first half Morocco attacked, but couldn't beat the agile Nigerian goalkeeper, Fregene. After half time, they moved the ball about more, while their chief schemer, Houmane, dribbled less. After 49 minutes, Filali put them ahead, but Nigeria immediately and surprisingly bounced back, Ine making an equaliser for his winger, Lawal. Feras got the winner after a right wing move, in the 62nd minute.

Then Morocco made sure of qualifying by defeating Sudan, at home. Their final two goals were scored by their centre-forward, Houmane, previously criticised on the grounds that he was not a "natural" striker, and preferred to drop back to deeper positions.

So Morocco survived where Scotland, Yugoslavia, Portugal and Argentina had fallen by the way. A strange World Cup.

September 14, 1969

Nigeria (2) 2	*Sudan* (2) 2
Okeye 2	Kowartu 2

September 21

Morocco (0) 2	*Nigeria* (0) 1
Filali, Feras	Lawal

October 3

Sudan (1) 3	*Nigeria* (0) 3
(Scorers unavailable)	

October 8

Sudan (0) 0	*Morocco* (0) 0

October 26

Morocco (1) 3	*Sudan* (0) 0
Houmane 2 Filali	

Chapter Three

European Cup, 1969/70

FOR the second consecutive year, a Dutch team reached the European Cup Final, but where Ajax went down so emphatically to Milan, Feyenoord prevailed with equal emphasis over Celtic.

Hopelessly unfavoured before the game, in Milan, they gave in the event a performance which grew mightily in stature as the game went on – into an extra time which should never have been needed. The Celtic manager and players themselves admitted as much, afterwards. Feyenoord reminded the intrigued Italians that *catenaccio* can be an offensive as well as a negative tactic, if you have such virile and marvellously skilful players as Israel, Jansen, Hasil, Kindvall, Van Hanegem and Moulijn. The night was a resounding triumph for Feyenoord's Austrian manager, Ernst Happel, once a centre-back in Austria's fine team of the 1950s.

As for Celtic, so bewilderingly inept at San Siro, they could take a little consolation from the majesty of their performances in the semi-final, when they beat Leeds – though admittedly, a weary Leeds – first away, then at home.

Milan, who had signed two new forwards in Fontana and Nestor Combin during the summer, had the easiest of beginnings to the tournament they won last season, drawing, and disposing of, the champions of Luxemburg.

Easier still was the task of Leeds United, who scored ten goals in their home match against poor Lyn Oslo, Mick Jones and Allan Clarke, the spearhead, accounting for half of them. Feyenoord, the Dutch champions, beat that, with twelve, Geels getting four and Ove Kindvall, the Swedish international, another three, against Reykjavik. But just in case this plethora of goals should lead people to believe that too many "minnows" were permitted in the tournament, Hibernians of Malta added to a previously brave home record – including a draw with Manchester United – by holding the Czech champions, Spartak Trnava, to 2–2, in Valetta. They could not, alas, do as much in the return, won by the Czechs 4–0, with two of the goals going to the endlessly durable Adamec.

Kiev Dynamo exploited F.K. Austria's current poor form by defeating them in Vienna. This, though Austria held a 1–0 lead at half-time. Kiev comfortably won the return, 3–1, though once again Austria led at the interval.

Celtic, who were going through an uncertain period when they were held to a goalless draw in Basel, won the return in Glasgow 2–0. Harry Hood scored an early first goal when Chalmers' shot bounced to him from a Swiss defender, and thereafter, it was largely a Celtic bombardment of Zurich's goal. Kunz played superbly as the visiting goalkeeper, but was unsighted when Gemmell drove a 30-yard shot past him. Fallon, meanwhile, had twice to make "double" saves from Swiss breakaways.

Legia Warsaw's eight goals at home to the Rumanian champions, Uta Arad, were an impressive surprise, after a close first game in Rumania. All eight goals came in the second half.

The most remarkable recovery was certainly St. Etienne's. So thoroughly beaten in Munich that the French critics were expatiating at length on the superiority of German football, they came brilliantly to life in the return, their talented strikers Keita and Revelli getting the three goals which put a surprised Bayern, and Beckenbauer, out of the Cup. Hervé Revelli thus confirmed his prolific recent form, which had included all three French goals away to Norway – and four in a friendly match, for his country.

In the Second Round, Leeds and Celtic opened in handsome style with 3–0 home victories on the same evening, Leeds over their old Fairs Cup Final rivals, Ferencvaros of Budapest, Celtic over the moulting lions of Benfica.

At Elland Road, where Ferencvaros, without Albert and Rakosi, made nothing of the heavy mud, it was a wonder that Leeds didn't score half-a-dozen. Themselves without Clarke and Cooper, they made a plenitude of chances against a Hungarian defence which, though heavily manned, was at times remarkably inept.

In less than two minutes, Bremner cleverly backheeled a return pass to Giles, who went through to score; both little men showed irresistible form, throughout. After twenty minutes, Gray crossed from the left, Lorimer from the right, and Mick Jones had no trouble in scoring. He had still less, ten minutes from half-time, when Giles ran through to find him in front of the goal, with Geczi alone to beat. This he did with calm efficiency – but it was to be the last of Leeds' goals, despite their superiority.

In Glasgow, Tommy Gemmell, who had just been put on the transfer list by his club, returned to the defence, and scored Celtic's first goal from a tearing free kick after only two minutes. Eusebio was twice thwarted by Fallon then, hobbling, receded from the game, to be replaced at half-time.

Jimmy Johnstone, robbing an opponent, made the second for Wallace who beat two defenders on the way; the third goal was scored with a header, by Hood from Murdoch's cross, after 69 minutes. Benfica, reduced to the offside game, could make little of Johnstone.

The return match was emphatically and astonishingly another story; Celtic went down 3–0 in their turn, scraped through on the toss of a coin, and probably owed their survival to the fact that Eusebio again had to leave the field at half-time. Not, however, before he had scored his team's first goal, nine minutes from the interval, with a superb header.

Graça then burst through on the right, took a return from Jorge, and shot in off the post to make it 2–0. Fallon and McNeill played gallantly in a besieged Celtic defence, throughout the second half, but at last Diamantino, with a plunging header, made it 3–0; and, on aggregate, 3–3. Fallon's save from Eusebio's half volley, after 20 minutes, was one of the best things in an enthralling match. It was an indictment of the competition that the victors should be so shabbily and arbitrarily decided.

In Budapest, Leeds had a much easier time of it, crushing Ferencvaros again in that Nep Stadium which has so often been the stage for British humiliations.

Only 5,400 spectators turned up in the rain to watch their flaccid team go down by the same score as at Elland Road: 3–0. Leeds held the Ferencvaros attack almost effortlessly, hit the post through Jones after five minutes and scored, again through the rampant Jones, after 36. Reaney crossed, Jones headed in, virtually untramelled. Nine minutes from time, he scored again, after robbing Juhasz. Finally, Lorimer's shot from 20 yards slithered home for the third. Leeds played with impressive poise, incision and skill, Paul Madeley yet again demonstrating his versatility, this time abetting Bremner in midfield.

The great surprise of the round was Milan's defeat by Feyenoord; revengers of Ajax, 1969's beaten Dutch finalists. At San Siro, the Rotterdam team held Milan, still suffering the reactions of their dire experiences in Buenos Aires, to a first half goal by Nestor Combin. In the return, Jansen wiped out that lead in the first half, after five minutes, and eight minutes from time, Van Hanegem headed the decisive goal. This, firmly scored from a left-wing cross, was an altogether more clear-cut affair than the first goal, when Cudicini surprisingly allowed Jansen's lob from the right-wing to pass over his head, plainly believing it would go out of play. Instead it clipped his right-hand post and rebounded into goal, giving Feyenoord an unexpected incentive, Milan a demoralising shock.

Another major surprise was the double defeat of Real Madrid by the excellent Standard Liège team, already enjoying another fine League season in Belgium.

It was not wholly unexpected that Real, much depleted and debilitated by injury for weeks past, should go down 1–0 in Liège – to a goal scored in the 41st minute by Standard's German centre-forward, Kostedde. It was most surprising that they could not even save, let alone win, the return match in Madrid, where they'd been virtually invincible for so long.

Louis Pilot, the Luxemburger captain and left-half of Standard's polyglot team, gave Standard a lead after only eight minutes with a shot Junquera might have saved. Velazquez equalised twelve minutes later, but a counter attack produced a second Belgian goal for Depireux. Again Real equalised, three minutes into the second half, – Gento scoring from the penalty spot after a foul on Amancio, and when Velazquez got the ball in the net again after a fusillade of shots, all seemed well for Real. But the goal was contentiously disallowed, for a previous Belgian offence, and Milan Galic, a Yugoslav substituting a German, Kostedde, scored the winner, seven minutes later.

Leeds United, in the quarter-finals, were a very different proposition, a team at its peak rather than one in decline. Exactly a week after five of the Standard players had been in the Belgian team well beaten by England in Brussels, Leeds, in very similar, wintry conditions, won in Liège. The goal was scored twenty minutes from time by Peter Lorimer; suitably enough, since only two fine saves by Piot had thwarted him in the first half. A long centre from the left by Terry Cooper was missed in the air by Dewalque, reaching Lorimer on the far post. The young Scot trapped the ball and shot from a very narrow angle, low into the far corner. Though Standard, who had always been full of running and enterprise in the heavy conditions, forced Gary Sprake to a couple of excellent late saves, Leeds held on to a victory they deserved. They had been cool, intelligent and, as the Standard manager said, physically very strong.

On the same evening, Celtic struck a blow for football in general, and Scottish football in particular, by thrashing a Fiorentina team cravenly huddled in defence; and not even doing it well.

Celtic, who know these tactics bitterly of old – not least from their games against Milan, the previous season – attacked consistently, which was not surprising, and successfully; which was. After 29 minutes John Hughes, so ill used that he gave way to Harry Hood, after half-time, pulled the ball back for Bertie Auld to score from 18 yards.

Four minutes after half-time, the indestructible Auld was involved in Celtic's second goal, when his cross was deflected by Carpenetti past his own goalkeeper. After 55 minutes Fiorentina called on Rizzo for Merlo and belatedly went over to the attack. This, as one knew, they were able to do with some style and colour. But it also opened them to counter-attack, and in the final minute Auld – again – crossed, Hood returned the ball into the middle, and Wallace headed in the important third.

The return, somewhat predictably, ended in a 1–0 win for Fiorentina, and victory on aggregate for Celtic. Chiarugi returned to the Fiorentina team and scored the goal after forty minutes with a cross shot from inside the penalty area.

Leeds, on the same night, had another 1–0 win over Standard, and although the goal came from a late penalty by Johnny Giles, they were well worth their success. Only a magnificent save, in the first half, by Piot from Clarke prevented their scoring earlier.

A high wind spoiled much of the game, and Leeds took most of the first half to gain control against Standard's compact, clever, forceful team. Eleven minutes from the end, Mick Jones was tripped in the area by Jeck, as he went through, and Giles calmly shot the penalty kick into the left-hand corner.

Legia Warsaw, the Polish champions, dealt as one expected they would with Galatassaray, the least likely of all the survivors; though in doing so, the Poles themselves became the team voted, so to speak, least likely to succeed. They drew in Turkey, after holding a one goal lead at half-time, and they won the return, in Warsaw, comfortably by two goals to nil. All three of their goals were scored by their experienced Polish international inside-forward, Brychzy.

Feyenoord were most piqued at having to play, in Berlin, on an atrocious pitch; frozen, it had been heavily sanded. At half-time, lorries came on to sand it again – and departed, leaving deep ruts. An error at a corner enabled Piepenburg to score the only goal of the game; any chance the Dutch may have had of recovery vanished when their full-back, Romeyn, idiotically struck an opponent, and was sent off.

But the Dutch champions did not err in the return, even if they had to wait for both their winning goals till the second half. The inevitable Ove Kindvall got the first, two minutes after half-time, and Wery, the right winger, added a second: the decider.

The semi-final round opened with the startling and merited victory of Celtic, at Leeds. Gaining the immense encouragement of a goal in the second minute, they went on to play beautifully measured, co-ordinated incisive football, defending in strength, counter attacking with bite. Only a very disputable decision prevented them doubling their lead early in the second half, and although Eddie Gray hit the bar late in the game, after dribbling superbly past two men, they very properly held out.

Leeds, who had put a reserve team out at Derby in a League match, two days earlier, and half a reserve side the previous Saturday, looked stale and uninventive. Connelly mastered Giles, who, like most of his team, was restricted to high lobs into the goal area. Bremner, well below his best, was taken off with concussion midway through the second half, giving way to Bates. Celtic later brought on Hughes for the excellent young Connelly, who had scored the goal; and driven home what might have been the second goal.

Madeley, deputising for Norman Hunter, was largely to blame for Celtic's scoring. He grievously missed a ball over on the right, and before he could recover, it was swept across the face of the goal. Connelly drove it, it hit Terry Cooper, and was deflected to the left of a becalmed Gary Sprake.

Though Williams once made a hash of a cross, to be violently berated by the confident Gemmell, he did not have one save to make till he smothered the ball at Clarke's feet, well into the second half. As against that, Sprake had to make several excellent saves, not least from Wallace, and Connelly, after Johnstone's run and pass, beat him all ends up just after the interval. The French referee gave an unexpected offside.

Little Jimmy Johnstone was perhaps the decisive player in the game. He ran superbly, dropping back to the edge of his own penalty area time and again to forage for the ball, beating his man at will, dribbling sinuously, forcing Cooper to keep an eye on him, so he scarcely began to overlap till well into the second half. All in all, a famous victory.

In Warsaw, Feyenoord, going deeper and deeper into defence as the match wore on, held Legia to a goalless draw in the Army Stadium. The match began in a drizzle, and ended under a drenching rain, the pitch reduced to a glutinous swamp.

When Leeds, four days after a Cup Final in which they had played extra time on an exhausting pitch, met Celtic in the return at Hampden, it was before 134,000 impassioned fans. They resisted as best they could, even held the lead at half-time through a remarkable opportunist's goal by Billy Bremner – then were crushed by a fresher, superior team.

Bremner's goal came after fourteen minutes of Celtic pressure. Receiving from Hunter, he perkily advanced to hit a long, splendid shot into the far, top corner of the goal, in off the post.

Celtic, with the brilliant Johnstone once again leading the United defence a fine dance, continued to attack, and both Madeley and Cooper were obliged to clear off the goal line. Mick Jones, the Leeds centre-forward, was carried off with a badly gashed leg, but bravely returned after the interval.

Within a couple of minutes, Celtic properly equalised. Hay pushed a short corner to Auld, at whose curling cross Hughes flung himself, to head a spectacular goal. It was after a collision with Hughes – deputising for Wallace – that Sprake was carried off with an injured leg, giving place to Harvey. Within five minutes, Celtic had scored the winner.

Johnstone once again electrically made himself space to centre, from the right. This time he pulled the ball back for the excellent Murdoch to hit it hard and true for the near corner. Harvey, who may well have been unsighted by one of his own defenders, could do little about it.

So Celtic deservedly, even majestically, reached their second European Final, after a victory in which they owed much to the dominance in midfield of Auld, Murdoch and the remarkable young "discovery", Connelly. Leeds could only brood on what might have been, had they not virtually been punished for their sheer success.

In the other semi-final, Feyenoord, as anticipated, despatched Legia

Warsaw. Not for the first time, the powerful Van Hanagem was their trump card, heading a goal after only three minutes. After 32 minutes, Hasil, the Austrian, scored the second from twenty yards. Feyenoord thus became the second successive Dutch club to reach the Final of the European Cup; impressive evidence of the improvement of the club game in Holland.

The Final provided an extraordinary game, which rose from a dull beginning, an undistinguished first half, to a thrilling crescendo, the belated winning goal coming only four minutes from the end of extra time.

Celtic, rather surprisingly and, as it proved, expensively, had decided on a 4–2–4 formation. Feyenoord played *catenaccio*, with Israel sweeping up with fine perception and agility behind the back four. Of the two midfield men, Van Hanegem generally played deep on the left, while Hasil, the Austrian international, perhaps the best man on the field, broke superbly into open spaces. The wingers, Wery and the veteran Coen Moulijn, were clever and resourceful while Ove Kindvall, the Swedish international centre-forward, though he missed two chances which greater quickness might have turned into goals, was a nagging danger.

The surprisingly ineffective form of little Jimmy Johnstone, hero of the semi-finals, accounted as much as any other factor for the poverty of Celtic's hectic, one pace, unintelligent display. Their solitary goal came on the half hour when Murdoch back-heeled a free kick to Gemmell, on the edge of the box, and the full-back thumped the ball in with enormous power. But two minutes later Celtic's own defence were standing still when, at a Feyenoord free kick, the ball was nodded across goal to Israel and by him off the far post and into the net, as casually as though it were all taking place on a hard tennis court.

In the second half, both sting and virtue had gone out of Celtic, and Feyenoord steadily dominated the play. Jansen often broke from defence, once giving Wery a through pass which should have meant a goal, while Hasil was a perpetual threat, hitting the post after 48 minutes. But the game went into extra time, and within thirty seconds, Hughes might have won it when he robbed an opponent, broke through and all but scored. Two minutes into the second period, Haak, the Dutch substitute, raced through from full-back, giving Kindvall the chance of a shot which Williams kept out with his feet. The goalkeeper then saved gallantly from Wery as he drove in the rebound.

But Celtic's luck could scarcely last. Four minutes from time, McNeill misjudged a long pass down the left and slipped, handling the ball as he fell. Kindvall, anticipating the mistake, ran on with the ball and beat Williams. Two minutes later, Hasil hit the underside of the bar, for good measure. A victory indeed.

EUROPEAN CUP 1969/70

Preliminary Round

Turku Palloseura 0	*KB Copenhagen* 1 Skouborg
KB Copenhagen 3 (Scorers unavailable)	*Turku Palloseura* (0) 0

First Round

Milan (1) 5 Prati 2, Rivera (penalty), Rognoni, Combin	*Avenir Beggen* (0) 0
Avenir Beggen (0) 0	*Milan* (1) 3 Combin, Sormani, Rivera
Leeds United (5) 10 Jones 3, Clarke 2, Giles 2, Bremner 2, O'Grady	*Lyn Oslo* (0) 0

Leeds United: Sprake; Reaney, Cooper; Bremner, Charlton, Hunter; Madeley, Clarke, Jones, Giles, O'Grady
Lyn Oslo: Olsen, S.; Rodvang, Kolle, Ostvold; Morisbak, Gulden; Borrehang, Christopherson, Berg, D. Olsen, Austnes.

Lyn Oslo (0) 0	*Leeds United* (3) 6 Belfitt 2, Hibbitt 2, Jones, Lorimer

Lyn Oslo: Olsen, S.; Rodvang, Ostvold, Borrehang, Kolle; Christopherson, Morisback; Hovdan, Berg, Olsen, O., Birkeland.
Leeds United: Sprake; Reaney, Cooper; Bremner, Madeley, Gray; Lorimer, Belfitt, Jones, Bates, Hibbitt.

Red Star (Belgrade) (5) 8 Karasi 2, Lazarevic 2, Klenkovski, Dzajic 2, Adamec	*Linfield* (0) 0

Red Star: Durkovic; Krivuca, Gevtic; Pavlovic, Dojcinoski, Klenkovski; Antonijevic, Karasi. Lazarevic, Acimovic, Dzajic.
Linfield: Gonigal; Gilliland, Patterson; Andrews, Bowyer, Hatton; Viollet, Millen, McGraw, Hamilton, Pavis.

Linfield (2) 2 McGraw 2	*Red Star (Belgrade)* (1) 4 Antonijevic 4
Basel (0) 0	*Celtic* (0) 0

Basel: Kunz; Kiefer, Michaud, Siegenthaler, Fischli; Ramseier, Odermatt; Hauser, Rahmon (Balmer), Benthaus, Wengen.
Celtic: Fallon; Craig, Gemmell; Brogan, McNeill, Clark; Johnstone, Chalmers, Wallace, Lennox, Hughes.

Celtic (1) 2	*Basel* (0) 0
Hood, Gemmell	

Celtic: Fallon; Hay, Gemmell; Clark, NcNeill, Callaghan; Johnstone, Wallace, Chalmers, Hood, Lennox.
Basel: Kunz; Michaud, Liefer, Ramseier, Siegenthaler, Fischli, Odermatt, Benthaus, Balmer, Hauser (Demarmeis), Wenger.

Hibernians Malta (0) 2	*Spartak Trnava* (0) 2
Cassar, Bonello	Adamec, Martinkov
Spartak Trnava (1) 4	*Hibernians Malta* (0) 0
Hrusecky, Adamec 2	
Azzopardi (own goal)	
Galatassaray (2) 2	*Waterford* (0) 0
Gokmen 2	
Waterford (0) 2	*Galatassaray* (1) 3
Buck, Morley	Ugur, Gokman, Ayhan
CSK Sofia (0) 2	*Ferencvaros* (0) 1
Jekov 2	Rakosi
Ferencvaros (2) 4	*CSK Sofia* (1) 1
Szoeke 2 (1 pen.),	Marosliev
Branikovics, Rakosi	
Arad (1) 1	*Legia Warsaw* (0) 2
Domide	Zmijewski, Gadocha
Legia Warsaw (0) 8	*Arad* (0) 0
Blaut, Gadocha 2, Brychzy,	
Sztachurski, Dejna, Zmijewski,	
Pieszko (penalty)	
Vorwaerts (0) 2	*Panathanaikos* (0) 0
Piepenberg 2	
Panathanaikos (1) 1	*Vorwaerts* (0) 1
Antoniades	Laslop
Bayern Munich (1) 2	*St. Etienne* (0) 0
Brenninger, Roth	

St. Etienne (1) 3 Revelli 2, Keita	*Bayern Munich* (0) 0
Standard Liege (2) 3 Kasmi (own goal), Depireux 2	*Nendori Tirana* (0) 0
Nendori Tirana (1) 1	*Standard Liege* (1) 1
Feyenoord (7) 12 Kindvall 3, Geels 4, Van Hanegem 2, Romeyn, Van Duivinsson, Wery	*Reykjavik* (0) 0
Reykjavik (0) 0	*Feyenoord* (2) 4 Geels 2, Kindvall, Wery

Played in Rotterdam

F.K. Austria (1) 1 Riedl	*Dynamo Kiev* (0) 2 Serber, Muntijan
Dynamo Kiev (0) 3 Muntian, Bychevetz, Pusach	*F.K. Austria* (1) 1 Aritz
Fiorentina (0) 1 Maraschi	*Oester* (*Sweden*) (0) 0
Oester (1) 1 Fjordestan	*Fiorentina* (1) 2 Amarildo, Esposito
Benfica (2) 2 Eusebio 2	*K.B. Copenhagen* (0) 0
K.B. Copenhagen (1) 2 Skovborg 2 (1 pen.)	*Benfica* (3) 3 Eusebio, Diamantino 2
Real Madrid (3) 8 Georgiou (own goal), Gento 2, Grosso, Fleitas 2 Grande, Pirri	*Olimpiakos Nicosia* (0) 0
Olimpiakos Nicosia (1) 1 Kettenis	*Real Madrid* (3) 6 De Diego 2, Planelles, Grande, Avramides (own goal) Fleitas

Played in Madrid

Second Round

Leeds United (3) 3	*Ferencvaros* (0) 0
Giles, Jones 2	

Leeds United: Sprake; Reaney, Madeley; Bremner, Charlton, Hunter; Lorimer, Bates, Jones, Giles, Gray.
Ferencvaros: Geczi; Novak, Pancsics, Balint, Horvath, Megyesi (Nemeth), Szoke, Juhasz, Szucs, Katona.

Ferencvaros (0) 0	*Leeds United* (1) 3
	Jones 2, Lorimer

Ferencvaros: Geczi; Novak, Balint, Megyesi, Juhasz, Szucs, Szoke, Branikovics, Horvath (Vaida), Nemeth, Katona.
Leeds United: Sprake; Reaney, Cooper; Bremner, Charlton, Hunter; Lorimer, Madeley, Jones, Giles, Gray.

Celtic (2) 3	*Benfica* (0) 0
Gemmell, Wallace, Hood	

Celtic: Fallon; Craig, Gemmell; Murdoch, McNeill, Clark; Johnstone, Hood, Wallace, Auld, Hughes.
Benfica: Henrique; Malta, Humberto, C., Zeca, Humberto, F., Graca, Coluna, Simoes, Torres, Eusebio (Augusto), Diamantino (Jorge).

Benfica (2) 3	*Celtic* (0) 0
Eusebio, Graca, Diamantino	

Celtic won on toss

Benfica: Henrique; Da Silva, Messias, Coluna, Adolfo, Toni, Graca, Aguas (Diamantino), Jorge, Eusebio (Martins), Simoes.
Celtic: Fallon; Craig, Gemmell; Brogan, McNeill, Murdoch; Johnstone, Callaghan (Connelly), Wallace, Auld (Hood), Hughes.

Dynamo Kiev (0) 1	*Fiorentina* (1) 2
Serebrianikov	Chiarugi, Maraschi
Fiorentina (0) 0	*Dynamo Kiev* (0) 0
Milan (1) 1	*Feyenoord* (0) 0
Combin	
Feyenoord (1) 2	*Milan* (0) 0
Jansen, Van Hanegem	
Spartak Trnava (0) 1	*Galatassaray* (0) 0
Kabat	

Galatassaray (0) 1 Ergun	*Spartak Trnava* (0) *Galatassray won toss*
St Legia Warsaw (0) 2 Plesko, Deyna	*St. Etienne* (1) 1 Revelli
St. Etienne (0) 0	*Legia Warsaw* (0) Deyna
Vorwaerts (1) 2 Fraessdorf, Begerad	*Red Star* (1) 1 Antonijevic
Red Star (1) 3 Karsi 2, Acimovic	*Vorwaerts* (1) 2 Begerad 2
Standard Liège (1) 1 Kostedde	*Real Madrid* (0) 0
Real Madrid (1) 2 Valazquez, Gento (penalty)	*Standard Liège* (2) 3 Pilot, Depireux, Galic

Quarter Finals

Standard Liège (0) 0	*Leeds United* (0) 1 Lorimer

Standard: Piot; Beurlet, Thyssen; Dewalque, Jeck, Van Moer; Semmeling, Pilot, Galic, Depireux, Takac.
Leeds United: Sprake; Reaney, Cooper; Bremner, Charlton, Hunter; Lorimer, Clarke, Jones, Giles, Madeley.

Leeds United (0) 1 Giles (penalty)	*Standard Liège* (0) 0

Leeds United: Sprake; Reaney, Cooper; Bremner, Charlton, Hunter; Lorimer, Clarke, Jones, Giles, Madeley.
Standard: Piot; Beurlet, Thyssen; Dewalque, Jeck, Pilot; Semmeling, Van Moer, Galic, Depireux, Takac.

Celtic (1) 3 Auld, Carpenetti (own goal), Wallace	*Fiorentina* (0) 0

Celtic: Williams; Hay, Gemmell; Murdoch, McNeill, Brogan; Johnstone, Lennox, Wallace, Auld, Hughes (Hood).
Fiorentina: Superchi; Rogora, Lomgoni, Carpenetti, Ferrante, Brizi, Esposito, Merlo (Rizzo), Maraschi, De Sisti, Amarildo.

Fiorentina (1) 1 Chiarugi	*Celtic* (0) 0

Fiorentina: Superchi; Rogora, Esposito, Ferrante, Lomgoni; Brizi, Merlo, De Sisti; Chiarugi, Maraschi, Amarildo.
Celtic: Williams; Hay, McNeill, Connelly, Gemmell; Brogan, Murdoch, Auld; Johnstone, Wallace, Lennox.

Galatassaray (0) 1 Mihat-Pacha	*Legia Warsaw* (1) 1 Brychzy
Legia Warsaw (1) 2 Brychzy 2	*Galatassaray* (0) 0
Vorwaerts (0) 1 Piepenburg	*Feyenoord* (0) 0
Feyenoord (0) 2 Kindvall, Wery	*Vorwaerts* (0) 0

Semi-Finals

Leeds United (0) 0	*Celtic* (1) 1 Connelly

Leeds United: Sprake; Reaney, Cooper; Bremner, (Bates), Charlton, Madeley; Lorimer, Clarke, Jones, Giles, Gray.
Celtic: Williams; Hay, Gemmell; Murdoch, McNeill, Brogan; Johnstone, Connelly, Wallace, Lennox, Auld.

Celtic (0) 2 Hughes, Murdoch	*Leeds United* (1) 1 Bremner

At Hampden Park

Celtic: Williams; Hay, Gemmell; Murdoch, McNeill, Brogan; Johnstone, Connelly, Hughes, Auld, Lennox.
Leeds United: Sprake; (Harvey), Madeley, Cooper; Bremner, Charlton, Hunter; Lorimer, (Bates), Clarke, Jones, Giles, Gray.

Legia Warsaw (0) 0	*Feyenoord* (0) 0
Feyenoord (2) 2 Van Hanegem, Hasil	*Legia Warsaw* (0) 0

FINAL *San Siro, Milan,* May 6, 1970

Feyenoord (1) 2	*Celtic* (1) 1
Israel, Kindvall	Gemmell

(*after extra time*)

Feyenoord: Pieters Graafland; Romeyn (Haak), Israel, Laseroms, Jansen, Van Duivenbode; Hasil, Van Hanegem; Wery, Kindvall, Moulijn.
Celtic: Williams; Hay, Gemmell; Murdoch, McNeill, Brogan; Johnstone, Wallace, Hughes, Auld (Connelly), Lennox.
Referee: Concetto Lo Bello (Italy).

Chapter Four

European Cupwinners' Cup 1969/70

Manchester City displayed their extraordinary capacity to rise to the occasion when they added the Cupwinners' Cup to the imposing list of trophies they have won in the past few seasons. They deservedly beat Gornik, the experienced Poles, in the Final, although they had to play without a key forward in Mike Summerbee, and lost the admirable Mike Doyle, early in the game. Their form in the competition vacillated, as it did throughout the season, but they came splendidly into their own in the return leg of the semi-final, at home to Schalke 04, and not unexpectedly became the third English club to win the competition. In the process, Francis Lee was able to demonstrate again that he is one of the most effective strikers in the world, while the value of the partnership between the shrewd Joe Mercer, as manager, and the explosive Malcolm Allison, as coach, was re-emphasised.

In a Preliminary Round match, Rapid Vienna eliminated Torpedo Moscow on the iniquitous basis of "away" goals. The first meeting between the clubs, in Vienna, ended in a 0–0 draw. In Moscow, under heavy, continuous rain, Torpedo did most of the pressing, but left Redl alone when he scored Rapid's vital goal after 54 minutes. Gershkovitsch managed to equalise two minutes from time, but his goal was of merely academic significance, Redl's was worth two....

Manchester City, setting out once more to frighten the cowards of Europe, received another fright themselves when Bilbao, managed by the former England international and Wolves manager Ronnie Allen took a 3–1 lead against them, in Spain. Bilbao were two ahead within eleven minutes, but Neil Young retrieved a goal in the vital minutes before half-time. The prolific Uriarte got a third, but Tommy Booth, City's young centre-half, scored in the 68th minute, and a courageous rally brought the equaliser near time. Colin Bell harried Echeverria into an own goal. The match gave ammunition to those who believed in City's attack, but less so in their defence. They were lucky to find Iribar, Bilbao's Spanish international goalkeeper, on such an untypically bad day.

He played well in the return, but not well enough to save Bilbao from defeat by an exuberant and much superior City team which attacked continuously. Oakes, in rampant form an attacking wing-half, put them ahead, a desperate scamper from goal by Iribar failed to avert a second goal, by Bell, and Bowyer got the third. All came in the second half – after a nasty incident in the tunnel between Doyle and Betzuen, who had to be substituted. A pity it should blemish so convincing and enterprising a display by City. Their unrelaxing pressure simply wore down Bilbao's packed defence.

Rangers, with two goals by their Scottish international forward, Johnston, took a comfortable lead against the Rumanians, Steaua. In the return match, they played a clever and effective defensive game, with Baxter skilful in midfield. Twice they broke away and came close to scoring through Watson and Jardine, but in the event a goalless draw was all they needed. Greig, their captain, was in good fettle.

Ards, doubtless encouraged by Swindon's very recent crushing of Roma, in the Football League Cupwinners' meetings, boldly held them to a goalless draw, in Ulster; another blow to Helenio Herrera's prestige.

Ards did not disgrace themselves in Rome, though almost inevitably they went down. A goal behind at half-time, the final score was 3–1, two of the goals going to the Roma centre-forward, the expensive Salvori.

Cardiff City, those weathered veterans of the competition, enjoyed themselves in Norway, scoring seven goals, four of them shared by their strikers, Clark and the much coveted John Toshack.

In the return, at Ninian Park, Cardiff strolled through easily. Three of their goals went to the 21-year-old reserve centre-forward, Sandy Allan, a Scot from Forfar. Peter King was responsible for the other two.

Shamrock Rovers surpassed themselves in Dublin, beating the German Cupholders, Schalke O4 of Gelsenkirchen, by the odd goal in three, both their goals being scored by Barber. It was clearly too much to expect them to do as well in the return, and they duly went down 3–0, in Gelsenkirchen.

Perhaps the most surprising result of the round was Dynamo Zagreb's 3–0 win over the Czech holders, Slovan Bratislava. Zagreb had long figured doughtily in European competition, but the ease of their success was highly unexpected. In the return, they held on in Bratislava to a goalless draw – so the holders had gone out in the very first round, as surprisingly eliminated as last season they had been unexpectedly successful.

In the Second Round, Manchester City took Lierse to pieces with some ease, in Belgium. Francis Lee shot in a header from Colin Bell, after seven minutes, then took a pass from Young – after 35 – beat a man and made it 2–0. He himself made the third goal for Bell, a minute from half-time.

At Maine Road, De Nul and Lierse gave City a great deal of trouble in the first half, though Mike Summerbee opened the score after 21 minutes. The second half saw Manchester dominant, setting a pace which finally annihilated Lierse and brought four more goals.

Rangers were toppled by Gornik, 3–1, in Poland, the formidable Lubanski scoring two of the goals. Two behind after nine minutes, Rangers protested that the third was scored after the ball had run out of play, Persson having previously made it 1–2.

In the return, Gornik surprisingly beat them by the same score at Ibrox, although Baxter gave them the lead with a strong right-foot shot after 17 minutes. Rangers dominated play but missed chances, and Olek broke away to equalise after 64 minutes. Lubanski scored a dazzling individual goal to put Gornik ahead, and their substitute, Skowronek, shot the third from 30 yards.

Cardiff City, usually so successful in this competition, were thoroughly beaten in Turkey by Goeztepe Izmir, who scored all their three goals in the first half.

Bird, substituting Lea, scored the only goal of the return, at Ninian Park, from long range but the tight Goeztepe defence allowed no more.

Manchester City found themselves, by the time they had to play the first leg of their quarter-final in Coimbra, in something of a trough; and only three days away from the League Cup Final. Their defensively organised team, with Pardoe, their left-back, a mock outside-right, gained a dull draw, without goals.

They were not much more impressive in the return, when they scraped through in the last minutes of extra time with a goal shot from twenty yards by their young substitute, Towers, who'd taken the place of Heslop, the burly defender, after the interval.

Coimbra, who had come to defend, and did it dourly, had no direct shot at goal until extra time. But although City were allowed to make the running, the tackling they faced was fast and hard. Seventeen minutes from time, they lost Colin Bell, who gave way to another youngster in Glennon. At long last Young crossed from the left, the ball was only half cleared, and Towers scored his goal.

In Rome, at the Stadio Olimpico, the Turks of Goeztepe, Smyrna, not only lost a boring game; they returned to the dressing-rooms to find that thieves had taken their money, watches and cigarettes.

Roma's 2–0 victory, by contrast, was no robbery, but it was obtained without flair or excitement against unenterprising opposition. Roma scored in the 31st minute of each half. A shot by Landini, which Ali might have saved, went in off a post, but the goalkeeper was unlucky when, after a brave intervention at the feet of Cordova, the ball flew upwards, for Cappelli to head an easy goal.

The return was another of those goalless draws in which Italian teams specialise, allowing Roma, and Helenio Herrera, to achieve the semi-final.

Fifty thousand spectators were present at a most exciting game in Sofia, Levski just getting the better of the Poles, Gornik Zabrze, 3–2; though they might have won more clearly. Gornik, who played a hard, physical game, exploited bad errors in the home defence with goals by Szoltysik and Banas, the first opening the score after six minutes. Asparoukhov, just back from a successful tour with the national team in Latin America, equalised on the half hour. Five minutes later, Panov gave Levski the advantage. In the 52nd minute, Banas equalised but Asparoukhov restored the Bulgarian lead, three minutes from the end.

It wasn't enough, however, to let them qualify. Gornik, with Lubanski and, once more, Banas getting the goals, beat them in Poland in front of an immense, 100,000 crowd, qualifying by virtue of their two away goals.

Schalke 04, improving with each round, had a splendid 3–1 away win over Dynamo Zagreb who, it will be remembered, had eliminated the holders. The return was, perhaps, a formality after this, but it was also harder going for the West Germans, who won only by a single goal – scored by Scheer, who came on as a substitute.

A splendid, characteristic individual goal by West Germany's outside-right, Libuda, beat Manchester City in their opening leg of the semi-final, away to Schalke 04. A quarter-of-an-hour from time, he raced fifty yards, beating Pardoe and Jefferies on the way, ending with a shot past Corrigan into the corner of the goal. Throughout the game, he ridiculed the heavy, slippery conditions.

Schalke, who largely called the tune after the first fifteen minutes, were particularly dominant after the interval, with Nauser, their inside-right, often dangerous.

In Rome, Gornik took a half-time lead through Banas, who scored after 23 minutes, but Salvori equalised after 52 minutes.

Manchester City, wildly unpredictable but full of possibilities, proceeded to tear Schalke 04 to shreds in the return at Maine Road, Lee, Bell and Summerbee, till he was injured, showing their most dynamic form, and Neil Young, recapturing his to score two fulminating goals. City's attacking play brimmed over with power, pace and invention.

After eight minutes, Lee got away, Oakes shot, and the ball was deflected to Mike Doyle, who scored. Next, Bell and Oakes gave Young the chance to control the ball coolly in the penalty box, and shoot in off the far post. Then, after Lee had dummied the German defence on Oakes' pass, Young ran through to score with a powerful left footer.

In the second half, Lee ran round the blind side after an elegant movement, to score the fourth, Young had a shot kicked off the line, then, in the 81st minute, Bell put in his long centre. It was no more than an anticlimax when the always combative Libuda got Schalke's one, irrelevant goal in injury time.

Roma, meanwhile, were drawing 2–2 away to Gornik in extra time; a fact which prevented them from qualifying on away goals. Capello gave Roma the lead from a penalty kick in the tenth minute, and it was only in the very last minute that another penalty kick, converted by Lubanski, equalised for Gornik.

After four minutes of extra time, Lubanski put Gornik ahead, but Roma, showing far more resilience than had been expected of them, equalised through Larosa in the final minute of injury time; the biter substantially bit.

Obliged to meet a third time, Gornik and Roma drew again, 1–1 after extra time, in Strasburg, and the villainous expedient of the toss sent Gornik luckily through to the Final. Lubanski, as usual, scored their goal, after 39 minutes; Capello equalised for Roma after 57.

The Final was played a week later in Vienna in pouring rain, before a minuscule crowd. Neil Young gave Manchester City the lead after 12 minutes, when Lee, whom Gornik never mastered, squeezed between two Polish defenders and beat Kostka with a shot that hit the post; Neil Young easily put in the loose ball. Four minutes later, Mike Doyle went off, injured, to be substituted, after some minutes, by Ian Bowyer, Colin Bell dropping deeper. Two minutes from half-time, City scored again, when Young, clean through, was fouled by Kostka. Lee took the penalty, hitting Kostka's legs with a shot which was still strong enough to score.

The die seemed cast. Lubanski, after a promising beginning, had been quite outshone by Lee, but twenty minutes from time, he juggled the ball on the edge of the six-yard box, and passed to Oslizlo, who had materialised, to score. City, however, held on for a well-deserved victory, the reward for much fluent football.

EUROPEAN CUPWINNERS' CUP 1969/70

Preliminary Round

Rapid Vienna (0) 0	*Torpedo Moscow* (0) 0
Torpedo Moscow (0) 1 Gerschkovitsch	*Rapid Vienna* (0) 1 Redl

First Round

Atletico Bilbao (2) 3 Argoitia, Clemente, Uriarte	*Manchester City* (1) 3 Young, Booth, Echeverria (own goal)

Bilbao: Iribar; Saez, Echeverria, Araguaren, Igartua; Larrauri, Argoitia; Uriarte, Arieta, Clemente, Rojo.
Manchester City: Corrigan; Book, Pardoe; Doyle, Booth, Oakes; Summerbee, Bell, Lee, Young, Bowyer.

Manchester City (0) 3 Oakes, Bell, Bowyer	*Atletico Bilbao* (0) 0

Manchester City: Corrigan; Book, Pardoe; Doyle, Booth, Oakes; Summerbee, Bell, Lee, Young, Bowyer.
Bilbao: Iribar; Zugzaga, Araguaren, Igartua, Echeverria; Larrauri, Argoitia; Betusszuen, Arieta, Clemente, Rojo.

Ards (0) 0	*Roma* (0) 0

Ards: Kydd; McCloy, Stewart; Nixon, Crothers, Bell; McAvoy, McAteer, Burke (Sands), Humphries, Welsh.
A.S. Roma: Ginulfi; Carpenetti, Cappelli; Santarini, Spinosi, Bet; Broglia (Enzo), Landini, Peirò, Capello, Scaratti.

Roma (1) 3 Salvori 2, Peirò	*Ards* (0) 1 Crothers

Roma: Ginulfi; Bet, Petrelli, Salvori, Cappelli; Santarini, Bertogna; Cappellini, Peirò, Capello, Cordova.
Ards: Kydd; McCloy, Crothers; Bell, Stewart, Nixon; Welsh, Humphries, McCoy, Anderson, McIntyre.

Rangers (2) 2 Johnston 2	*Steaua* (*Bucharest*) (0) 0

Rangers: Neef; Johansen, Provan; Greig, McKinnon, Baxter; Henderson, Jardine, Stein, Johnston, Persson.
Steaua: Lujtsuciu; Cristache, Satmareanu, Vigu, Dumitru, Halmageanu, Pantea, Tataru, Voinea, Negrea, Creiniceanu.

Steaua (Bucharest) (0) 0 — *Rangers* (0) 0

Steaua: Suciu; Cristache, Satmareanu, Halmageanu, Vigu; Dumitru (Nicolae), Negrea; Pantea, Tataru, Voinea, Manea (Stefanescu).
Rangers: Neef; Johansen, Provan; Greig, McKinnon, Baxter; Henderson, Watson (Smith), Stein, Jardine, Johnston.

Mjoendalen (1) 1 — *Cardiff City* (3) 7
Olsen — Clark 2, Toshack 2, Lea, Sutton, King

Mjoendalen: Nilsen; Broch, Jonsrud, Loe, Svendsen; Brede, Skistad; Kristiansen; Solberg, Holmen (Larsen), Boye Skistad, Olsen.
Cardiff City: Davies; Derrett, Carver, Sutton, Murray; Harris, Phillips (Jones); Clark, Lea, Toshack, King.

Cardiff City (4) 5 — *Mjoendalen* (1) 1
King 2, Allan 3 — Solberg

Cardiff City: Davies; Carver, Bell, Sutton, Murray, Lewis, Jones; Clark, Allan, Toshack, King.
Mjoendalen: Larsen, J.; Broch, Jonsrud; Loe, Svendsen, Skistad; Kristiansen, Solberg, E., Holmen (Solberg, J.), Larsen, S., Olsen.

Shamrock Rovers (1) 2 — *Schalke* 04 (1) 1
Barber 2 — Pirkner

Schalke 04 (1) 3 — *Shamrock Rovers* (0) 0
Libuda, Pirkner, Wittkamp

F.C. Magdeburg (1) 1 — *MTK Budapest* (0) 0
Sparwasser

MTK Budapest (1) 1 — *F.C. Magdeburg* (0) 1
Takacs — Sparwasser
after extra time

Dukla Prague (1) 1 — *Olympique Marseilles* (0) 0
Hudec

Olympique Marseilles (1) 2 — *Dukla Prague* (0) 0
Loubet 2

Rapid Vienna (1) 1 — *PSV Eindhoven* (2) 2
Bjerregaard — Veenstra, Schmidt-Hansen

PSV Eindhoven (2) 4 — *Rapid Vienna* (1) 2
Van der Kuylen, Veenstra, Schmidt-Hansen 2 — Floegel, Bjerregaard

Frem (2) 2 Henning, Hansen	*St. Gallen* (1) 1 Nafziger
St. Gallen (0) 1 Cornioley	*Frem* (0) 0
Norkopping (3) 5 Asfeldim 2, Nordblad, Jonsson 2	*Sliema Malta* (1) 1 Bonnet
Sliema Malta (0) 1	*Norkopping* (0) 0
Dynamo Zagreb (1) 3 Milkjovic, Novak, Gucmirtl	*Slovan Bratislava* (0) 0
Slovan Braitslava (0) 0	*Dynamo Zagreb* (0) 0
Lierse (5) 10 Vermeyen 3, De Nul 4, Put, Janssens 2	*Apoel* (*Cyprus*) (0) 1 Agathocleus
Apoel (*Cyprus*) (0) 0	*Lierse* (1) 1 De Nul

(*played at Lierse*)

Olimpiakos (0) 2 Joutsos, Sideris	*Gornik* (2) 2 Wilczek 2
Gornik (1) 5 Wilczek, Skowronek, Szoltysik, Banas 2 (1 penalty)	*Olimpiakos* (0) 0
Goztepe Izmir (1) 3 Gursel, Fevzi, Halil	*Union Luxembourg* (0) 0
Union Luxembourg (0) 2	*Goztepe Izmir* (2) 3
IBV Reykjavik (0) 0	*Levski* 4 Panov 2, Veselinov, Asparoukhov
Levski (1) 4 Kotkov 3, Galdarski	*IBV Reykjavik* (0) 0
Academica (0) 0	*Palloseura Kuspio* (0) 0
Palloseura (0) 0	*Academica* (0) 1 Nele

Second Round

Lierse (0) 0	*Manchester City* (3) 3
	Lee 2, Bell

Lierse: Engelen; Diereckx, Bogaerts, Michielsen, Van Den Eynde, Willems, Vermeyen, Van Opstal, De Nul, De Ceulaer, Janssens.
Manchester City: Corrigan; Book, Pardoe; Doyle (Heslop), Booth, Oakes; Summerbee, Bell, Lee, Young, Bowyer.

Manchester City (1) 5	*Lierse* (0) 0
Summerbee, Bell 2, Lee 2	

Manchester City: Mulhearn; Book, Pardoe; Doyle, Booth, Oakes (Towers); Summerbee, Bell, Lee, Jeffries, Bowyer.
Lierse: Engelen; Van Den Eynde, Bogaerts, Michielsen, Martens, Willems, Van Opstal, Janssens, De Ceulaer, De Nul, Min (Put).

Gornik Zabrze (2) 3	*Rangers* (0) 1
Lubanski 2, Szoltysik	Persson

Gornik: Kostka; Latocha, Oslizlo; Gorgon, Florenski, Szoltysik; Wilczek, Olek, Banas, Lubanski, Szarynski.
Rangers: Neef; Johansen, Heron; Greig, McKinnon, Baxter; Henderson, Penman, Stein, Johnston, Persson.

Rangers (1) 1	*Gornik Zabrze* (0) 3
Baxter	Olek, Lubanski, Skowzonek

Rangers: Neef; Johansen (Jardine), Heron; Greig, McKinnon, Baxter; Henderson, Penman, Stein, Johnston, Persson (McDonald).
Gornik: Kostka; Kutchka, Oslizlo, Gorgon, Latocha, Szoltysik, Wilczek, Olek, Banas, Lubanski, Szarynski. sub: Skowzonek.

Goeztepe Izmir (3) 3	*Cardiff City* (0) 0
Fevzi, Ertan, Nielssen	

Goeztepe Izmir: Mehmet, I., Caglayan, Ihsan; Mehmet, A., Ozer, Nevsat; Fevzi, Ertan, Nielssen, Gersel, Mehmet, F.
Cardiff City: Davies; Carver, Bell; Harris, Murray, Sutton; Lea, Clark, King, Toshack, Sharp.

Cardiff City (0) 1	*Goeztepe Izmir* (0) 0
Bird	

Cardiff City: Davies; Carver, Bell; Sutton, Murray, Harris; Allan, Clark, Lea, Toshack, King. subs: Bird, Coldrick.
Goeztepe: Mehmet, I.; Caglayan, Ozer, Mehmet, A., Azi, Nevsat, Fevzi, Ertan, Nielssen, Gursel, Mehmet, F.

Roma (0) 1 Capello	*P.S.V. Eindhoven* (0) 0
P.S.V. Eindhoven (0) 1 Van der Kuylen	*Roma* (0) 0

(*after extra time: Roma won toss*)

Norkopping (0) 0	*Schalke* 04 (0) 0
Schalke 04 (1) 1 Scheer	*Norkopping* (0) 0
Levski (2) 4 Kostov, Panov, Mitkov, Kirilov	*St. Gallen* (0) 0
St. Gallen (0) 0	*Levski* (0) 0
F.C. Magdeburg (1) 1 Sparwasser	*Academica Coimbra* (0) 0
Academica Coimbra (0) 2 Alinho, Mario Campos	*F.C. Magdeburg* (0) 0
Marseilles (1) 1 Loubet	*Dynamo Zagreb* (0) 1 Cercek
Dynamo Zagreb (0) 0	*Marseilles* (0) 0

Quarter-Finals

Academica Coimbra (0) 0	*Manchester City* (0) 0

Academica Coimbra: Cardoso; Artur, Albino, Rodriguez, Marques, Rocha, Campos, M., Campos, V., Jorge, Nene, Serafim.
Manchester City: Corrigan; Book, Mann; Doyle, Booth, Oakes; Pardoe, Bell, Summerbee, Lee, Young.

Manchester City (0) 1 Towers *after extra time*	*Academica Coimbra* (0) 0

Manchester City: Corrigan; Book, Mann; Booth, Heslop (Towers), Oakes; Doyle, Bell (Glennon), Lee, Young, Pardoe.
Academica Coimbra: Cardoso; Artur, Albino, Rodriguez, Marques, Rocha; Campos, M., Campos, V., Antonio, Nene, Serafim.

Roma (1) 2 Landini, Cappelli	*Goeztepe Izmir* (0) 0
Goeztepe Izmir (0) 0	*Roma* (0) 0

Levski Sofia (2) 3	*Gornik* (1) 2
Asparoukhov 2, Banov	Szoltysik, Banas
Gornik (1) 2	*Levski Sofia* (0) 1
Lubanski, Banas	Kivilov
Dynamo Zagreb (0) 1	*Schalke* 04 (1) 3
Cercek	Pirkner, Fichtel, Becher
Schalke 04 (0) 1	*Dynamo Zagreb* (0) 0
Scheer	

Semi-Finals

Schalke 04 (0) 1	*Manchester City* (0) 0
Libuda	
Manchester City (3) 5	*Schalke* 04 (0) 1
Doyle, Young 2, Lee, Bell	Libuda

Manchester City: Corrigan; Book, Pardoe; Doyle, Booth, Oakes; Towers, Bell, Summerbee (Carrodus), Lee, Young.
Schalke 04: Nigbur; Slomiany, Becher, Russman, Fichtel, Wiitkamp; Libuda, Neuser, Poh Ischmidt, Erlhoff, Van Haaren. sub: Scheer.

Roma (0) 1	*Gornik* (1) 1
Banas	Salvori
Gornik (0) 2	*Roma* (1) 2
Lubanski 2 (1 penalty)	Capello (penalty), Larosa

Semi-final play-off: *Strasbourg*

Gornik (1) 1	*Roma* (0) 1
Lubanski	Capello

(*after extra time: Gornik won on toss*)

FINAL, *Vienna,* April 29, 1970

Manchester City (2) 2	*Gornik* (0) 1
Young, Lee (penalty)	Oslizlo

Manchester City: Corrigan; Book, Booth, Heslop, Pardoe, Doyle (Bowyer), Oakes, Towers, Bell, Lee, Young.
Gornik: Kostka; Gorgon, Oslizlo, Latocha, Florenski (Deja), Olek, Szoltysik, Wilczek (Skowronck), Banas, Lubanski, Szarynski.

Chapter Five

European Fairs Cup 1969/70

For the first time since 1953, a major honour came to Highbury when Arsenal, against all the odds, won the European Fairs Cup; thus becoming the third successive English club to do so. When Newcastle United, the holders, went out on "away goals" to Anderlecht in the quarter-finals, there seemed little hope of the Cup remaining in England. But Arsenal rose above themselves magnificently, first to put out Ajax, the 1969 European Cup finalists, in the semi-final, then to beat Anderlecht, after losing 3–1 in Brussels, by a ringing and well deserved 3–0.

Arsenal's home form against both Ajax and Anderlecht was extraordinarily good; and earlier in the competition they had made Sporting Lisbon, who ran away with the Portuguese championship, look a poor side. Though they paid £100,000 during the season for the Hibernian winger, Peter Marinello, the irony was that he did not even play in the Final, when they owed so much to their own, home-developed youngsters, such as the brilliant 18-year-old half-back Eddie Kelly, the local forward, Charlie George, and the indomitable George Armstrong. Kelly's goal, in the Final, was one of the most brilliantly taken of the season, and it was heartening, after the game, to witness such scenes of triumph again at Highbury.

Newcastle, the holders, who had begun the season well but then run into a losing sequence, recovered just in time to win away to Dundee United, 2–1. For this, they had to thank the remarkable heading powers of Wyn Davies, who struck the crossbar three times in the first half, with his headers, then, in the second half, headed two goals. Both came from right wing centres; the first by the overlapping Craggs, the second from Robson. Ian Scott's later goal for Dundee United was also headed.

Newcastle continued to play poorly in the League, and when they scrambled home against the Scots club in the return, thanks to Dyson's goal in the second minute of injury time, it was only their second victory in eight games; the other being at Dundee. Reid was in excellent form for the visitors, who were more than a match for the holders, after a deceptively good start. In the last ten minutes, however, Newcastle crowded on sail again – and scored.

Arsenal overcame Glentoran 3–0 after dominating the first half, George Graham, in splendidly accurate form at the time, scored two of their goals, exploiting his ability in the air.

The return match was surprisingly won 1–0 by Glentoran, Henderson exploiting a penalty kick for hands against Neill after only 90 seconds. Charlie George, Arsenal's 18-year-old striker, was sent off in the second half, apparently for insulting a linesman, but the defence held out without trouble.

Liverpool crushed Dundalk in a welter of goals. Dunfermline, running well in the Scottish League at the time, defeated Bordeaux after an eventful second half in which two of the "Girondins", Dortomb and Durdino, were sent off, before ten minutes had gone. They lost 2–0 in the return, but had enough goals in hand to survive the defeat.

Kilmarnock recovered well to knock out Zurich, losing the first tie by the odd goal (after leading 2–0), but prevailing in the second, thanks largely to a fine display on the right wing by little Tommy McLean. He made two of the goals and got the other himself, following up his own penalty kick.

Southampton, in their first leg, were surprised by Rosenborg Trondheim, in Norway; a team, ironically enough, coached by their erstwhile left-half, George Curtis. True, Ron Davies, Southampton's chief striker, had to be substituted at half-time, thanks to a groin injury. True, the Norwegian goal was a thoroughly dubious one, scored when Iverson blocked Martin's clearance with his raised foot, and Sunde put the ball in. But Trondheim showed fine compactness in defence; on a night when their fellow Norwegians Lyn and Mjoendalen, in the other competitions, were letting in seventeen goals between them to British teams.

As expected, Southampton won the return leg by sufficient goals (just) to qualify. The game was described by the *Times* as "metronomic and soporific". It was also frequently very rough. Ron Davies, whose head was the target for endless hopeful crosses, nodded one of them, from Kirkup, home, and Terry Paine eventually scored a second, when Christiansen's silly back pass put him onside, and inexorably away. Davies, distracted by Norwegian defenders who kept wandering into the box, subsequently missed a penalty kick.

Coleraine, having lost 3–2 away to Jeunesse, in Luxemburg, came to life in the return after the Jeunesse man, Langer, was sent off the field 11 minutes from time, adding three goals in the last six minutes, to qualify.

Arsenal, though much criticised at the time by their supporters, played impressively well to hold Sporting to a goalless draw in Lisbon in the second round. Sporting had most of the play against a coolly defensive Arsenal, who occasionally broke away with effect. Once, Damas made a fine save from Sammels. The most notable save of the match, however, was Geoff Barnett's from Peres' penalty; Simpson had felled Marinho in the area. Arsenal, however, deserved their draw.

So did Southampton, the following week, in Guimaraes. Instead of playing defensively against the Portuguese team, they used two wingers, twice equalised, went ahead in their turn, and were caught by a penalty in the very last minute.

Mendes put Vitoria ahead from 25 yards, Channon headed in Paine's centre to equalise, Mendes gave Vitoria back the lead from a free kick, 14 minutes into the second half, Davies headed in Byrne's cross, then Paine volleyed Southampton's third goal. The penalty occurred when Byrne brought down Ademir, and Pinto scored. Using

Sydenham's speed to advantage, Southampton had shown a good deal of enterprise; a contrast to their beginning, in Norway.

The return match, played on a quagmire at The Dell, they won with rather surprising ease. Though they hadn't won in the League for well over two months, they overplayed Vitoria, especially in the second half, when they got four of their goals. They led through an own goal after a corner, Davies increased the lead from a rather severe penalty, the forceful Gabriel headed a third, then Ademir scored Vitoria's goal. Terry Paine laid the basis for further goals, by Channon and Ron Davies, in the last five minutes.

Liverpool, on the same night, lost 1–0 in Portugal to another Vitoria, Setubal. Setubal had more of the play on a slippery pitch, but mistakenly relied on high crosses against Liverpool's tall defence. By the end, Liverpool commanded, though they didn't force a corner till 11 minutes from time and Yeats missed a fine chance in the last minute. The only goal came five minutes from half time when Cardoso hit the bar and Tome put in the rebound. Guerreiro missed a fine chance to increase the lead, 18 minutes from the end, when he headed wide with Lawrence at sea.

In the event, this mistake was not decisive. Vitoria did lose at Liverpool, but only, and in the death throes of the game, by 3–2; a margin which gave them a comfortable lead on away goals.

Liverpool had only themselves to blame; it was the untypical prodigality of their defence which gave Vitoria both their goals and effectively torpedoed their hopes; despite the late flourish, the ultimate, meaningless victory. Vital, the splendid Setubal goalkeeper, also had much to do with their disappointment.

After 23 minutes, Lawler and Yeats inattentively left the ball to one another. Guerreiro dashed in between them, Lawrence felled him, Wagner converted the penalty. At half-time, Liverpool replaced Graham and Peplow with Hunt and Evans and exerted steady pressure. Alas for them, Vitoria could counterattack as well as cover; breaking away, down the left, they scored again when Tome crossed and Strong put into his own goal. 2–0.

Three goals down on aggregate, there was plainly little hope of Liverpool saving the tie; yet they rallied. When Carrico punched off the line a shot by Hunt, Smith scored from the second penalty of the game. Vital saved no fewer than five dangerous shots before Evans equalised. Finally, with almost the last kick of the game, Hunt won it for Liverpool, 3–2; an academic if faintly consoling victory.

Arsenal, on the same evening, were beating Sporting Lisbon with surprising ease. Though Marinho shot against the bar with the score 0–0, they dominated the first half, finding super-abundant space against a defence which, despite playing with a sweeper, lacked both physical challenge and close marking. It threw away the first goal when Baptista hopelessly miskicked at a left wing centre, giving Radford the chance to spin and shoot. Damas palmed the ball into his own goal.

Graham headed the second, placing a right wing centre, this time, coolly wide of Damas; again a good goal but a rather "soft" one. The third, in the second half, arrived when McNab shot through a crowd of players and Graham, who may have been offside, got the last touch before the ball reached goal.

Kilmarnock went into the Third Round by defeating the strong Bulgarian side, Slavia Sofia, running up enough goals in the first leg,at home, to allow them to survivethe return. Two up at half-time at Rugby Park, they put on two goals in a minute – Mathie, scoring his second, and Gilmour – in the late second half; Chalamanov, Slavia's distinguished right-back, got back a goal two minutes from the end. In Sofia, Kilmarnock went down 2–0, but held out in the second half, to qualify.

Dunfermline had most of the play but were often troubled by the counter attacks of Gwardia, the Polish team. McLean gave Dunfermline the lead in merely eight minutes, but Marczak equalised for the Poles after 62; only for Gardner ten minutes later, to give his team a tenuous lead to take to Warsaw.

There, they not only held it but increased it – as early as the third minute when their left half, Renton, scored with a drive from thirty yards. Gwardia thereafter attacked desperately, but found Martin, in Dunfermline's goal, too good for them.

Coleraine were simply overwhelmed by the experienced Belgians, Anderlecht, so used to the more demanding battles of the European Cup. Winning 6–1 at home, Anderlecht had six more in the net, away, without reply, before half-time. In the second half, they brought on Mair as substitute goalkeeper, and Dickson dribbled round him to score in the first minute. He also scored after 72 minutes – a couple of minutes after Irwin had got a second. But all this was mere academy, and Puis' second penalty of the match raised Anderlecht's score to seven. The best you could say for Coleraine was that they didn't lose heart.

Newcastle held on to their trophy, again belying their poor form in the League by holding Porto, away, to a 0–0 draw. Their performance in the return, at St. James' Park, however, faithfully reflected their recent failings, for they made hard work of winning a dull game 1–0. Two inches of snow and a strong wind made conditions heavily in Newcastle's favour; yet they managed to score only one goal, Jim Scott running on to a pass by Wyn Davies and going past two defenders, before beating Rui.

In the Third Round, Newcastle found themselves drawn against another English club, Southampton, emulating them by making their first appearance in European competition. Though Southampton's League form had been still more indifferent than Newcastle's, they surprised them by holding them to a goalless draw at St. James' Park. In the "Battle of the Davieses", Ron came out better than Wyn; indeed, only a brave effort by McFaul once prevented him scoring. Wyn began very well against the ex-Newcastle centre-half, McGrath, but when Mc-

Grath went off, injured, Southampton's defence surprisingly played better. They were worth their draw.

Luck, however, was decisively against them in the return, at The Dell. Having recently thrashed Newcastle 3–0 in an F.A. Cup tie, they celebrated yet another return by Ron Davies, dominating a match in which they made quite enough chances to win. They were especially ill done by when Clark, the Newcastle back, seemed to punch out Channon's header, in the second half, at a time when they were already leading through a goal headed by Channon from Paine's centre. As it was, Newcastle were enabled to score a rather messy equaliser six minutes from time, after Smith had crossed into the Southampton area. So Newcastle went through on "away goals".

In Rouen, Arsenal played cautiously for a draw, and got it without overmuch difficulty. They made the best attempt of a dull night, when Kelly, their young substitute, tried Rigoni with a ferocious volley, but otherwise had scarcely a shot – while Rouen had only a couple which were potentially dangerous. Some of Rouen's tackling was most unceremonious, and George Graham suffered a badly twisted ankle.

The return match was penitentially dull, with Rouen totally defensive, Arsenal almost as wholly sterile. When, a minute from time, George headed on Neill's free kick and Sammels flicked it home, the chief feeling must have been one of relief that extra time would not compound the tedium of the ninety drab minutes.

Rigoni, after a somewhat haphazard beginning, played well in the Rouen goal, and made a couple of fine saves in the second half from a header and a volley by Marinello, playing his first home game for Arsenal after a £100,000 transfer from Hibernian. But by and large, Arsenal were pitifully lacking in ideas and attacking method.

Kilmarnock, held to a draw in their first match, at home to Baku, went out 2–0 in the return. Dunfermline, however, were distinctly unfortunate to be beaten on "away" goals, after turning the tables on the powerful Anderlecht team, 3–2.

McLean wiped out Anderlecht's previous lead, after nine minutes. Eight minutes later Gardner hit the post with a penalty, but Dunfermline continued to attack and led again a minute after half-time, when Mitchell headed in Edwards' cross. Anderlecht then came vigorously to life. Van Himst got a goal back, Mulder equalised five minutes from the end, and although McLean got the winner two minutes later, it was not enough.

Internazionale, who, like Barcelona, had been having a poor time of it in their league, got the better of the Spaniards on their own ground, a few days after losing in Bologna; a disappointment for the new Barcelona regime of Vic Buckingham and Ted Drake.

In the return, Inter were winning 1–0 at San Siro, and seemed to be moving smoothly towards qualification when fog caused the match to be abandoned. When it was replayed, Barcelona put up a much better show, holding Inter to a 1–1 draw; though it was not enough to prevent the Milanese team from qualifying.

Karl Zeiss Jena impressively defeated Ujpest, confirming the decline right across the board of Hungarian football. But perhaps the most extraordinary achievement of the round was that of Ajax Amsterdam; in the person of a reserve defender called Ruud Surendonk.

In the return leg against Naples, Ajax wiped out their 1–0 deficit through Swart, dominated the play, but couldn't score again by the end of normal time. Their manager, Rinus Michels, in a stroke of inspiration, pulled off the international forward Van Dijk and substituted Surendonk, usually a defender. Surendonk scored three in seven minutes, and Ajax won, 4–0!

So to the quarter-finals, which began somewhat anticlimactically when Internazionale sent to Berlin a team consisting of six first choices and five reserves, pronouncing themselves pleased to lose only 1–0 to Hertha.

On an icy pitch, Hertha predictably forced the pace in a game played in an unwontedly good spirit. Horr, after 22 minutes, scored the only goal of the game, with a cross shot. The sub-zero temperature did not prevent nearly 50,000 spectators watching in the Olympic Stadium.

The fact that only 15,000 watched the return proved Milan's continuing indifference to the competition. Boninsegna scored both the game's goals, and Inter went through.

Ajax went down away to the surprising Karl Zeiss Jena, but again displayed their recuperative powers when they thrashed them 5–1 at home in the return, having wiped out the deficit by half-time.

The two English survivors made sharply contrasted beginnings; Newcastle were soundly beaten in Belgium, Arsenal won in a canter in Rumania.

In Brussels, Newcastle gave what Joe Harvey, their manager, described as their poorest performance ever, in the competition. They were, it's true, unfortunate to meet an Anderlecht team which had just, belatedly, run into form, scoring six times in its previous League game. Six, at least, might have gone into the Newcastle net, and it was no real extenuation to say that Newcastle lacked their first-choice full-backs. Craggs and Guthrie did very well in their place, in an overrun defence.

Anderlecht, dominating midfield, first scored after half-an-hour. Mulder, the clever Dutchman, pulled the ball back for Desanghere to score. Puis got the second from a splendid, swerving free kick to the top corner, thirty minutes later. United made only one true chance, and then Smith wasted it by shooting, when Dyson stood unmarked.

In Bucharest, Arsenal found the going much easier against Baku Dynamo. Their refurbished team, after weeks of sterility, shrugged off biased refereeing to win comfortably, after a cautious start.

Arsenal took the lead after 57 minutes, George shot against the underside of the bar from Storey's pass, and Sammels exploited the rebound. Ten minutes from time, Radford calmly headed in McNab's centre, for the second.

At Highbury, they won the return with ludicrous ease; so much so that one marvelled at the fact that Baku had gone so far, had beaten

Kilmarnock on the way. Though their international forward, Dembrovski, returned in midfield, he made no more than transient contributions; a clever, long-legged footballer who tended to hold on to the ball too long.

The perfectly inept goalkeeping of the tall Ghita, after a fine early save from the excellent young Kelly, had much to do with the debacle. He gave away two absurdly soft headed goals by standing transfixed on his line, while the defence in front of him showed that mere numbers are not enough. The open spaces, the sheer lack of challenge, were bewildering.

Arsenal, with Kelly an irresistible force in midfield, John Radford, a powerful centre-forward, and Jon Sammels always looking for goals, made it a holiday. They scored seven without too much trouble, and the crowd at the North end were not unreasonable in chanting, "We want ten!" There was that great a difference between the teams.

Newcastle were less fortunate; their elimination was bitterly ironical and morally unjust – though they themselves, after all, had had their narrow squeaks and lucky breaks, the previous season.

Most unexpectedly, Anderlecht came to St. James' Park, and were overrun. After four minutes, Bryan Robson headed a goal; after twenty, he scored from twenty yards. Clark, Newcastle's left-back, had to go off with damaged ligaments and be substituted after 25 minutes, but Newcastle did not lose their hold on the game. Five minutes from time, Keith Dyson converted Bobby Moncur's free kick to score the goal which, it seemed, would take United into the semi-finals. But with two minutes left, Thomas Nordahl – son of the formidable Gunnar – took a leaf out of his father's book by shooting home from twenty yards. So Anderlecht, by virtue of that away goal, survived dubiously on aggregate.

Internazionale, in fine fettle after an excellent win against Fiorentina in the League, three days earler, defeated Anderlecht on their own ground, through the inevitable Boninsegna's goal, in the first leg of the semi-finals.

With Ivanoe Fraizzoli, Inter's President, offering his men a two million lire (£1200) bonus if they won the tournament, qualification for the Final, at least, seemed inevitable. At last, it seemed, a Milanese team was taking the Fairs Cup seriously. Whereupon Anderlecht came to San Siro, scored two first half goals, and won, 2–0! Bergholtz, their Dutch striker, got both of them.

Arsenal most unexpectedly thrashed Ajaz 3–0 in the first leg of their semi-final at Highbury, after it seemed that Ajax's cravenly misguided defensive policy would limit their success to a goal. This was scored after 17 minutes by George, after McNab's cross was headed out. The shot, first time and indifferent, passed just inside the near post while Bals, who later said he was unsighted, remained motionless.

With Johan Cruyff hovering cleverly with intent on the left wing, for occasional forays, this seemed all the goals that a virile but prosaic Arsenal would score, even when they brought on Armstrong for the less stalwart Marinello. Suddenly Ajax wilted. A defence which employed Vasovic wastefully as sweeper wilted twelve minutes from time, leaving Sammels unmarked to Armstrong's centre. His first shot hit Bals, his second flew home. Then Graham was tripped by Swart on the edge of the area, and George scored from the penalty. It was an inspiring night for Arsenal, succeeding where other English clubs had failed against this experienced, talented Dutch team. Young players like George and Kelly acquitted themselves unusually well, while Radford ploughed powerfully through the heavy going.

In the return, Arsenal played as defensively as had Ajax, at Highbury; with the difference that they kept the score down to a single goal. This was scored in the 18th minute by Muhren, after Wilson had saved but couldn't hold a powerful shot by Keizer.

Somewhat desperate in the first half, Arsenal played with more poise in the second, against an attack led once more with great subtlety by Johan Cruyff. Eddie Kelly confirmed his great promise as a midfield player, while Peter Simpson was admirable in defence.

Anderlecht, gathering strength and returning at last to their familiar form, were much too good for Arsenal in the first leg of the Final, played in Brussels. For much of the game, they simply overwhelmed the London team, who had to rely on the brave goalkeeping of Bob Wilson to keep down the score. They were deservedly 3–0 down when, five minutes from time, the 18-year-old Kennedy, who had come in as substitute for Charlie George, splendidly headed a goal from Armstrong's centre, to keep the tie at least nominally open.

Anderlecht's inside-forwards, Devrindt, Mulder and Van Himst, were devastatingly good. Soon after George had forced Trappeniers to make one of his rare difficult saves, Nordahl found Devrindt, who shot cleverly between Wilson and the post.

Devrindt made the second goal for Mulder, who scored with a fulminating shot from the edge of the penalty box, and fifteen minutes from time, after some elegant interpassing with Devrindt, Mulder also got the third.

The return game was a much different story, even though for the first 26 minutes Anderlecht's clever, star-encrusted forward-line was as dangerous as Arsenal's, so that the Londoners established no kind of dominance. But the weakness of Trappeniers, the blond, international goalkeeper, in the air was already apparent – and suddenly Kelly's marvellous goal gave Arsenal hope.

Collecting the ball just outside the crowded penalty area, the 18-year-old right-half flicked it, with staggering calm, from left foot to right, then shot powerfully wide of the right hand of a motionless Trappeniers. The second half followed almost exactly the pattern of the first. Though Anderlecht's defence looked curiously shaky, with the black Kialunda highly vulnerable, Desanghere more robust than authoritative, Arsenal made little progress. Indeed, Nordahl hit a post and Mulder was always a threat. Then, after 27 minutes, Graham sent McNab down the left, and a perfect cross was perfectly and powerfully headed in by John Radford. Within a minute, George had swept a long ball from the left across goal to the unmarked Sammels – almost a repetition of the Ajax game – and Sammels drove a low, splendidly powerful cross shot into the net. Arsenal had done it; and at the finish, we had the sight of their players, joyful and bare chested in the bleak rain, being carried round the pitch by their ecstatic fans. A resounding achievement for a team which had been so often and so bitterly criticized during the season.

EUROPEAN FAIRS CUP 1969/70

First Round

Arsenal (3) 3 — *Glentoran* (0) 0
Graham 2, Gould

Arsenal: Wilson; Storey, McNab (Nelson); McLintock, Simpson, Graham; Robertson, Court (Kelly), Gould, Sammels, Armstrong.
Glentoran: Finlay; Coyle, McKeag; Stewart, McCullough, Macken; Weatherup, Bruce, Henderson, Morrow, Hill.

Glentoran (1) 1 — *Arsenal* (0) 0
Henderson (penalty)

Glentoran: Finlay; Hill, McKeag; Coyle, McCullough, Mackin; Weatherup, Stewart, Henderson, Bruce, Morrow. subs: Patterson, Lemon.
Arsenal: Webster; Rice, McNab, Court, Neill, Simpson; Robertson, Sammels, Radford, Gould, George. sub: Kennedy.

Dundee United (0) 1 — *Newcastle United* (0) 2
Scott, — Davies 2

Dundee United: Mackay; Rolland, J., Cameron; Gillespie, Smith, Markland; Wilson, Reid, Cameron, K., Scott, Mitchell.
Newcastle United: McFaul; Craggs, Clark; Gibbs, Burton, Moncur; Robson, Dyson, Davies, Arentoft, Smith, J.

Newcastle United (0) 1 — *Dundee United* (0) 0
Dyson

Newcastle United: McFaul; Craig, Clark; Gibb, McNamee, Moncur; Robson, Dyson, Davies, Smith, Foggon (Arentoft.)
Dundee United: Mackay; Rolland, Cameron, J.; Gillespie, Smith, Markland; Hogg, Reid, Gordon, Scott, Mitchell.

Liverpool (5) 10 — *Dundalk* (0) 0
Evans 2, Smith 2, Graham 2, Lawler, Lindsay, Thompson, Callaghan

Liverpool: Clemence; Lawler, Strong; Smith, Yeats, Hughes; Callaghan, Graham, Lindsay, Evans, Thompson.
Dundalk: Swan; Brennan, O'Reilly, Murray, McConville, Hendricks, Gilmore (Stokes), Turner, O'Connor, Bartley, Carroll.

Dundalk (0)	*Liverpool* (2) 4 Thompson 2, Graham, Callaghan

Dundalk: Swan; Brennan, O'Riley; Murray, McConville, Millington; Kinsella (Gilmore), Turner, O'Connor, Bartley, Carroll (Stokes).
Liverpool: Clemence; Lawler, Strong; Smith, Lloyd, Hughes; Thompson (Callaghan), Evans, Graham (Hunt), St. John, Boersma.

Partizan (0) 2 Djordjevic 2	*Ujpest* (0) 1 Dunai

Note re sub

Only in brackets if it is known who the sub replaced.

Ujpest (0) 2 Bene, A. Dunai	*Partizan* (0) 0
Sabadell (1) 2 Garzon, Cristo	*Bruges* (0) 0
Bruges (3) 5 Carteus, Lambert 2, Turesson 2	*Sabadell* (0) 1
Las Palmas (0) 0	*Hertha Berlin* (0) 0
Hertha Berlin (0) 1 Patzke (penalty)	*Las Palmas* (0) 0
Wiener Sportklub 4	*Ruch Chorzow* 2
Ruch Chorzow 4	*Wiener Sportklub* 1
Rouen (1) 2 Pospichal, Rustichelli	*Twente* (0) 0
Twente (1) 1 Dvost	*Rouen* (0) 0
Vitoria Guimaraes (1) 1 Manual	*Banik* (0) 0

Banik (0) 1	*Vitoria Guimaraes* (0) 1
Sporting Lisbon (1) 4 Pedras, Gonçalves, Peres (pen.), Lourenço	*Linz* (0) 0
Linz (1) 2 Wurdinger, Leitnev	*Sporting Lisbon* (1) 2 Gonçalves, Lourenço
Jena (0) 1 Stein	*Altay Izmir* (0) 0
Altay Izmir (0) 0	*Jena* (0) 0
Lausanne (1) 1 Chapuisat	*Vasas Gyor* (2) 2 Gyorfi 2
Vasas Gyor (0) 2 Korsos, Somogy	*Lausanne* (0) 1 Duerr
Trondheim Rosenborg (1) 1 Sunde	*Southampton* (0) 0

Trondheim Rosenborg: Fossen; Ronnes, Rime; Eggan, Hvidsand, Christiansen; Naess, Pedersen, Iversen, Sunde (Haagenrud), Loraas. (Oiasaeter).
Southampton: Martin; Jones, Kirkup; Fisher, Gabriel, Walker; Paine, Channon, Davies (Saul), Stokes, Byrne.

Southampton (1) 2 Davies, Paine	*Trondheim Rosenborg* (0) 0

Southampton: Martin; Kirkup, Hollywood; Kemp, McGrath, Gabriel; Paine, Stokes, Davies (Fisher), Byrne, Sydenham.
Trondheim Rosenborg: Fossen; Ronnes, Rime, Eggan, Hvidsand, Christiansen, Naess, Pedersen, Sunde, Iversen, Oiasaeter (Sjovold.)

Hansa Rostock (1) 3 Drews 2, Pankau	*Panionios* (0) 0
Panionios (0) 2 Spyropoulos, Dedes	*Hansa Rostock* (0) 0
Baku Dynamo (3) 6 Dembrouschi 3, Ene 2, Baluta	*Floriana Valetta* (0) 0

Floriana Valetta 0	*Baku Dynamo* 1 Balutza
Slavia Sofia (1) 2 Grigorov, Kolev	*Valencia* (0) 0
Valencia (0) 1	*Slavia Sofia* (1) 1
Internazionale (0) 3 Boninsegna 2, Reif	*Sparta Prague* (0) 0
Sparta Prague (0) 0	*Internazionale* (1) 1 Boninsegna
Juventus (2) 3 Vieri (penalty), Leonardi, Castano	*Lokomotiv* (1) 1 Vasiliev
Lokomotiv (0) 1 Vasiliev	*Juventus* (1) 2 Leonardi. Anastasi
VfB Stuttgart (1) 3 Bjorklung (own goal), Olsson, Haug	*Plazs Malmo* (0) 0
Plazs Malmo (0) 1 Larsson	*VfB Stuttgart* (1) 1 Weidmann
Hanover 96 (2) 2 Heynckes, Skoblar	*Ajax* (1) 1 Swart
Ajax (1) 3 Cruyff, Swart, Muehren	*Hanover* 96 (0) 0
Aris Salonika (1) 1 Spyridon	*Cagliari* (0) 1 Martiradonna
Cagliari (2) 3 Domenghini, Riva, Gori	*Aris Salonika* (0) 0

(*match abandoned owing to brawl*)

Metz (0) 1 Schzepaniak	*Naples* (1) 1 Bosdaves
Naples 2 Bianchi, Improta	*Metz* 1 Hausser

Barcelona (3) 4 Ejlersen (own goal), Zaldua, Celosia 2	*Odense* (0) 0
Odense (0) 0	*Barcelona* (0) 2 Rexach 2
Gwardia (*Warsaw*) (1) 1 Lipinski	*Vojvodina* (0) 0
Vojvodina (0) 1 Dakich	*Gwardia* (*Warsaw*) (1) 1 Wisnieski
Dunfermline (1) 4 Paton 2, Mitchell, Gardner	*Bordeaux* (0) 0

Dunfermline: Duff; Callaghan, Lunn, McGarty, Baillie, Renton, Mitchell, Paton, Edwards, Gardner, McLean.

Bordeaux: Montes; Papin, Grabowski, Andrien, Desremaux, Durdino, Dortumb, Simon, Ruiter, Betta, Petyt.

Bordeaux (1) 2 Othily, Wojiak	*Dunfermline* (0) 0

Bordeaux: Montes; Papin, Grabowski; Betta, Desremaux, Texier; Otchily, Simon, Ruiter, Dortumb, Wojiak.

Dunfermline: Duff; Callaghan, Lunn; McGarty, Baillie, Renton; Mitchell, Paton, Edwards, Gardner, McLean.

Zurich (2) 3 Volkert (penalty), Kunzli, Grunig	*Kilmarnock* (2) 2 McLean, (T) Mathie

Zurich: Grob; Munch, Hasler, Rebozzi, Kuhn, Grunig, Winiger, Martinelli, Kunzli, Quentin, Volkert.

Kilmarnock: McLaughlin; King, Dickson, Gilmour, McGrory, Beattie, McLean, T., Strachan, Morrison, McLean, J., Mathie.

Kilmarnock (1) 3 McGrory, Morrison, McLean (T)	*Zurich* (0) 1 Grunig

Kilmarnock: McLaughlan; King, Dickson; Gilmour, McGrory, Strachan; McLean, T., Morrison, Mathie, McLean, J., Cook.

Zurich: Grob; Munch, Hasler; Rebozzi, Kuhn, Grunig; Winiger, Kygurtz, Kunzli, Quentin, Volkert.

Munich 1860 (1) 2 Fischer 2	*Skeid Oslo* (0) 2 Johansen, Sjoeberg
Skeid Oslo (1) 2 Sjoeberg 2	*Munich* 1860 (1) 1 Keller
Valur Reykjavik 0	*Anderlecht* 6
Anderlecht (1) 2 Nordahl, Mulder	*Valur Reykjavik* (0) 0
Charleroi 2	*Zagreb* 1
Zagreb (0) 1 Huttmancheré (own goal)	*Charleroi* (1) 3 Bertoncello, Bissot 2
Hvidovre (0) 1 Soerensen	*Porto* (1) 2 Helder 2
Porto (1) 2 Selim, Rolando	*Hvidovre* (0) 0
Jeunesse d'Esch (0) 3 Allamano 3	*Coleraine* (1) 2 Hunter, Murray

Jeunesse: Hoffman, R.; Da Grava, Kosmala, Hoffman, J., Morocutti, Feyder, Drouet, Allamano, Di Genova, Langer, Bartolacci.

Coleraine: Hunter; McCurdy, Campbell; O'Doherty, Jackson, Murray; Dunlop, Curley, Wilson, Dickson, Jennings.

Coleraine (1) 4 Wilson, Dickson 2, Jennings	*Jeunesse d'Esch* (0) 0

Coleraine: Hunter; McCurdy, Campbell; O'Doherty, Jackson, Murray; Dunlop, Curley, Wilson, Dickinson, Jennings.
Jeunesse: Hoffman, R.; Da Grava, Kosmala; Hoffman, J., Morocutti, Drouet; Seyden, Allamano, Di Genova, Langer, Bartolacci.

Vitoria Setubal (1) 3 Jacinto Jao, Guerreiro, José Maria	*Rapid Bucharest* (0) 1 Meague
Rapid Bucharest (0) 1 Stelian	*Vitoria Setubal* (2) 4 Wagner 2 (2 penalties), José Maria 2

Second Round

Sporting Lisbon (0) 0 — *Arsenal* (0) 0

Sporting: Damas; Gomez, Calo, Carlos, Hilario, Goncalves, Peres, Morais, Nelson, Lourenco, Marinho, subs: Celestino, Dani.
Arsenal: Barnett; Storey, McNab; Court, Neill, Simpson; Robertson, Sammels, Radford, Graham, Armstrong.

Arsenal (2) 3 — *Sporting Lisbon* (0) 0
Radford, Graham 2

Arsenal: Barnett; Storey, McNab; Court, Neill, Simpson; Robertson, Sammels, Radford, Graham, Armstrong.
Sporting: Damas; Gomez, Celestino (Manaca), Goncalves, Baptista, Calo, Morais, Nelson (Lourenco), Marinho, Peres, Dinis.

Anderlecht (3) 6 — *Coleraine* (1) 1
Van Himst, Mulder 2, Van Binst, Hanon, Devrindt — Murray

Anderlecht: Vandenbossche; Heylens, Velkeneers; Van Welle, Cornelis, Hanon; Stierli, Van Binst, Mulder, Van Himst, Martens (Devrindt.)
Coleraine: Hunter; McCurdy, O'Doherty; Jackson, Campbell, Murray; Wilson (Irwin), Dunlop, Dickson, Curley, Jennings.

Coleraine (0) 3 — *Anderlecht* (6) 7
Dickson 2, Irwin — Van Himst 3, Puis 3 (2 penalties), Devrindt

Coleraine: Hunter; McCurdy, Gordon; Campbell, Jackson, Murray; Dunlop, Curley, Dickson, Jennings, Irwin.
Anderlecht: Vandenbossche (Mair); Heylens, Velkeneers, Kialunda, Stierli, Hanon, Nordahl, Devrindt, Mulder, Van Himst, Puis.

Vitoria Setubal (1) 1 — *Liverpool* (0) 0
Tome

Setubal: Vital; Conceicao, Cardoso, Alfredo (Arcanjo), Carrico, Tome, Maria, Wagner, Guerreiro, Figueiredo, Joao.
Liverpool: Lawrence; Lawler, Wall; Smith, Yeats, Hughes; Callaghan, Ross, Graham (St. John), Strong, Thompson.

Liverpool (0) 3 — *Vitoria Setubal* (1) 2
Smith (penalty), Evans, Hunt — Wagner (penalty), Strong (own goal)

Liverpool: Lawrence; Lawler, Strong; Smith, Yeats, Hughes; Cal-

laghan, Peplow (Hunt), Graham (Evans), St. John, Thompson.
Vitoria Setubal: Vital; Rebelo, Cardoso, Moreira, Carrico, Tome, Maria, Wagner, Guerreiro, Arcanjo, Jacinto.

Porto (0) 0	*Newcastle United* (0) 0

Porto: Rui; Gualter, Sucena; Pavao, Vieira, Nunes, Valdemar; Rolando, Seninho, Pinto, Salim, Nobrega.
Newcastle United: McFaul; Craig, Clark; Gibb, Burton, Moncur; Robson, Dyson, Davies, Guthrie (Craggs), Arentoft.

Newcastle United (1) 1 Scott	*Porto* (0) 0

Newcastle United: McFaul; Craig, Clark; Gibb, Burton, Moncur; Scott, Robson, Davies, Arentoft, Foggon.
Porto: Rui (Anibal); Gualter, Valdemar, Nunes, Sucena, Rolando (Joao), Salim, Albano, Pavao, Pinto, Nobrega.

Ajax (2) 7 Vasovic 2, Swart, Cruyff 2, Van Dijk 2	*Ruch Chorzow* (0) 0
Ruch Chorzow (1) 1 Piechniczek	*Ajax* (1) 2 Muhren, Van Dijk
Hansa Rostock (0) 2 Hergesell, Sackritz	*Internazionale* (1) 1 Boninsegna
Internazionale (3) 3 Jair, Suarez, Mazzola	*Hansa Rostock* (0) 0
Karl Zeiss Jena (0) 2 Rock, Irmscher	*Cagliari* (0) 0
Cagliari (0) 0	*Carl Zeiss Jena* (1) 1 Stein
Hertha Berlin (2) 3 Gayer, Wild, Lagen, S.	*Juventus* (1) 1 Anastasi
Juventus (0) 0	*Hertha Berlin* (0) 0
Vasas Gyor 2 Varsanyi, Orban	*Barcelona* 3 Zaldua 2, Pellices

Barcelona (1) 2	*Vasa Gyor* (0) 0
Pujol, Zaldua	
VfB Stuttgart (0) 0	*Naples* (0) 0
Naples (0) 1	*VfB Stuttgart* (0) 0
Canzi	
Kilmarnock (2) 4	*Slavia Sofia* (0) 1
Mathie 2, Cook, Gilmour	Chalamanov

Kilmarnock: McLaughlan; King, Dickson; Gilmour, McGrory, Beattie; McLean, T., Morrison, Mathie, McLean, J., (Waddell), Cook.
Slavia: Zolov; Chalamanov, Christakiev; Aleksiev, Petrov, Davidov; Dimitrov, Georgiev, Mihailov, Kolev, Kotzev.

Slavia Sofia (2) 2	*Kilmarnock* (0) 0
King (own goal), Mihailov	

Slavia: Tisolov; Gerov, Petrov; Aleksiev, Davidov, Kolev; Dimitrov, Georgiev, Mihailov, Gregorov, Kotzev.
Kilmarnock: McLaughlan; King, Dickson; Gilmour, McGrory, Beattie; McLean, T., Morrison, Mathie, Strachan, Cook.

Bruges (2) 5	*Ujpest Dosza* (1) 2
Rensenbrink 3, Turesson 2	Juhasz, Fazekas
Ujpest Dosza (1) 3	*Bruges* (0) 0
Fazekas 2, Bene	
Skeid Oslo (0) 0	*Baku Dynamo* (0) 0
Baku Dynamo (0) 2	*Skeid Oslo* (0) 0
Dembrovski 2	
Charleroi (3) 3	*Rouen* (1) 1
Bissot 2, Spaute	Villa
Rouen (1) 2	*Charleroi* (0) 0
Rustichelli, Villa	
Victoria Guimaraes (1) 3	*Southampton* (1) 3
Mendes 2, Pinto	Davies, Channon 2

Victoria Guimaraes: Rodrigues; de Velha, Pinto, Jorge, Costeado, Artur, Birreiro, Manuel, Mendes, Perez, Carlos (Ademir).
Southampton: Martin; Kirkup, Byrne; Fisher (Hollywood), McGrath, Gabriel; Paine, Channon (Saul), Davies, Walker, Sydenham.

Southampton (1) 5	*Victoria Guimaraes* (0) 1
Costeado (own goal), Davies 2 (1 penalty), Gabriel, Channon	Ademir

Southampton: Martin; Kirkup, Byrne; Fisher, McGrath, Gabriel; Paine, Channon, Davies, Walker, Sydenham.
Victoria Guimaraes: Rodrigues; de Velha, Pinto, Jorge, Costeado, Artur, Birreiro, Manuel, Mendes, Perez (Augusto), Ademir.

Dunfermline (1) 2	*Gwardia Warsaw* (0) 1
McLean, Gardner	Marczak

Dunfermline: Martin; Callaghan, Lunn; McGarty, Baillie, Renton; Mitchell, McKimmie (Robertson), Edwards, Gardner, McLean.
Gwardia: Pocialik; Jurczak, Kielak; Sroka, Michalik, Dawidczynski, Szymczak, Biernacki, Maszatalev, Marczak.

Gwardia Warsaw (0) 0	*Dunfermline* (1) 1
	Renton

Gwardia: Pocialik; Sroka, Jurczak, Michalik, Kielak, Wisniewski, Marczak, Lipinski, Szymczak, Dawidczynski, Maszatalev.
Dunfermline: Martin; Callaghan, Lunn; McGarty, Baillie, Renton; Mitchell, Paton, Edwards, Gardner, McLean.

Third Round

Newcastle United (0) 0	*Southampton* (0) 0

Newcastle United: McFaul; Craig, Clark; Gibb, Burton, Moncur; Robson, Dyson, Davies, W., Arentoft, Scott.
Southampton: Martin; Kirkup, Byrne; Fisher, McGrath (Stokes), Gabriel; Paine, Channon, Davies, R., Walker, Jenkins.

Southampton (1) 1	*Newcastle United* (0) 1
Channon	Robson

Southampton: Martin; Kirkup, Byrne; Fisher, Gabriel, Walker; Jenkins, Channon, Davies R., Paine, Sydenham (Stokes.)

Newcastle United: McFaul; Craig, Clark; Gibb, McNamee, Moncur; Robson, Smith, Davies, W., Young (Guthrie), Ford.

Anderlecht (1) 1	*Dunfermline* (0) 0
Devrindt	

Anderlecht: Vandenbossche; Heylens, Cornelis; Peeters, Velkeneers, Kialunda; Nordahl, Bergholtz (Hanon), Mulder, Devrindt, Puis.

Dunfermline: Duff; Callaghan, Lunn; McNicoll, Baillie, McLean; Edwards, McLaren, Mitchell, Gardner, Robertson.

Dunfermline (1) 3	*Anderlecht* (0) 2
McLean 2, Mitchell	Van Himst, Mulder

Dunfermline: Duff; Callaghan, Lunn; McNicoll, Baillie, McLean; Edwards, McLaren, Mitchell, Gardner, Gillespie.

Anderlecht: Trappeniers; Heylens, Cornelis; Peeters, Velkeneers, Kialunda; Mulder, Nordahl, Van Himst, Deraeve, Puis.

Rouen (0) 0	*Arsenal* (0) 0

Rouen: Rigoni; Largouet, Merelle, Rio, Senechal, Pospichal, Rustichelli, Dos Santos, Villa, Leroy, Brugnant.

Arsenal: Wilson; Storey, McNab; Court, Neill, Simpson; Robertson, Sammels, Radford, Graham (Kelly), Armstrong.

Arsenal (0) 1	*Rouen* (0) 0
Sammels	

Arsenal: Wilson; Storey, Nelson; Court, Neill, Simpson; Marinello, Sammels, Radford, George, Armstrong (Graham).

Rouen: Rigoni; Largouet, Merelle, Rio, Senechal, Druda, Rustichelli, Dos Santos, Villa, Pospichal, Bruant (Douis.)

Kilmarnock (0) 1	*Dynamo Baku* (0) 1
Mathie	Balutza

Kilmarnock: McLaughlin; King, Dickson; Gilmour, McGrory, Beattie; Cook, Mathie, Morrison, Waddell, McLean T.

Baku: Ghita; Comanescu, Nedelcu; Kiss, Vatafu, Velicu; Pana, Dembrovski, Ene Daniel, Dutan, Balutza.

Dynamo Baku (1) 2	*Kilmarnock* (0) 0
Ene Daniel 2	

Baku: Ghita; Comanescu, Nedelcu; Velicu, Kiss, Vatafu; Dutan, Pana, Dembrovski, Ene Daniel, Balutza (Meumayer.)

Kilmarnock: McLaughlin; King, Dickson; Gilmour (Maxwell), McGrory, Strachan; McLean, J., McLean, T., Morrison, Mathie, Sheed.

Karl Zeiss Jena (0) 1	*Ujpest* (0) 0
Krauss	

Ujpest (0) 0	*Karl Zeiss Jena* (2) 3 Scheitler, Stein, Ducke, P.
Barcelona (1) 1 Fuste	*Internazionale* (2) 2 Boninsegna, Bertini
Internazionale (1) 1 Boninsegna	*Barcelona* (1) 1 Rexach
Vitoria Setubal (1) 1 Tome	*Hertha Berlin* (1) 1 Horr
Hertha Berlin (0) 1 Steffenhagen	*Vitoria Setubal* (0) 0
Naples 1 Manservisi	*Ajax* (0) 0
Ajax (1) 4 Swart, Surendonk 3	*Naples* (0) 0

(*after extra time*)

Quarter-Finals

Carl Zeiss Jena (3) 3 Ducke, R., Stein, Ducke, P.	*Ajax* (0) 1 Vasovic
Ajax (3) 5 Swart 2, Vasovic, Keizer, Cruyff	*Carl Zeiss Jena* (1) 1 Ducke P.
Hertha (1) 1 Horr	*Internazionale* (0) 0
Internazionale (0) 2 Boninsegna 2	*Hertha* (0) 0
Anderlecht (1) 2 Desanghere, Puis	*Newcastle United* (0) 0

Anderlecht: Trappeniers; Heylens, Velkeneers, Kialunda, Maertens; Nordahl, Desanghere, Puis; Devrindt, Mulder, Van Himst.

Newcastle United: McFaul; Craggs, Guthrie; Gibb, McNamee (Burton), Moncur; Robson, Smith (Elliott), Davies, Foggon, Dyson.

Newcastle United (2) 3 Robson 2, Dyson	*Anderlecht* (0) 1 Nordahl

Newcastle United: McFaul; Craig, Clark; Gibb, Burton, Moncur; Robson, Dyson, Davies, Guthrie, Foggon.

Anderlecht: Trappeniers; Heylens, Martens; Nordahl, Velkeneers, Kialunda; Desanghere, Devrindt, Mulder, Van Himst, Puis.

Dynamo Baku (0) 0	*Arsenal* (0) 2 Sammels, Radford

Baku: Ghita; Cominescu, Nedelcu, Velicu, Kiss, Vatafu, Dutan, Neumaier, Pana, Ene, David (Siminceanu.)

Arsenal: Wilson; Storey, McNab; McLintock, Simpson, Kelly; Graham, Sammels, Marinello, Radford, George.

Arsenal (4) 7 Radford 2, George 2, Graham, Sammels 2	*Dynamo Baku* (1) 1 Balutza

Arsenal: Wilson; Storey, McNab; Kelly, McLintock, Simpson; Marinello, Sammels, Radford, George, Graham (Armstrong.)

Baku: Ghita; Cominescu, Nedelcu, David, Vatafu, Velicu, Pana, Dembrovski, Ene, Dutan, Balutza.

Semi-Finals

Anderlecht (0) 0	*Internazionale* (0) 1 Boninsegna
Internazionale (0) 0	*Anderlecht* (2) 2 Bergholtz 2
Arsenal (1) 3 George 2, Sammels (1 penalty)	*Ajax* (0) 0

Arsenal: Wilson; Storey, McNab; Kelly, McLintock, Simpson; Marinello (Armstrong), Sammels, Radford, George, Graham.

Ajax: Bals; Vasovic, Suurbier, Hulshoff, Krol, Reynders, Muhren, Swart, Cruyff, Van Dijk, Keizer (Surendonk.)

Ajax (1) 1 Muhren	*Arsenal* (0) 0

Ajax: Bals; Suurbier, Hulshoff, Vasovic, Krol, Reynders, Muhren, Swart, Cruyff, Van Dijk, Keizer.

Arsenal: Wilson; Storey, McNab; Kelly, McLintock, Simpson; Armstrong, Sammels, Radford, George, Graham.

FINAL

First leg. *Brussels*, April 22, 1970

Anderlecht (2) 3 — Devrindt, Mulder 2
Arsenal (0) 1 — Kennedy

Anderlecht: Trappeniers; Heylens, Velkeneers, Kialunda, Cornelis (Peeters), Desenghere, Nordahl; Devrindt, Mulder, Van Himst, Puis.

Arsenal: Wilson; Storey, McNab; Kelly, McLintock, Simpson; Armstrong, Sammels, Radford, Graham, George (Kennedy).

Second leg. *Highbury*, April 28, 1970

Arsenal (1) 3 — Kelly, Radford, Sammels
Anderlecht (0) 0

Arsenal: Wilson; Storey, McNab; Kelly, McLintock, Simpson; Armstrong, Sammels, Radford, George, Graham.

Anderlecht: Trappeniers; Heylens, Velkeneers, Kialunda, Martens; Nordahl, Desanghere; Devrindt, Mulder, Van Himst, Puis.

(*Arsenal won on aggregate*, 4–3)

Chapter Six

Liberators

ONCE again, the Copa de Los Libertadores included no Brazilian teams, which largely deprived it of significance. Once again, the holders, the dreaded Estudiantes, were exempted until the semi-finals.

The four qualifying pools ended thus:

GROUP I

	P	W	D	L	F	A	Pts.
Boca Juniors	6	5	1	0	14	4	11
River Plate	6	3	1	2	15	6	7
Bolivar	6	1	2	3	7	9	4
Universitario	6	0	2	4	2	19	2

GROUP II

	P	W	D	L	F	A	Pts.
Nacional	6	4	2	0	13	3	10
Penarol	6	3	3	0	18	4	9
Valencia	6	2	1	3	9	19	5
Deportivo Galicia	6	0	0	6	2	16	0

GROUP III

	P	W	D	L	F	A	Pts.
Guarani	10	5	5	0	12	4	15
Universidad de Chile	10	5	3	2	19	11	13
Olimpia	10	4	4	2	19	11	12
Deportivo Cali	10	5	2	3	18	16	12
America	10	1	3	6	12	22	5
Rangers	10	1	1	8	11	27	3

GROUP IV

	P	W	D	L	F	A	Pts.
Universitario	6	4	1	1	11	4	9
Liga. D. Universitaria	6	3	1	2	10	6	7
Defensor Arica	6	1	3	2	5	6	5
America	6	1	1	4	4	14	3

SEMI-FINALS

Estudiantes showed that time had not withered their remarkable if sometimes dubious capacity for winning important Cup ties, even away from home. They fully deserved their 1–0 win in Buenos Aires over River Plate, counter-attacking with great effect. Indeed, not only did their dangerous left winger, Juan Veron, exploit a long pass to score, just after half-time, but another goal, by Flores, was disallowed for offside. After Veron's goal, Estudiantes closed up the game; River's attacking play at first exposed them to the winning goal, and later proved ineffectual.

Estudiantes duly won the return, thus confirming their reputation as extraordinary Cup fighters, whatever their previous moral failings.

The remaining semi-finalists left by the play-offs were Penarol, hampered by the fact that so many of their players were required for World Cup preparation, and Universidad de Chile. Winning 2–0 in Montevideo, Penarol lost the return in Santiago, 1–0. This meant a play-off, which ended in a 2–2 draw, after extra time. Goal aggregate is decisive in such cases, and Penarol therefore scraped through.

Semi-finals

River Plate (0) 0	*Estudiantes* (0) 1 Veron
Estudiantes 3	*River Plate* 1
Penarol 2	*Universidad de Chile* 0
Universidad 1	*Penarol* 0
Penarol 2	*Universidad* 2

after extra time

Penarol qualify on aggregate

The Final, between Penarol and Estudiantes, was ridiculed by the fact that all Penarol's Uruguayan internationals, among them Rocha and Mazurkiewiecz, were unavailable, since they were in training with the World Cup team. Thus it was no surprise when Estudiantes won a harsh game in the first leg, at Buenos Aires, by the only goal, scored after 42 minutes by the defender, Togneri. A few seconds from the end, Nestor Goncalvez, the Penarol captain, was sent off, after a violent foul on Veron. Togneri's goal came from a shot from outside the penalty area, after a Penarol clearance.

Final

May 20

Estudiantes (0) 1	*Penarol* (0) 0
Togneri	

Estudiantes: Errea, Pagnanini, Spadaro, Togneri, Pachame, Solari, Bilardo, Echecopar, Conigliaro, Flores (Rudzky), Veron.

Penarol: Pintos, Soria (Gonzalez), Figueroa, Peralta, Martinez, Viera, Concalves, Lamas (Caceres), Acuna, Onega, Lamberck.

May 27

Penarol (0) 0	*Estudiantes* (0) 0

Penarol: Pintos, Soria (Speranza), Figueroa, Peralta, Martinez, Viera, Concalves, Lamas, Acuna, Onega, Lamberck.

Estudiantes: Errea, Pagnanini, Spadaro, Togneri, Medina, Bilardo, Pachame, Solari, Conigliaro (Aguilar), Echecopar (Rudzky), Veron.

Chapter Seven

World Club Championship 1969

THIS nasty, unnecessary tournament brought its habitual quota of Argentinian brutality, Estudiantes this time surpassing themselves at the expense of Milan – who nevertheless defeated them, for the trophy. The most maltreated victim of the team which, in 1968, had similarly dealt with Manchester United, was a fellow Argentinian, Nestor Combin. During the first match, when he raced through the Estudiantes defence to score Milan's second goal, he left the field with a bleeding mouth. In the second, in Buenos Aires, Estudiantes made a proper job of it. Combin went off the field, bleeding again, this time on a stretcher with a broken nose – the victim of a vicious elbow in the face by Aguirre Suarez, who was sent off by a courageous referee. Manera was similarly banished. Poletti viciously kicked Prati as he lay on the ground.

General Ongania, the military dictator of Argentina, who had previously warned his World Cup team after their violent display in Bolivia, had three of the Estudiantes men arrested: Aguirre Suarez, Poletti, the goalkeeper, and Manera. Dictators, too, have their fleeting moments of grace. . . . Poletti was suspended for life, the other two for long periods.

In the first leg, Milan overcame Estudiantes' various skulduggeries to win 3–0 with fast, enterprising football. The big Brazilian outside-right, Angelo Sormani, headed a goal after eight minutes, from Pierino Prati's centre, Combin dribbled a long pass by Rosato round two men before scoring the second, a minute from half-time; Sormani got the third.

This left Estudiantes with a virtually impossible deficit, the rules of the competition now making aggregate of goals decisive, where before a victory by each team necessitated a play off, regardless of who had scored more goals. Estudiantes were reported to have offered their players *the entire gate receipts* if they could reverse the three-goal deficit. If so, Estudiantes' natural belligerence received an alarming further charge.

After the game at San Siro, Rivera, who scored the first goal of the match in Buenos Aires, remarked that he was afraid it would be his last: "If one always had to play like this, it would be better to invent another game." Lodetti, the midfield player, observed, "A permanent crime against the spirit of football," while Nereo Rocco, Milan's coach, rumbled, "A footballer risks his career against the Argentinians." Now, I wonder, will people think that we of the British Press who went to Buenos Aires for the 1968 game exaggerated?

Estudiantes scored twice in the two minutes before half time, to take the lead; a right-footed drive by Aguirre Suarez, after Conigliaro had a shot blocked, a drive by Conigliaro, after a pass by Bilardo. In the second half, Milan shut up shop and that was that.

Poor Combin, however, found insult added to injury when he reached the dressing-rooms on his stretcher; the police arrested him on a charge of evading the draft (he'd left Argentina to play for Lyon before conscription.) Once more, Ongania intervened, to have him released.

When, one reflected, was FIFA going to put an end to the whole squalid business? And what sort of a world championship was it, in any case, when the Brazilian clubs stayed out of the South American Cup, year by year?

San Siro, October 8, 1969

Milan (2) 3 — *Estudiantes de la Plata* (0) 0

Sormani 2, Combin

Milan: Cudicini; Malatrasi; Anquilletti, Rosato, Schnellinger; Lodetti, Rivera, Fogli; Sormani, Combin (Rognoni), Prati.

Estudiantes: Poletti; Aguirre Suarez, Manera, Madero, Malbernat; Bilardo, Togneri, Echecopar; Flores, Conigliaro, Veron.

Buenos Aires, October 22

Estudiantes de la Plata (2) 2 — *Milan* (1) 1
Aguirre Suarez, Conigliaro — Rivera

Estudiantes: Poletti; Manera, Aguirre Suarez, Madero, Malbernat; Bilardo (Echecopar), Romeo, Togneri; Conigliaro, Taverna, Veron.

Milan: Cudicini; Malatrasi (Fogli); Anquilletti, Maldera, Rosato, Schnellinger; Lodetti, Rivera; Sormani, Combin, Prati (Rognoni.)

Milan, under the new dispensation whereby goal aggregate is decisive, won by 4 goals to 2.

THE FOOTBALL LEAGUE CUP 1969/70

Though it produced this season an all-First Division Final between two distinguished Cup fighting teams, Manchester City and West Bromwich Albion, the League Cup still could not rid itself of its overtones of ambiguity. How hard, to put it crudely, was everybody trying? Did we see the full power, say, of Leeds United when they went out 2–0 at Chelsea, or were they saving it for the battles of the European Cup and the League?

There is no doubt that Manchester United did their very utmost to win the trophy, but that was surely less for its intrinsic importance than for the carrot hung before the donkey: that of participation in the Fairs Cup (*if* you are a First Division club). United eventually fell in a memorable two-legged semi-final, the second of which produced a 63,000 gate at Old Trafford, to Manchester City.

A late penalty at Maine Road, a late free kick at Old Trafford, each by Francis Lee, turned the trick. It was 1–1 at Maine Road when Ure tripped Lee, who shot home the penalty. It was 2–1 to United in the return when Lee, rashly it first seemed, decided to have a direct shot from an indirect free-kick. Alex Stepney had a moment of still greater aberration; he parried it, and Summerbee ran the ball home, to take City through.

West Bromwich, meanwhile, thrashed Carlisle United, Chelsea's conquerors, 4–1 at The Hawthorns, after losing the first leg, at Carlisle. So they went to their second League Final at Wembley since 1967, their third League Final since 1966; not to mention their winning F.A. Cup Final of 1968. For City, it was a swift return to Wembley after taking the F.A. Cup there in 1969.

Their victory allowed them to complete an unusual and impressive "treble," since they'd won the Championship in 1968 and the F.A. Cup in 1969. They were not, at the time the game was played, remotely in form; a fact emphasized when they drew 0–0 away to Academica Coimbra in the Portuguese sunshine, three days earlier, in the Cup-winners' Cup.

So they picked a cautious team, which included George Heslop as an extra centre-half, no wingers, and Pardoe in midfield. The supreme irony of it all was that, having packed the middle of their defence with tall men, they should give away a highly avoidable goal after only five minutes, yet prevail in the end not least because the plodding, heavy men were suited to the grimly heavy conditions.

Albion began with a bang and went out with a whimper. When Ray Wilson, their left-back, crossed long and high from the left, it was a classical goalkeeper's ball; but the 6 foot 4 inch Joe Corrigan allowed himself to be outjumped by Jeff Astle, who headed in. At no time, indeed, did City's defence look dominant in the air, but the brilliance of Francis Lee and a fine second half by Colin Bell made up for everything.

Lee, who had recently been in something of a trough, was superbly effective. In the first half, he twice nearly scored with headers and once, with splendid virtuosity, almost made a goal for Mike Summerbee.

In the event it was Summerbee, just after receiving an injury which put him off the field, who played a part in the equaliser. He hooked on Pardoe's right-wing corner, Colin Bell got his head to it, and Mike Doyle ran in on the blind side, to score.

Albion's little, light men tired on the very taxing surface, and it was rather a surprise that the game should go into extra time. Eleven minutes of the first period had been played when Lee, again superbly beating a man and crossing from near the right-hand post, this time saw Bell flick the ball on with his head, and Pardoe turn it home, for the winner.

Football League Cup Final

Wembley Stadium, March 7, 1970

Manchester City (0) 2	*West Bromwich Albion* (1) 1
Doyle, Pardoe	Astle

(*after extra time*)

Chapter Eight
British International Tournament 1969-70

BRITISH INTERNATIONAL TOURNAMENT 1969-70

A MISERABLY devalued British Championship was shared by England, Scotland and Wales with four points each. Though circumstances to some extent conspired against it, with a truncated season, a replayed F.A. Cup Final, Celtic and Manchester City reaching European finals, it was still perfectly clear that the idea of playing off the whole competition in eight days at the end of the season was a failure. The whole thing now appeared as an afterthought, an anticlimax, something to be endured by weary players, emerging from the taxing realities of Cup and League play. Over the whole affair, meanwhile, lay the shadow of the European cup competitions, as it so easily might in the future, besides.

The tournament began on Saturday, April 18 with a drab performance by England in Cardiff, and the sending off of George Best in Belfast, where what amounted to a Scotland B XI defeated Northern Ireland, 1–0.

Midway through the second half, Best seemed completely to lose control of himself, after disagreeing with a decision by a permissive referee in Mr. Jennings. He chased him, appeared to spit in disgust, and finally threw a handful of mud at Jennings, who had no alternative but to send him off. Previously, he had missed a couple of chances, and had generally been well held by Newcastle's Bobby Moncur.

Once he had gone, a previously indifferent Scottish team began to take control of the game and might have scored a couple of times through their substitute, Colin Stein. Their only goal, in fact, came from a breakaway after a corner. Alan Gilzean, who had an effective match, found McLean, whose good cross was headed in by Derby's O'Hare, winning his first cap. Another first cap went to the splendid young Celtic right-back, Hay, his club's only player in the side – the other candidates having been allowed a rest.

Jimmy Nicholson, who had played so well all season for Huddersfield Town, had an outstanding game for Ireland.

At Cardiff, the best player on the field was Terry Hennessey, released from his customary postion in Wales' back four, as second stopper, to run superbly free in midfield. His tackling, control and use of a difficult ball in a high wind were all exemplary, while Ron Davies gave Brian Labone great difficulty.

England looked pale and ineffectual. They would have fallen a goal behind after 21 minutes had Banks not been awfully quick to dive at the feet of the galloping Davies, put through by Rees. As it was, Dick Kryzwicki scored for Wales five minutes from the interval. Peters lost the ball in the Welsh half and didn't chase, Alan Durban capped a long run with a through pass on to which Kryzwicki ran, as the English defence stood square, obviously believing him offside.

It was only in the 71st minute that England equalised, with a superb goal by Francis Lee. Receiving from Ball, he cut in from the left wing for a thrilling right-footed shot which tore past Millington and into the far, top corner of the goal. Surprising, in the circumstances, that Ramsey did not give a few of his hungry young lions a chance to roar.

Two of them were thrown into the fray the following Tuesday, against Northern Ireland at Wembley, though in all fairness to Ramsey it can't be said that either made a great impact. Brian Kidd did become more relaxed and thrustful in the second half, when he headed against the bar, but Ralph Coates never looked happy as a straightforward winger, clearly preferring the midfield.

The game was notable above all as Bobby Charlton's 100th for England, and he had a suitably effective match, putting over the corner from which Martin Peters headed England's first goal, and himself scoring the third, after Jennings had failed to hold a left wing cross from Hughes.

The finest goal of the match, however, was unquestionably scored by

George Best – playing despite the disapproval of FIFA, who felt with some justice that he should automatically have been suspended. Early in the second half, Best collected a long pass on the right, beautifully beat Stiles with his right foot on the outside, then pivoted to beat Banks with a glorious left-footed shot on the turn.

England, who, as Alf Ramsey admitted, had been lucky to lead at half-time, then awoke. Clements allowed Newton to break down the right on an overlap, and cross a ball which Geoff Hurst headed into goal, via a defender; then came Charlton's goal. England, with all three centre-halves injured, played Bobby Moore in the position, and he gradually mastered Dougan. But once again the appalling pitch seriously affected play; a tax on the limbs, and a menace to any attempt at fine accuracy.

Scotland, with another makeshift team, were held, the following day, to a goalless draw at Hampden, by Wales. The Welsh team again played defensively, with two strikers up, breaking now and again with speed and bite. There was one occasion in the second half when Cruickshank had to make a fine save on the ground from Ron Davies' header, and another as Rodrigues drove in the rebound.

Generally, however, Scotland had the better of things on a soaked pitch, and Colin Stein twice hit defenders when the ball seemed to be going in – with a header in the first half, a shot in the second.

On the Saturday, over 137,000 fans packed Hampden to watch a goalless draw between what amounted to a Scotland XI and an England XI. Scotland had immensely the better of it, even if they managed only two direct shots throughout the game, both in the final seven minutes, and neither giving Gordon Banks much trouble.

With Jimmy Johnstone in ebullient form, and needing all the efforts of a splendid Nobby Stiles to help contain him, Scotland dominated play. Why they did not get a penalty when Labone ruthlessly tripped Colin Stein, after 20 minutes, is something only the West German referee, Herr Schulenberg, will know. Stein, a splendid thruster, had beaten Newton and left Labone stranded when he was chopped down at thigh height. In the second half, O'Hare missed two fine chances within a couple of minutes, and England survived. They even had the ball in the net two minutes from time, Hurst putting in a cross by Peters, but the linesman rather mysteriously disallowed it for offside against Jeff Astle. It would certainly have been a travesty had Scotland lost. Though their team lacked a creative midfield – Carr still lacks experience, Hay is no midfield player, Greig has power rather than subtlety – it was unquestionably superior.

England's spearhead was hardly seen, Bobby Moncur dealing manfully with everything he had to – including a shot by Peters which knocked him out. Ball had one of his least effective games.

In Swansea, Wales were lucky to beat a Northern Ireland team which, though without Derek Dougan, had much the better of the second half. The only goal was scored when Craig collided with his goalkeeper,

McFaul – preferred to Pat Jennings – and Ronnie Rees toe-ended the ball into the net.

George Best was subjected to some unpleasant fouling, especially by Moore and Powell, but came briskly to life in the second half, when Ireland deserved at least to save the game, if not win it. In midfield, Terry Hennessey was this time eclipsed by Ireland's Jimmy Nicholson, capping his fine season for club and country.

Cardiff, April 18, 1970

Wales (1) 1	*England* (0) 1
Krzywicki	Lee

Wales: Millington (Swansea); Rodrigues (Leicester City), Thomas (Swindon Town); Hennessey (Derby County), England (Spurs), Powell (Sheffield United); Krzywicki (Huddersfield Town), Durban (Derby County), Davies, R. (Southampton), Moore (Charlton Athletic), Rees (Nottingham Forest).
England: Banks (Stoke City); Wright (Everton), Hughes (Liverpool); Mullery (Spurs), Labone (Everton), Moore (West Ham United); Lee (Manchester City), Ball (Everton), Charlton (Manchester United), Hurst (West Ham United), Peters (Spurs).

Belfast

Northern Ireland (0) 0	*Scotland* (1) 1
	O'Hare

Northern Ireland: Jennings (Spurs); Craig (Newcastle United), Clements (Coventry City); Todd (Burnley), Neill (Arsenal), Nicholson (Huddersfield Town); Campbell (Dundee), Lutton (Wolves), Dougan (Wolves), McMordie (Middlesbough), Best (Manchester United). subs: Dickson (Coleraine), O'Kane (Nottingham Forest).
Scotland: Clark (Aberdeen); Hay (Celtic), Dickson (Kilmarnock); McLintock (Arsenal), McKinnon (Rangers), Moncur (Newcastle United); McLean (Kilmarnock), Carr (Coventry City), O'Hare (Derby County), Gilzean (Spurs), Johnstone (Rangers). sub: Stein (Rangers).

Wembley Stadium, April 21

England (1) 3	*Northern Ireland* (0) 1
Peters, Hurst,	Best
Charlton	

England: Banks (Stoke City); Newton (Everton), Bell (Manchester City)), Hughes (Liverpool); Mullery (Spurs), Moore (West Ham United), Stiles (Manchester United); Coates (Burnley), Kidd (Manchester United), Charlton (Manchester United), Hurst (West Ham United), Peters (Tottenham Hotspur).
Northern Ireland: Jennings (Spurs); Craig (Newcastle United), Clements (Coventry City); O'Kane (Nottingham Forest), Neill (Arsenal), Nicholson (Huddersfield Town); McMordie (Middlesbrough), Best

(Manchester United), Dougan (Wolves), O'Doherty (Coleraine), Cowan (Newcastle United), Lutton (Wolves) (Nelson (Arsenal)).

Hampden Park, April 22

Scotland (0) 0 — *Wales* (0) 0

Scotland: Cruickshank (Hearts); Callaghan (Dunfermline), Dickson (Kilmarnock); Greig (Rangers), McKinnon (Rangers), Moncur (Newcastle United); McLean (Kilmarnock), Hay (Celtic), Stein (Rangers), O'Hare (Derby County), Carr (Coventry City). sub: Lennox (Celtic).

Wales: Millington (Swansea); Rodrigues (Leicester City), Thomas (Swindon Town); Hennessey (Derby County), England (Spurs), Powell (Sheffield United); Krzywicki (Huddersfield Town), Durban (Derby County), Davies, R. (Southampton), Moore (Charlton Athletic), Rees (Nottingham Forest).

Hampden Park, April 25

Scotland (0) 0 — *England* (0) 0

Scotland: Cruickshank (Hearts); Gemmell (Celtic), Dickson (Kilmarnock); Greig (Rangers), McKinnon (Rangers), Moncur (Newcastle United) (Gilzean (Spurs)); Johnstone (Celtic), Hay (Celtic), Stein (Rangers), O'Hare (Derby County), Carr (Coventry City).

England: Banks (Stoke City); Newton (Everton), Hughes (Liverpool); Stiles (Manchester United), Labone (Everton), Moore (West Ham United); Thompson (Liverpool), Mullery (Spurs)), Ball (Everton), Astle (West Bromwich Albion), Hurst (West Ham United), Peters (Tottenham Hotspur).

Swansea

Wales (1) 1 — *Northern Ireland* (0) 0

Rees

Wales: Millington (Swansea Town); Rodrigues (Leicester City), Thoma (Swindon Town), Hennessey (Derby County), England (Spurs Powell (Sheffield United); Krzywicki (Huddersfield Town), Durbar (Derby County), Davies, R. (Southampton), Moore (Charlton Athletic), Rees (Nottingham Forest).

Northern Ireland: McFaul (Newcastle United); Craig (Newcastl United), Nelson (Arsenal); O'Kane (Nottingham Forest), Nei (Arsenal), Nicholson (Huddersfield Town); Campbell (Dundee), Be (Manchester United), Dickson (Coleraine), McMordie (Middle brough), Clements (Coventry City). O'Doherty (Coleraine).

	P	W	D	L	F	A	P
Scotland	3	1	2	0	1	0	[illegible]
England	3	1	2	0	4	2	4
Wales	3	1	2	0	2	1	4
Northern Ireland	3	0	0	3	1	5	0

WALES v THE UNITED KINGDOM
Cardiff, July 28, 1969

Played to celebrate the investitute of the Prince of Wales, this fixture produced, despite the heavy rain, a lively, entertaining and talented game. Wales were without Wyn Davies and Powell, recalling the veteran Cliff Jones; the U.K. did not have the services of such obvious candidates as Moore and Banks, while the splendid Lee played only half the match. Nevertheless, the standard was a high one.

Making considerably more chances, the U.K. deserved success. In the first half, Thomas kicked off the line after Lee had dribbled round Sprake and shot into goal, but when Dougan cleverly held off England, shot, and Sprake could only block the shot, no one could stop Lee putting in the winning goal. In the second half, Jennings had to make a couple of fine saves from Cliff and Barrie Jones; but as against that, Rodrigues cleared off the line from Jackie Charlton's header, while Sprake saved gallantly from the inextinguishable Billy Bremner, his club captain.

Wales (0) 0	*United Kingdom* (1) 1
	Lee

Wales: Sprake (Leeds United); Rodrigues (Leicester City), Thomas (Swindon Town); Hennessey (Nottingham Forest), England (Spurs), Moore (Charlton Athletic); Jones, B. (Cardiff City), Jones, C. (Fulham), Davies R. (Southampton), Toshack (Cardiff City), Rees (Nottingham Forest). (sub. Reece (Sheffield United)).

United Kingdom: Jennings (Spurs and Ireland); Gemmell (Celtic and Scotland), Cooper (Leeds United and England) (sub. Newton (Blackburn Rovers and England)); Bremner (Leeds United and Scotland), Charlton, J. (Leeds United and England), Mullery (Spurs and England); Best (Manchester United and Ireland), Lee (Manchester City and England), sub. Henderson (Rangers and Scotland), Dougan (Wolves and Ireland), Charlton, R. (Manchester United and England), Hughes (Celtic and Scotland).

EUROPEAN NATIONS CUP 1970/72

The draw for the fourth European Nations Cup was made in Rome on March 20. Once again, the contestants were divided into qualifying groups, the eight winners reaching the quarter-finals, when the tournament becomes a knock-out one. England's fortunes were considerably greater than those of the other home countries.

GROUP 1: Rumania, Czechoslovakia, WALES, Finland.
GROUP 2: Bulgaria, Hungary, France, Norway.
GROUP 3: ENGLAND, Greece, Switzerland, Malta.
GROUP 4: Russia, NORTHERN IRELAND, Spain, Cyprus.
GROUP 5: Belgium, SCOTLAND, Portugal, Denmark.
GROUP 6: Italy (Holders), Sweden, Austria, Eire.

GROUP 7: Yugoslavia, East Germany, Holland, Luxemburg.
GROUP 8: West Germany, Poland, Turkey, Albania.

Chapter Nine

Friendly Internationals Against Foreign Teams 1969-70

SCOTLAND were the first to play such a match; a somewhat misguided Sunday fixture against Eire, in Dublin, entailing predictable absenteeism; and a wretched Scottish performance. Eire, in fact, were palpably the better team and should have won, though they, too, suffered from some late defections.

At Manchester, in October, England's first Under 23 international against Russia ended with a 2–0 win, after a rather sterile first half. In this period, the Russians were more inventive and better together; they nearly scored when Larin lobbed against Corrigan's bar.

After half-time, England struck up more of an understanding and, with John Hurst in excellent form, began to make chances. Osgood made a goal for Husband after 64 minutes, Kidd, with a fine run on the left, a second for Joe Royle, three minutes from time.

England opened their season with an encouraging, if scarcely spectacular, 1–0 win away to Holland, in Amsterdam. Injury kept out a number of players, among them Ball, Banks and Labone, while Emlyn Hughes of Liverpool was given a first cap, at left-back.

Bell, who headed against the crossbar just on half-time, confirmed his opportunism by scoring the only goal, late in the game, exploiting what was a misplaced shot rather than a pass, from Bobby Charlton. Lee played with his usual dynamism, while the brilliant Cruyff contrived two very awkward situations for England in the second half. Bonetti was admirably alive to them.

Scotland's Under 23 team then dealt impressively with a far from untalented French side, whom they beat with considerable ease, at Hampden Park. Two of the goals went to the square-shouldered Derby County centre-forward, John O'Hare, while little Willie Carr, of Coventry, and Robb, of Aberdeen, were also very dangerous.

At Wembley, England opened their home season with a miserably disappointing performance against a much depleted Portuguese team – without Eusebio, Coluna, Torres and Simoes. Jackie Charlton headed the solitary goal, on the near post, from his brother, Bobby's, inswinging corner. Bobby himself hit a post and Francis Lee, in the second half, missed a penalty, awarded when Astle was pulled down by the goalkeeper when about to score. Lee had played splendidly for a busy hour.

But it was three superb saves by Peter Bonetti, at or after free-kicks, which allowed England to take the game. Their 4–4–2 formation showed manifest failings, even if the absence of Hurst, Labone and Newton, among others, had to be taken into account.

The next game, at home to the Dutch, was drearier still, and did not even provide the consolation of a victory, however meagre. Sir Alf Ramsey made a number of somewhat haphazard changes, giving Hunter one of his rare excursions, in place of Bobby Moore, restoring Mick Jones to the team after an absence of nearly five years, capping Ian Storey-Moore of Nottingham Forest for the first time. The result was sheer incoherence. Moore did, it's true, once head past Van Beveren, for the goal to be disallowed, while Bobby Charlton put the ball in the net just after the final whistle. But in general a cool Dutch team gave as good as they got, defended in style, and often broke dangerously, especially through the talented, finely economical Johan Cruyff. At last a much put-upon crowd lost patience with its team, and the end came to the accompaniment of the slow handclap, booing, and choruses of, "What a load of rubbish!"

Things clearly had to improve; and they did when England played their next international away to Belgium in Brussels, the following February. Eager to win, and improve their morale for the World Cup, Belgium played the game not in the Heysels Stadium, their normal home ground, but in the smaller Anderlecht Stadium.

Ramsey, on this occasion, at last cast out the mediocrities, and belatedly and rather grudgingly gave a chance to Chelsea's Peter Osgood; who came in after Bobby Charlton and Colin Bell dropped out.

The improved form of Geoff Hurst, the return of Moore and Ball, the revival of Peters, the skills of Osgood, allowed England to weather a first half largely dominated by Belgium; and to win.

Their first goal, a manifest breakaway in the 28th minute, came after a fine run by Osgood, through the mud and sleet, a quick, clever flurry of passes between Peters and Hurst, quick anticipation and a shot by Alan Ball.

In the second half, 13 minutes had gone when Peters made one of his West Ham near-post goals for Hurst's immaculate head. Belgium reduced the deficit when Dockx drove his free kick through the English wall. England, however, replied almost immediately with another goal by Ball, after Hurst had headed back Cooper's centre. A warming performance.

In April, England's Under 23 team resumed its activities when a highly experimental team proved far too strong for the young Bulgarians, at Plymouth. Left-wingers played well for both sides, Roger Morgan of the Spurs scoring two goals in the second half for England, Mitkov, five minutes from time, running through alone after beating Smith, to get the solitary Bulgarian goal.

England dominated the first half, but had only Nish's lobbed goal, in injury time, to show for it. With Dave Thomas running strongly and crossing well from the right, the second half brought three more, before

Bulgaria at last replied. Four Second Division players took part in the victory – and only two members of the World Cup party, Hughes and Shilton, a sign of the depth of England's resources.

Having spent two quiet weeks acclimatising to altitude in Mexico City, England then embarked on a brief tour of even higher points, in South America, playing two matches both in Bogota and Quito; and winning all four.

There was a good deal of difference in the manner of these victories, much the handsomest being gained by the full national team over Colombia in Bogota, a night game which followed a curtain raiser played, and won 1–0, by the second team. This was a match of little distinction. The England XI began well, with Stiles driving them on from midfield and Osgood making an impressive start, but by half-time, they no longer held the edge on midfield. Though the defence, not least Bob McNab, who was one of the six omitted later from the World Cup 22, was in sturdy form. The only goal was scored after 31 minutes of the second half by Jeff Astle, who had come on as substitute for Brian Kidd. When Zape, an unimpressive goalkeeper, dropped the ball, he pushed it into the net.

The full England team, by contrast, scored after only 90 seconds, when Geoff Hurst headed on Bobby Charlton's inswinging right wing corner, and Martin Peters sharply headed it in. England, thus encouraged, took charge of midfield, with Peters in superb form, well abetted by Alan Ball, and with a Bobby Charlton showing far more appetite for the game than in previous internationals.

Peters headed a second goal six minutes from half time, again from Charlton's inswinging right wing corner, after Hurst had cleverly lured the defence away. Both these goals had, in fact, been planned that morning, after a conference with the trainer, Harold Shepherdson.

In the second half, England continued to play splendid football against a weak and ingenuous Colombian team, making astonishingly light of the 8,000 feet altitude. Two more goals came; one smashed in by Charlton's left foot in the 57th. minute, after a movement in which Peters played a great part, the other headed by Ball, from Cooper's centre.

Only four days later, the two teams played in the morning and early afternoon at Quito, 9,300 feet up, in Ecuador. This time, it was the B team, playing the local champions, Liga Deportiva Universitaria, who showed the more commanding form, after appearing to lose their grip of the game.

They opened the score after 23 minutes, Astle sending home a tremendous volley after the goalkeeper had feebly pushed out Clarke's overhead kick, following a corner.

Liga, however, rallied to equalise, their clever Uruguayan striker, Barreto, receiving from Salazar and dribbling skilfully across the face of the defence, from left to right, before scoring with a ferocious shot.

By half time, the English side seemed to be in difficulties, but the deadly finishing of Astle won them the game. Two minutes after McNab and Coates had replaced Clarke and Thompson, and fourteen minutes into the second half, he beat the goalkeeper to a cross by Colin Bell, and Munoz could only help the ball into the goal.

Six minutes later, he timed perfectly his run on to Bell's free kick, and sent his header low into the right hand corner of the goal, the referee very properly ignoring demands for offside. Finally, eleven minutes from time, after a shot by Emlyn Hughes rebounded from the post, Osgood played the ball calmly across, and Astle's hard shot again rebounded in, from a defender.

The first team, now palpably showing the effects of altitude – no great shame, when one game followed so hard on the other, in Bogota – again had the encouragement of an early goal. This time it was scored by Francis Lee. Mullery passed to Newton, whose right wing cross sailed over the defence and the jumping Hurst, to be rushed in by Lee.

The Ecuadorians, however, proved tougher customers than the Colombians, and should certainly have equalised when Ball inexplicably passed back, straight into the path of Penaherrera, who had a long, clear run to goal. Banks, however, was out in a flash, to make a superb, smothering save. During the second half, Penaherrera missed another chance, and England were thus able to break away to score a second.

Twelve minutes from time, Peters crossed high from the right, Hurst leaped to back head the ball, and Kidd, who had been called as a substitute, flung himself for a brave, low, successful header. 2–0 was perhaps mildly flattering to England, but with the exception of those two errors, the defence had held up well.

Dublin, September 21

Eire (1) 1	*Scotland* (1) 1
Givens	Stein

Eire: Kelly (Preston North End); Brennan (Manchester United), Meagan (Drogheda); Finucane (Limerick), Mulligan (Shamrock Rovers), Conway (Fulham); Rogers (Blackburn Rovers), Giles (Leeds United), Givens (Manchester United), Hale (Waterford), Treacy (Charlton Athletic).

Scotland: McGarr (Aberdeen); Greig (Rangers), Gemmell (Celtic); Stanton (Hibernian), McKinnon (Rangers), Moncur (Newcastle United); Henderson (Rangers), Bremner (Leeds United), Stein (Rangers), Cormack (Hibernian), Hughes (Celtic). subs: Herriot (Birmingham City), Callaghan (Dunfermline).

Old Trafford, October 22

England Under 23 (0) 2	*Russia Under 23* (0) 0
Husband, Royle	

England: Corrigan (Manchester City); Parkin (Wolves), Hughes (Liverpool); Todd (Sunderland), Ellis (Sheffield Wednesday), Hurst (Everton); Husband (Everton), Osgood (Chelsea), Royle (Everton), Kidd (Manchester United), Nish (Leicester City).

Russia: Tkatschenko; Lisneko, Reschko, Smirnov, Chochoedze, Kalinov, Bogovik, Koslov, Zintschenko, Larin, Stekolnikov.

Amsterdam, November 5

Holland (0) 0	*England* (0) 1
	Bell

Holland: Treitjel; Drost, Israel, Eikjenbroek, Krol; Veenstra (Van Dijk), Rijnders; Cruyff, Mulder, Van Hanegem (Muhren), Rensenbrink.
England: Bonetti (Chelsea); Wright (Everton), Hughes (Liverpool); Mullery (Spurs), Charlton, J. (Leeds United), Moore (West Ham United); Lee (Manchester City), Bell (Manchester City), Charlton, R. (Manchester United), Hurst (West Ham United), Peters (West Ham United).

Glasgow, December 3

Scotland Under 23 (1) 4	*France Under 23* (0) 0
O'Hare 2	
Lorimer 2 (1 penalty)	

Scotland: Hughes (Chelsea); Malone (Ayr United), Hay (Celtic); Blackley (Hibernian), Thomson (Hearts), Munro (Wolves); Lorimer (Leeds United), Carr (Coventry City), O'Hare (Derby County), Robb (Aberdeen) Marinello (Hibernian), Johnston (Rangers).

France: Baratelli; Camerini, Rostagni, Osman, Vanucci, Huck, Eo (Mezy), Hardouin, Vergnes, Larqué, Dellamore.

Wembley, December 10

England (1) 1	*Portugal* (0) 0
Charlton, J.	

England: Bonetti (Chelsea); Reaney (Leeds United), Hughes (Liverpool); Mullery (Spurs), Charlton, J. (Leeds United), Moore (West Ham United); Lee (Manchester City), Bell (Manchester City) Peters, (West Ham United), Astle (West Bromwich Albion), Charlton, R. (Manchester United), Ball (Everton).
Portugal: José Henrique; Conceicao, Cardoso, José Carlos, Murca, Tome, Toni, Graça (Pedro Gomes), Guerreiro, Antonio (Figueiredo), Jacinto Joao.

Wembley, January 15, 1970

England (0) 0	*Holland* (0) 0

England: Banks (Stoke City); Newton (Blackburn Rovers), Cooper (Leeds United); Peters (West Ham United), Charlton, J. (Leeds United), Hunter (Leeds United); Lee (Manchester City), (Mullery (Spurs), Bell (Manchester City), Jones (Leeds United) (Hurst (West Ham United)), Charlton, R. (Manchester United), Storey-Moore (Nottingham Forest).
Holland: Van Beeveren; Drost, Israel, Eikjenbroek, Krol, Jansen, Rijnders (Muhren), Van Dijk, Cruyff, Van Hanegem (Weenstra), Keizer.

Brussels, February 25, 1970

Belgium (0) 1 — *England* (1) 3
Dockx — Ball 2, Hurst

Belgium: Trappeniers; Heylens, Dewalque, Jeck, Thissen; Van Moer, Dockx, Polleunis (Verheyen); Semmeling, Devrindt, Van Himst.

England: Banks (Stoke City); Wright (Everton), Cooper (Leeds United), Hughes (Liverpool), Labone (Everton), Moore (West Ham United); Lee (Manchester City), Ball (Everton), Osgood (Chelsea), Hurst (West Ham United), Peters (West Ham United).

Plymouth, April 8

England Under 23 (1) 4 — *Bulgaria Under 23* (0) 1
Nish, Currie, Morgan 2 — Mitkov

England: Shilton (Leicester City); Smith (Sheffield Wednesday), Parkin (Wolves); Nish (Leicester City), Dobson (Burnley), Hughes (Liverpool); (Edwards (Manchester United)); Thomas (Burnley), Piper (Plymouth Argyle), Dyson (Newcastle United), Currie (Sheffield United), Morgan (Spurs) (Garland (Bristol City)).
Bulgaria: Kamenski; Zafirov, Ivkor; Gaidarski, Kolev, Radjev; Denev (Panov), Paunov, Mitev (Kotsev), Mihailov, Mitkov.

Bogota, May 20

Colombia B (0) 0 — *England XI* (0) 1
Astle

Colombia B: Zape; Riascos, Soto, Verdugo, Viafara; Arboleda, Velasquez; Ospina, Torres, Canpaz, Hurtado (Morales.)

England XI: Bonetti (Chelsea); Wright (Everton), McNab (Arsenal); Stiles (Manchester United), (Coates (Burnley)), Charlton (Leeds United), Hunter (Leeds United); Kidd (Manchester United), (Astle (West Bromwich Albion), Bell (Manchester City), Osgood (Chelsea), Clarke (Leeds United), Hughes (Liverpool.)

Bogota, May 20

Colombia (0) 0 — *England* (2) 4
Peters 2, Charlton, Ball

Colombia: Quintana; Segovia, Segrera, D. Lopez, Hernandez; Canon, O. Lopez, Garcia; Paz (Arango), Brand, Gallego.
England: Banks (Stoke City); Newton (Everton), Labone (Everton), Moore (West Ham United), Cooper (Leeds United); Mullery (Spurs), Ball (Everton), Peters (Tottenham Hotspur); Lee (Manchester City), Charlton (Manchester United), Hurst (West Ham United.)

Quito, May 24

Liga Deportiva Universitaria (1) 1 — *England XI* (1) 4
Barreto — Astle 4

Liga: Montoya; Tobar, Zambrano, Munoz, Cabrero; Ale, Soussman; Salazar (Moreno), Barreto (Garzon), Tapia, Pintado.

England XI: Bonetti (Chelsea); Wright (Everton), Charlton (Leeds United), Hunter (Leeds United), Hughes (Liverpool); Stiles (Manchester United), Osgood (Chelsea), Bell (Manchester City); Clarke (Leeds United), (McNab (Arsenal)) Astle (West Bromwich Albion), Thompson (Liverpool), (Coates (Burnley)).

Quito, May 24		
	Ecuador (0) 0	*England* (1) 2 Lee, Kidd

Ecuador: Mejia; Utreras, Campoverde, Portilla, Valencia; Cardenas, Bolaños; Munoz (Cabezas), Peñaherrera, Carrera (Rodriguez), Larrea.
England: Banks (Stoke City); Newton (Everton), Cooper (Leeds United); Mullery (Spurs), Labone (Everton), Moore (West Ham United); Lee (Manchester City), Ball (Everton), Charlton (Manchester United) Hurst (West Ham United), Peters (Spurs.)

Chapter Ten

Friendly Internationals Between Foreign Teams

August 1969 – May 1970

August 6	*Russia* (0) 0	*Sweden* (0) 1 Eklund
August 25	*Sweden* (2) 3 Danielsson 2 Eriksson (penalty)	*Israel* (1) 1 Ramin
August 27	*Poland* 6 Lubanski 2, Marks 2, Dejna, Brychzy	*Norway* 1 Iversen
September 21	*Norway* (2) 2 Olsen, D., Saethrang	*Denmark* (0) 0
September 21	*Austria* (1) 1 Pirkner	*West Germany* (1) 1 Muller
September 24	*Bulgaria* (0) 0	*West Germany* (1) 1 Doerfel
September 24	*Turkey* (2) 3 Melin, Nihat, Can	*Switzerland* (0) 0
September 24	*Yugoslavia* (1) 1	*Russia* (2) 3

	Dzajic	Asatiani, Nodina, Bychevetz
September 24	*Sweden* (0) 2	*Hungary* (0) 0
	Nicklasson, Grahn	
October 8	*East Germany* (0) 1	*Poland* (2) 2
	Nowotny	Lubanski, Stachurski
November 5	*Mexico* (1) 1	*Belgium* (0) 0
	Onofre	
November 12	*Mexico* (2) 4	*Norway* (0) 0
	Onofre, Padilla, Ponce 2	
November 14	*Guatemala* 1	*Norway* 3
December 28	*Morocco* (2) 3	*Bulgaria* (0) 0
	Maaroufi 2 (1 penalty), Ghazouani	
December 31	*Malta* (0) 1	*Luxemburg* (1) 1
	Cini	Hoffmann, N.
February 15	*Peru* (0) 0	*Russia* (0) 0
February 15	*Mexico* (1) 1	*Bulgaria* (0) 1
	Diaz	Marachliev
February 21	*Peru* (0) 0	*Russia* (0) 2
		Pusach, Khmelnitski
February 18	*Spain* (2) 2	*West Germany* (0) 0
	Arieta 2	
February 22	*Peru* (1) 1	*Bulgaria* (0) 3
	Sotil	Penev, Petkov, Marachliev
February 20	*Mexico* (0) 2	*Bulgaria* (0) 0
	Rivas, Basaguren	
February 21	*Spain* (2) 2	*Italy* (2) 2
	Salvadore (2 own goals)	Anastasi, Riva
February 22	*Mexico* (0) 0	*Sweden* (0) 0
February 23	*El Salvador* (0) 0	*Russia* (1) 2
		Pusach, Serebrianikov
February 25	*Peru* (0) 5	*Bulgaria* (1) 3
	Sotil 3, Challe, Cubillas	Dermendjiev, Asparoukhov 2
February 26	*Mexico* (0) 0	*Russia* (0) 0
February 26	*Costa Rica* (1) 2	*El Salvador* (0) 0
	Saenz, Daniels	
February 28	*Mexico* (0) 0	*Sweden* (0) 1
		Eiderstedt
March 4	*Brazil* (0) 0	*Argentina* (0) 2
		Mas, Conigliaro
March 8	*Brazil* (1) 2	*Argentina* (1) 1
	Jairzinho, Pelé	Brindisi
March 5	*Peru* (0) 0	*Mexico* (0) 1
		Basaguren

March 8	*Peru* (1) 1 Leon	*Mexico* (0) 0
March 15	*Mexico* (2) 3 Padilla, Onofre, Lopez	*Peru* (1) 1 Challe
March 21	*Brazil* (4) 5 Pelé 2, Gerson Roberto 2	*Chile* (0) 0
March 27	*Brazil* (0) 2 Carlos Alberto, Rivelino	*Chile* (1) 1 Castro
March 31	*Uruguay* (2) 2 Maniero, Cubilla	*Peru* (0) 0
April 8	*France* (1) 1 Michel	*Bulgaria* (1) 1 Jekov
April 8	*West Germany* (1) 1 Overath	*Rumania* (1) 1 Neagu
April 8	*Yugoslavia* (0) 1 Bajevic	*Austria* (1) 1 Redl
April 12	*Yugoslavia* (1) 2 Pancsics (own goal), Gracanin	*Hungary* (1) 2 Bene, Fazekas
April 12	*Austria* (0) 1 Kreuz	Czechoslovakia (3) 3 Albrecht, Hrdlicka, Adamec
April 13	*Brazil* (0) 0	*Paraguay* (0) 0
April 18	*Peru* (1) 4 Reyes 2, Baylon, Gallardo	*Uruguay* (0) 2 Bareno, Ancheta
April 21	*Peru* (0) 3 Gallardo, Sotil, Castillo	*El Salvador* (0) 0
April 21	*Switzerland* (0) 0	*Spain* (1) 1 Rojo
April 28	*France* (2) 2 Loubet, Djorkaeff (penalty)	*Rumania* (0) 0
April 29	*Brazil* (1) 1 Rivelino	*Austria* (0) 0
May 2	*Hungary* (0) 2 Fazekas, Karsai	*Poland* (0) 0
May 3	*Switzerland* (1) 2 Blaettler 2	*France* (0) 1 Revelli
May 6	*Rumania* (0) 0	*Yugoslavia* (0) 0
May 9	*West Germany* (1) 2 Seeler, Loehr	*Eire* (0) 1 Mulligan
May 5	*Bulgaria* (1) 3	*Russia* (2) 3

	Jekov 2, Bonev	Evriuzhikin, Nodia, Bychevetz
May 7	*Poland* (2) 2 Kozovski, Szoltysik	*Eire* (0) 1 Gibbons
May 9	*Luxemburg* (0) 0	*Czechoslovakia* (1) 1 Jurkanin
May 13	*West Germany* (1) 1 Seeler	*Yugoslavia* (0) 0
May 13	*Norway* (0) 0	*Czechoslovakia* (1) 2 Olassen (own goal), Adamec
May 10	*Portugal* (0) 1 Coelho	*Italy* (1) 2 Riva 2
May 16	*Hungary* (1) 1 Fazekas	*Sweden* (0) 2 Persson, Eiderstedt
May 16	*Poland* (1) 1 Deyna	*East Germany* (1) 1 Vogel

Chapter Eleven
F.A. Cup 1960-70

In the first replayed Cup Final since 1912, the first ever not to be resolved at Wembley, Chelsea beat Leeds United to win the trophy at last. They won it at Manchester, 55 years after their first attempt to do so was frustrated there by Sheffield United, in the so-called Khaki Final. They had to come from behind both at Wembley and Old Trafford, and play both matches without their key midfield player, young Alan Hudson. For Leeds, frustrated in three major competitions, their defeat in extra time by Webb's goal was an especially bitter experience. They scarcely deserved to be beaten, but weariness had something to do with it.

Manchester United's was also an interesting progress. In the Fourth Round, they had abundant revenge for their defeat by Manchester City in the League Cup, thrashing them 3–0 at Old Trafford without George Best – but with Brian Kidd in splendid form. Then Best returned – scoring six out of eight goals away to Northampton Town. By contrast, Middlesbrough gave United a severe passage. They were unlucky not to beat them on Teesside, and very unlucky to go out at Old Trafford, where a careless back pass by Hickton, leading to a penalty and the winning goal by Morgan, was decisive.

Leeds, by contrast, had the easiest of runs to the semi-final, though they made heavy weather of knocking out Swansea 2–1, at home, in the Third Round. Only when Mel Nurse, Swansea's centre-half, was sent off did they really get a hold on the game. Easy victories against Sutton United, the Isthmian League amateurs (6–0, away, after which they signed John Faulkner, the Sutton centre-half), Mansfield Town and Swindon, away, followed.

Watford did splendidly to defeat two First Division clubs in Stoke City, with a long-range shot by Franks, and Liverpool, with a fine header by Endean, at Vicarage Road, in the Fifth and Sixth Rounds. This qualified them, for the first time in their history, for the semi-final. They were drawn against Chelsea, who in the previous round had comfortably won away to a Queen's Park Rangers team which had just eliminated Derby County. Chelsea had been forced to a replay by Burnley, in the Fourth Round, after losing a two goal advantage at Stamford Bridge, but won impressively, 3–1, at Turf Moor.

Their semi-final against Watford, on the abominable pitch at Tottenham, was a match only for forty-five minutes. David Webb scored after only three minutes, but Watford equalised when a long shot by Garbutt bounced fiendishly, to deceive Bonetti.

Thus encouraged, they gave as good as they got until half-time. But when Osgood firmly and fiercely restored Chelsea's lead, that was the end of it. Peter Houseman, switching to the right, scored twice, Ian Hutchinson once, and Chelsea were in their third Cup Final.

Manchester United and Leeds, in the other semi-final, entered a prolonged, prodigious combat. There were no goals at Hillsborough, no goals at Villa Park – after extra time. At Sheffield, United, rather surprisingly, had the better of the first half, when the young, red-haired Italian, Carlo Sartori, played splendidly in midfield – though both he and Best might have scored.

In the second half, Leeds steadily became dominant, but Alex Stepney's goalkeeping frustrated them; just as it had in the opening minutes, when Ure's miskick allowed Mick Jones to race through. Sartori tired after the interval, and Leeds seemed likely to have won, had the game gone into extra time.

At Birmingham it did; but again United held out. Indeed, for 75 minutes, they'd been the better side, Brian Kidd missing early chances, Denis Law, coming on as substitute for Sartori, late ones. With both goalkeepers and both teams in exhilarating form, though Ure and Norman Hunter were missing, a draw was quite just, even if Manchester United had abundant chances to win.

A splendid serial came to its protracted end at Bolton, two days later. Billy Bremner scored the only, and decisive goal in the ninth minute, when Leeds broke away after a corner, Clarke headed the ball down, and it skidded off Jones' foot, for Bremner to shoot in with his left.

At Wembley, a Cup Final more dramatic than distinguished, full of excitement rather than outstanding football, ended in a draw after extra time. The players, Leeds' overworked side in particular, were to be congratulated in putting on any kind of show on a disgracefully inadequate surface. Great quantities of sand had been rolled into the pitch, which made movement a constant physical effort, and the bounce of the ball so uncertain that it probably caused two of the goals.

Chelsea lacked Alan Hudson, their splendid 18-year-old mid-field player, still recovering from an ankle injury, while Ron Harris, their skipper, played though still suffering pain from a damaged hamstring. Leeds were without their England full-back, Paul Reaney, who had broken his leg at West Ham. The omnicompetent Madeley serenely took his place.

After a somewhat uneasy beginning, Leeds dominated play for some twenty minutes, and had Billy Bremner not then tired, after some ebullient play, might have won with some ease. Chelsea palpably missed Hudson, while Osgood had a poor game.

Leeds went ahead, after 21 minutes, with a curious, unsatisfactory goal. From Gray's inswinging corner, Charlton got his head to the ball, Bonetti appeared to be impeded as he came out, and as McCreadie swung his foot to clear, the bounce of the ball deceived him on the sandy ground, and it trickled over the line.

Two minutes later, McCreadie had the satisfaction of lobbing in the centre which brought his team's equaliser. Hutchinson headed the ball down and Peter Houseman, taking Hudson's place in midfield, half-volleyed a cross shot. Gary Sprake went down to make what should have been an easy save, but he too may well have been deceived by the bounce of the ball, as it passed through his hands.

But with Eddie Gray beating Webb time and again with humiliating ease, and generally finishing with great power, Leeds seemed to have the advantage. If Chelsea almost scored, after a break down the left and some clever work, when Sprake blocked Hutchinson's shot and Hunter kicked Osgood's off the line, Leeds were the more consistent. Gray's shot beat Bonetti but hit the bar; then, six minutes from time, Clarke – always lurking and dangerous – dived to Giles' low cross, to head against the inside of the post. Jones seized on the rebound, to score.

Chelsea seemed down and out; yet within two minutes, they had equalised. Harris tapped a free kick on the left to Hollins, who sent over an inswinging cross. Hutchinson, always brave and incisive, moved across the defence to head into the near corner.

In extra time, Leeds had the better of it, Clarke, in the first period, hitting wood yet again, when he volleyed against the bar. Yet in fairness to Chelsea, a last ditch tackle in the goalmouth by Madeley and Charlton's lunging save on the line, in the first half, deserve to be remembered. So the game was drawn; the first Cup Final ever to be drawn at Wembley.

The replay, an evening match at Old Trafford before 62,000 spectators, was hard, nasty, ill-tempered, undistinguished and ineptly refereed. Fouls proliferated, most of them ignored or insufficiently punished. Chelsea were probably more often guilty than Leeds, but the fact remains that one of the worst and potentially most decisive fouls was by Mick Jones of Leeds, on Chelsea's Peter Bonetti, whose left knee was injured by a kick. Whether Bonetti would have reached the shot with which Jones gave his club the lead soon afterwards, in the 36th minute, is debatable. Bonetti thought he would; perhaps he might. In any event, it was a fine goal. Allan Clarke began it with a superb, sustained run, taking out three Chelsea players, before sending through Jones, on the right. The centre-forward, too, ran powerfully and bravely, before scoring with a fierce right-footed cross shot.

Leeds took heart from the goal, and there seemed some excuse for their fans to sing, "We've won the Cup". Though Ron Harris, switched to right-back after Webb's embarrassments at Wembley, had subdued Gray with hard and sometimes cruel tackling, Cooper was running marvellously, Madeley playing majestically, and the absence of Hudson was sadly evident in Chelsea's flimsy midfield.

But with only ten minutes left, Chelsea equalised. A run on the right by Charlie Cooke, an elegant chip, and there was Peter Osgood running in on the blind side to head immaculately past Harvey's right hand.

This meant extra time again, and after 105 minutes, Chelsea scored the goal which laid so many myths and legends. Ian Hutchinson took one of his astonishing long throws from the left. As the ball floated over the goalmouth, Jackie Charlton jumped for it but succeeded only in back heading it further across goal, to the far post. There, with a jack-in-the-box leap, David Webb reached it to head into the net; a splendid atonement for his failings at Wembley.

It would be pleasant to say that an occasion so momentous for Chelsea was equally pleasing to a neutral spectator. But when history had been given its due, the principal feeling was relief that so ill-tempered an affair was over.

F.A. CUP FINAL. *Wembley*, April 11, 1970

Chelsea (1) 2	*Leeds United* (1) 2
Houseman, Hutchinson	Charlton, Jones

(*after extra time*)

Chelsea: Bonetti; Webb, McCreadie; Hollins, Dempsey, Harris (Hinton); Baldwin, Houseman, Osgood, Hutchinson, Cooke.

Leeds United: Sprake; Madeley, Cooper; Bremner, Charlton, Hunter; Lorimer, Clarke, Jones, Giles, Gray.
Referee: Mr. E. Jennings (Stourbridge).

Replay, *Old Trafford*, April 29, 1970

Chelsea (0) 2	*Leeds United* (1) 1
Osgood, Webb	Jones

(*after extra time*)

Chelsea: Bonetti; Harris, McCreadie; Hollins, Dempsey, Webb; Baldwin, Cooke, Osgood, Hutchinson, Houseman. (Hinton.)

Leeds United: Harvey; Madeley, Cooper; Bremner, Charlton, Hunter; Lorimer, Clarke, Jones, Giles, Gray.

SCOTTISH LEAGUE CHAMPIONSHIP 1969/70

After a beginning in which Hibernian and St. Johnstone briefly figured, the Scottish Championship settled down to its inevitable pattern of dominance by Celtic, formally pursued by Rangers. The latter flagged, finally, during March, when they suddenly and unexpectedly lost three games by the odd goal, leaving Celtic in an unassailable position.

Celtic's powerful, enterprising team was modified in one or two positions, notably at right-back, where Hay won a regular place, in goal, where Williams established himself in succession to Simpson and Fallon, and at inside-right, where a place went to the young Lou Macari, occasionally.

The virtual impossibility of any Scottish club sustaining a challenge to Celtic and Rangers was shown by the fact that Hibernian were forced to sell first Peter Marinello, for £100,000, to Arsenal, then, late in March, after an infinity of rumours – and suspensions – Peter Cormack, for £80,000, to Nottingham Forest.

Rangers sacked their manager half way through the season and appointed their former Scottish international outside-right, the ex-manager of Kilmarnock, Willy Waddell. It was rather too late for him to reverse the tide at that point.

SCOTTISH CUP 1970

In a remarkable crescendo, an Aberdeen team which went into the Cup Final the most distant outsiders clearly beat a Celtic team which had just won majestically at Leeds in the European Cup. Aberdeen had not won the tournament since 1947.

Celtic and Rangers met, this time, as early as the quarter-final; a bruisingly ill-tempered one in which there was much violence off the field and far too much on it. Celtic, again, prevailed, but were run surprisingly close in the semi-final, thanks largely to the fine goal-keeping of Dundee's Donaldson.

Aberdeen had got through 1–0, thanks to a goal in the first half by their new right-winger, Derek McKay, against Kilmarnock, but there was no reason to favour their chances against the mighty Celtic team, at Hampden.

It is true that Aberdeen might have gone behind after only 16 minutes, when their defence was split but Hermiston got a foot to Murdoch's shot; equally true that Aberdeen went ahead from an extremely doubtful penalty for hands, 12 minutes later – taken by Harper. But Aberdeen settled down, and when Celtic applied pressure after half-time, Buchan splendidly inspired a tight defence. With Celtic often falling into a clever offside trap, Hughes ineffectual up front, Murdoch obscure in midfield, Celtic at last replaced the former with Hughes, 12 minutes from time.

A couple of minutes later, Aberdeen broke out; and scored. McKay and Harper brought the ball out of defence, Williams blocked Forrest's shot, and McKay put the loose ball in. A minute later, Lennox, at the other end, shot wide from an easy chance, then redeemed himself, by scoring.

Away came Aberdeen again, and the teen-aged McKay, with calm precocity, took another chance, to make it 3–1. Temperament, indeed!

Scottish Cup Final, *Hampden Park,* April 11, 1970

Aberdeen (1) 3	*Celtic* (0) 1
Harper (penalty),	Lennox
McKay, 2	

Aberdeen: Clark; Boel, Murray; Hermiston, McMillan, Buchan, M.; McKay, Robb, Forrest, Harper, Graham. (Buchan G.)
Celtic: Williams; Hay, Gemmell; Murdoch, McNeill, Brogan; Johnstone, Wallace, Connelly, Lennox, Hughes. (Auld.)

Chapter Twelve

Football League Championship 1969-70

An absurd accumulation of fixtures, caused by the top-heavy nature of the League, transformed a thrilling battle for the Championship into sad, eventual anticlimax; though Everton were distinguished winners.

After at first threatening to be a one-horse race, with Everton romping away at some leisure, the First Division settled in due course into a two-horse affair. Everton, who beat Leeds most convincingly at Goodison early in the season, were still five points out in front at the turn; but Leeds' inexorable form allowed them to recover their lost ground.

Though Newcastle surprisingly beat them in a dourly hard match at St. James' Park, just before Christmas, they promptly and deservedly beat an Everton team made rough by desperation, at Elland Road; then went into a long unbeaten run while Everton kept dropping points.

Everton were seriously affected by the loss of Colin Harvey, so important in midfield, for many weeks, with an eye infection. His return was promptly followed by a long suspension for the still more important Alan Ball. While Everton were running well, the only fault one could find with them was an unwillingness to express their talent in away matches; which certainly cost them an unexpected defeat by the refreshing Derby County team.

When, early in March, however, Everton won a midweek game at Tottenham which had twice been put off, they went into the lead again by a single point, and the race was open once more.

It remained so until, late in March, Leeds were involved both in their series of three semi-finals against Manchester United in the F.A. Cup, and in the European Cup, besides. Exhausted after two replays with

Manchester United, one going into bruising extra time, in three days, they had to put out a skeleton team at home to Southampton, on Easter Saturday, and lost most unluckily after going a goal ahead and looking much the superior team. Two own goals and a most doubtful penalty torpedoed them. Meanwhile, Everton were thrashing a surprisingly feeble Chelsea team 5–2 at Goodison, taking full advantage of the weak goalkeeping of Bonetti's substitute, Tommy Hughes, as Leeds had at Stamford Bridge, earlier in the year.

The following Monday, Leeds abandoned all pretence of retaining their Championship when they fielded a complete reserve team against Derby County and lost 4–1, while Everton were winning at Stoke. It was all, virtually, over.

The moral of it was clearly that there are still far too many clubs in the First Division; even if the Football League could properly claim that this, the World Cup season, was a compressed and truncated one. But the wretched form of the bottom five clubs, the unimpressive showing of the leading First Division teams, made it embarrassingly plain that only eighteen clubs, at most, are worth First Division status. The abolition of the maximum wage may well have contributed to this; but not entirely. Centres of population as large as Sunderland and Sheffield (Wednesday) are perfectly capable of financing good teams, other things, such as good organization, being equal. Precisely the same, of course, may be said of Birmingham, where Aston Villa experienced the most disastrous season in their history, sacking Tommy Doherty, their manager, in mid-season.

The new board of directors, which had finally and triumphantly swept the bewhiskered old guard aside, proved still less capable of building Villa the team its traditions deserve.

Relegated with Villa to the Second Division was, by a strange, unhappy irony, the other great club of the late 1880s and early 1890s, Preston North End, who dismissed their manager, Bobby Seith, and trainer, shortly before the final blow fell. Charlton Athletic, who had already sacked *their* manager, Eddie Firmani, struggled free by the skin of their teeth. For Villa, there was some consolation in the fact that support remained almost astonishingly loyal and high, crowds of as many as 30,000 presiding at the last rites. Clearly there was every hope that, under their new manager, Vic Crowe, they would quickly and properly come up again.

Huddersfield Town, most ably managed by the old Manchester United back, Ian Greaves, strolled away with the Championship of the Second Division, even if their team was more functional than exciting. Jimmy Nicholson was a brilliant midfield half-back, Hutt a most promising left-back, from a club which has produced so many down the years, but it was as well when, late in the season, Greaves strengthened a dull attack by signing Dick Krzywicki, West Bromwich's thrustful Welsh international. The indications were that Huddersfield would hold their own, but scarcely do more, in the First Division.

For final league tables see page 279

FOOTBALL LEAGUE INTERNATIONALS

The increasingly pointless fixture between the Football League and the part-time players of the League of Ireland was this season properly relegated to Barnsley: and was very dull. Bryan Robson, the lively young Newcastle forward, headed a fine goal from Morrissey's cross after only 20 seconds. There was then a yawning hiatus till Bailey and Summerbee scored two more within a minute, soon after half-time. But the Irish defence stuck gamely to its task.

Next in this marginal, anticlimactic series was a game between the Scottish League, who turned out an almost contemptuously *ersatz* team, and the Irish League. The Scots won it without overmuch trouble, but only 5,000 bothered to turn up to watch it. This was scarcely a surprise.

The competition – or rather, the series – then lay dormant until the following March, when the Irish League visited London and defeated the League of Ireland with some comfort, 2–0, in a dull game.

The following day, the Football League took on the Scottish League in an interesting game at Coventry. It could scarcely be said to be representative, since the somewhat inept choice of the date meant that both Leeds and Celtic were involved in the European Cup, and needed all their players. The Scottish League were unquestionably the worse sufferers – but after being outplayed for much of the first half, they exploited a couple of English mistakes to revive, in the second.

The game was notable largely for the dazzling form of Ralph Coates, the splendid little blond Burnley forward, playing with equal, devastating effect in midfield in the first half, and in the firing line, in the second, when the newly transferred Martin Peters succeeded the injured Kidd.

Jeff Astle headed the first goal, following a strong run by Don Rogers – a successful late choice – and a cross by Brian Kidd, from the left. A fine individual run and long cross by Coates led to the second, McKinnon, challenged by Astle, playing the ball straight to Rogers.

Confusion between McFarland and Glazier led to Cormack scoring, after half-time. Coates' run and cross made another for Astle; Johnstone made another Scottish goal for Graham, who'd come on as a substitute.

Barnsley, September 10

Football League (1) 3	*League of Ireland* (0) 0
Robson, Bailey, Summerbee	

Football League: Bonetti (Chelsea); Reaney (Leeds United), Clark (Newcastle United); Harvey (Everton), Madeley, Hunter (Leeds United); Robson (Newcastle United), Lee, Summerbee (Manchester City), Bailey (Wolves), Morrissey (Everton).

League of Ireland: Thomas; Bryan (Waterford), Meagan, (Drogheda); Finucane (Limerick), Mulligan, Kiernan; O'Neill (Shamrock Rovers),

Davenport, Wigginston (Cork Hibernian), Leech (Shamrock Rovers), Matthews (Waterford).

Ibrox Park, Glasgow, November 19

Scottish League (3) 5	*Irish League* (1) 2
Harper 2, Robb,	McCaffrey 2
Cormack, Johnston	

Scottish League: Donaldson (Dundee); Clunie (Hearts), Greig (Rangers), Thomson (Hearts), Sweeney (Morton), Stanton (Hibernian), Cormack (Hibernian), Harper (Aberdeen), Ingram (Ayr United), Robb (Aberdeen), Johnston (Rangers).

Irish League: Finley (Glentoran); Hill (Glentoran), Hutton (Crusaders), Macken (Glentoran), McCullough (Glentoran), Nixon (Ards), Humphries (Ards), McCaffrey (Distillery), Mulgrew (Bangor), Rowland (Derry City), Weatherup (Glentoran).

Dalymount Park, Dublin, March 17, 1970

League of Ireland (0) 0	*Irish League* (0) 2
	O'Doherty,
	Sheehan (own goal)

League of Ireland: Thomas (Waterford); Gannon (Shelbourne), Herrick (Cork Hibernians); Finucane (Limerick), Pugh (Sligo), Meagan (Drogheda) – sub. Sheehan (Cork Hibernians) – O'Neill (Shamrock Rovers), Leech (Shamrock Rovers), Wigginston (Cork Hibernians), McEvoy (Limerick), Matthews (Waterford).

Irish League: Finlay (Glentoran); Patton (Glenavon), McKeag (Glentoran); O'Doherty (Coleraine), McCullough (Glentoran), Bowyer (Linfield); Humphries (Ards), Hamilton (Linfield), Mullan (Coleraine), McCaffrey (Glentoran), Smith (Derry), (Lunn (Porterdown)).

Coventry, March 18, 1970

Football League (2) 3	*Scottish League* (0) 2
Astle 2, Rogers	Cormack, Graham

Football League: Stepney (Manchester United) (Glazier (Coventry City)); Smith (Sheffield Wednesday), Hughes (Liverpool); Newton (Nottingham Forest), McFarland (Derby County), Todd (Sunderland); Coates (Burnley), Kidd (Manchester United) (Peters (Tottenham Hotspur)), Astle (West Bromwich Albion), Harvey (Everton), Rogers (Swindon Town).

Scottish League: McCrae (Motherwell); Callaghan (Dunfermline), Dickson (Kilmarnock); Smith (Rangers), McKinnon (Rangers), Stanton (Hibernian); Cormack (Hibernian), Greig (Rangers), McLean (Kilmarnock), Hall (St. Johnstone) (Graham (Hibernian)), Johnston (Rangers).

Manchester City: Corrigan; Book, Mann; Doyle, Booth, Oakes; Heslop, Bell, Summerbee, Lee, Pardoe. (Bowyer).

West Bromwich Albion; Osborne; Fraser, Wilson; Brown, Talbut, Kaye; Cantello, Suggett, Astle, Hartford, Hope. (Krzywicki.)

BRITISH MANAGERS IN EUROPE

An intriguing feature of the season was the re-emergence of British club managers in Europe. Ronnie Allen, who had been sacked by Wolves, was astonishingly successful as manager of Atletico Bilbao, where tighter discipline and training methods produced a team capable of thrashing Real Madrid 5–0, and setting a hectic pace in the Spanish Championship. The wealthy Barcelona club followed suit by appointing Vic Buckingham, the former Spurs player and manager of Sheffield Wednesday, West Bromwich and Fulham. He in turn brought as his assistant the old Arsenal centre-forward and Chelsea manager, Ted Drake.

Porto, the celebrated Portuguese club, followed suit by appointing Tommy Docherty, after Aston Villa had dismissed him. He had previously been sought both by Bilbao and by another Spanish club, Malaga.

Chapter Thirteen

African Nations Cup, 1970

BENEFITING enormously and unquestionably from home advantage and the impetus given them by an ecstatic crowd, the Sudan won an African Nations Cup which turned, at the end, into a form of endurance test. They and the runners-up, Ghana, were not, by general agreement, the two most talented teams, but they were the two most durable.

By and large, the competition was lively and exciting, emphasising the great talent and brio of African players – which still seem, however, to need harnessing to a European regimen.

The undoubted star was Laurent Pokou, a strongly made centre-forward who scored seven goals for the gifted but erratic Ivory Coast team; five in one game against much diminished Ethiopia.

The tournament was divided into two groups. In Khartoum, the qualifiers were the Ivory Coast and the hosts, Sudan. In the first match, Ivory Coast, holding a 2–0 lead thanks to two goals by Pokou, were overtaken in the second half. Two of the Cameroons' goals were scored by Koum, who flew in from Grenoble.

Sudan easily beat Ethiopia, 3–0, playing with solid efficiency against a poor Ethiopian team, hindered by an injury to their goalkeeper.

The Cameroons then narrowly overcame Ethiopia 3–2, obviously missing Koum, who'd temporarily returned to France. A thrilling game between Sudan and the Ivory Coast was won literally at the last second by the latter, 1–0. Ivory Coast then proceeded to walk over

Ethiopia, 6–1, and Sudan exploited defensive errors by the Cameroons to win a tight match, 2–1. Unlucky Cameroons: they thus failed to qualify, merely on goal average.

In Group B, at Wad Manani, it quickly became clear that the 1968 winners, Congo Kinshasa, were not the same force. In their opening match, a reprise of the 1968 Final, they lost 2–0 to Ghana. The Ghanaians, massed in defence, breaking powerfully, thanks to the huge centre-forward Owusu – scorer of their two goals – looked an impressive team.

So did the United Arab Republic, two of whose goals in a 4–1 win over Guinea were scored by the clever Abugreisha.

Congo and Guinea proceeded to draw 2–2, while the U.A.R. and Ghana drew 1–1. The Egyptians equalised from a late penalty, given by the excellent little Cameroons referee, Kandem, after Ghana's goal-keeper had punched an opponent, rather than the ball.

Ghana were then surprisingly held to a draw by Guinea. This time it was the Ghanaians who had to grope their way to a point with a belated penalty kick. The U.A.R. had quite a hard time winning 1–0 over Kinshasa, unlucky to lose their inspiration, the midfield half-back Kidumo, at half-time. Abugreisha headed a pleasing winner.

So the U.A.R. finished top, Ghana second.

Both semi-finals ran into extra time. Ghana improved on their two previous performances, beating an overconfident Ivory Coast. The winning goal was scored after 100 minutes by Malik.

In the other game, Sudan squeezed through 2–1 against their ancient foes, Egypt – otherwise the U.A.R. The Sudanese did well to shrug off an injury, just before half-time, to their right-back. Besheir put them ahead 12 minutes from time, Chazli equalised four minutes later, only for Besheir to score again, after 104 minutes. Delirium on the terraces.

The Arab Republic beat a tired Ivory Coast team 3–1 to take third place, Pokou getting yet another goal and becoming, comfortably, leading scorer for the second successive African Nations Cup. Chazli scored all three Egyptian goals.

Then, in a rather disappointing Final, Sudan beat Ghana by the only goal, scored by Hasabu, their left winger, as early as the eleventh minute.

Final:
Khartoum, February 19, 1970

Sudan (1) 1	*Ghana* (0) 0
Hasabu	

Sudan: Aziz; El Sir, James, Amin (Magmeldin), Souliman, Bushra, Isaid, Bushara, Izeldeen, Jacksa, Hasabu.
Ghana: Mensah; Boye, Mingle, Eshun, Acquah, Ghartey, Sunday, Yankey, Jones, Owusu, Malik.

Chapter Fourteen
Fifty World Stars

ALBERT, Florian (Ferencvaros and Hungary). Born Budapest, 1940. A beautifully fluent centre-forward, with fine ball control; a most penetrative striker near goal. Albert, a journalist, was capped for the first time in 1958, succeeding the great Nandor Hidegkuti when he was only 17. He made his name as an inside-right, and there are indications of this in his mastery of the ball. He scored twice against England, when Hungary beat them 2–0 in May 1960 – and again when Hungary beat them at Rancagua, in the 1960 World Cup. This he followed with a hat trick against Bulgaria. Superb against Brazil at Everton, 1966. He was named European footballer of the year for 1967, played for Rest of the World v. Brazil, 1968.

AMANCIO, Amaro (Real Madrid and Spain). The best native forward Spain has produced since Suarez and Del Sol, Amancio, like Suarez, is from the province of La Coruna. At 18, he was playing for Deportivo Coruna in the Second Division. Real brought him to Madrid in 1962 as an inside-right, turned him with brilliant success into an outside-right, then converted him back to inside-forward. He is very quick, has fine ball control – some say he holds on too long – and is a ready opportunist. He played a large part in Real's passage to the European Final of 1964, a still larger one in Spain's victory in the Nations Cup. He was generally acclaimed their best player. In 1966 his goal equalised against Partizan in the European Final, while in 1968 he played for the Rest of the World v. Brazil.

ANASTASI, Pietro (Juventus and Italy). When Anastasi joined Juventus from Varese in 1968 for a fee equivalent to more than £400,000, the young centre-forward became the most expensive player in the world. He is that great rarity, a Sicilian who has made his mark in Italian football. Born in Catania on April 7, 1948, he developed with Massiminiana, a local club, went to Varese in 1966, made his Serie A debut in September, 1967, and immediately after joining Juventus was thrown in at the deep end by Italy. He in fact made his debut in Rome in the 1968 European Nations Cup Final against Jugoslavia, scoring a fine goal in the replay.

ASPAROUKHOV, Gundi (Levski and Bulgaria). One of the outstanding successes of season 1965/6. In Florence, on December 29, 1965, his two goals most surprisingly knocked Belgium out of the World Cup in a play-off match. A few weeks earlier, he had scored both goals for Levski in Lisbon, when they won 3–2 to Inter in a European Cup tie. So well did he play that he won the admiration of their manager, Bela Guttmann. Asparoukhov, an ex-basketball player who had one rather ill-starred game at Rancagua in Bulgaria's 1962 World Cup side – they lost 6–1 to Hungary – has now established himself as one of the most promising leaders in Europe. A centre-forward unworried by the closest of marking, clever in control, brave in the goal area, very strong in the air, a powerful shot with either foot. An injured ankle hampered him in the 1966 World Cup, but he returned to England in 1968 to score a fine goal at Wembley.

BALL, Alan (Everton and England). The outstanding and probably decisive player of the 1966 World Cup Final, when he ran Schnellinger of Germany into the ground, and produced a series of devastating passes. Outside-right in that game, and the English World Cup team, he was first capped in his natural position of inside-forward in May, 1965, against Yugoslavia in Belgrade, when he'd just turned 20. Small, red haired, tirelessly active, Ball is the son of a former Birmingham professional, utterly dedicated to the game. Wolves and Bolton turned him down, Blackpool signed him, reluctantly transferring him to Everton for over £100,000 in the summer of 1966.

BANKS, Gordon (Stoke City and England). Certainly the most consistent, and improved, goalkeeper of the 1966 World Cup, when he played a major part in England's success. At once solid and spectacular, he was born in Sheffield, developed, like other fine goalkeepers, with Chesterfield, before joining Leicester City. England first capped him in 1963 against Brazil, at Wembley; he went on to make the England European tour. Tall, strongly built, an intelligent distributor of the ball, he was 28 when Stoke bought him for £52,500, on April 17, 1967.

BAYLON, Julio (Alianza, Lima and Peru). A black outside-right – or left – recognised after his brilliant form in the World Cup qualifying competition as probably the best in South America, and one of the best orthodox wingers in the world. Very fast and direct, with superb ball control and a fulminating shot, Baylon was one of the principal reasons that Peru overcame Argentina, to qualify. Though normally a ring winger, he switched effectively to the left for the final, decisive match in Buenos Aires, against Argentina.

BECKENBAUER, Franz (Bayern Munich and West Germany). At 21, he was perhaps the outstanding all round half-back of the 1966 World Cup, an elegant ball player, strong, intelligent and versatile. Came up through the German schoolboy and youth teams, winning his first full caps in 1965; both at defensive wing-half, and at inside-forward. Some feel that Germany paid the penalty for using him too cautiously against England in the 1966 Final; he can score goals, as he proved against Switzerland and Uruguay, as well as make them.

BENE, Ferenc (Ujpest and Hungary). After Hidegkuti, Albert and after Albert, with almost indecent speed – Bene, hero of the 1964 Olympic

Tournament, centre-forward of almost every gift. He has marvellous acceleration, glorious control, a fine shot and uncanny self-possession, while his movement off the ball is always highly intelligent. Bene won his first cap as an outside-right, when barely 18, moved inside for the 1964 Finals of the Nations Cup (he scored in each game) but really found himself when leading the Olympic attack in Tokyo. Opening the tournament with six goals against Morocco, the 19-year-old centre-forward closed it, against Czechoslovakia, with a goal of outstanding individual brilliance, running half the field. The one he scored against Brazil in the 1966 World Cup was even better.

BEST, George (Manchester United and Ireland). Dazzling in European Final, 1968. The most talented Irish winger since the war, he himself would rather play inside-forward, where he began, as a Belfast schoolboy. But it doesn't trouble him to play largely outside-left, though he's a naturally right-footed player. Coming to Old Trafford as a 15-year-old, he was homesick, returned to Belfast, but was eventually persuaded back to Manchester. Though small and slight, his astonishing balance, control and swerve make him infinitely dangerous. First capped against Wales, 1964. Footballer of the year, 1968: both in England and Europe.

BREMNER, Billy (Leeds United and Scotland). One of the chief motivating forces of the Leeds team which forced its way to the front in the latter sixties and early seventies, Bremner joined the club as a fifteen-year-old schoolboy outside-right. It was in this position that he made his League debut in the Second Division, but he moved successively to inside-right then right-half, where his lack of height and weight are more than made up for by his courage, bite and stamina. Red-haired, with the temperament generally associated with red-haired Scottish half-backs, he has become cooler and more restrained with time. His play has skill and imagination as well as drive; as witnessed by the fact that Leeds made him their captain. He played for them in two League Cup Finals, the F.A. Cup Final of 1965, when he scored a typically opportunist goal, and was a major figure in their record League Championship season of 1968/9. For Scotland, he figured in the unsuccessful qualifying tournaments for the 1966 and 1970 World Cup. He was first capped in 1966, against England at Hampden. He stands 5–5½, weighs about 10 stone, and was born at Stirling.

BYCHEVETZ, Anatoli (Kiev Dynamo and Russia). A winger – more accurately, a striker – who emerged during 1967 as one of the most dangerous forwards in the game, though still only 21. Owed his chance in the Kiev Dynamo team to the fact that so many of their players were "conscripted" for the Russian 1966 World Cup side. Bychevetz took it emphatically, his opportunism being greatly responsible for Kiev's victory in the Russian Championship. In 1967, he was one of the stars of the Russian victory over Scotland at Hampden Park, returning to Glasgow a few months later to score and play a large part in their

European Cup defeat of the holders, Celtic. Strong, fast, brave, well balanced, cool and an excellent ball player, he is dangerous alike with foot and head.

CHARLTON, Bobby (Manchester United and England). An outside-left who began his career as an inside-left, and has also played for England at centre-forward and inside-right, Bobby was taught football by his mother in Ashington, Northumberland. Newcastle United, where his uncle, Jackie Milburn, played, wanted him, but he signed as a junior for Manchester United. He survived the Munich disaster of 1958 to play in his second consecutive Cup Final, but it wasn't till 1963 that he got a winner's medal. Went to Sweden in 1958 with England's World Cup party but didn't get a game; played in all four in 1962 in Chile. A beautiful mover with a superb shot in either foot. Height 5 ft. 9 in. Weight 12 st. 2 lb. A major star of the 1966 World Cup, voted European footballer of the year. Beat England scoring record with his 45th at Wembley v. Sweden, May 1968. Over 100 caps.

CHESTERNIJEV, Albert (Red Army and Russia). A powerful, devoted, intelligent centre-half – often the sweeper – Chesternijev did not turn to football until he was in his late teens. Until then he had been a successful athlete. Progress was very quick. In the 1966 World Cup, he played the first five matches for Russia, though he missed the third place game. Two years earlier, he was a member of the Russian team which reached the Final of the European Nations Cup in Madrid, and lost 2–1 to Spain, while in 1968, he figured in the team which lost the third place match to England in Rome, in the same competition. He then captained the Russian team which qualified, at the expense of Northern Ireland, for the finals of the 1970 World Cup. He is married to an international skating champion.

COLUNA, Mario (Benfica and Portugal). Born in Mozambique, possessor of one of the finest left feet in the game. Coluna graced all four Benfica European Cup Final sides, scoring in 1961 and 1962, and playing splendidly till forced by injury to leave the field in 1963. A coloured footballer with an endless capacity for work, he was inside-left in the first two Finals, left-half in the third. Born in Lourenço Marques on August 6, 1935, his chief interest at first was athletics, and he set a long-jump record for Mozambique. The local club Deportivo transferred him to Benfica as a centre-forward, then he played at outside-left, and ultimately inside-forward. His first cap, though, came at centre-forward. A fine 1966 World Cup captain, skippered Benfica to 1968 European Final.

CRUYFF, Johan (Ajax Amsterdam and Holland). A fast, tough, clever centre-forward who was altogether too much for Liverpool when Ajax thrust them out of the European Cup in 1966. Previously, he'd been suspended for a year by the Dutch Federation after an incident in the match against Czechoslovakia; but he was reprieved at the beginning of season 1967/8. Made his début for Ajax at 19 in season 1965/6, with immediate impact.

DAVIES, Ron (Southampton and Wales). One of the best headers of a football in the world and one of today's most dangerous centre-forwards, Davies would bring £200,000 if Southampton ever agreed to transfer him. Manchester United seemed prepared to pay that after Davies had majestically headed four goals against them at Old Trafford, in 1969. Tall, strong, a superb jumper, and by no means ungifted on the ground, it took him some time to mature. He began obscurely with Chester, moved on to score many goals for Luton, from there was transferred to Norwich, won his first cap for Wales in 1964, and at last reached First Division status with Southampton. Among his talents are those of a caricaturist, whose work has been published in magazines. Born Holywell. Height 6–0, weight 12-6.

DZAJIC, Dragan (Red Star and Yugoslavia). Outside-left. At the age of 22, he was the most brilliant forward in the European Nations Finals of 1968, when he scored both against England in the semi-finals (the only goal) and against Italy in the first Final, in Rome. Enormously quick and very brave, he was picked the following November for the Rest of the World against Brazil.

ENGLAND, Mike (Tottenham Hotspur and Wales). This authoritative, powerfully built centre-half first played for his country in 1962, against Ireland; a 4–0 win for Wales. Almost unbeatable in the air and a surprisingly quick mover, Blackburn, who signed him from Welsh junior football, tried him at centre-forward, in 1965–6. It was in 1966 that Spurs signed him for £90,000.

EUSEBIO, Ferreira de Silva (Benfica and Portugal). This coloured inside-forward, born in Mozambique, like Coluna, had an astonishingly swift rise. He had played barely 25 professional games in Portugal before being capped in 1961. Earlier he had shown marvellous form in the Paris International tournament, and was flown out as an immensely successful last-minute substitute for Benfica, playing Penarol in Montevideo for the World Club title. Eusebio has a fulminating right foot, with which he scored goals in the 1962 and 1963 Finals. In the latter he gave Benfica a lead they couldn't hold. Despite his fame, he was still barely 21 at the time. Top scorer in 1966 World Cup. Helped Benfica to 1968 Final.

FACCHETTI, Giacinto (Internazionale and Italy). No full-back in the world scores as many goals as this towering player. Facchetti has said that if he couldn't go into the attack, he wouldn't play in defence. Born July 18, 1942, at Treviglio, he joined Inter at the age of 18 from his local club, was first capped against Turkey, in Istanbul, in March 1963. Played in Inter's successful European and world finals of 1964 and 1965, and captained Italy in 1970 World Cup Final.

GERSON (Sao Paolo and Brazil). One of the outstanding players in the 1970 World Cup, Gerson was Brazil's incomparable general in midfield and a splendid striker, besides; witness his fine goal against Italy. Naturally it was scored with his formidably accurate and powerful left foot. A Rio man who began with Flamengo, moved to Botafogo, and moved again, to Sao Paolo, rather unexpectedly, in early 1970, he played for Brazil in the 1960 Olympic tournament in Rome. He was also a member of the unsuccessful 1966 World Cup side in England, when one didn't see him at his best. In Mexico, however, this stocky, incisive player expressed his full, remarkable potential.

HALLER, Helmut (Juventus and West Germany). This fair-haired, extremely versatile inside-right was playing his third World Cup tournament in 1970. In 1966 he coolly scored Germany's first goal of the World Cup Final against England, at Wembley. In 1962, in Chile, he played two qualifying group matches and the quarter-finals – on the right wing – for his country. Haller was born in Augsburg, on 21.7.1939, developed with the local club, and should have been sold to Bologna before 1962, when he went to them, after the World Cup. There, he had a successful but rather unsettled six years, before he went to Juventus for a huge fee in 1968. Clever in control, perceptive in his passing, Haller has tended over the years to modulate into a mid-field player; but he can still take his goals well.

HURST, Geoff (West Ham United and England). Seldom has a player been so quickly and astonishingly transformed as Hurst, in and by the 1966 World Cup. After a mediocre European tour with England, he came into the World Cup side against Argentina, when his beautifully headed goal won the quarter-final. In the Final, he scored three times – with head and each foot – to set a new record. Now a striking inside-left, he came up through West Ham's youth teams as a wing-half. He is tall, powerfully built, splendid in the air, with a ferocious shot in both feet. First capped for England against West Germany at Wembley in February, 1966. Born Ashton-under-Lyne, the son of a footballer. Height 5 ft. 11 in. Weight 13 st.

JAIRZINHO (Botafogo and Brazil). Came into the Botafogo side as a teenaged centre-forward, his favourite position, but moved to the right wing when injury put Garrincha out of the side. His international début was brilliantly made against Portugal in the Little World Cup of 1964, in Rio, when he scored a spectacular goal. Jairzinho is small but tough; very fast, very skilful, an excellent finisher. Went on Brazil's 1965 European tour, played in the 1966 World Cup, recovered bravely from a series of operations to his leg, in 1967. An irresistable force in Brazil's 1970 World Cup attack.

JOHNSTONE, Jimmy (Celtic and Scotland). Tiny, red-haired outside-right who emerged as a major star in season 1966/7, when he played a magnificent part in Celtic's European Cup victory. A splendid ball player, fast, direct and admirably courageous, he is a living reminder that orthodox wing-play is very far from dead. The previous season, he'd shown memorable form against England, for Scotland, at Hampden. Played in all three World Club Final matches in 1967/8.

KEITA, Salif (St. Etienne and Mali). Centre-forward. A tall, slim player who arrived in France in 1968, went almost immediately into the St. Etienne League team and, despite the heavy conditions, at once established himself as a superbly equipped player. He comes from Bamako, where he was born on December 6, 1946.

KINDVALL, Ove (Feyenoord and Sweden). In 1969 Kindvall became only the second Swedish footballer ever to become his country's Sportsman of the Year. It was a recognition not only of his great goal-scoring abilities but of the part he had played in helping Sweden to qualify for the World Cup in Mexico. He scored both their goals in the vital home match against France, won 2–0. It was two goals scored in Gothenburg for Sweden against Brazil which initially made his name, just before the World Cup series of 1966. He scored them with characteristically strong, determined bursts; the kind of play which has subsequently made him a well-paid professional with Feyenoord, in the Dutch League; in which he is a prolific scorer. Though not very large, he is enormously quick, incisive and brave, and can accelerate or change pace devastatingly. His Swedish club was, like another great centre-forward, Gunnar Nordahl, Norkopping.

KVASNIAK, Andrej (Malines and Czechoslovakia). A tall, loping midfield player, always thoughtful, never hurried, Kvasniak played well for Czechoslovakia in the World Cup Final of 1962 in Santiago, against Brazil. In 1970, his excellent generalship in midfield enabled them to conquer Hungary and go to Latin America for another World Cup. Kvasniak, the only survivor from the 1962 World Cup Final team, had by then left Spartak of Prague for the Malines club, of the Belgian Second Division; he was mysteriously rejected in France. He is largely a left-footed player, whether he is cleverly sending long passes, or powerfully shooting at goal.

LABONE, Brian (Everton and England). First capped in 1962, Brian Labone didn't command a regular place at centre-half in England's team till he succeeded Jackie Charlton in 1967/8; and then, ironically, it was at a time when he was thinking of retiring. Playing in the European Nations Cup finals of 1968, he was finally persuaded to change his mind early the following year. A thoughtful footballer who believes centre half to be "a dying position", he was born in 1940 and has been at Goodison Park since he left school. Twice captained Everton in the Cup Final. Height 6 ft. 1 in. Weight 12 st. 11 lb.

LEE, Francis (Manchester City and England), When Lee joined Manchester City from Bolton Wanderers at a £60,000 fee in 1967, he had never been picked for the England Under 23 team, though he had been a First Division player at sixteen, a League footballer ever since. With City, this fast, compact, direct, blond forward, quite happy to play either on the right wing or in the middle, suddenly blossomed. Ramsey chose him on the England right wing against Bulgaria in 1968, and he had a splendidly adventurous game. He was mysteriously omitted against Rumania, but then returned to establish himself as the finest English forward to emerge since the World Cup. He virtually won a hard game against Northern Ireland in Belfast single-handed, and had an impressive 1969 tour of South America. Lee, who lives with his family in a converted Tudor cottage in Westhoughton, has numerous business interests outside football. Height 5 ft. 7½ in. Weight 12 st. 2 lb.

LUBANSKI, Wlodek (Gornik and Poland). Fair-haired centre-or inside-forward, considered the finest player Poland has produced since the war. Born in 1947, officially classified as a student, he'd played 20 international games before he was 20 years old. A frequent and spectacular goal scorer. His progress has been the more remarkable in that he missed two years, recovering from a severe illness caused when he over-enthusiastically took too large a quantity of pills, while under treatment.

MAGNUSSON, Roger (Marseilles and Sweden). The best Swedish outside-right since Hamrin, he was born at Blomstermala, March 20, 1954, and played for Atvidaberg. Juventus signed him in 1965, but the Italian ban on foreigners prevented him playing regularly for them. At first lent to Cologne in the Bundesliga, he appeared in the Juventus European Cup attack in season 1967/8, and the following season went to Olympique Marseilles, where he at once began to show splendid form. Tall and powerful, he has a magnificent swerve "outside" the back.

MAZURKIEWICZ, Ladislao (Penarol and Uruguay). Goalkeeper who played in the second half for the Rest of the World against Brazil in November, 1968. Most impressive in the 1966 World Cup, he later that year helped Penarol to win the world club title against Real Madrid, having played for them in the South American Cup Finals of 1965 and 1966. As his name would indicate, he is of Polish descent; spectacular but brave and safe.

MOORE, Bobby (West Ham United and England). Born in East London, Moore joined West Ham from school, as a centre-half, and received youth caps for England. It was only on being switched to wing-half, however, that he showed his full potential; a tremendous tackler, and a fine user of the long ball. England capped him for the first time against Peru in Lima on the way to the 1962 World Cup, in which he played every game. By the following year, he was captain of the side. Tall, fair-haired, powerfully built, he captained West Ham to the European Cupwinners' Cup of 1965. Splendidly captained England's 1966 World Cup winning team, and their 1968 European Nations side, and their 1970 team in Mexico.

MULLER, Gerd (Bayern Munich and West Germany). A centre-forward, immensely powerful in the thighs, who has been the heaviest scorer in West German football since Uwe Seeler – whom he somewhat resembles. Born on November 3, 1945, at Noerdlingen, in Bavaria, Muller was 17 when he was first picked for the local amateur side, for whom he scored 46 goals in a season. Curiously, two Bavarian clubs had the chance to sign him, TSV Munich and Nuremberg, and even the manager of Bayern, Zlatko Cjaicowski, had to be forced by his President to take Muller on. Lucky for Bayern. His heavy scoring has since helped them to win the Cup, the Championship and the European Cupwinners' Cup; and it materially assisted West Germany to reach the 1970 World Cup Finals. His toughness is evidenced by the fact that, four weeks after breaking an arm in Belgrade playing for West Germany against Yugoslavia, he figured in the Cupwinners' Cup Final against Rangers. Leading World Cup scorer in Mexico, 1970.

MURDOCH, Bobby (Celtic and Scotland). Originally an inside-right, now usually a right-half. In either position, a midfield player of great poise and intelligence. Joined Celtic when he was a Motherwell schoolboy, 1959; he was born on August 17, 1944. Played in Celtic's 1967 European Cup winning and world club finals teams. An enthusiastic golfer.

PELÉ (Santos and Brazil). Probably the greatest inside-forward of his generation, a remarkable goal-scorer of astonishing gymnastic powers. Pelé was a Brazilian international at the age of 16, scored two goals in the World Cup Final of 1958 at 17, and has been progressing ever since. Alas, a muscle injury kept him out of all but two Brazilian World Cup games in Chile, but he made up for that with his irresistible brilliance when inspiring Santos to thrash Benfica for the World Club title. Pelé comes from a poor coloured family in Bauru – Santos got him from the little local team of Noroeste. In 1957 he became a national name when scoring eight goals for a combined Santos-Vasco de Gama team in the Marumbuy Cup; a cap against Argentina soon followed. No player is more indiarubber in recovery and more difficult to control. He is already a rich young man, with interests in building and a contract to publicise Brazilian coffee; but intense pressures both on and off the field see to it that he earns every penny. He scored his 1000th goal in 1969. Scored one, made two in 1970 World Cup final.

PERFUMO, Roberto (Racing Club and Argentina). Right-back – playing in the centre of the defensive line, or sweeping-up. A player at once strong and skilful, mobile and perceptive, he captained Racing to victory in the South American Cup and world club finals of 1967. In 1966, his acrobatic, resourceful play did much to make the Argentinian defence as formidable as it was. Born in Buenos Aires, October 3, 1942.

PETERS, Martin (Tottenham Hotspur and England). A linking half-back of high technical skill and a flair for breaking through to score, Peters' role in the England World Cup team was that of a midfield man, though he wore a left-winger's shirt. A local development, born in Plaistow, he was a successful schoolboy and youth international player; can turn out at inside- or even centre-forward. England first capped him at home to Yugoslavia in May, 1966, after which he made their Scandinavian tour. So to the World Cup tournament, in which he played all but the first game, scoring against Germany in the Final. In March, 1970, he joined Spurs for a fee of £125,000, plus Jimmy Greaves.

PIRRI, José Martinez Sanchez (Real Madrid and Spain). Right-half; a greatly gifted midfield footballer, strong, intelligent, beautifully balanced and an excellent ball player. Figured in Spain's World Cup team of 1966, heading their goal against West Germany, two months after helping Real win the European Cup Final. He was then only 21. A Real Madrid development, he frequently comes forward to score goals, and has a cool temperament surprising in one of his relatively green years.

POLLEUNIS, Odilon (St. Trond and Belgium). Equally effective in midfield or as a striker – he prefers midfield – Polleunis burst on to the scene just in time to play a major part in Belgium's fine performance in the 1968/9 World Cup eliminators. Capped as a striker against Finland, he scored three; reverting to midfield, he got another two against the Yugoslavs – both World Cup matches. Belgian Footballer of the Year for 1968.

RIVA, Luigi (Cagliari and Italy). Despite breaking a leg in the middle of season 1966/7, this powerful outside-left ended it as leading scorer of the Italian Championship. The following season, Switzerland's manager, Foni, called him "the most dangerous left winger in the world". Born at Leggiuno in the province of Varese, where he frequently returns to fish, on November 7, 1944, Riva was orphaned at an early age. He began with Legnano, signed for Cagliari in 1963 and helped the Sardinian club to promotion. First capped against Hungary in Budapest, June 27, 1965, he wasn't picked again till the match against Austria just before the 1966 World Cup; in which he didn't play. But 1967 saw him consolidate his place, with a flurry of goals, and he played a major part in Italy's qualification for the 1970 World Cup.

RIVELINO (Corinthians and Brazil). A midfield player, inside-forward, who became, at 22, a regular member of the Brazilian national team in 1968, when he toured Europe and South America with them, and scored against the Rest of the World. A fine technician with a powerful left foot, his one problem appears to be that of stamina.

RIVERA, Gianni (Milan and Italy). Inside-forward who at 16 was bought by Milan from Alessandria (his home town) for £65,000 – on a half-share basis! Milan already held the other half. Rivera is a slight, shy, almost gazelle-like figure of precocious maturity, both on and off the field. A member of the gifted young Italian Olympic team of 1960, just before he turned 17, he won a regular place in Milan's side only after Jimmy Greaves had gone home in 1961 – and at once proceeded to inspire their attack to the Championship. The following season he was a major force in their winning the European Cup. Indeed, his pass made the decisive goal for Altafini. The son of a railway official who moved to Milan to be with him, Rivera is reckoned by the Italians to be their finest home-grown product since the war, a graceful, clairvoyant player with fine ball control and a surprisingly powerful shot. First capped in Brussels against Belgium on May 13, 1962, he went on to play in the World Cup in Chile, England and Mexico, captained Milan to the European Cup and World Championship of 1969.

ROCHA, Pedro (Penarol and Uruguay). Scorer of the winning goal for Uruguay against Argentina in the Final of the 1967 South American Championship in Montevideo, Rocha had, earlier in the season, helped Penarol to win the world clubs championship. A tall, graceful inside-left who can play cleverly in midfield or, if necessary, get goals, he has represented Uruguay in the World Cups of 1962, in Chile, and 1966, in England. Won his first caps in 1962, at the age of 19.

SZUCS, Lajos (Honved and Hungary). An attacking wing-half who had the unusual distinction of going straight from Hungary's Olympic winning team in Mexico into the Rest of the World team against Brazil in Rio; November, 1968. Powerfully built, Szucs has a tremendous shot in either foot. He scored three goals against Japan in the Olympic semi-finals. In 1969 he left Ferencvaros for Honved, but since his old club resisted the transfer, he had to serve a year's automatic suspension.

TORRES, José (Benfica and Portugal). It was confidence in the massive, towering young centre-forward which made Benfica let Aguas go. At first Torres seemed to have little but his height and heading to offer, though he led the attack through to the European Cup Final of 1963. But he has improved on the ground – and is now almost unbeatable in the air. His father encouraged him to give up football for keeping pigeons. One day he lost his temper, killed the pigeons and, in a fit of remorse, allowed Torres to play football again. Beginning with Desportivo di Torres Novas, he found his way to Benfica. Four goals against Fiorentina in the 1963 Cadiz Tournament showed he was there to remain. Probably the best centre-forward of the 1966 World Cup and a major star of the 1967/8 European Cup.

photo: United Press International

England's Geoff Hurst heads for goal despite the efforts of Willi Schulz and Sepp Maier of West Germany in the World Cup quarter final match.

photo: United Press International

Gerd Mueller of West Germany scores the winning goal against England in the quarter final of the World Cup. Peter Bonetti is the beaten goalkeeper.

photo: United Press International

Brazil captain Carlos Alberto holds the Jules Rimet Trophy aloft after his country had beaten Italy 4-1 in the 1970 World Cup final.

photo: United Press International

Jairzinho scores Brazil's third goal in the 1970 World Cup final despite a desperate attempt to clear by Giacinto Facchetti of Italy.

photo: United Press International

Jackie Charlton (not in picture) scores the first goal of the 1970 FA Cup final. Eddie McCreadie and Ron Harris of Chelsea both fail to stop the ball from crossing the line.

photo: United Press International

Jackie Charlton scoops the ball off the Leeds' goalline to prevent Chelsea from scoring in the 1970 FA Cup final.

photo: United Press International

Neil Young scores the first goal for Manchester City in the 1970 European Cup Winners Cup final played in Vienna. The Gornik Zabre goalkeeper is Hubert Kostka.

photo: United Press International

Wim Jansen of Feyenoord and Willie Wallace of Celtic contest possession during the 1970 European Cup final.

TOSTAO (Cruzeiro and Brazil). Only 19 when he made an appearance for Brazil in the World Cup at Everton in 1966, scoring a fine goal against Hungary, Tostao by 1970 had proved himself one of the game's most talented and dangerous strikers. Brave, quick and very incisive, he scored one goal and made the other when Brazil turned a 1–0 deficit into victory against England in Rio, in June, 1969. He proceeded to score no fewer than nine goals in Brazil's World Cup qualifying group that August, but alas, when at the height of his effectiveness, he suffered a detached retina after being hit in the face by the ball. This led to a difficult operation in Houston, and though he was cleared to play early in 1970, there was no minimising the gravity of his injury. Tostao, whose real name is Eduardo Concalves de Andrade, is a student of economics. By an intriguing coincidence, he made his initial impact on international football in the same game as Ove Kindvall; the Brazil v. Sweden match in Gothenburg just before the 1966 World Cup in which each of them scored two goals. Brazil won, 3–2.

VAN HIMST, Paul (Anderlecht and Belgium). Shares with Rik Coppens and Jef Mermans the distinction of being the most accomplished centre-forward produced by Belgium since the war. A player of precociously assured temperament, he was born on October 2, 1943 – and at 17 was chosen Footballer of the Year. A season later the jury chose him again, but he showed no sign of immodesty – and continued to turn up for training on a bicycle. Anderlecht use him as a striking inside-forward, a position he fills with equal force and skill. His hobbies include jazz, films, books and the theatre.

ZOFF, Dino (Naples and Italy). Goalkeeper who played most capably for Italy when they won the European Nations Cup in Rome, in 1968. Born in Friuli, February 2, 1942, up in the north east of Italy, he was spotted and developed, like so many Italian stars, by Udinese. Mantova signed him in 1963, and four years later, he was transferred to Naples.

Chapter Fifteen

World Cup History

The World Cup – or to give it its proper name, the Jules Rimet Trophy was first played in Montevideo in 1930, but the principle of it was agreed by FIFA, the federation of international football associations, at their Antwerp Congress of 1920. No man did more to further the idea than Jules Rimet, President of the French Football Federation, who was elected FIFA President in Antwerp, and it was thus that the attractive gold cup came to be given his name.

By 1930 the four British associations had withdrawn from FIFA, and it was not for another twenty years that British teams competed for a World Cup. Whether they would have won it between the wars is open to question. The fact that they did not undergo the test allowed the myth of British superiority in football to last a generation longer than it might otherwise have done. In 1934, just before the Italian version of the World Cup, Hugo Meisl, the brilliant manager of the Austrians, expressed the view that England, had they competed, would not even have reached the semi-final.

Four years later, England were invited to compete in the Finals without qualifying, to take the place of Austria, overrun by the Nazis. But the invitation was refused.

In 1930 the competing countries were divided into four pools, the qualifiers going into the semi-finals, which were played on the normal Cup tie basis of "sudden death". In 1934 and 1938 the World Cup finals were played as a straight knock-out tournament, but in 1950 the four pools were reconstituted, with one main difference. The four winners went into a further pool, to contest the title. It was thus only a matter of chance that the last match between Brazil and Uruguay, one of the most passionate and exciting in the history of the tournament, should also turn out to be the decider.

In 1958 and 1962 four groups were again constituted, but on these occasions, two teams from each went into the quarter-finals after which, as in 1930, the tournament followed the pattern of a straight knock-out contest. In 1966, when the World Cup was played in England, the same dubious formula applied. In 1970, goal "difference" replaced goal average.

WORLD CUP, 1930 – Montevideo

Though the tournament was won by a very fine team – Uruguay had previously come to Europe to take the Olympic titles of 1924 and 1928 – it hardly drew a representative entry.

In the 1926 FIFA Congress Henri Delaunay, the French Federation's excellent secretary, expressed the view that football could no longer be confined to the Olympics: "Many countries where professionalism is now recognised and organised cannot any longer be represented there by their best players." In 1928, FIFA passed his resolution to hold a World Cup tournament at once. Only the Scandinavian block, and Esthonia, voted against it! Odd that Sweden should eventually stage a World Cup and play in the Final.

Uruguay got the competition for a variety of reasons; their Olympic success, their promise to pay every competing team's full expenses and to build a new stadium, the fact that 1930 was their centenary.

But distance and the need to pay their players for a couple of months, led to most of the big European powers withdrawing: Italy, Spain, Austria, Hungary, Germany, Switzerland, Czechoslovakia, Britain, of course, were out of FIFA. It was only thanks to King Carol himself that Rumania entered; he not only picked the team but got time off for the players from their firms. France, Belgium and Yugoslavia were the other three: lower middle-class European teams of that era. The stage was set for a South American domination.

It was the United States who provided the surprise. Their team, made up largely of ex-British professionals jokingly christened "the shot putters" by the French, because of their massive physiques, showed great stamina and drive, and actually qualified for the semi-finals. There, an excellent Argentinian eleven – beaten 2–1 in the replayed 1928 Olympic Final, by Uruguay – brushed them aside.

Uruguay, however, again proved irresistible. They prepared with the dedication one has come to expect over the past fifteen years from leading South American teams; but then, it was quite new. For two months, their players were "in concentration" at an expensive hotel in the middle of the Prado park. When Mazzali, the brilliant goalkeeper, sneaked home late one night, he was thrown out of the team.

A splendid half-back line (playing in the old attacking centre-half-back style) was Uruguay's strength: José Andrade, Lorenzo Fernandez and Alvaro Gestido. José Nasazzi, the captain and right-back, was a great force, and in the forward-line Scarone and Petrone (now slightly over the hill) were superb technicians and dangerous goalscorers.

The tournament began on July 13, 1930. France surprised Argentina in an early match, losing only 1–0, after the crowd had invaded the pitch, when the referee blew for time six minutes early – then had to clear the pitch and restart the game. The Argentinians, who had the ruthless but effective Monti at centre-half, and the clever Stabile at centre-forward, duly won that group. Their match with Chile included a violent free-for-all, provoked by Monti.

Yugoslavia, beating Brazil 2–1 in their first match, also qualified. The brave Americans won their pool without conceding a goal, while Uruguay, too, kept their defence intact, though Peru ran them very close. This was the first match to be played at the new Centenary Stadium, which still wasn't ready when the competition started.

In the semi-finals, Argentina and Uruguay both had 6–1 wins, against the U.S.A. and Yugoslavia respectively. In the Final, Uruguay had to take the field without their new star, the young centre-forward Anselmo, who was unfit. But Argentina's new man, Stabile, first capped in their opening game, was able to lead their attack.

The match took place on July 30, 1930. Uruguay deservedly won, but their team seemed to lack the confidence it had shown in the two Olympic successes. An argument about the ball led to each side playing one half with a ball of native manufacture. Argentina survived an early goal by Pablo Dorado, the Uruguayan outside-right, to lead 2–1 at half-time, through Peucelle and Stabile. But a splendid dribble by Pedro Cea was crowned by the equaliser, after which Iriarte and Castro made it 4–2. Montevideo went wild – the following day was a national holiday.

DETAILS
POOL I

France 4, *Mexico* 1 (3–0)
France: Thépot; Mattler, Capelle; Villaplane (capt.), Pinel, Chantrel; Liberati, Delfour, Maschinot, Laurent, Langiller.
Mexico: Bonfiglio; Gutierrez, R. (capt.), Rosas, M.; Rosas, F., Sanchez, Amezcua; Perez, Carreno, Mejia, Ruiz, Lopez.
Scorers: Laurent, Langiller, Maschinot (2) for France, Carreno for Mexico.

Argentina 1, *France* 0 (0–0)
Argentina: Bossio; Della Torre, Muttis; Suarez, Monti, Evaristo, J.; Perinetti, Varallo, Ferreira (capt.), Cierra, Evaristo, M.
France: Thépot, Mattler, Capelle; Villaplane (capt.), Pinel, Chantrel, Liberati, Delfour, Maschinot, Laurent, Langiller.
Scorer: Monti for Argentina.

Chile 3, *Mexico* 0 (1–0)
Chile: Cortes; Morales, Poirier; Torres, A., Saavedra, Helgueta; Ojeda, Subiabre, Villalobos, Vidal, Schneeberger (capt.).
Mexico: Sota; Guitierrez, R. (capt.), Rosas, M.,; Rosas, F., Sanchez, Amezcua; Perez, Carreno, Ruiz, Gayon, Lopez.
Scorers: Vidal, Subiabre (2) for Chile.

Chile 1, *France* 0 (0–0)
Chile: Cortes; Ciaparro, Morales; Torres, A., Saavedra, Torres, C.; Ojeda, Subiabre, Villalobos, Vidal, Schneeberger (capt.).
France: Thépot; Mattler, Capella; Chantrel, Delmer, Villaplane (capt.); Liberati, Delfour, Pinel, Veinante, Langiller.
Scorer: Subiabre for Chile.

Argentina 6, *Mexico* 3 (3–0)
Argentina: Bossio; Della Torre, Paternoster; Cividini, Zumelzu (capt.), Orlandini; Eucelle, Varallo, Stabile, Demaria, Spadaro.
Mexico: Bonfiglio; Gutierrez, R. (capt.), Gutierrez, F.; Rosas, M., Sanchez, Rodriguez; Rosas, F., Lopez, Gayon, Carreno, Olivares.
Scorers: Stabile (3), Varallo (2), Zumelzu for Argentina, Lopez, Rosas, F., Rosas, M., for Mexico.

Argentina 3, *Chile* 1 (2–1)
Argentina: Bossio; Della Torre, Paternoster; Evaristo, J., Monti, Orlandini; Eucelle, Varallo, Stabile, Ferreira, Evaristo, M.
Chile: Cortes; Ciaparro, Morales; Torres, A., Saavedra, Torres, C.; Arellanc, Subiabre (capt.), Villalobos, Vida, Aguilera.
Scorers: Stabile 2, Evaristo, M. for Argentina, Subiabre for Chile.

POOL II

Yugoslavia 2, *Brazil* 1 (2–0)
Yugoslavia: Yavocic; Ivkovic (capt.), Milhailovic; Arsenievic, Stefanovic, Djokic; Tirnanic, Marianovic, Beck, Vujadinovic, Seculic.
Brazil: Montiero; Costa, Gervasoni; Fonseca, Santos, Guidicelli; Ribeiro, Braga, Patsuca, Neto, Pereira.
Scorers: Tirnanic, Beck for Yugoslavia, Neto for Brazil.

Yugoslavia 4, *Bolivia* 0 (0–0)
Yugoslavia: Yavocic; Ivkovic (capt.), Milhailovic; Arsenievic, Stefanovic, Djokic; Tirnanic, Marianovic, Beck, Vujadinovic, Naidanovic.

Bolivia: Bermudez; Durandal, Civarria; Argote, Lara, Valderama; Gomez, Bustamante, Mendez (capt.), Alborta, Fernandez.
Scorers: Beck (2), Marianovic, Vujadinovic for Yugoslavia.

Brazil 4, *Bolivia* 0 (1–0)
Brazil: Velloso; Gervasoni, Oliveira; Fonseca, Santos, Giudicelli; Meneses, Quieroz, Leite, Neto (capt.), Visintainer.
Bolivia: Bermudez; Durandal, Ciavarria; Sainz, Lara, Valderama; Oritiz, Bustamante, Mendez (capt.), Alborta, Fernandez.
Scorers: Visintainer (2), Neto (2), for Brazil.

POOL III

Rumania 3, *Peru* 1 (1–0)
Rumania: Lapuseanu; Steiner, Burger; Rafinski, Vogl (capt.), Eisembeisser; Covaci, Desu, Wetzer, Staucin, Barbu.
Peru: Valdivieso; De las Casas (capt.), Soria; Galindo, Garcia, Valle; Flores, Villanueva, Denegri, Neira, Souza.
Scorers: Staucin (2), Barbu for Rumania, Souza for Peru.

Uruguay 1, *Peru* 0 (0–0)
Uruguay: Ballesteros; Nasazzi (capt.), Tejera; Andrade, Fernandez, Gestido; Urdinaran, Castro, Petrone, Cea, Iriarte.
Peru: Pardon; De las Casas, Maquilon (capt.); Denegri, Galindo, Astengo; Lavalle, Flores, Villanueva, Neira, Souza.
Scorer: Castro for Uruguay.

Uruguay 4, *Rumania* 0 (4–0)
Uruguay: Ballesteros; Nasazzi (capt.), Mascheroni; Andrade, Fernandez, Gestido; Dorado, Scarone, Anselmo, Cea, Iriarte.
Rumania: Lapuseanu; Burger, Tacu; Robe, Vogl (capt.), Eisembeisser; Covaci, Desu, Wetzer, Rafinski, Barbu.
Scorers: Dorado, Scarone, Anselmo, Cea for Uruguay.

POOL IV

United States 3, *Belgium* 0 (2–0)

United States: Douglas; Wood, Moorhouse; Gallacher, Tracey, Brown; Gonsalvez, Florie (capt.), Patenaude, Auld, McGhee.
Belgium: Badjou; Nouwens, Hoydonckx; Braine (capt.), Hellemans, De Clercq; Diddens, Moeschal, Adams, Voorhoof, Versijp.
Scorers: McGhee (2), Patenaude for U.S.A.

United States 3, *Paraguay* 0 (2–0)
United States: Douglas; Wood, Moorhouse; Gallacher, Tracey, Auld; Brown, Gonsalvez, Patenaude, Florie (capt.), McGhee.
Paraguay: Denis; Olmedo, Miracca; Etcheverri, Diaz, Aguirre; Nessi, Romero, Dominguez, Gonzales, Caceres, Pena (capt.).
Scorers: Patenaude (2), Florie for U.S.A.

Paraguay 1, *Belgium* 0 (1–0)
Paraguay: Benitez, P.; Olmedo, Flores; Benitez, S., Diaz, Garcete; Nessi, Romero, Gonzales, Carceres, Pena (capt.).
Belgium: Badjou; De Deken, Hoydonckx; Braine (capt.), Hellemans, Moeschal; Versijp, Delbeke, Adams, Nouwens, Diddens.
Scorer: Pena for Paraguay.

PLACINGS

Pool I

	P	W	D	L	Goals F	Goals A	Pts.
Argentina	3	3	0	0	10	4	6
Chile	3	2	0	1	5	3	4
France	3	1	0	2	4	3	2
Mexico	3	0	0	3	4	13	0

Pool II

	P	W	D	L	F	A	Pts.
Yugoslavia	2	2	0	0	6	1	4
Brazil	2	1	0	1	5	2	2
Bolivia	2	0	0	2	0	8	0

Pool III

	P	W	D	L	F	A	Pts.
Uruguay	2	2	0	0	5	0	4
Rumania	2	1	0	1	3	5	2
Peru	2	0	0	2	1	4	0

Pool IV

	P	W	D	L	F	A	Pts.
United States	2	2	0	0	6	0	4
Paraguay	2	1	0	1	1	3	2
Belgium	2	0	0	2	0	4	0

SEMI-FINALS

Argentina 6, *United States* 1 (1–0)
Argentina: Botasso; Della Torre, Paternoster; Evaristo, J., Monti,

Orlandini; Eucelle, Scopelli, Stabile, Ferraira (capt.), Evaristo, M.
U.S.A.: Douglas; Wood, Moorhouse; Gallacher, Tracey, Auld; Brown, Gonsalvez, Patenaude, Florie (capt.), McGhee.
Scorers: Monti; Scopelli, Stabile (2), Paucelle (2) for Argentina. Brown for U.S.A.

Uruguay 6, *Yugoslavia* 1 (3–1)
Uruguay: Ballesteros; Nassazzi (capt.), Mascheroni; Andrade, Fernandez, Gestido; Dorado, Scarone, Anselmo, Cea, Iriarte.
Yugoslavia: Yavocic; Ivkovic (capt.), Milhailovic; Arsenievic, Stefanovic, Djokic; Tirnanic, Marianovic, Beck, Vujadinovic, Seculic.
Scorers: Cea (3), Anselmo (2), Iriarte for Uruguay, Seculic for Yugoslavia.

FINAL

Uruguay 4, *Argentina* 2 (1–2)
Uruguay: Ballesteros; Nasazzi (capt.), Mascheroni; Andrade, Fernandez, Gestido; Dorado, Scarone, Castro, Cea, Iriarte.
Argentina: Botasso; Della Torre, Paternoster; Evaristo, J., Monti, Suarez; Eucelle, Varallo, Stabile, Ferreira (capt.), Evaristo, M.
Scorers: Dorado, Cea, Iriarte, Castro for Uruguay, Peucelle, Stabile for Argentina.
Leading scorer: Stabile (Argentina) 8.

WORLD CUP, 1934 – Italy

The 1934 World Cup was altogether more representative and better attended, even though Uruguay, piqued by the way the European powers had snubbed them, stayed away and Argentina, fearful to lose more of their stars to Italian clubs, did not take part at full strength. Eight FIFA conferences were needed before Italy was chosen as the host. It had been realised that future World Cups could no longer be played in a single city nor could they be put on by any but a wealthy football federation. Italy, whose Fascist government looked on the powerful national team as a fine instrument of propaganda, eagerly put forward her claims. "The ultimate purpose of the tournament," said General Vaccaro, a political appointment as President of the Italian federation (FIGC), "was to show that Fascist sport partakes of a great quality of the ideal."

"Italy wanted to win," wrote the Belgian referee, John Langenus, "it was natural. But they allowed it to be seen too clearly."

Italy's remarkable team manager, Vittorio Pozzo, drew from the inflated, martial spirit of the times the authority and inspiration to build a fine team. It contained three Argentinians – Monti, Guaita and Orsi – of Italian extraction, whose inclusion Pozzo justified on the grounds that they would have been eligible to fight for Italy in the first world war. "If they were able to die for Italy, they could certainly play for Italy."

His team pivoted round a strong, attacking centre-half in Monti; had a splendid goalkeeper in Combi; a powerful defence, and a clever attack in which Meazza, one of the most gifted Italian forwards of all time, figured as a "striking" inside-right.

Austria, Italy's great rivals, were a tired team, and their equally gifted manager, Hugo Meisl, was convinced they could not win the tournament. Nevertheless in Seszta, their rugged left-back, Smistik, the roving centre-half, and Sindelar, the brilliantly elusive, ball-playing centre-forward, they had players of world class. The previous February Austria's *wunderteam* had beaten Italy 4–2, in Turin.

Hungary and Spain were the strongest "outsiders". Hungary had a fine centre-forward in Dr. Georges Sarosi, later to become an attacking centre-half. Their technique was brilliant, but their finishing poor. Both they and the Czechs had beaten England 2–1, on England's May tour of Europe. Spain had their great veteran, Ricardo Zamora, in goal, and the excellent Quincoces at left-back. The Czechs had an equally famous and experienced goalkeeper in Planicka and a smooth, clever forward-line.

Then there was Germany, playing a rigid third-back game, captained by the blond and versatile Franz Szepan.

Italy kicked off in Rome with an easy win against the U.S.A., fielding only three of their 1930 team. The surprise of the first round was France's excellent performance against Austria in Turin. As in 1930, the French rose to the occasion. They nearly scored in the first minute when Seszta's mistake was brilliantly retrieved by Peter Platzer, Austria's goalkeeper, and would probably have won, had it not been for an injury to Nicolas, their captain and centre-forward, who had to go on the wing. He scored almost at once, but that was virtually his last contribution. Despite the handicap, France dominated the second half, and it was only a doubtful goal by Schall, in extra-time – he looked offside – which really beat them. In later years, Schall himself said it was offside.

Germany, beating Belgium in Florence, looked uninspired; only Szepan, at centre-half, rose above mediocrity. The Czechs were another disappointment, needing two fine saves by Planicka to survive against the Rumanians, in Trieste, Egypt gave Hungary a fright at Naples, going down 4–2, and both South American challengers went out at once, Brazil to Spain, Argentina to Sweden.

In the second round in Florence, a marvellous exhibition of goal-keeping by Zamora enabled Spain to hold Italy to a 1–1 draw, but so roughly was he handled in a feebly refereed match that he could not take part in the replay. This was still more lamentably refereed, so much so that the Swiss official, Mercet, was suspended by his own Federation. Italy got through, thanks to a goal by Meazza, in a game that left a very nasty aftertaste.

The other match of the second round was that which opposed the classical Danubian rivals, Hungary and Austria. "It was a brawl," said Meisl, "not an exhibition of football." He brought the lively Horwath into his attack, and Horwath rewarded him with a goal after only seven minutes. Markos, Hungary's outside-right, was sent off, soon after Sarosi (on a poor day) had got Hungary's only goal from a penalty.

Rumania: Zambori; Vogl, Albu; Deheleanu, Cotormani (capt.), Moravet; Bindea, Covaci, Depi, Bodola, Dobai.
Scorers: Puc, Nejedly for Czechoslovakia, Dobai for Rumania.

Germany 5, *Belgium* 2 (1–2). *Florence*
Germany: Kress; Haringer, Schwarz; Janes, Szepan (capt.), Zielinksi; Lehner, Hohmann, Conen, Siffling, Kobierski.
Belgium: Van de Weyer; Smellinckx, Joacim; Peeraer, Welkenhuyzen (capt.), Klaessens; Devries, Voorhoof, Capelle, Grimmonprez, Herremans.
Scorers: Voorhoof (2) for Belgium, Conen (3), Kobierski (2) for Germany.

Austria 3, *France* 2 (1–1) (1–1) after extra time. *Turin*
Austria: Platzer; Cisar, Seszta; Wagner, Smistik (capt.), Urbanek; Zischek, Bican, Sindelar, Schall, Viertel.
France: Thépot; Mairesse, Mattler; Delfour, Verriest, Llense; Keller, Alcazar, Nicolas (capt.), Rio, Aston.
Scorers: Nicolas, Verriest (penalty) for France, Sindelar, Schall, Bican for Austria.

Spain 3, *Brazil* 1 (3–1). *Genoa*
Spain: Zamora (capt.); Ciriaco, Quincoces; Cillauren, Muguerza, Marculeta; Lafuente, Iraragorri, Langara, Lecue, Gorostiza.
Brazil: Pedrosa; Mazzi, Luz; Tinoco, Zaccone, Canilli; Oliviera, De Britto, Leonidas, Silva, Bartesko.
Scorers: Iraragorri (penalty), Langara (2) for Spain, Silva for Brazil.

Switzerland 3, *Holland* 2 (2–1). *Milan*
Switzerland: Sechehaye; Minelli, Weiler (capt.); Guinchard, Jaccard, Hufschmid; Von Kaenel, Passello, Kielholz, Abegglen III, Bossi.
Holland: Van der Meulen; Weber, Van Run; Rellikaan, Andeniesen (capt.), Van Heel; Wels, Vente, Bakhuijs, Smit, Van Nellen
Scorers: Kielholz (2), Abegglen III for Switzerland, Smit, Vente for Holland.

Sweden 3, *Argentina* 2 (1–1). *Bologna*
Sweden: Rydberg; Axelsson, Andersson, S.; Carlsson, Rosen (capt.), Andersson, E.; Dunker, Gustafsson, Jonasson, Keller, Kroon.
Argentina: Freschi; Pedevilla, Belis; Nehin, Sosa-Urbieta, Lopez; Rua, Wilde, De Vincenzi (capt.), Galateo, Iraneta.
Scorers: Bellis, Galateo for Argentina, Jonasson (2), Kroon for Sweden.

Hungary 4, *Egypt* 2 (2–1). *Naples*
Hungary: Szabo, A.; Futo, Sternberg; Palotas, Szucs, Lazar; Markos, Vincze, Teleky, Toldi, Szabo, F.
Egypt: Moustafa Kamel; Ali Caf, Hamitu; El Far, Refaat, Rayab; Latif, Fawzi, Muktar (capt.), Masoud Kamel, Hassan.
Scorers: Teleky, Toldi (2), Vincze for Hungary, Fawzi (2) for Egypt.

The Austrians just about deserved their 2–1 win. Germany beat a Swedish team reduced for most of the match to ten men, and the Czechs beat Switzerland 3–2 in Turin, in the most thrilling match of the round. Nejedly got the winning goal seven minutes from the end.

The semi-finals pitted Italy against Austria in Milan, Germany against Czechoslovakia in Rome. Italy deservedly got through, on a muddy ground, thanks to a goal by Guaita after 18 minutes, showing amazing stamina after their hard replay against Spain, only two days before. Austria did not have a shot until the 42nd minute.

The Czechs, surviving the trauma of a ridiculous equalising goal, when Planicka inexplicably let the ball sail over his head, were much too clever for the Germans, and beat them 3–1. Thus, they would meet Italy in the Final.

Meanwhile, in the third place match, a dejected Austrian team surprisingly went down 3–2 at Naples to the plodding Germans, who scored in 24 seconds.

Fortified by gargantuan presents of food, the Czechs gave Italy a tremendous run for their money in the Final. Short passing cleverly, making use of Puc's thrust on the left wing, with Planicka at his best in goal, they had slightly the better of the first half. Twenty minutes from time, Puc took a corner, and when the ball came back to him, drove it past Combi for the first goal.

Czechoslovakia should have clinched it, then. Sobotka missed a fine chance, Svoboda hit the post. Then Guaita and Schiavio switched, the Italian attack began to move better, and a freak goal by Orsi equalised. His curling, right-footed shot swerved in the air, and went over Planicka's hands. Next day, in practice, he tried twenty times, without success, to repeat it.

In the seventh minute of extra time, the injured Meazza got the ball on the wing, centred to Guaita, and the ball was moved on to Schiavio, who scored. Italy had done it, with little to spare. Neutral experts believed that home ground, frenzied support, the consequent intimidation of referees, may have been decisive. Nevertheless, theirs was a fine splendidly fit and dedicated team.

FIRST ROUND

Italy 7, *U.S.A.* 1 (3–0). *Rome*
Italy: Combi; Rosetta (capt.), Allemandi; Pizziolo, Monti, Bertolini; Guarisi, Meazza, Schiavio, Ferrari, Orsi.
U.S.A.: Hjulian; Czerchiewicz, Moorhouse (capt.); Pietras, Gonsalvez, Florie; Ryan, Nilsen, Donelli, Dick, Maclean.
Scorers: Schiavio (3), Orsi (2), Meazza, Ferrari for Italy, Donelli for U.S.A.

Czechoslovakia 2, *Rumania* 1 (0–1). *Trieste*
Czechoslovakia: Planicka (capt.); Zenisek, Ctyroky; Kostalek, Cambal, Krcil; Junek, Silny, Sobotka, Nejedly, Puc.

SECOND ROUND

Germany 2, *Sweden* 1 (1–0). *Milan*
Germany: Kress; Haringer, Busch; Gramlich, Szepan (capt.), Zielinski; Lehner, Hohmann, Conen, Siffling, Kobierski.
Sweden: Rydberg; Axelsson, Andersson, S.; Carlsson, Rosen (capt.), Andersson, E.; Dunker, Jonasson, Gustafsson, Keller, Kroon.
Scorers: Hohmann (2) for Germany, Dunker for Sweden.

Austria 2, *Hungary* 1 (1–0). *Bologna*
Austria: Platzer; Disar, Seszta; Wagner, Smistik (capt.), Urbanek; Zischek, Bican, Sindelar, Horwarth, Viertel.
Hungary: Szabo, A.; Vago, Sternberg; Palotas, Szucs, Szalay; Markos, Avar, Sarosi, Toldi, Kemeny.
Scorers: Horwarth, Zischek for Austria, Sarosi (penalty) for Hungary.

Italy 1, *Spain* 1 (0–1) (1–1) after extra time. *Florence*
Italy: Combi (capt.); Monzeglio, Allemandi; Pizziolo, Monti, Castellazzzi; Guaita, Meazza, Schiavio, Ferrari, Orsi.
Spain: Zamora (capt.); Ciriaco, Quincoces; Cillauren, Muguerza, Fede; Lafuente, Iraragorri, Langara, Regueiro, Gorostiza.
Scorers: Regueiro for Spain, Ferrari for Italy.

Italy 1, *Spain* 0 (1–0) Replay. *Florence*
Italy: Combi (capt.); Monzeglio, Allemandi; Ferraris IV, Monti, Bertolini; Guaita, Meazza, Borel, De Maria, Orsi.
Spain: Noguet; Zabalo, Quincoces (capt.); Gillauren, Muguerza, Lecue; Ventolra, Regueiro, Campanal, Chacho, Bosch.
Scorer: Meazza for Italy.

Czechoslovakia 3, *Switzerland* 2 (1–1) *Turin*
Czechoslovakia: Planicka; Zenisek, Ctyroky; Kostalek, Cambal, Krcil; Junek, Svoboda, Sobotka, Nejedly, Puc.
Switzerland: Sechehaye; Minelli, Weiler; Guinchard, Jaccard, Hufschmid; Von Kaenel, Jaeggi IV, Kielholz, Abegglen III, Jaeck.
Scorers: Kielholz, Abegglen III for Switzerland, Svoboda, Sobotka, Nejedly for Czechoslovakia.

SEMI-FINALS

Czechoslovakia 3, *Germany* 1 (1–0). *Rome*
Czechoslovakia: Planika (capt.); Burger, Ctyroky; Kostalek, Cambal, Krcil; Junek, Svoboda, Sobotka, Nejedly, Puc.
Germany: Kress; Haringer, Busch; Zielinksi, Szepan (capt.), Bender; Lehner, Siffling, Conen, Noack, Kobierski.
Scorers: Nejedly (2), Krcil for Czechoslovakia, Noack for Germany.

Italy 1, *Austria* 0 (1–0). *Milan*
Italy: Combi (capt.); Monzeglio, Allemandi; Ferraris IV, Monti, Bertolini; Guaita, Meazza, Schiavio, Ferrari, Orsi.
Austria: Platzer; Cisar, Seszta; Wagner, Smistik (capt.), Urbanek; Zischek, Bican, Sindelar, Schall, Viertel.
Scorer: Guaita for Italy.

THIRD PLACE MATCH

Germany 3, *Austria* 2 (3–1). *Naples*
Germany: Jakob; Janes, Busch; Zielinksi, Muenzenberg, Bender; Lehner, Siffling, Conen, Szepan (capt.), Heidemann.
Austria: Platzer; Cisar, Sesztar; Wagner, Smistik (capt.), Urbanek; Zischek, Braun, Bican, Horwath, Viertel.
Scorers: Lehner 2, Conen for Germany, Horwath, Seszta for Austria.

FINAL

Italy 2, *Czechoslovakia* 1 (0–0) (1–1) after extra time. *Rome*
Italy: Combi (capt.); Monzeglio, Allemandi; Ferraris IV, Monti, Bertolini; Guaita, Meazza, Schiavio, Ferrari, Orsi.
Czechoslovakia: Planicka (capt.); Żenisek, Ctyroky; Kostalek, Cambal, Krcil; Junek, Svoboda, Sobotka, Nejedly, Puc.
Scorers: Orsi, Schiavio for Italy, Puc for Czechoslovakia.
Leading Scorers: Schiavio (Italy), Nejedly (Czechoslovakia), Conen (Germany) each 4.

WORLD CUP 1938 – France

Italy were the winners again, but this time their win was more convincing. For the first time, indeed, a host nation failed to take the World Cup. Pozzo himself has said that on grounds of pure football, his 1938 side was superior to the team of 1934. Only the inside-forwards, Meazza and Ferrari, survived from that eleven. Monti's place at centre-half had been taken by another South American, Andreolo, from Uruguay. Foni and Rava, full-backs in the successful Italian Olympic side of 1936, were now in the full national side. Olivieri, an excellent goalkeeper, was a fitting successor to Combi. At centre-forward, the tall, powerful Silvio Piola rivalled Meazza (and overhauled him in 1951!) as the most prolific Italian goalscorer of all time.

Argentina wanted to put on this World Cup, but the claims of France were preferred. Austria and Spain had to withdraw for political reasons, Uruguay, still worried by the crisis of professionalism (another factor in their refusal to compete in 1934) refused again to take part. So did Argentina – whose fans demonstrated their displeasure outside the offices of the Federation.

But Brazil, a much improved side, were there again, with the great Leonidas at centre-forward, and Da Guia at full-back. Sarosi was in great form for Hungary, who had not long since beaten the Czechs 8–3 – he had fine support from Szengeller, the 22-year-old inside-left. Planicka, Nejedly and Puc survived from the Czechs' 1934 team, and Germany, now under Sepp Herberger, was still recovering from a 6–3 home defeat by England. The Swiss looked strong.

In the first round, the hardest fought tie was that between Germany – England's victims – and Switzerland, who had beaten England 2–1 a few days later, in Zurich. The Germans fielded four Austrians in the first match, one of whom, the outside-left, Pesser, was sent off in extra time. Gauchel gave Germany the lead from Pesser's centre. Abegglen headed an equaliser, and extra time brought no more goals. The teams had a good five days to gird themselves for the replay. This time, Germany fielded three Austrians, and brought back their talented 1934 captain, Szepan, to play at inside-left. They went into a 2–0 lead – one from Hahnemann, an unlucky own goal by Loertscher, the Swiss left-half – at half-time. Wallasshek made it 1–2 early in the second half, but when the Swiss left-winger Aebi went off injured, the die seemed cast.

Not a bit of it. The Swiss held out till Aebi came back, Bickel equalised and Abegglen, the star of the match, rounded it off with two fine goals.

The greatest surprise was Cuba's defeat of Rumania, after a 3–3 draw in Toulouse. Half the Rumanian side had previous World Cup experience, three had played in Uruguay. But the Cubans played with great speed and *brio*, and were 3–2 ahead in extra time, when the Rumanians equalised. In the replay, they surprisingly dropped their star goalkeeper, Carvajales, who was brilliantly replaced by Ayra, and won, after being a goal down. The winner, according to the French linesman, was offside, but the German referee allowed it. What has happened to Cuban football since 1938? Obscurely, it has sunk without trace.

The Czechs, with four 1934 men, beat Holland 3–0 in Le Havre, but then needed extra time to do it, and were fortunate that Holland lacked Bakhuijs, their leading scorer. Two of the Czech goals came from their half-backs; the celebrated Nejedly got the other.

At Strasbourg, a marvellous match between Brazil and Poland ended at 4–4. Poland had had a fine season, culminating with a 6–1 win over Ireland, and victory by 4–1 aggregate over Yugoslavia, in the eliminators for the World Cup. Their inside-forward, Ernest Willimowski, was one of the most talented in Europe, and a notable goalscorer. Brazil had six players making their international début. Their magnificent centre-forward Leonidas, the Black Diamond, did the hat trick for them in the first half, but in the second, the Polish half-backs took control, and ordinary time ended at 4–4. In extra time, Leonidas and Willimowski each got his fourth goal, but another by Romeo, for Brazil, was decisive – 6–5.

In Marseilles, Italy got the shock of their lives from little Norway.

Within two minutes, Ferrari had given Italy the lead, but Norway tightened their grip on Piola and their own centre-forward, the powerful Brunyldsen, gave Andreolo a terrible time of it. Three times the Italian posts and bar were hit; at others Olivieri saved them. In the second half, Brustand, an excellent left-winger, made it 1–1, but Piola eventually got the winner from a rebound.

Pozzo, however, revived his team's morale, and in the next round they won comfortably, 3–1 against France in Paris, before 58,000 spectators, the biggest crowd of that World Cup. Foni replaced Monzeglio at right-back, and Biavati, the winger with the fluttering foot, took over from Paserati.

For France, Delfour and Mattler were playing their third World Cup, the star was Piola. His two goals in the second half won the game, after France had rashly thrown themselves into attack.

Sweden, exempt from the first round, managed by Nagy, a Hungarian, and smarting from their humiliation by Japan in the last Olympiad, put an end to the Cuban illusion, winning 8–0. Torre Keller, their 35-year-old right-half and captain, was celebrating fourteen years of international competition. The fair-haired right-winger, Gustav Wetterstroem, was, however, the chief destroyer. Four of the goals were his.

In Lille, a tired Swiss team lost 2–0 to a technically superior Hungary; the Swiss felt the lack of Minelli and Aebi.

In Bordeaux, where the new municipal stadium was inaugurated, Czechoslovakia, 1934 finalists, played Brazil the now joint favourites with Italy. It was a holocaust; three players sent off, two Brazilians and a Czech while Planicka with a broken arm, and Nejedly, with a broken leg, finished in hospital. Zeze, violently kicking Nejedly, for no apparent reason – and getting himself sent off – began it. Leonidas gave Brazil the lead, Nejedly equalised from a penalty in the second half, and the depleted Czechs held out against the nine-man Brazilians, in extra time.

Curiously enough, the replay was conducted in the mildest of climates. The Brazilians made nine changes, the Czechs six. The Czechs led at half time through the energetic Kopecky, moved up to the attack, but they badly missed the passing of Nejedly. Worse, Kopecky had to leave the field injured, a shot by Senecky seemed to be over the line before the Brazilian 'keeper cleared it – and Leonidas was at his best. He it was who equalised, Roberto who got the winning goal.

In the semi-finals, Brazil paid the penalty for over-confidence, inexplicably omitting Leonidas and the brilliant Tim, against the Italians at Marseilles, and Colaussi scored the opening goal and Meezza clinched the game from a penalty after Domingas had rashly fouled Piola. Thus it was 2–0, and Romeo's goal for Brazil had no real significance. For all his folly, Domingas had impressed Pozzo as "one of the greatest defenders one is likely to meet."

In the other semi-final, Hungary thrashed Sweden 5–1 in Paris. Nyberg got a 35-second goal for Sweden, but the Hungarians took it in their stride. They were 3–1 up by half-time – two for Szengeller –

and he and Sarosi added goals in the second half. There could have been many more.

Sweden again took the lead in the third place match, at Bordeaux, and led 2–1 against Brazil at half time. Then Leonidas turned it on, scored two goals, and Brazil won 4–2.

On June 19, at the Stade Colombes, the Hungarians played graceful, short-passing football, the Italians showed rhythm and bite. Again, Colaussi got the first goal. Sarosi equalised within a minute – he was Hungary's great hope – but Meazza, getting too much room all the while, made one for Piola, and Italy led 2–1. By half-time Colaussi, put through by Meazza, had scored again 3–1.

In the second half, Sarosi got another in a scramble, but the Italian defence was in control. Colaussi was too fast for Polgar, while Biavati and Piola were too quick for the whole defence when Piola scored from Biavati's ultimate back-heel. A swift, strong, ruthless team had kept Italy the World Cup.

FIRST ROUND

Switzerland 1, *Germany* 1 (1–1) (1–1) after extra time. *Paris*
Switzerland: Huber; Minelli (capt.), Lehmann; Springer, Vernati, Loertscher; Amado, Wallaschek, Bickel, Abegglen III, Abei.
Germany: Raftl; Janes, Schnaus; Kupfer, Mock (capt.), Kitzinger; Lehner, Gellesch, Geuchel, Hahnemann, Pesser.
Scorers: Gauchel for Germany, Abegglen III for Switzerland.

Switzerland 4, *Germany* 2 (0–2). Replay. *Paris* (Parc des Princes)
Switzerland: Huber; Minelli (capt.), Lehmann; Springer, Vernati, Loertscher; Amado, Abegglen III, Bickel, Wallaschek, Aebi.
Germany: Raftl; Janes, Strietel; Kupfer, Goldbrunner, Skoumal; Lehner, Stroh, Hahnemann, Szepan (capt.), Haumer.
Scorers: Hahnemann, Loetscher own goal for Germany, Walleschek, Bickel, Abegglen III (2) for Switzerland.

Cuba 3, *Rumania* 3 (0–1) after extra time. *Toulouse*
Cuba: Cavajeles; Barquin, Chorens (capt.); Arias, Rodriquez, Berges; Maquina, Fernandez, Socorro, Tunas, Sosa.
Rumania: Palovici; Burger, Chiroiu; Vintila, Rasinaru (capt.), Rafinski; Bindea, Covaci, Baratki, Bodola, Dobai.
Scorers: Covaci, Baratki, Dobai for Rumania, Tunas, Maquina, Sosa for Cuba.

Cuba 2, *Rumania* 1 (0–1) Replay. *Toulouse*
Cuba: Ayra; Barquin, Chorens (capt.); Arias, Rodriquez, Berges; Maquina, Fernandez, Socorro, Tunas, Sosa.

Rumania: Sadowski; Burger, Felecan; Barbulescu, Rasinaru, Rafinski; Bogden, Moldoveanu, Baratki, Pranzler, Dobai.
Scorers: Dobai for Rumania, Socorro, Maquina for Cuba.

Hungary 6, *Dutch East Indies* 0 (4–0) *Reims*
Hungary: Hada; Koranyi, Biro; Lazar, Turai, Balogh; Sas, Szengeller, Sarosi (capt.), Toldi, Kohut.
Dutch East Indies: Mo Heng; Hu Kom, Samuels; Nawir, Meng (capt.), Anwar; Hang Djin, Soedarmadji, Sommers, Pattiwael, Taihuttu.
Scorers: Kohut, Tolid, Sarosi (2), Szengeller (2) for Hungary.

France 3, *Belgium* 1 (2–1). *Paris, Colombes*
France: Di Lorto; Czenave, Mattler (capt.); Bastien, Jordan, Diagne; Aston, Heisserer, Nicolas, Delfour, Vienante.
Belgium: Badjou; Pavrick (capt.), Sayes; Van Alphen, Stynen, De Winter; Van de Wouwer, Voorhoof, Isemborghs, Braine, R., Byle.
Scorers: Vienante, Nicolas (2) for France, Isemborghs for Belgium.

Czechoslovakia 3, *Holland* 0 (0–0) (0–0) after extra time. *Le Havre*
Czechoslovakia: Planicka; Burger, Daucik; Kostalek, Boucek (capt.), Kopechy; Riha, Simunek, Zeman, Nejedly, Puc.
Holland: Van Male; Weber, Caldenhove; Pawae, Anderiesen, (capt.), Van Heel; Wels, Van der Veen, Smit, Vente, De Harder.
Scorers: Kostalek, Boucek, Nejedly for Czechoslovakia.

Brazil 6, *Poland* 5 (3–1) (4–4) after extra time. *Strasbourg*
Brazil: Batatoes; Domingas Da Guia, Machados; Zeze, Martin (capt.), Alfonsinho; Lopez, Romeo, Leonidas, Peracio, Hercules.
Poland: Madejski;, Szcepaniak, Galecki; Gora, Nytz (capt.), Dytko; Piec I, Piontek, Szerfke, Willimowski, Wodarz.
Scorers: Leonidas (4), Peracio, Romeo for Brazil, Willimowski (4), Piontek for Poland.

Italy 2, *Norway* 1 (1–0) (1–1) after extra time. *Marseilles*
Italy: Olivieri; Monzeglio, Rava; Serantoni, Andreolo, Locatelli; Paserati, Meazza (capt.), Piola, Ferrari, Ferraris.
Norway: Johansen, H.; Johansen, R. (capt.), Holmsen; Henriksen, Eriksen, Homberg; Frantzen, Kwammen, Brunylden, Isaksen, Brustad.
Scorers: Ferrari, Piola for Italy, Brustad for Norway.

SECOND ROUND

Sweden 8, *Cuba* 0 (4–0). *Antibes*
Sweden: Abrahamson; Eriksson, Kjellgren; Almgren, Jacobsson, Svanstroem; Wetterstroem, Keller, Andersson H., Jonasson, Nyberg.

Cuba: Carvajeles; Barquin, Chorens; Arias, Rodriquez, Berges; Ferrer, Fernandez, Socorro, Tunas, Alonzo.
Scorers: Andersson, Wetterstroem (4), Jonasson, Nyberg, Keller.

Hungary 2, *Switzerland* 0 (1–0). *Lille*
Hungary: Szabo; Koranyi, Biro; Szalay, Turai, Lazar; Sas, Vincze, Sarosi (capt.), Szengeller, Kohut.
Switzerland: Huber; Stelzer, Lehmann (capt.); Springer, Vernati, Loertscher; Amadado, Wallaschek, Bickel, Abegglen III, Grassi.
Scorers: Szengeller (2) for Hungary.

Italy 3, *France* 1 (1–1). *Paris, Colombes*
Italy: Olivieri; Foni, Rava; Serantoni, Andreolo, Locatelli; Biavati, Meazza (capt.), Piola, Ferrari, Colaussi.
France: Di Lorto; Czenava, Mattler (capt.); Bastien, Jordan, Diagne; Aston, Heisserer, Nicolas, Delfour, Vienante.
Scorers: Colaussi, Piola (2) for Italy, Heisserer for France.

Brazil 1, *Czechoslovakia* 1 (1–1) (1–1) after extra time. *Bordeaux*
Brazil: Walter; Domingas Da Guia, Machados; Zeze, Martin (capt.), Alfonsinho; Lopez, Romeo, Leonidas, Peracio, Hercules.
Czechoslovakia: Planicka; Berger, Daucik; Kostalek, Bocek (capt.), Kopecky; Riha, Simunek, Ludl, Nejedly, Puc.
Scorers: Leonidas for Brazil, Nejedly (penalty) for Czechoslovakia.

Brazil 2, *Czechoslovakia* 1 (0–1) replay. *Bordeaux*
Brazil: Walter; Jahu, Nariz; Britto, Brandao (capt.), Algemiro; Roberto, Luisinho, Leonidas, Tim, Patesko.
Czechoslovakia: Burkert; Berger, Daucik; Kostalek, Bocek (capt.), Ludl; Horak, Senecky, Kreutz, Kopecky, Rulc.
Scorers: Kopecky for Czechoslovakia, Leonidas, Roberto for Brazil.

SEMI-FINALS

Italy 2, *Brazil* 1 (2–0). *Marseilles*
Italy: Olivieri; Foni, Rava; Serantoni, Andreolo, Locatelli; Biavati, Meazza (capt.), Piola, Ferrari, Colaussi.
Brazil: Walter; Domingas Da Guia, Machados; Zeze, Martin (capt.), Alfonsinho; Lopez, Luisinho, Peracio, Romeo, Patesko.
Scorers: Colaussi, Meazza (penalty) for Italy, Romeo for Brazil.

Hungary 5, *Sweden* 1 (3–1). *Paris, Colombes*
Hungary: Szabo, Koranyi, Biro; Szalay, Turai, Lazar; Sas, Szengeller, Sarosi (capt.), Toldi, Titkos.
Sweden: Abrahamson; Eriksson, Kjellgren; Almgren, Jacobsson, Svanstroem; Wetterstroem, Keller (capt.), Andersson H., Jonasson, Nyberg.
Scorers: Szengeller (3), Titkos, Sarosi for Hungary, Nyberg for Sweden.

THIRD PLACE MATCH

Brazil 4, *Sweden* 2 (1–2). *Bordeaux*
Brazil: Batatoes; Domingas Da Guia, Machados; Zeze, Brandao, Alfonsinho; Roberto, Romeo, Leonidas (capt.), Peracio, Patesko.
Sweden: Abrahamson; Eriksson, Nilssen; Almgren, Linderholm, Svanstroem (capt.); Berssen, Andersson H., Jonasson, Andersson, A., Nyberg.
Scorers: Jonasson, Nyberg for Sweden, Romeo, Leonidas (2) Peracio for Brazil.

FINAL

Italy 4, *Hungary* 2 (3–1). *Paris, Colombes*
Italy: Olivieri; Foni, Rava; Serantoni, Andreolo, Locatelli; Biavati, Meazza (capt.), Piola, Ferrari, Colaussi.
Hungary: Szabo; Polgar, Biro; Szalay, Szucs, Lazar; Sas, Vincze, Sarosi (capt.), Szengeller, Titkos.
Scorers: Colaussi (2), Piola (2) for Italy, Titkos, Sarosi for Hungary.

WORLD CUP 1950 – Brazil

The first World Cup for twelve years, the first since the outbreak of war, was in many ways the most vivid and impassioned yet. If Brazil were the moral victors, Uruguay's success was a marvellous anti-climax, emphasising the uncertainties of the game. Certainly the Uruguayans were most fortunate to have their qualifying pool reduced to a single, ludicrous match against Bolivia – but in the Final the defensive prowess of Varela, Andrade and Maspoli, and the counter-attacking of Schiaffino and Ghiggia, were worthy of success.

For the first – and so far last – time the competition was organised on the curious basis of four qualifying pools and a final pool. Again, there were several distinguished absentees; Austria, Hungary, Czechoslovakia, Argentina. The Austrians, who seem to suffer from a periodic inferiority complex (they were to withdraw again in 1962) said quaintly that their team was too inexperienced – and then proceeded to beat Italy in Vienna. Russia stayed out, and Germany were still excluded from FIFA. But the British countries took part for the first time, their own International Championship charitably being recognised as a qualifying group, in which the first two would go through to the finals. Scotland, with baffling insularity and pique, decided that if they did not win the title they would not go to Brazil. England beat them 1–0 at Hampden – and they stayed at home to sulk.

England and Brazil were the favourites; Brazil as talented hosts, England for, presumably, historical reasons. Their chances were diminished by the withdrawal of Neil Franklin, their gifted centre-half, who flew off to play in Bogota, Colombia, then unregistered with FIFA. Injuries had blunted the edge of the gallant Mortensen, a splendid opportunist, but there were still such giants as Matthews,

Finney, Williams, Ramsey, Mannion. In retrospect, the team looks better than one felt it to be in prospect.

Brazil approached the tournament with all the intense dedication shown by Uruguay in 1930 – and Italy in 1934. Managed by Flavio Costa, a lean, intense man with the inevitable South American moustache, they took up monastic residence in a house just outside Rio, with vitamin drinks, ten o'clock curfew and a ban on wives. Local firms accoutred the house for nothing. There were two doctors, two masseurs, three chefs.

The massive Maracana Stadium – shades of Uruguay in 1930 – was still being completed (capacity 200,000) when the teams arrived – and when they left. Its seats had been painted blue; allegedly a pacifying colour.

France, angered by the amount of travelling they would have to do, withdrew at the last moment; this, after having been eliminated, then invited to take the place of Turkey, another country that withdrew. Though the French attitude was hardly defensible, there's no doubt that the travelling arrangements strongly favoured Brazil. So did the thin air of Rio.

Brazil kicked off against Mexico in a stadium that was still no more than an ambitious shambles. Brazil won 2–0, both goals coming from their lithe and brilliant centre-forward, Ademir. In São Paulo, a brave Swedish team sprang the first surprise of the competition by beating Italy. George Raynor, their clever little Yorkshire coach, had brilliantly rebuilt an Olympic winning team pillaged of its stars by – the Italians. In Nacka Skoglund and Kalle Palmer, he had unearthed two delicate and subtle inside-forwards, flanking a powerful leader in the fair-haired Hasse Jeppson who completely mastered the great Carlo Parola. Italy had picked a strange team with Campatelli, a veteran left-half, at inside-left – after three years out of the national side. Carapallese, the Italian captain and outside-left, gave them the lead before a crowd that was full of Italo-Brazilians, but the hefty Knud Nordahl dominated Gino Cappello, their centre-forward. Jeppson equalised, Andersson gave Sweden the lead with a long shot, and a mistake in the second half by Sentimenti IV, in goal, allowed Jeppson to clinch it. Muccinelli pulled back a goal, Carapellese hit the bar – but that was as near as Italy could get.

In the other matches, the United States roused echoes of 1930 by leading Spain at half-time, fighting gallantly, and going down only by 3–1. Spain, with fine wingers in Basora and Gainza, and a tough centre-forward in Zarra, were greatly surprised. At the hard little Belo Horizonte ground, Yugoslavia easily beat Switzerland, with Cjaicowski, at right-half, Mitic and Bobek, at inside-forward, standing out for their skill.

England's win against Chile, in Rio, was laboured, but in their next match they suffered one of the greatest humiliations in world football history; they were beaten 1–0 by the United States in Belo Horizonte. So casually did the Americans take the game that most of them were up till the small hours. Everything seemed set for England; crisp mountain air; a British mining firm to put them up; a forward line of stars. But gallant defence by Borghi, in goal, Colombo at centre-half, and Eddie McIlvenny, a Scotsman discarded eighteen months earlier by Third Division Wrexham on a free transfer, held them out; and after 37 minutes America scored. Gaetjens got his head to a cross by Bahr, to beat Williams; and all England's pressure could not bring an equaliser. Did Mullen's header from Ramsey's free kick cross Borghi's line? Perhaps; but America deserved their win for their courage.

In São Paulo, Brazil, too, faltered; held to a 2–2 draw by little Switzerland, who equalised two minutes from the end. Costa had picked a team full of *paulistas*, to flatter São Paulo, and the gesture had very nearly been expensive.

Italy beat Paraguay, who had drawn with Sweden, but the die was cast. Brazil, who had to beat Yugoslavia, conquerors of Mexico, in Rio, to qualify, got through by the skin of their teeth. Indeed, had it not been for a wretchedly unlucky head injury to Mitic, on a steel girder outside the dressing-room, who knows what might have happened?

In the third minute, Ademir took a pass from the splendid right-half, Bauer, and opened the score. Yugoslavia, however, gave as good as they got. Cjaicowski II missed a fine chance to equalise, Bauer found the inimitable Zizinho – playing his first game of the tournament – and the inside-right wriggled through to clinch a difficult game. The Brazilians, playing "diagonal" defence with a wandering centre-half and half-backs on the flanks, had made heavy weather of qualifying. Uruguay, 8–0 conquerors of Bolivia, had no trouble at all.

As for England, they went down 1–0 to Spain (a goal headed by Zarra) in Rio, and that was the end of them. Changes brought in Eddie Baily of Spurs at inside-left, Stanley Matthews on the right wing, Jackie Milburn at centre-forward, but the forward-line was still dogged by bad luck, and when Milburn did get the ball in the net, he was very dubiously given offside. Chile, winning 5–2 against the United States, emphasised England's shame.

In their first matches of the final pool, Brazil played some of the finest football that has ever graced the World Cup. Their inside-forward trio of Zizinho, Ademir and Jair, with its pyrotechnical ball play, its marvellous understanding, was practically unstoppable, and Bauer gave it marvellous support. Raynor planned for Sweden to get an early goal, but two early chances went begging, and after that Brazil swept them aside. It was sheer execution. A second-half penalty by Andersson was the most Sweden could do against seven Brazilian goals, four of them Ademir's.

Spain went the same way, giving one goal less away. This time Jair and Chico got two each, Ademir did not score. Meanwhile Spain had held Uruguay to a bad-tempered 2–2 draw, Basora getting two more goals, despite the marking of Andrade. It seemed doubtful indeed whether the Uruguayans, bogeys of Brazil though they were, could hold them this time, when they were under full sail.

Against Sweden, in São Paulo, the Uruguayans scraped through 3–2, after being a goal down at half-time. Skoglund's off day and a bad foul by M. Gonzales on Johnsson – not to mention Uruguay's far easier programme – weighed against Sweden in the second half.

Thus to the deciding match, played before 200,000 impassioned fans at the Maracana; a match which Brazil had only to draw to take the World Cup. For three-quarters of an hour they pounded a superb Uruguayan defence, brilliantly marshalled by their veteran centre-half, Obdulio Varela. Not till two minutes after half-time did Friaça meet a cross from the left to beat the astonishing Maspoli. Then Uruguay began to hit back, Varela turned to the attack, and after 20 minutes sent the fragile Ghiggia away on the right. Tall, pale, slender Juan Schiaffino controlled his centre, unmarked, advanced, shot – and scored. Eleven minutes from time, Ghiggia took a return from Perez, ran on, and scored the winner.

Sweden, beating Spain 3–1 with a sudden late show of life, bravely took third place. And Brazil had to wait another eight years for ultimate satisfaction.

POOL I

Brazil 4, *Mexico* 0 (1–0). *Rio*
Brazil: Barbosa; Augusto (capt.), Juvenal; Eli, Danilo, Bigode; Meneca, Ademir, Baltazar, Jair, Friaça.
Mexico: Carbajal; Zetter, Montemajor; Ruiz, Ochoa, Roca; Septien, Ortis, Casarin, Perez, Velasquez (capt.).
Scorers: Ademir (2), Jair, Baltazar for Brazil.

Yugoslavia 3, *Switzerland* 0 (3–0). *Belo Horizonte*
Yugoslavia: Mrkusic; Horvat, Stankovic; Cjaicowski I (capt.), Jovanovic, Djaic; Ognanov, Mitic, Tomasevic, Bobek, Vukas.
Switzerland: Corrodi; Gyger, Rey; Bocquet, Eggimann, Neury; Bickel (capt.), Antenen, Tamini, Bader, Fatton.
Scorers: Tomasevic (2), Ognanov for Yugoslavia.

Yugoslavia 4, *Mexico* 1 (2–0). *Porto Alegre*
Yugoslavia: Mrkusic; Horvat, Stankovic; Cjaicowski I (capt.), Jovanovic, Djaic; Mihailovic, Mitic, Tomasevic, Bobek, Cjaicowski II.
Mexico: Carbajal; Gutierrez, Ruiz; Gomez, Ochao, Ortiz; Flores, Naranjo, Casarin, Perez, Velasquez (capt.).
Scorers: Bobek, Cjaicowski II (2), Tomasevic for Yugoslavia, Casarin for Mexico.

Brazil 2, *Switzerland* 2 (2–1). *São Paulo*
Brazil: Barbosa; Augusto (capt.), Jucenal; Bauer, Ruy, Noronha;

Alfredo, Maneca, Baltazar, Ademir, Friaça.
Switzerland: Stuber; Neury, Bocquet; Lasenti, Eggimann, Quinche; Tamini, Bickel (capt.), Antenen, Bader, Fatton.
Scorers: Alfredo, Baltazar for Brazil, Fatton, Tamini for Switzerland.

Brazil 2, *Yugoslavia* 0 (1–0). *Rio*
Brazil: Barbosa; Augusto (capt.), Juvenal; Bauer, Danilo, Bigode; Maneca, Zizinho, Ademir, Jair, Chico.
Yugoslavia: Mrkusic; Horvat, Brokela; Cjaicowski I (capt.), Jovanovic, Djaic; Vukas, Mitic, Tomasevic, Bobek, Cjaicowski II.
Scorers: Ademir, Zizinho for Brazil.

Switzerland 2, *Mexico* 1 (2–0). *Porto Alegre*
Switzerland: Hug; Neury, Bocquet; Lusenti, Eggimann (capt.), Kerner; Tamini, Antenen, Friedlander, Bader, Fatton.
Mexico: Carbajal; Gutierrez, Gomez; Roca, Oritz, Vuburu; Flores, Naranjo, Casarin, Borbolla, Velasquez (Capt.).
Scorers: Bader, Fatton for Switzerland, Velasquez for Mexico.

POOL II

Spain 3, *United States* 1 (0–1). *Curitiba*
Spain: Eizaguirre; Asensi, Alonzo; Gonzalvo III, Gonzalvo II, Puchades; Basora, Hernandez, Zarra, Igoa, Gainza.

U.S.A.: Borghi; Keough, Maca; McIlvenny (capt.), Colombo, Bahr; Craddock, Souza, J., Gaetjens, Pariani, Valentini.
Scorers: Souza, J. for U.S.A. Barora (2), Zarra for Spain.

England 2, *Chile* 0 (1–0). *Rio*
England: Williams; Ramsey, Aston; Wright, (Capt.) Hughes, Dickinson; Finney, Mortensen, Bentley, Mannion, Mullen.
Chile: Livingstone; Faerias, Roldon; Alvarez, Busquez (capt.), Carvalho; Malanej, Cremaschi, Robledo, Munoz, Diaz.
Scorers: Mortensen, Mannion for England.

United States 1, *England* 0 (1–0). *Belo Horizonte*
U.S.A.: Borghi; Keough, Maca; McIlvenny (capt.), Colombo, Bahr; Wallace, Pariani, Gaetjens, Souza, J., Souza, E.
England: Williams; Ramsey, Aston; Wright (capt.), Hughes, Dickinson; Finney, Mortensen, Bentley, Mannion, Mullen.
Scorer: Gaetjens for U.S.A.

Spain 2, *Chile* 0 (2–0). *Rio*
Spain: Eizaguirre; Alonzo, Pana; Gonzalvo III, Antunez, Purchades;

Basora, Igoa, Zarra, Panizo, Gainza.
Chile: Livingstone; Faerias, Roldon; Alvarez, Brusquez (capt.), Valho; Prieto, Cremaschi, Robledo, Munoz, Diaz.
Scorers: Basora, Zarra for Spain.

Spain 1, *England* 0 (0–0). *Rio*
Spain: Ramallets; Asensi, Alonzo; Gonzalvo III, Antunez, Puchades; Basora, Igoa, Zarra, Panizo, Gainza.
England: Williams; Ramsey, Eckersley; Wright (capt.), Hughes, Dickinson; Matthews, Mortensen, Milburn, Baily, Finney.
Scorer: Zarra for Spain.

Chile 5, *United States* 2 (2–0). *Recife*
Chile: Livingstone; Machuca Roldon; Alvarez, Busquez (capt.), Faerias; Munoz, Cremaschi, Robledo, Prieto, Ibanez.
U.S.A.: Borghi; Keough, Maca; McIlvenny (capt.), Colombo, Bahr; Wallace, Pariani, Gaetjens, Souza, J., Souza, E.
Scorers: Robledo, Cremaschi 3, Prieto for Chile, Pariani, Souza, J. (penalty) for U.S.A.

POOL III
Sweden 3, *Italy* 2 (2–1). *São Paulo*
Sweden: Svensson; Samuelsson, Nilsson G. (capt.); Andersson, Nordahl, K., Gard; Sundqvist, Palmer, Jeppson, Skoglund, Nilsson, S.
Italy: Sentimenti IV; Giovannini, Furiassi; Annovazzi, Parola, Magli; Muccinelli, Boniperti, Cappello, Campatelli, Carapallese (capt.).
Scorers: Jeppson 2, Andersson for Sweden, Carapellese, Muccinelli for Italy.

Sweden 2, *Paraguay* 2 (2–1). *Curitiba*
Sweden: Svensson; Samuelsson, Nilsson, E. (capt.); Andersson, Nordahl, K., Gard; Johnsson, Palmer, Jeppson, Skoglund, Sundqvist.
Paraguay: Vargas; Gonzalito, Cespedes; Gavilan, Lequizamon, Cantero; Avalos, Lopez, A., Jara, Lopez, F., Unzaim.
Scorers: Sundqvist, Palmer for Sweden, Lopez, A., Lopez, F. for Paraguay.

Italy 2, *Paraguay* 0 (1–0). *São Paulo*
Italy: Moro; Blason, Furiassi; Fattori, Remondini, Mari; Muccinelli, Pandolfini, Amadei, Cappello, Carapellese.
Paraguay: Vargas; Gonzalito, Cespedes; Gavilan, Lequizamon, Cantero; Avalos, Lopez, A., Jara, Lopez, F., Unzaim.
Scorers: Carapellese, Pandolfini for Italy.

POOL IV

Uruguay 8, *Bolivia* 0 (4–0). *Recife*

Uruguay: Maspoli; Gonzales, M., Tejera; Gonzales, W., Varela (capt.), Andrade; Ghiggia, Perez, Miguez, Schiaffino, Vidal.
Bolivia: Gutierrez I; Achs, Bustamente; Greco, Valencia, Ferrel; Alganaraz, Ugarte, Caparelli, Gutierrez II, Maldonado.
Scorers: Schiaffino 4, Miguez 2, Vidal, Ghiggia for Uruguay.

PLACINGS

	P	W	D	L	Goals F	Goals A	Pts.
Pool I							
Brazil	3	2	1	0	8	2	5
Yugoslavia	3	2	0	1	7	3	4
Switzerland	3	1	1	1	4	6	3
Mexico	3	0	0	3	2	10	0
Pool II							
Spain	3	3	0	0	6	1	6
England	3	1	0	2	2	2	2
Chile	3	1	0	2	5	6	2
United States	3	1	0	2	4	8	2
Pool III							
Sweden	2	1	1	0	5	4	3
Italy	2	1	0	1	4	3	2
Paraguay	2	0	1	1	1	4	1
Pool IV							
Uruguay	1	1	0	0	8	0	2
Bolivia	1	0	0	1	0	8	0

FINAL POOL

Uruguay 2, *Spain* 2 (1–2). *São Paulo*

Uruguay: Maspoli; Gonzales, M., Tejera; Gonzales, W., Verela (capt.), Andrade; Ghiggia, Perez, Miguez, Schiaffino, Vidal.
Spain: Ramallets; Alonzo, Gonzalvo II; Gonzalvo III, Parra, Puchades; Basora, Igoa, Zarra, Molowny, Gainza.
Scorers: Ghiggia, Varela for Uruguay, Basora 2 for Spain.

Brazil 7, *Sweden* 1 (3–1). *Rio*

Brazil: Barbosa; Augusto (capt.), Juvenal; Bauer, Danilo, Bigode; Maneca, Zizinho, Ademir, Jair, Chico.
Sweden: Svensson; Samuelsson, Nilsson, E.; Andersson, Nordahl, K., Gard; Sundqvist, Palmer, Jeppson, Skoglund, Nilsson, S.

Scorers: Ademir 4, Chico 2, Maneca for Brazil, Andersson (penalty) for Sweden.

Uruguay 3, *Sweden* 2 (1–2). *São Paulo*

Uruguay: Paz; Gonzales, M., Tejera; Gambetta, Varela (capt.), Andrade; Ghiggia, Perez, Miguez, Schiaffino, Vidal.
Sweden: Svensson; Samuelsson, Nilsson, E.; Andersson, Johansson, Gard; Johnsson, Palmer, Melberg, Skoglund, Sundqvist.
Scorers: Palmer, Sundqvist for Sweden, Ghiggia, Miguez 2 for Uruguay.

Brazil 6, *Spain* 1 (3–0). *Rio*

Brazil: Barbosa; Augusto (capt.), Juvenal; Bauer, Danilo, Bigode; Friaça, Zizinho, Ademir, Jair, Chico.
Spain: Eizaguirre; Alonzo, Gonzalvo II; Gonzalvo III, Parra, Puchades; Basora, Igoa, Zarra, Panizo, Gainza.
Scorers: Jair 2, Chico 2, Zizinho, Parra (own goal) for Brazil, Igoa for Spain.

Sweden 3, *Spain* 1 (2–0). *São Paulo*

Sweden: Svensson; Samuelsson, Nilsson, E.; Andersson, Johansson, Gard; Sundqvist, Mellberg, Rydell, Palmer, Johnsson.
Spain: Eizaguirre; Asensi, Alonzo; Silva, Parra, Puchades; Basora, Fernandez, Zarra, Panizo, Juncosa.
Scorers: Johansson, Mellberg, Palmer for Sweden, Zarra for Spain.

Uruguay 2, *Brazil* 1 (0–0). *Rio*

Uruguay: Maspoli; Gonzales, M., Tejera; Gambetta, Varela (capt.), Andrade; Ghiggia, Perez, Miguez, Schiaffino, Moran.
Brazil: Barbosa; Augusto (capt.), Juvenal; Bauer, Danilo, Bigode; Friaça, Zizinho, Ademir, Jair, Chico.
Scorers: Friaça for Brazil, Schiaffino, Ghiggia for Uruguay.

FINAL POSITIONS

					Goals		
	P	W	D	L	F	A	Pts.
Uruguay	3	2	1	0	7	5	5
Brazil	3	2	0	1	14	4	4
Sweden	3	1	0	2	6	11	2
Spain	3	0	1	2	4	11	1

Leading Scorers: Ademir (Brazil) 7, Schiaffino (Uruguay), Basora (Spain) 5.

WORLD CUP 1954 – Switzerland

The 1954 World Cup, which rolled over little, under-organised Switzerland like a tidal wave over some peaceful village, was another instance of the Cup being won, at the last gasp, by the "wrong" team. This time, the "wrong" team was Sepp Herberger's cunningly managed Germany, the "wronged" team, the brilliant Hungarians.

Hungary, who had smashed England's unbeaten home record against foreign teams 6–3 at Wembley the previous November, then beaten them again 7–1 in Budapest, as an aperitif to the World Cup, had the finest team the world had seen since the 1950 Brazilians; and probably the best Europe has ever seen.

The organisation of the tournament settled down into the somewhat hybrid and equally unsatisfactory form it has retained ever since. Four qualifying groups provided two qualifiers each, which then met in the quarter-finals, those which had finished first playing those which had finished second. Again, the British Championship was charitably designated as a qualifying group, and this time, Scotland, again runner-up to England, deigned to enter. Their team paid a heavy penalty for the insularity of their Association in 1950.

Uruguay at last entered a European World Cup; they had yet to lose a match in the competition. Of the victorious 1950 team, still playing with a roving centre-half and "bolt" defence, Maspoli, Andrade, Varela, Miguez and Schiaffino all remained. There were splendid new wingers in Abbadie and Borges, and a powerful stopper in the fair-haired Santamaria, later to become a bulwark of Real Madrid.

Even so, Hungary remained favourites, with their marvellous attack, pivoting on Boszik, the right-half, and Nandor Hidegkuti, the deep-lying centre-forward; most of their goals scored with the remarkable head of Sandor Kocsis or the matchlessly powerful left foot of the captain, Ferenc Puskas, whose injury was probably to decide the series.

Austria, whose European dominance was ended by Hungary, had the remains of a fine team, a superb half-back in the tall, dark, strong Ernest Ocwirk, formerly their roving centre-half, now a wing-half. Austria had at last abandoned the classic Vienna School for the third back game which Meisl would have loathed.

Sweden, robbed of their stars by Italian clubs and eliminated by Belgium, were not there. Italy, under the management of the Hungarian Lajos Czeizler, basing their defence on the Inter (Milan) block, had a good recent record. Brazil had largely rebuilt their side. The great inside-forward trio had disappeared *en bloc*. Only Bauer and Baltazar remained, but the black Djalma Santos and his elegant namesake Nilton, were fine backs, and Julinho came with a forbidding reputation for power and brilliance on the right wing. The defence still clung to the old, "diagonal" system and had not mastered the third-back game. Costa had given way to Zeze Moreira, as the manager.

Yugoslavia, with the experience of Mitic, Bobek and Cjaicowski I, the acrobatic goalkeeping of Beara, the skill and finishing power of the excellent Zebec and Vukas, were obviously good outsiders. One should add that an absurd omission in the rules made it necessary for extra time to be played *whenever* two teams were level at full-time. Each pool included two "seeded" teams.

The tournament began with France losing by a single goal to Yugoslavia – a goal scored by the young Milutinovic, who was later to play for Racing Club de Paris. Brazil, with Didi directing operations, gobbled up Mexico. Hungary had an even easier task against little Korea in Pool II. Germany disposed of Turkey without trouble.

Scotland played well against the talented Austrian side in Zürich, and their remodelled defence, with new backs in Willy Cunningham and Aird, looked promisingly solid. In attack, they missed the punch of Lawrie Reilly, who had been ill. Scotland gave Schmied in the Austrian goal much more to do than had their own goalkeeper; their half-backs were excellent, and it was only Schmied's late, daring save from centre-forward Mochan, which allowed them to hang on to Probst's first-half goal.

England, still tottering from the travesty of Budapest, threw away all Matthews' brilliant work, in a 4–4 draw with Belgium. Pol Anoul, the fair-haired inside-forward, gave Belgium the lead after only five minutes, fifteen minutes from time England were 3–1 in the lead thanks to the finishing of Ivor Broadis and Nat Lofthouse, who divided the goals between them. Over-complacent, they allowed Belgium to wipe out the lead through Anoul again, and their talented compact centre-forward, the unpredictable Rik Coppens. That meant – under the farcical rules of the competition – extra time.

For half an hour, England were dominant, but Matthews, the inspiration of the side, here, there and everywhere, pulled a muscle, and two minutes after Lofthouse had crowned a fine inter-passing movement between Broadis and Manchester United's Tommy Taylor, Dickinson headed Dries' free kick past Merrick, for the Belgian equaliser.

In the meantime, Italy surprisingly came a cropper at Lausanne against Switzerland. The days of Pozzo, present only in his capacity of journalist, were distant indeed. Bad refereeing by Viana of Brazil unsettled the players and led to a holocaust of fouls and bad temper. Italy had the play, Switzerland got the goals, Hugi, who had switched to outside-right, scoring the winner twelve minutes from time. Two Swiss players were kicked in the stomach, and the Italians chased Viana off the field after he had dubiously ruled out a goal by Benito Lorenzi, who had persistently argued with him. Not for nothing was Lorenzi nicknamed "*Veleno*" – Poison.

The next round of matches included what was perhaps the decisive moment of the competition; the kick, accidental perhaps, with which Germany's centre-half Werner Liebrich injured Ferenc Puskas, and put him out of action till a Final in which he should not really have taken part. Sepp Herberger cleverly decided to throw away this match, fielding a team which consisted largely of reserves, convinced that Germany would easily dispose of Turkey in the play-off. The Hungarians tore Germany apart, getting eight goals, four of them by Kocsis, whose heading was remarkable. The fact that a team could be thus overwhelmed and still come back to win a *cup* competition was as good a comment on the organisation of this World Cup as one could require. Three of Hungary's goals came in the last fifteen minutes, when Puskas was off the field.

Uruguay, who had conquered the mud in Berne to beat an uninspired Czech team, now exploited the firmer going in Basel to humiliate Scotland 7–0. Schiaffino, tall, pale, lean, a wonderful ball-player and strategist, with a splendid understanding with his centre-forward, Miguez, tore Scotland's defence to pieces. Borges and Abbadie, the wingers, got five of the goals between them against a wretched Scottish team, which had not been helped by dissension among its officials. Andy Beattie, the team manager, had resigned after the Austrian game.

Austria, meanwhile, showed dazzling form in thrashing the Czechs 5–0, Ocwirk and the polished Gerhard Hanappi cleverly supporting an attack in which inside-forwards Probst and Stojaspal divided the goals.

But the finest match of all, perhaps the best of the whole tournament, with the exception of the Hungary–Uruguay semi-final, was Brazil's draw with Yugoslavia in Pool I.

On the pretty Lausanne ground overlooking Lake Geneva, the Yugoslavs gave a splendid exhibition, Cjaicowski and Boskov dominating midfields, with Beara superb in goal. But the only goal was by Zebec, three minutes from half-time. In the second half Brazil came to life and Didi, after sustained pressure, got an equaliser with a spectacular drive. There were no more goals in extra time.

In the play-offs, Germany, with a full team again, swamped Turkey while Italy, who had revived to beat Belgium 4–1, lost by the same score to Switzerland; a bafflingly inconsistent team. England, who had beaten the Swiss 2–0 in a dull game in Berne, were already through. They had strengthened their defence by moving Wright to centre-half in place of the injured Owen, a move which would bear abundant fruit in the years to come.

In the quarter-finals, England's 4–2 defeat by Uruguay has subsequently been put down to the goalkeeping of Merrick, as though England really deserved to win. In fact, the Uruguayans did remarkably well to defeat England, with both Varela and Andrade pulling muscles and Abbadie limping for much of the game.

England, with Matthews back in the side and shining again, did well, Lofthouse rubbing out Borges' fifth-minute goal. Varela's long-distance volley gave Uruguay a lead they did not deserve on the play – Merrick might have saved it; then after Varela had taken a free kick "from hand," Schiaffino made it 3–1; again with a shot that could have been saved. Schiaffino's later excellence at left-half saw to it that England did not save the game. Finney's goal made it 2–3, Matthews hit the post, but at last Ambrois slipped through for the fourth, and England were eliminated.

In Lausanne, Austria, again on form, won an astonishing twelve-goal match with the Swiss; a score unthinkable two World Cups later! Using the speed of the Koerners down the wings and shooting, untypically, from long range, Austria had the star of the match in the classical Ocwirk. The best Swiss player was their dark inside-right, Roger Vonlanthen, who was behind most of their goals.

Meanwhile, the Brazilians met the Hungarians in what has come to be known as the Battle of Berne; a potentially great match which degenerated into a shocking display of violence.

Hungary made one of their spectacular starts, Hidegkuti scoring from a corner in the third minute, and getting his shorts ripped off for his pains. Then, five minutes later, he centred for Kocsis to head in. As the rain poured down, tackling grew ferocious. Buzansky knocked Indio down, big Djalma Santos scored from the penalty and Hungary, without Puskas, were faltering.

A quarter of an hour after half time, they too scored from a penalty – by Lantos, after Pinheiro had handled – but a marvellous run and shot by Julinho made it 3–2. Nilton Santos and Boszik came to blows, and Arthur Ellis, the Halifax referee, sent both off the field. Hostilities were well and truly open. Four minutes from time, when the field resembled a boxing ring, Ellis sent off Humberto Tozzi, Brazil's inside-left, for kicking at an opponent, and in the last minute, Koscis headed the fourth for Hungary. Then the battle was transferred to the dressing-rooms. . . .

In Geneva, Yugoslavia dominated Germany for an hour without being able to score. But the towering Horvat put past his own goalkeeper. The Slav forwards again finished poorly; Kohlmeyer kicked off the German line three times, and at last a breakaway goal by the bull-like Helmut Rahn, Germany's splendid outside-right, settled matters.

The Lausanne Hungary-Uruguay semi-final was unforgettable, though Hungary missed Puskas, Czibor gave Hungary a fifteen-minute lead, from Kocsis' header, and Hidegkuti's head made it 2–0 just before half-time.

That seemed to be that but with only a quarter of an hour left Schiaffino put the Argentinian-born Hohberg through to make it 2–1 – and repeated the move three minutes from the end.

In the first half of extra time, Hohberg was through a third time, but his shot hit the post and Hungary survived. Two splendid headers from Kocsis in the last fifteen minutes gave them a wonderful match.

Germany meanwhile, to the general astonishment, routed Austria, not least because goalkeeper Walter Zeman had a tragic game. The Germans, splendidly marshalled by their captain, Fritz Walter, backed up by his Kaiserslautern "block", scored twice from corners, twice from centres, twice from penalties. Germany's switching, Walter's scheming and his cunning corners gave Austria a nightmare second half, in which they conceded five goals.

In the third place match, in Zürich, Austria gained consolation. Unlike the equivalent game of 1934, they started underdogs, yet won – against a tired, demoralised Uruguay. A first-half injury to Schiaffino put the lid on it; Stojaspal emerged as the game's cleverest forward, and Ocwirk was magisterial. It was Ocwirk who shot the third goal from 25 yards, in a tepid second half.

And so to Berne, and the dramatic, unexpected Final.

Hungary, with Puskas insisting that he play, might have demoralised Germany with their opening attack. After six minutes Boszik put Koscis through, his shot was blocked, but Puskas followed up to score. Two minutes more and Czibor, on the right wing, made it 2–0.

What saved Germany was their swift reply – Morlock putting in Fritz Walter's fast centre. Rahn scored from a corner – and the game was open again. Turek, in Germany's goal, made save after dazzling save, Hidegkuti hit a post, Kocsis the bar, and Kohlmeyer kicked off the line. Then Eckel and Mai got a tighter grip on the Hungarian inside-forwards, Fritz Walter brought his wingers into the game and at last Boszik mispassed. Schaefer found Fritz Walter, the cross was pushed out – and Rahn smashed the ball in. Germany had won. When Puskas, coming to life again, raced on to Toth's pass to score, the goal was flagged offside. And when Czibor shot Turek made another marvellous save.

Hungary, tired in body and spirit by their battles with the South Americans, may have been the moral victors, but Germany's success was none the less a memorable one.

POOL I

Yugoslavia 1, *France* 0 (1–0). *Lausanne*

Yugoslavia: Beara; Stankovic, Crnkovic; Cjaicowski I (capt.), Horvat, Boskov; Milutinovic, Mitic, Vukas, Bobek, Zebec.
France: Remetter; Gianessi, Kaelbel; Penverne, Jonquet (capt.), Marcel; Kopa, Glovacki, Strappe, Dereuddre, Vincent.
Scorer: Milutinovic for Yugoslavia.

Brazil 5, *Mexico* 0 (4–0). *Geneva*

Brazil: Castilho; Santos, D., Santos, N.; Brandaozinho, Pinheiro (capt.), Bauer; Julinho, Didi, Baltazar, Pinga, Rodriguez.
Mexico: Mota; Lopez, Gomez; Cardenas, Romo, Avalos; Torres, Naranjo (capt.), Lamadrid, Balcazar, Arellano.
Scorers: Baltazar, Didi, Pinga (2), Julinho for Brazil.

France 3, *Mexico* 2 (1–0). *Geneva*

France: Remetter; Gianessi, Marche (capt.); Marcel, Kaelbel, Mahjoub; Kopa, Dereuddre, Strappe, Ben Tifour, Vincent.
Mexico: Carbajal; Lopez, Romo; Cardenas, Avalos, Martinez; Torres, Naranjo (capt.), Lamadrid, Balcazar, Arellano.

Scorers: Vincent, Cardenas (own goal), Kopa (penalty) for France, Naranjo, Balcazar for Mexico.

Brazil 1, *Yugoslavia* 1 (0–0) (1–1) after extra time. *Lausanne*

Brazil: Castilho; Santos, D., Santos, N.; Brandaozinho, Pinheiro (capt.), Bauer; Julinho, Didi, Baltazar, Pinga, Rodriguez.
Yugoslavia: Beara; Stankovic, Crnkovic; Cjaicowski I (capt.), Horvat, Boskov; Milutinovic, Mitic, Zebec, Vukas, Dvornic.
Scorers: Zebec for Yugoslavia, Didi for Brazil.

POOL II

Hungary 9, *Korea* 0 (4–0). *Zürich*

Hungary: Grosics; Buzansky, Lantos; Boszik, Lorant, Szojka; Budai, Kocsis, Palotas, Puskas (capt.), Czibor.
Korea: Hong; Park, K., Kang; Min (capt.), Park, Y., Chu; Chung, Park, I., Sung, Woo, Choi.
Scorers: Czibor, Kocsis (3), Puskas (2), Lantos, Palotas (2) for Hungary.

Germany 4, *Turkey* 1 (1–1). *Berne*

Germany: Turek; Laband, Kohlmeyer; Eckel, Posipal, Mai; Klodt, Morlock, Walter, O., Walter, F. (capt.), Schaefer.
Turkey: Turgay (capt.); Ridvan, Basti; Mustafa, Cetin, Rober; Erol, Suat, Feridun, Burhan, Lefter.
Scorers: Suat for Turkey, Klodt, Morlock, Schaefer, Walter for Germany.

Hungary 8, *Germany* 3 (3–1). *Basel*

Hungary: Grosics; Buzansky, Lantos; Boszik, Lorant, Zakarias; Toth, J., Kocsis, Hidegkuti, Puskas (capt.), Czibor.
Germany: Kwiatowski; Bauer, Kohlmeyer; Posipal, Liebrich, Mebus; Rahn, Eckel, Walter, F. (capt.), Pfaff, Herrmann.
Scorers: Hidegkuti (2), Kocsis (4), Puskas, Toth for Hungary, Pfaff, Herrmann, Rahn for Germany.

Turkey 7, *Korea* 0 (4–0). *Geneva*

Turkey: Turgay (capt.); Ridvan Basri; Mustafa, Cetin, Rober; Erol, Suat, Necmettin, Lefter, Burhan.
Korea: Hong; Park, K. (capt.) Kang; Han, Lee, C. K., Kim; Choi, Lee, S., Lee, G. C., Woo, Chung.
Scorers: Burhan (3), Erol, Lefter, Suat (2) for Turkey.

PLAY-OFF

Germany 7, *Turkey* 2 (3–1), *Zürich*

Germany: Turek; Laband, Bauer; Eckel, Posipal, Mai; Klodt, Morlock, Walter, O., Walter, F. (capt.), Schaefer.

Turkey: Sukru; Ridvan, Basri; Mehmet, Cetin (capt.), Rober; Erol, Mustafa, Necmettin, Soskun, Lefter.
Scorers: Morlock (3), Walter, O., Schaefer (2), Walter, F. for Germany, Mustafa, Lefter for Turkey.

POOL III

Austria 1, *Scotland* 0 (1–0). *Zürich*
Austria: Schmied; Hanappi, Barschandt; Ocwirk (capt.), Happel, Koller; Koerner, R., Schleger, Dienst, Probst, Koerner, A.
Scotland: Martin; Cunningham (capt.), Aird; Docherty, Davidson, Cowie; McKenzie, Fernie, Mochan, Brown, Ormond.
Scorer: Probst for Austria.

Uruguay 2, *Czechoslovakia* 0 (0–0). *Berne*
Uruguay: Maspoli; Santamaria, Martinez; Andrade, Varela (capt.), Cruz; Abbadie, Ambroid, Miguez, Schiaffino, Borges.
Czechoslovakia: Reiman; Safranek, Novak (capt.); Trnka, Hledik, Hertl; Hlavacek, Hemele, Kacani, Pazicky, Krauss.
Scorers: Miguez, Schiaffino for Uruguay.

Austria 5, *Czechoslovakia* 0 (4–0). *Zürich*
Austria: Schmied; Hanappi, Barschandt; Ocwirk (capt.), Happel, Koller; Koerner, R., Wagner, Stojaspal, Probst, Koerner, A.
Czechoslovakia: Stacho; Safranek, Novak (capt.); Trnka, Pluskal, Hertl; Hlavacek, Hemele, Kacani, Pazicky, Krauss.
Scorers: Stojaspal (2), Probst (3) for Austria.

Uruguay 7, *Scotland* 0 (2–0). *Basel*
Uruguay: Maspoli; Santamaria, Martinez; Andrade, Varela (capt.), Cruz; Abbadie, Ambrois, Miguez, Schiaffino, Borges.
Scotland: Martin; Cunningham (capt.). Aird; Docherty, Davidson, Cowie; McKenzie, Fernie, Mochan, Brown, Ormond.
Scorers: Borges (3), Miguez (2), Abbadie (2) for Uruguay.

POOL IV

England 4, *Belgium* 4 (2–1) (3–3) after extra time. *Basel*
England: Merrick; Staniforth, Byrne; Wright (capt.), Owen, Dickinson; Matthews, Broadis, Lofthouse, Taylor, Finney.
Belgium: Gerneay; Dries (capt.), Van Brandt; Huysmans, Carré, Mees; Mermans, Houf, Coppens, Anoul, Van den Bosch (P.).
Scorers: Anoul (2), Coppens, Dickinson (own goal) for Belgium, Broadis (2), Lofthouse (2) for England.

England 2, *Switzerland* 0 (1–0). *Berne*
England: Merrick; Staniforth, Byrne; McGarry, Wright (capt.), Dickinson; Finney, Broadis, Wilshaw, Taylor, Mullen.
Switzerland: Parlier; Neury, Kernen; Eggimann, Bocquet (capt.),

Bigler; Antenen, Vonlanthen, Meier, Ballaman, Fatton.
Scorers: Mullen, Wilshaw for England.

Switzerland 2, *Italy* 1 (1–1). *Lausanne*
Switzerland: Parlier; Neury, Kernen; Flueckiger, Bocquet (capt.), Casali; Ballaman, Vonlanthen, Hugi, Meier, Fatton.

Italy: Ghezzi; Vincenzi, Giacomazzi; Neri, Tognon, Nesti; Muccinell Boniperti (capt.), Galli, Pandolfini, Lorenzi.
Scorers: Ballaman, Hugi for Switzerland, Boniperti for Italy.

Italy 4, *Belgium* 1 (1–0). *Lugano*
Italy: Ghezzi; Magnini, Giacomazzi (capt.); Neri, Tognon, Nesti; Frignani, Cappello, Galli, Pandolfini, Lorenzi.
Belgium: Gernaey; Dries (capt.), Van Brandt; Huysmans, Carré, Mees; Mermans, Van den Bosch, H., Coppens, Anoul, Van den Bosch, P.
Scorers: Pandolfini (penalty), Galli, Frignani, Lorenzi for Italy, Anoul for Belgium.

PLAY-OFF

Switzerland 4, *Italy* 1 (1–0). *Basel*
Switzerland: Parlier; Neury, Kernan; Eggimann, Bocquet (capt.), Casali; Antenen, Vonlanthen, Hugi, Ballaman, Fatton.
Italy: Viola; Vincenzi, Giacomazzi (capt.), Neri, Tognon, Nesti; Muccinelli, Pandolfini, Lorenzi, Segato, Frignani.
Scorers: Hugi (2), Ballaman, Fatton for Switzerland, Nesti for Italy.

PLACINGS

POOL I

	P	W	D	L	Goals F	Goals A	Pts.
Brazil	2	1	1	0	6	1	3
Yugoslavia	2	1	1	0	2	1	3
France	2	1	0	1	3	3	2
Mexico	2	0	0	2	2	8	0

POOL II

	P	W	D	L	Goals F	Goals A	Pts.
Hungary	2	2	0	0	17	3	4
Germany	2	1	0	1	7	9	2
Turkey	2	1	0	1	8	4	2
Korea	2	0	0	2	0	16	0

POOL III

	P	W	D	L	Goals F	Goals A	Pts.
Uruguay	2	2	0	0	9	0	4
Austria	2	2	0	0	6	0	4
Czechoslovakia	2	0	0	2	0	7	0
Scotland	2	0	0	2	0	8	0

Pool IV

England	2	1	1	0	6	4	3
Italy	2	1	0	1	5	3	2
Switzerland	2	1	0	1	2	3	1
Belgium	2	0	1	1	5	8	2

QUARTER-FINALS

Germany 2, *Yugoslovia* 0 (1–0). *Geneva*
Germany: Turek; Laband, Kohlmeyer; Eckel, Liebrich, Mai; Rahn, Morlock, Walter, O., Walter, F. (capt.), Schaefer.
Yugoslavia: Beara; Stankovic, Crnkovic; Cjaicowski I, Horvat, Boskov; Milutinovic, Mitic (capt.), Vukas, Bobek, Zebec.
Scorers: Horvat (own goal), Rahn for Germany.

Hungary 4, *Brazil* 2 (2–1). *Berne*
Hungary: Grosics; Buzansky, Lantos; Boszik (capt.), Lorant, Zakarias; Toth, M., Kocsis, Hidegkuti, Czibor, Toth, J.

Brazil: Castilho; Santos, D., Santos, N.; Brandaozinho, Pinheiro (capt.), Bauer; Julinho, Didi, Indio, Tozzi, Maurinho.
Scorers: Hidegkuti (2), Kocsis, Lantos (penalty) for Hungary, Santos, D. (penalty), Julinho for Brazil.

Austria 7, *Switzerland* 5 (2–4). *Lausanne*
Austria: Schmied; Hanappi, Barschandt; Ocwirk (capt.), Happel, Koller; Koerner, R., Wagner, Stojaspal, Probst, Koerner, A.
Switzerland: Parlier; Neury, Kernen, Eggimann, Bocquet (capt.), Casali; Antenen, Vonlanthen, Hugi, Ballaman, Fatton.
Scorers: Ballaman (2), Hugi (2), Hannappi (own goal) for Switzerland, Koerner, A. (2), Ocwirk, Wagner (3), Probst for Austria.

Uruguay 4, *England* 2 (2–1). *Basel*
Uruguay: Maspoli; Santamaria, Martinez; Andrade, Varela (capt.), Cruz; Abbadie, Ambrois, Miguez, Schiaffino, Borges.
England: Merrick; Staniforth, Byrne; McGarry, Wright (capt.), Dickinson; Matthews, Broadis, Lofthouse, Wilshaw, Finney.
Scorers: Borges, Varela, Schiaffino, Ambrois for Uruguay, Lofthouse, Finney for England.

SEMI-FINALS

Germany 6, *Austria* 1 (1–0). *Basel*
Germany: Turek; Posipal, Kohlmeyer; Eckel, Liebrich, Mai; Rahn, Morlock, Walter, O., Walter, F. (capt.), Schaefer.

Austria: Zeman; Hanappi, Schleger; Ocwirk (capt.), Happel, Koller; Koerner, R., Wagner, Stojaspal, Probst, Koerner, A.
Scorers: Schaefer, Morlock, Walter, F. (2 penalties), Walter. O, (2) for Germany, Probst for Austria.

Hungary 4, *Uruguay* 2 (1–0) (2–2) after extra time. *Lausanne*
Hungary: Grosics; Buzansky, Lantos; Boszik (capt.), Lorant, Zakarias; Budai, Kocsis, Palotas, Hidegkuti, Czibor.

Uruguay: Maspoli; Santamaria, Martinez; Andrade (capt.), Carballo, Cruz; Souto, Ambrois, Schiaffino, Hohberg, Borges.
Scorers: Czibor, Hidegkuti, Kocsis (2) for Hungary, Hohberg (2) for Uruguay.

THIRD PLACE MATCH *Zürich*

Austria 3, *Uruguay* 1 (1–1)
Austria: Schmied; Hanappi, Barschandt; Ocwirk (capt.), Kollmann, Koller; Koerner, R., Wagner, Dienst, Stojaspal, Probst.
Uruguay: Mospoli; Santamaria, Martinez; Andrade (capt.), Carballo, Cruz; Abbadie, Hohberg, Mendez, Schiaffino, Borges.
Scorers: Stojaspal (penalty), Cruz (own goal), Ocwirk for Austria, Hohberg for Uruguay.

FINAL *Berne*

Germany 3, *Hungary* 2 (2–2)
Germany: Turek; Posipal, Kohlmeyer; Eckel, Liebrich, Mai; Rahn, Morlock, Walter, O., Walter, F., Schaefer.
Hungary: Grosics; Buzansky, Lantos; Boszik, Lorant, Zakarias; Czibor, Kocsis, Hidegkuti, Puskas, Toth, J.
Scorers: Puskas, Czibor for Hungary, Morlock, Rahn (2) for Germany.
Leading Scorer: Kocsis (Hungary) 11.

WORLD CUP 1958 – Sweden

At long last, after the disappointment of 1950, and the violent elimination of 1954, Brazil carried off the World Cup in spectacular fashion, with a performance, in the Final against Sweden, which rivalled the greatest ever seen. There, on the rain-soaked stadium of Rasunda, the Brazilian forwards juggled, gyrated and, above all, finished with marvellous, gymnastic skill. There, Garrincha, the outside-right, and Pelé, the 17-year-old inside-left, together with the incomparable Didi, wrote themselves indelibly into the history of the game.

It was a World Cup which began greyly, and built up to an ultimate crescendo; a World Cup heavy with nostalgia, thanks to the return of Sweden's stars. Professionals now, the Swedes could recall Nacka

Skoglund, a hero of their 1950 World Cup team – and Nils Liedholm and Gunnar Gren, from their great 1948 Olympic team. They could also bring back from Italy Julli Gustavsson, their splendid centre-half, and Kurt Hamrin, a dazzling little outside-right. To begin with, their supporters were pessimistic, but as round succeeded round and George Raynor's elderly team marched on to the Final, nationalist feeling mounted alarmingly, culminating in the Gothenburg semi-final.

Brazil had toured Europe in 1956 without much success, but they had learned from their tour. Now they brought with them the 4–2–4 formation which was soon to sweep the world. Four defenders in line, two pivotal players in midfield, four forwards up to strike. They were established, if a little precariously, as the favourites.

England's chances had been gravely affected by the tragic air disaster at Munich, in which their Manchester United stars, Tommy Taylor, Roger Byrne and the mighty Duncan Edwards, had perished.

The Russians, included with England, Brazil and Austria in quite the most powerful qualifying group of all (this time, all three teams would play one another), had just drawn 1–1 with England in Moscow. This was their first World Cup, but they had won the Olympic tournament in Australia two years before, while in Lev Yachin they had one of the finest goalkeepers in the game.

Italy and Uruguay were out; Uruguay thrashed 5–0 in Asuncion by Paraguay, Italy eliminated by brave little Northern Ireland. The Irish, brilliantly captained by their elegant right-half Danny Blanchflower, generalled in attack by Jimmy McIlroy, were the surprise of the eliminators. After a black game of violence in Belfast, when the referee, Hungary's Zsolt, was fog bound, and the World Cup game was turned into a friendly, Chiappella of Italy was sent off and the crowd swarmed on to the pitch. The rematch saw Ireland victorious 2–1. But the Munich crash deprived them of Jackie Blanchflower, a key man at centre-half.

Wales was there on the most fragile grounds. Already eliminated, they were given a second chance when FIFA decided Israel could not qualify by forfeit alone after Uruguay had refused to come back into the competition. So Wales had the fairly easy task of eliminating Israel, which they did surprisingly well.

Scotland, who had eliminated Spain, were in mediocre form, and had been humiliated by England in Glasgow 4–0. Germany, the holders, captained again by Fritz Walter, had the burly Helmut Rahn on the right wing, but had turned Hans Schaefer into an inside-forward. A new star was the powerful, ruthless wing-half, Horst Szymaniak. Clearly they would take some beating.

Sweden opened the tournament on June 8 in Stockholm, with an easy 3–0 win over Mexico. Two of the goals were scored by their strong, fair-haired centre-forward, Ange Simonsson. Nils Liedholm got the other goal from a penalty. Bror Mellberg, a 1950 World Cup man, played at inside-right.

In the same group, Hungary, shorn of Puskas, Kocsis and Czibor, who had stayed in the West after the 1956 Revolution, were held to a

1–1 draw by Wales. Jack Kelsey, Wales' calm, strong goalkeeper, a hero of the tournament, was dazzled by the sun when Boszik scored after four minutes, but the massive John Charles, recalled from Italy, headed the equaliser from a corner.

In Gothenburg, England and Russia had an exciting battle in which England rallied for a somewhat lucky draw. The power of Voinov and Tsarev (left-half and captain Igor Netto was injured) plus the skill of Salnikov, in midfield, the goalkeeping of Yachin and the domination of Krijevski, enabled Russia to take a 2–0 lead. But Kevan headed in a free kick and at last Tom Finney, injured in a ruthless tackle and destined to take no further part in the competition, equalised with a penalty.

The Brazilians accounted for Austria 3–0 in Boras, but their team was still in the melting-pot. Pelé, canvassed as their *wunderkind*, was injured, and some wanted the unorthodox Garrincha on the right wing. Team manager Feola himself preferred Vavà to Mazzola at centre-forward, despite the fact that Mazzola (real name José Altafini) scored two of the three goals.

In Group I, the brave Irish at once showed their quality by defeating the Czechs 1–0 at Halmstad, tough little Wilbur Cush, their versatile inside-right, getting the goal. Harry Gregg had a fine game in goal, but the absence of Jackie Blanchflower forced his brother, Danny, much deeper into defence.

At Malmö, Germany were too strong and efficient for an Argentine side which, having brilliantly won the South American Championship the previous year, at once lost its chief stars to Italy. Their style looked old-fashioned, and they had no answer to Rahn, who added two more to his tally of World Cup goals.

No one had expected anything from the French, yet here they were in Norrköping, thrashing Paraguay 7–3, their inside-forward trio of Fontaine (who had expected to be a reserve), Kopa, back from Real Madrid and playing deep, and Piantoni doing remarkable things. Three of the goals were from Kopa. In fact the weeks in training camp at Kopparberg, under Paul Nicolas, had transformed the French morale.

Scotland, meanwhile, undeterred by the fact that Yugoslavia had recently beaten England 5–0, held them to a 1–1 draw at Vasteras. Stamina and determination saved the game after an anxious first half and a seven-minute goal by Petakovic. At right-half, the 35-year-old Eddie Turnbull was in splendid form for the Scots.

The second "round" was full of surprises. In Gothenburg, an English defence cleverly organised to the prescription of Bill Nicholson, the team coach, held up Brazil's forwards. Howe, the right-back, played in the middle, Clamp, the right half, on the flank, while Slater marked Didì out of the game. Brazil were rather lucky not to give away a penalty in the second half when Bellini felled Kevan, but England, on the other hand, owed much to the cool elegance in goal of Colin McDonald of Burnley. There was no score.

At Boras, Russia, too, accounted for an ageing Austria.

In Group I, Ireland had a shock from the Argentinians, who brought back 40-year-old Angel Labruna at inside-left, and gave them a casual lesson in the skills of the game, to beat them 3–1. The stars were Labruna and another veteran, the roving centre-half Nestor Rossi.

Germany, two down, rallied to draw with the Czechs, both goals going to the rejuvenated Helmut Rahn, who'd been written off between the two World Cups.

Yugoslavia, who had Branko Zebec, their Rest of Europe left-winger, at centre-half, surprised France to win with a breakaway goal three minutes from time. At Norrköping, a tired-looking Scottish team went down to Paraguay, inspired by Silvio Parodi, from inside-forward. Bobby Evans, the red-haired Celtic centre-half, laboured in vain against a thrustful Paraguayan attack.

Wales, feeble in attack, were held to a draw by Mexico, in Stockholm, and the following day, again at Rasunda, the Swedes rather unconvincingly beat Hungary. Hungary, with Boszik of all people at deep centre-forward, were laboured in attack, with only the ferocious shooting of Tichy to keep them in the game. Did Tichy score in the fifty-fifth minute with a shot that beat Svensson and hit the underside of the bar? The referee thought not, and half a minute later Hamrin's lob was deflected past Grosics to make it 2–0. Tichy's goal, when it did come, was irrelevant.

The shock of the final round was Czechoslovakia's 6–1 crushing of Argentina at Halsingborg, the sequel to which was a bombardment of rubbish for the Argentine players when they got back to Buenos Aires airport. The Czechs were altogether too fast, with Borovicka and Molnar unstoppable.

Ireland and Germany drew 2–2 in one of the best matches of the competition, with Gregg superb in goal, and Rahn having a superb first half but fading in the second. Peter McParland, Ireland's tough outside-left, twice gave them the lead, but Uwe Seeler, a new young star at centre-forward, equalised 11 minutes from time; so Ireland had to play off against the Czechs.

England, in Boras, stubbornly unchanged by their manager, Walter Winterbottom, toiled to a mediocre draw with Austria, so they too had to replay. Haynes, the general, and Douglas, on the right wing, were plainly exhausted after the effort they had made to drag their respective clubs out of Division II; Kevan remained a blunt instrument; Finney was still injured. In Gothenburg, meanwhile, Brazil, at the plea of their own players, at last gave a chance to Garrincha, who mesmerised the Russian defence. Pelé had his first game, and the clever Zito replaced Dino as linking right-half. Russia used Netto to shadow Didì, but Didì was the dominant player of the match. Vavà, replacing Mazzola at centre-forward, scored in the 3rd and 77th minutes, but the 2–0 score flattered Russia. Brazil had found their team, and their form.

In Group II, France just got home against a Scottish team well served by Bill Brown, making his début in goal, while Paraguay held the Yugoslavs to a draw. Sweden, fielding five reserves, were satisfied with a goalless draw with Wales, who thus had to meet Hungary (easy conquerors of Mexico) in the play-off.

This they bravely and surprisingly won 2–1 with John Charles back in defence. Tichy opened the score; Ivor Allchurch equalised with a superb forty-yard volley, and, five minutes later, Terry Medwin intercepted Grosics' short goal kick to win the game. Sipos was sent off for kicking Hewitt, and Wales hung on to win and to qualify. A famous victory.

Equally famous was Ireland's defeat of the Czechs. Peter Doherty, once a great Irish inside-forward, now an inspirational team manager, had expressed his confidence that what they had done once, they could do again; and so they did. Injuries to Uprichard, in goal, and to Bertie Peacock did not hold them back. A goal down and forced to play half an hour's extra time, they won in the 100th minute, when McParland converted Blanchflower's free kick. Again, the winger scored both goals.

England, at last making changes, throwing Peter Broadbent and Peter Brabrook in the deep end, unluckily went down to Russia in Gothenburg. Twice Brabrook hit the post, but when Russia's Ilyin hit the post, the ball went in. England were eliminated.

In the quarter-finals, the weary, depleted Irish went down 4–0 to France at Nörrkoping, Casey playing despite just having had four stitches in his shin and Gregg keeping goal on one leg. But theirs had been a glorious achievement.

Wales too went out, defending superbly against Brazil, but falling at last to a goal by Pelé, deflected past the splendid Kelsey by the equally splendid Williams. John Charles was unfit to play, but his brother, Mel, was a superb centre-half and Hopkins cleverly contained Garrincha.

Sweden, with Hamrin irresistible, knocked out the Russians. The little winger headed the first goal, and made the second for Simonsson. Finally, a ruthless German team knocked out the Yugoslavs in Malmö with Rahn, inevitably getting the goal. As in Switzerland, four years earlier, the Slavs dominated the game, but just could not score.

In the semi-finals, France's luck deserted them. For 37 minutes, at the Rasunda, they held Brazil, but with the score 1–1, Jonquet, their elegant centre-half, was hurt, and that was that. Didi's thirty-yard swerver gave Brazil the lead, and Pelé, at last showing his quality, got three more in the second half.

In Gothenburg, a chanting, nationalistic crowd mustered by official cheer leaders, was urging Sweden on to victory against the Germans. It was rather an unsatisfactory match in many ways. Schaefer brilliantly volleyed Germany into the lead – but Sweden equalised after Liedholm had handled with impunity. In the second half, the game turned on Juskowiak's flash of temper. He kicked Hamrin, was sent off, and the way was clear for Gren, nine minutes from time, and Hamrin himself – a wonderfully impertinent, dribbling goal – to take Sweden into the Final.

France thrashed Germany 6–3 on that same ground, in the third-place match, four of the goals going to the rampant Fontaine, brilliantly combining with Kopa. This was one of the finest partnerships the World Cup has seen, giving Fontaine a new scoring record for the competition.

It rained in Stockholm on the day of the Final, but the crowd, its cheer leaders now properly banned, was quiet, and even Liedholm's fine, early goal, as he picked his way through the Brazilian penalty area, did not decide the game. The Brazilians, scornful of George Raynor's forecast that if they gave away an early goal, "they'd panic all over the show," stubbornly held on. Six minutes later, Garrincha, with marvellous swerve and acceleration, left Axbom and Parling standing, and made the equaliser for Vavà. Pelé hit a post; Zagalo, always ready to drop deep, cleared from under his own bar; but it was clear that the two full-backs Santos (with Djalma playing his first game of the tournament) had the measure of Sweden's little wingers.

After thirty-two minutes Garrincha repeated his astonishing *tour de force*, and Vavà scored again. In the second half, he gave way to the incredible Pelé, who coolly juggled the ball to smash in a third. Zito and Didì were immaculate now in midfield, while Zagalo had sandwiched a goal of his own between Pelé's and the Swedes' second, making it 4–2. Then came the final goal, a brilliant header from Pelé, with the Brazilian fans shouting, "*Samba, samba*!" It had been a dazzling exhibition of the arts of the game, and victory, at last, for the team which morally deserved it.

POOL I

Germany 3, *Argentina* 1 (2–1). *Malmö*
Germany: Herkenrath; Stollenwerk, Juskowiak; Eckel, Erhardt, Szymaniak; Rahn, Walter, Seeler, Schmidt, Schaefer.
Argentina: Carrizo; Lombardo, Vairo; Rossi, Dellacha, Varacka; Corbatta, Prado, Menendez, Rojas, Cruz.
Scorers: Rahn (2), Schmidt for Germany, Corbatta for Argentina.

Ireland 1, *Czechoslovakia* 0 (1–0). *Halmstad*
Ireland: Gregg; Keith, McMichael; Blanchflower, Cunningham, Peacock; Bingham, Cush, Dougan, McIlroy, McParland.
Czechoslovakia: Dolejsi; Marz, Novak; Pluskal, Cadek, Masopust; Hovorka, Dvorak, Borovicka, Hartl, Kraus.
Scorer: Cush for Ireland.

Germany 2, *Czechoslovakia* 2 (1–0). *Halsingborg*
Germany: Herkenrath; Stollenwerk, Juskowiak; Schnellinger, Erhardt, Szymaniak; Rahn, Walter, Seeler, Schaefer, Klodt.
Czechoslovakia: Dolejsi; Mraz, Novak; Pluskal, Popluhar, Masopust; Hovorka, Dvorak, Molnar, Feureisl, Zikan.

Scorers: Rahn (2) for Germany, Dvorak (penalty), Zikan for Czechoslovakia.

Argentina 3, *Ireland* 1 (1–1). *Ha msta*
Argentina: Carrizo; Lombardo, Vario; Rossi, Dellacha, Varacka; Corbatta, Avio, Menendez, Labruna, Boggio.
Ireland: Gregg; Keith, McMichael; Blanchflower, Cunningham, Peacock; Bingham, Cush, Casey, McIlroy, McParland.
Scorers: Corbatta (2) (one penalty), Menendez for Argentina, McParland for Ireland.

Germany 2, *Ireland* 2 (1–1). *Malmö*
Germany: Herkenrath; Stollenwerk, Juskowiak; Eckel, Erhardt, Szymaniak; Rahn, Walter, Seeler, Schaefer, Klodt.
Ireland: Gregg; Keith, McMichael; Blanchflower, Cunningham, Peacock; Bingham, Cush, Casey, McIlroy, McParland.
Scorers: Rahn, Seeler for Germany, McParland (2) for Ireland.

Czechoslovakia 6, *Argentina* 1 (3–1). *Halsingborg*
Czechoslovakia: Dolejsi; Mraz, Novak; Dvorak, Popluhar, Masopust; Hovorka, Borovicka, Molnar, Feureisl, Zikan.
Argentina: Carrizo; Lombardo, Vario; Rossi, Dellacha, Varacka; Corbatta, Avio, Menendez, Labruna, Cruz.
Scorers: Dvorak, Zikan (2), Feureisl, Hovorka (2) for Czechoslovakia, Corbatta for Argentina.

Qualifying Match

Ireland 2, *Czechoslovakia* 1 (1–1) after extra time. *Malmö*
Ireland: Uprichard; Keith, McMichael; Blanchflower, Cunningham, Peacock; Bingham, Cush, Scott, McIlroy, McParland.
Czechoslovakia: Dolejsi; Mraz, Novak; Bubernik, Popluhar, Masopust; Dvorak, Borovicka, Feureisl, Molnar, Zikan.
Scorers: McParland (2) for Ireland, Zikan for Czechoslovakia.

POOL II

France 7, *Paraguay* 3 (2–2). *Norrköping*
France: Remetter; Kaelbel, Lerond; Penverne, Jonquet, Marcel; Wisnieski, Fontaine, Kopa. Piantoni, Vincent.
Paraguay: Mayeregger; Arevalo, Miranda; Achucarro, Lezcano, Villalba; Aguero, Parodi, Romero, Re, Amarilla.
Scorers: Fontaine (3), Piantoni, Wisnieski, Kopa, Vincent for France, Amarilla (2) (1 penalty), Romero for Paraguay.

Yugoslavia 1, *Scotland* 1 (1–0). *Vasteras*
Yugoslavia: Beara; Sijakovic, Crnkovic; Krstic, Zebec, Boskov; Petakovic, Veselinovic, Milutinovic, Sekularac, Rajkov.
Scotland: Younger; Caldow, Hewie; Turnbull, Evans, Cowie; Leggat, Murray, Mudie, Collins, Imlach.

Scorers: Petakovic for Yugoslavia, Murray for Scotland.

Yugoslavia 3, *France* 2 (1–1). *Vasteras*
Yugoslavia: Beara; Tomic, Crnkovic; Krstic, Zebec, Boskov; Petakovic, Veselinovic, Milutinovic, Sekularac, Rajkov.
France: Remetter; Kaelbel, Marche; Penverne, Jonquet, Lerond; Wisnieski, Fontaine, Kopa, Piantoni, Vincent.
Scorers: Petakovic, Veselinovic (2) for Yugoslavia, Fontaine (2) for France.

Paraguay 3, *Scotland* 2 (2–1). *Norrköping*
Paraguay: Aguilar; Arevalo, Enhague; Achucarro, Lezcano, Villalba; Aguero, Parodi, Romero, Re, Amarilla.
Scotland: Younger; Parker, Caldow; Turnbull, Evans, Cowie; Leggat, Collins, Mudie, Robertson, Fernie.
Scorers: Aguero, Re, Parodi for Paraguay, Mudie, Collins for Scotland.

France 2, *Scotland* 1 (2–0). *Cerebro*
France: Abbes; Kaelbel, Lerond; Penverne, Jonquet, Marcel; Wisnieski, Fontaine, Kopa, Piantoni, Vincent.
Scotland: Brown; Caldow, Hewie; Turnbull, Evans, Mackay; Collins, Murray, Mudie, Baird, Imlach.
Scorers: Kopa, Fontaine for France, Baird for Scotland.

Yugoslavia 3, *Paraguay* 3 (2–1). *Ekilstuna*
Yugoslavia: Beara; Tomic, Crnkovic; Boskov, Zebec, Kristic; Petakovic, Veselinovic, Ognjanovic, Sekularac, Rajkov.
Paraguay: Aguilar; Arevalo, Echague; Villalba, Lezcano, Achucarro; Aguero, Parodi, Romero, Re, Amarilla.
Scorers: Ognjanovic, Veselinovic, Rajkov for Yugoslavia, Parodi, Aguero, Romero for Paraguay.

POOL III

Sweden 3, *Mexico* 0 (1–0). *Stockholm*
Sweden: Svensson; Bergmark, Axbom; Liedholm, Gustavsson, Parling; Hamrin, Mellberg, Simonsson, Gren, Skoglund.
Mexico: Carbajal; Del Muro, Gutierrez; Cardenas, Romo, Flores; Hernandez, Reyes, Calderon, Gutierrez, Seema.
Scorers: Simonsson 2, Liedholm (penalty) for Sweden.

Hungary 1, *Wales* 1 (1–1). *Sandviken*
Hungary: Grosics; Matray, Sarosi; Boszik, Sipos, Berendi; Sandor, Tichy, Hidegkuti, Bundzsak, Fenyvesi.
Wales: Kelsey; Williams, Hopkins; Sullivan. Charles, M., Bowen; Webster, Medwin, Charles, J., Allchurch, Jones.
Scorers: Boszik for Hungary, Charles, J., for Wales.

Wales 1, *Mexico* 1 (1–1). *Stockholm*

Wales: Kelsey; Williams, Hopkins; Baker, Charles, M., Bowen; Webster, Medwin, Charles, J., Allchurch, Jones.
Mexico: Carbajal; Del Muro, Gutierrez; Cardenas, Romo, Flores; Belmonte, Reyes, Blanco, Gonzales, Sesma.
Scorers: Allchurch for Wales, Belmonte for Mexico.

Sweden 2, *Hungary* 1 (1–0). *Stockholm*

Sweden: Svensson; Bergmark, Axbom; Liedholm, Gustavsson, Parling; Hamrin, Melberg, Simonsson, Gren, Skoglund.
Hungary: Grosics; Matray, Sarosi; Szojka, Sipos, Berendi; Sandor, Tichy, Boszik, Bundzsak, Fenyvesi.
Scorers: Hamrin 2 for Sweden, Tichv for Hungary.

Sweden 0, *Wales* 0 (0–0). *Stockholm*

Sweden: Svensson; Bergmark, Axbom; Boerjesson, Gustavsson, Parling; Berndtsson, Kaelgren, Lofgren, Skoglund.
Wales: Kelsey; Williams, Hopkins; Sullivan, Charles, M., Bowen; Vernon, Hewitt, Charles J., Allchurch, Jones.

Hungary 4, *Mexico* 0 (1–0). *Sandviken*

Hungary: Ilku; Matray, Sarosi; Boszik, Sipos, Kotasz; Budai, Bencsics, Tichy, Bundzsak, Fenyvesi.
Mexico: Carbajal; Del Muro, Gutierrez; Cardenas, Sepulvedo, Flores; Belmonte, Reyes, Blanco, Gonzales, Sesma.
Scorers: Tichy 2, Sandor, Bencsics for Hungary.

Play-off

Wales 2, *Hungary* 1 (0–1). *Stockholm*

Wales: Kelsey; Williams, Hopkins; Sullivan, Charles, M., Bowen; Medwin, Hewitt, Charles, J., Allchurch, Jones.
Hungary: Grosics; Mattray, Sarosi; Boszik, Sipos, Kotasz; Budai, Bencsics, Tichy, Bundzsak, Fenyvesi.
Scorers: Allchurch, Medwin for Wales, Tichy for Hungary.

POOL IV

England 2, *Russia* 2 (0–1). *Gothenburg*

England: McDonald; Howe, Banks; Clamp, Wright, Slater; Douglas, Robson, Kevan, Haynes, Finney.
Russia: Yachin; Kessarev, Kuznetsov; Voinov, Krijevski, Tsarev; Ivanov, A., Ivanov, V., Simonian, Salnikov, Ilyin.
Scorers: Simonian, Ivanov, A., for Russia, Kevan, Finney (penalty) for England.

Brazil 3, *Austria* 0 (1–0). *Boras*

Brazil: Gilmar; De Sordi, Santos, N.; Dino, Bellini, Orlando; Joel, Dida, Mazzola, Didì, Zagalo.
Austria: Szanwald; Halla, Swoboda; Hanappi, Happel, Koller; Horak, Senekowitsch, Buzek, Koerner, Schleger.
Scorers: Mazzola (2), Santos for Brazil.

England 0, *Brazil* 0 (0–0). *Gothenburg*

England: McDonald; Howe, Banks; Clamp, Wright, Slater; Douglas, Robson, Kevan, Haynes, A'Court.
Brazil: Gilmar; De Sordi, Santos, N.; Dino, Bellini, Orlando; Joel, Didì, Mazzola, Vavà, Zagalo.

Russia 2, *Austria* 0 (1–0). *Boras*

Russia: Yachin; Kessarev, Kuznetsov; Voinov, Krijevski, Tsarev; Ivanov, A., Ivanov, V., Simonian, Salnikov, Ilyin.
Austria: Schmied; Kozlicek, E., Swoboda; Hanappi, Stotz, Koller; Horak, Kozlicek, P., Buzek, Koerner, Senekowitsch.
Scorers: Ilyin, Ivanov, V., for Russia.

Brazil 2, *Russia* 0 (1–0). *Gothenburg*

Brazil: Gilmar; De Sordi, Santos, N.; Zito, Bellini, Orlando; Garrincha, Didì, Vavà, Pelé, Zagalo.
Russia: Yachin; Kessarev, Kuznetsov; Voinov, Krijevski, Tsarev; Ivanov, A., Ivanov, V., Simonian, Netto, Ilyin.
Scorer: Vavà (2) for Brazil.

England 2, *Austria* 2 (0–1). *Boras*

England: McDonald; Howe, Banks; Clamp, Wright, Slater; Douglas, Robson, Kevan, Haynes, A'Court.
Austria: Szanwald; Kollmann, Swoboda; Hanappi, Happel, Koller; Kozlicek, E., Kozlicek, P., Buzek, Koerner, Senekowitsch.
Scorers: Koller, Koerner for Austria, Haynes, Kevan for England.

PLAY OFF

Russia 1, *England* 0 (0–0). *Gothenburg*

Russia: Yachin; Kessarev, Kuznetsov; Voinov, Krijevski, Tsarev; Apoukhtin, Ivanov, V., Simonian, Falin, Ilyin.
England: McDonald; Howe, Banks; Clayton, Wright, Slater; Brabrook, Broadbent, Kevan, Haynes, A'Court.
Scorer: Ilyin for Russia.

PLACINGS

		POOL I				Goals	
	P	W	D	L	F	A	Pts.
Germany	3	1	2	0	7	5	4
Czechoslovakia	3	1	1	1	8	4	3
Ireland	3	1	1	1	4	5	3
Argentina	3	1	0	2	5	10	2
		POOL II					
France	3	2	0	1	11	7	4
Yugoslavia	3	1	2	0	7	6	4
Paraguay	3	1	1	1	9	12	3
Scotland	3	0	1	2	4	6	1
		POOL III					
Sweden	3	2	1	0	5	1	5
Hungary	3	1	1	1	6	3	3
Wales	3	0	3	0	2	2	3
Mexico	3	0	1	2	1	8	1
		POOL IV					
Brazil	3	2	1	0	5	0	5
England	3	0	3	0	4	4	3
Russia	3	1	1	1	4	4	3
Austria	3	0	1	2	2	7	1

QUARTER-FINALS

France 4, *Ireland* 0 (1–0). *Norrköping*
France: Abbes; Kaelbel, Lerond; Penverne, Jonquet, Marcel; Wisnieski, Fontaine, Kopa, Piantoni, Vincent.
Ireland: Gregg; Keith, McMichael; Blanchflower, Cunningham, Cush; Bingham, Casey, Scott, McIlroy, McParland.
Scorers: Wisnieski, Fontaine (2), Piantoni for France.

Germany 1, *Yugoslavia* 0 (1–0). *Malmö*
Germany: Herkenrath; Stollenwerk, Juskowiak; Eckel, Erhardt, Szymaniak; Rahn, Walter, Seeler, Schmidt, Schaefer.
Yugoslavia: Krivocuka; Sijakovic, Crnkovic; Kristic, Zebec, Boskov; Petakovic, Veselinovic, Milutinovic, Ognjanovic, Rajkov.
Scorer: Rahn for Germany.

Sweden 2, *Russia* 0 (0–0). *Stockholm*
Sweden: Svensson; Bergmark, Axbom; Boerjesson, Gustavsson, Parling; Hamrin, Gren, Simonsson, Liedholm, Skoglund.

Russia: Yachin; Kessarev, Kuznetsov; Voinov, Krijevski, Tsarev; Ivanov, A., Ivanov, V., Simonian, Salnikov, Ilyin.
Scorers: Hamrin, Simonsson for Sweden.

Brazil 1, *Wales* 0 (0–0). *Gothenburg*
Brazil: Gilmar; De Sordi, Santos, N.; Zito, Bellini, Orlando; Garrincha, Didì, Mazzola, Pelé, Zagalo.
Wales: Kelsey; Williams, Hopkins; Sullivan, Charles, M., Bowen; Medwin, Hewitt, Webster, Allchurch, Jones.
Scorer: Pelé for Brazil.

SEMI-FINALS

Brazil 5, *France* 2 (2–1). *Stockholm*
Brazil: Gilmar; De Sordi, Santos, N.; Zito, Bellini, Orlando; Garrincha, Didì, Vavà, Pelé, Zagalo.
France: Abbes; Kaelbel, Lerond; Penverne, Jonquet, Marcel; Wisnieski, Fontaine, Kopa, Piantoni, Vincent.
Scorers: Vavà, Didì, Pelé (3) for Brazil, Fontaine, Piantoni for France.

Sweden 3, *Germany* 1 (1–1). *Gothenburg*
Sweden: Svensson; Bergmark, Axbom; Boerjesson, Gustavsson, Parling; Hamrin, Gren, Simonsson, Liedholm, Skoglund.
Germany: Herkenrath; Stollenwerk, Juskowiak; Eckel, Erhardt, Szymaniak; Rahn, Walter, Seeler, Schaefer, Cieslarczyk.
Scorers: Schaefer for Germany, Skoglund, Gren, Hamrin for Sweden.

THIRD PLACE MATCH *Gothenburg*

France 6, *Germany* 3 (0–0)
France: Abbes; Kaelbel, Lerond; Penverne, Lafont, Marcel; Wisnieski, Douis, Kopa, Fontaine, Vincent.
Germany: Kwiatowski; Stollenwerk, Erhardt; Schnellinger, Wewers, Szymaniak; Rahn, Sturm, Kelbassa, Schaefer, Cieslarzcyk.
Scorers: Fontaine (4) Kopa (penalty), Douis for France, Cieslarczyk, Rahn, Schaefer for Germany.

FINAL *Stockholm*

Brazil 5, *Sweden* 2 (2–1)
Brazil: Gilmar; Santos, D., Santos, N.; Zito, Bellini, Orlando; Garrincha, Didì, Vavà, Pelé, Zagalo.
Sweden: Svensson; Bergmark, Axbom; Boerjesson, Gustavsson, Parling; Hamrin, Gren, Simonsson, Liedholm, Skoglund.
Scorers: Liedholm, Simonsson for Sweden, Vavà (2), Pelé (2), Zagalo for Brazil.
Leading Scorer: Fontaine 13 (present record total).

WORLD CUP 1962 – Chile

The selection of Chile as host to the 1962 World Cup was a surprising one, determined largely by sentiment and by the pressures of Chile's representative to FIFA, the late Carlos Dittborn: "We have nothing, that is why we must have the World Cup." Chile had recently suffered a disastrous earthquake, but Dittborn promised all would be ready in time. Argentina, the logical choice, had a poor record in terms of loyalty to the tournament and, in fact, Chile made a good enough job of the organisation, though the insanely high prices kept out an impoverished working class, and there was flagrant profiteering by hotels and agencies.

Once again, the four-pool qualifying system was employed, this time with such disastrous effects (goal average was counted) as to cast doubt not only on the system but on the whole future of the game. Manic defence, eight men in the penalty box, reduced many of the qualifying matches to farce.

Brazil and Russia were the favourites, Russia because, on their recent South American tour, they had beaten Argentina, Uruguay and Chile. Otherwise, the field looked a mediocre one. England had just lost to Scotland in Glasgow for the first time for twenty-five years; Hungary, Argentina and Italy were in decline; Germany as tough as ever, but lacking a Fritz Walter, Chile had the great advantage of playing at home, and the experienced managership of Fernando Riera, but nobody much favoured them.

In their opening match, at the fine new Santiago stadium, they easily beat the Swiss 3–1. Brazil, kicking off at the beautiful little seaside ground at Viña del Mar – also especially constructed – beat Mexico 2–0, but with great difficulty. Their team, rather to the general surprise, showed but two changes from 1958; Mauro (Santos) replacing Bellini as centre-half and captain, and Zozimo coming in for Orlando, now in Argentina. Vavà, back from Spain, displaced Santos' Coutinho at centre-forward, and Zagalo, destined to be used deep in a virtual 4–3–3 formation, had regained his position on the left wing. Pelé, making the first goal for Zagalo, and scoring the second himself, saved a Brazilian team which seemed to be hardening in its arteries.

The following day, the Czechs surprised Helenio Herrera's Spain 1–0, although they were lacking their star finisher, Rudolf Kucera, left at home for a cartilage operation. The great Di Stefano, suffering from a pulled muscle, did not play for Spain at all.

In the Rancagua stadium, Argentina scored the only goal of a tedious, defensive match against the destructive Bulgarians, who had eliminated France. The following day, Hungary, much more relaxed, surprised an uninspired England team, feeble and straightforward in attack. A long-range goal by Tichy, a penalty equaliser by Flowers, then the game was decided by a brilliant individual goal by Florian Albert, the young Hungarian centre-forward. Right-half Solymosi, tall, fair-haired, infinitely relaxed, was perhaps the best player on the field.

Up in the far north, at Arica, Uruguay squeezed home 2–1 against

Colombia. Sanchez played splendidly in goal for the Colombians, who were to spring yet another great surprise.

Next day Russia won a violent game against the Yugoslavs 2–0; nevertheless it was the best game played in the group, and the only one in which Yachin, in goal, justified his mighty reputation. A serious foul by Mujic put Dubinski out of the game, and the tournament, with a broken leg. Both Russian goals in the second half were owed to their powerful centre-forward, Victor Ponedelnik. For the first, Ponedelnik hit the bar with a free kick, and Ivanov beat Soskic to the ball. For the second, four minutes from time and soon after Dubinski's injury, Ponedelnik both began and finished the movement.

Netto, back in the team again as captain, had a fine match, as did Ivanov, while Dragoslav Sekularac showed his immense class for the impassioned Yugoslav side.

In Pool II, Germany and Italy drew goallessly in Santiago. Both teams played with an extra man in defence. The Italians, admirably marshalled by their pivot, Maldini, stood up well to the Germans' physical power but were lucky when Uwe Seeler hit the bar.

The second "round" saw tragedy afflict Brazil. Playing against the Czechs, Pelé severely pulled a muscle, and that was the last of him we saw in the tournament. A left-footed shot against the foot of the post after twenty-five minutes provoked the injury. Both sides closed up in defence; the Czechs, with Schroiff excellent in goal, and Popluhar a strapping centre-half, gave nothing away, and there was not a goal.

Spain, thanks to a goal by Perió of Madrid Athletic, a minute from the end, squeezed home against the gallant Mexicans, for whom the veteran Carbajal was a splendid goalkeeper.

In Rancagua, England found better form, and deservedly beat the Argentinians, Alan Peacock making an excellent début at centre-forward. The tall, slim, blond Sacchi and Marzolini, in Argentine's defence, were their only stars; Sanfilippo's goal came too late to matter.

Hungary thrashed the Bulgars 6–1, with Albert scoring a brilliant hat-trick. The Bulgarians, without their best forwards, Diev and Iliev, looked vulnerable indeed.

Group II, in Santiago, also produced the notorious and distasteful match between Italy and Chile. At the root of the trouble was a couple of foolish, inflammatory articles written by Italian journalists in Chile; the first, and more offensive, was the work of a non sports-writer. Later, the Italians alleged that the Chileans had deliberately used these articles to create an atmosphere hostile to their team. Certainly that atmosphere existed. The Italian players claimed that the Chileans were, from the start, spitting in their faces and insulting them. When Leonel Sanchez, the Chilean left-winger, felled Maschio, Italy's Argentinian inside-forward, with a left hook, Mr. Ken Aston, the English referee, had his back to the incident; his linesmen claimed they had seen nothing, and play went on, with Maschio nursing a broken nose. It was somewhat ironic that the two players eventually sent off in a vicious, brawling travesty of a game should both be Italian; Ferrini for a scything tackle on Landa, and David for allegedly kicking an opponent.

The Italians, who had made wholesale and somewhat ill-advised changes, were thus reduced to nine men, and Chile duly scored in the 75th and 89th minutes through Ramirez and their strong impressive inside-right, Jorge Toro. To this day, the Italians bitterly blame Mr. Aston for their defeat. He himself said the game was literally uncontrollable; the French, neutral parties, felt he was weak, and lacked authority. In the circumstances it would have required the authority of a Hercules.

Germany, meanwhile, beat the Swiss 2–1 in a thoroughly tedious match, during which a ruthless tackle by Szymaniak put Eschmann, Switzerland's inside-left, off with a broken leg. The Germans did not look impressive. In their final qualifying match against Chile, they were an offence to the eye; negative, destructive winners thanks to an early penalty and a late breakaway goal, headed by Seeler. The Chileans, faced by a defence reinforced by Szymaniak, nominally an inside-right, attacked with naïve enthusiasm, but were limited to long drives from outside the box, often by their strong left-half, Eladio Rojas.

Germany thus qualified, with Chile, and Italy's 3–0 win over the Swiss was of mere academic value.

In Viña del Mar, a brave last-ditch rally by Spain, fielding a lively young experimental side, nearly accounted for Brazil. Indeed, it was only two goals late in the game by Pelé's excellent young substitute, Amarildo, which won it for Brazil. Adelardo's 34th-minute goal for Spain stood for nearly 40 minutes. One bright spot for Brazil was the improved form of Garrincha late in the game; form which was to be brilliantly maintained.

As for the Czechs, they went down 3–1 to a Mexican team which was one of the revelations of the tournament, this, despite the fact that Masek put the Czechs ahead in the very first minute. Not a bit perturbed, the Mexicans hit back with three goals, the second of which was scored after a superb individual run by their outside-right, Del Aguila. They had gone out – but with much more honour than in their previous World Cup disappointments.

There were no goals at all in the concluding matches at Rancagua, between Hungary and Argentina, and England and Bulgaria. The latter game was of infinite tedium, Bulgaria massing in defence for no obvious reason – they had already been eliminated – and England growing content with a draw, as the game wore wearily on. This they were rather lucky to get, when Kolev, his side's one star, eluded Armfield near the end, and put across a centre which should surely have been exploited.

Up at Arica, there had been high jinks. Russia, in the second round, had been held to a most unexpected 4–4 draw by the undervalued Colombians. It was a bad day for Yachin, a very good one for the gifted little black Colombian inside-left Klinger. A French critic described the match, in retrospect, as "one of the great surprises of modern football". Russia led 3–0 after a quarter of an hour. With twenty-two minutes left it was 4–1; then the Colombians hit back. Yachin, explicably, let the ball in straight from Coll's corner. Galvanized, Colombia added two goals more; and two fine saves by Yachin prevented others. But the French claim that the match signified "the end of the greatest goalkeeper of modern times" was ridiculed by Yachin's memorable display for FIFA at Wembley in 1963.

The draw with Russia seemed to exhaust Colombia, who crashed 5–0 in their last match, against Yugoslavia. The Slavs, inspired by Sekularac, had ridden a goal by Cabrera to beat Uruguay 3–1. At the end of the match, the sporting Uruguayans carried the little inside-forward off in triumph. He set far too deep a problem for Colombia. As for the Russians, they beat Uruguay 2–1 and were lucky to do so, the Uruguayans being depleted by injury to Eliseo Alvarez. Yet they dominated the second half, hitting the post three times. Ivanov's winning goal came in the last minute.

In the quarter-finals, Brazil, "at home" in Viña del Mar, won a curious match against England, who had to take the field without the injured Peacock. Garrincha was in unstoppable form, his swerve and acceleration as irresistible as in Sweden. After 31 minutes, he showed another talent, getting up splendidly to head in a corner. England should have been two down when Flowers unaccountably passed across his own goal to Amarildo, but Springett saved brilliantly, and Hitchens equalised after Greaves' header came back from the bar.

Alas for Springett, however, he allowed Garrincha's second-half free kick to come back off his chest, for Vavà to score easily, and later he was tricked by Garrincha's clever swerving long shot. Brazil were through, but they had been a little lucky.

In Arica, Chile, whose fans were growing more and more crazily excited, put out Russia. Again, Yachin had a poor game, badly placed for Leonel Sanchez's goal straight from a free kick after ten minutes; still more at fault with Eladio Rojas' 35-yard second. Chislenko replied a couple of minutes later, but the 4–2–4 Chilean team held on to a narrow success.

Surprisingly, the Czechs beat the Hungarians 1–0 in Rancagua. For 80 minutes they were penned in their own half, while Hungary beat a tattoo on their goalposts. Schroiff, in goal, was unbeatable, and Scherer's breakaway goal in the 13th minute won the match. Tichy's "equaliser" was ruled, disputably, offside.

In Santiago, the much more creative Yugoslavs beat Germany 1–0, at last revenging themselves for previous World Cup defeats at the hands of Germany. Radakovic, a head injury bandaged, smashed in Galic's pass four minutes from the end, to win a match which seemed bound for extra time.

In the semi-finals, Garrincha dashed Chile's hopes, with another marvellous display. A magnificent 20-yard left-footer after nine minutes put Brazil ahead; a header from a corner doubled the lead. Toro, with a mighty free kick, made it 2–1, but just after half-time, Vavà headed a vital goal from Garrincha's dropping corner-kick: 3–1. Leonel Sanchez made it 3–2, from a penalty, but Vavà tied up the match, heading in Zagalo's centre. Zagalo had worked with boundless stamina and decisive effect.

In a displeasing finale, Landa, Chile's centre-forward, and Garrincha were in turn sent off the field. Garrincha for kicking Rojas, Landa for a foul on Zito. As he made his way round the track. Garrincha had his head cut by a missile thrown from a frantically partisan crowd.

The Czechs, to everyone's amazement, prevailed again – over the talented Yugoslavs. At Viña del Mar, watched by a mere and miserable 5,000, Schroiff was again the determining player. The Slavs had most of the game but, weak on the wings, could not turn their domination into more than Jerkovic's equalising goal. A breakaway allowed Scherer to give the Czechs the lead again; a silly handling offence by Markovic allowed the same player to decide the match, from the penalty spot.

A tired Yugoslav team, with Sekularac even so the best player on the field, lost 1–0 to Chile in the third place game. Rojas' long shot, deflected, beat an excellent Soskic for the only goal of a dreary match.

In the Final, Brazil once more had to play without Pelé. Playing at a slow, steady rhythm, with Kvasniak tireless and long-legged in midfield, the Czechs cleverly took the lead when Masopust ran on to Scherer's through pass. But alas for the Czechs, this was not to be a good day for Schroiff. He should have stopped Amarildo's equaliser from the narrowest of angles. In the second half, Amarildo whiplashed past his man to make a headed goal, under the bar, for Zito, and, 13 minutes from time, poor Schroiff dropped a high lob into the sun by Djalma Santos, and that was number three. Not a Brazilian victory to be compared with Stockholm; this was an older, more cautious team, without Pelé, with a slower Didì, with Garrincha well controlled by the experienced Czech defence. The Czechs had been distinguished losers. With Kucera, who knows how much better they might have done?

GROUP I *Arica*

Uruguay 2, *Colombia* 1 (0–1)

Uruguay: Sosa; Troche, Em. Alvarez; El. Alvarez, Mendez, Goncalves; Rocha, Perez, Langon, Sasia, Cubilla.
Colombia: Sanchez; Zaluaga, Gonzalez, Lopez, Etcheverri; Silva, Coll; Aceros, Klinger, Gamboa, Arias.
Scorers: Zaluaga for Colombia, Cubilla, Sasia for Uruguay.

Russia 2, *Yugoslavia* 0 (0–0)

Russia: Yachin; Dubinski, Ostrovski; Voronin, Maslenkin, Netto; Metreveli, Ivanov, Ponedelnik, Kanevski, Meschki.

Yugoslavia: Soskic; Durkovic, Jusufi; Matus, Markovic, Popovic; Mujic, Sekularac, Jerkovic, Galic, Skoblar.
Scorers: Ivanov, Ponedelnik for Russia.

Yugoslavia 3, *Uruguay* 1 (2–1)

Yugoslavia: Soskic; Durkovic, Jusufi; Radakovic, Markovic, Popovic; Melic, Sekularac, Jerkovic, Galic, Skoblar.
Uruguay: Sosa; Troche, Em. Alvarez, El. Alvarez, Mendez; Goncalves, Rocha; Cubilla, Cabrera, Sasia, Perez.
Scorers: Cabrera for Uruguay, Skoblar, Galic, Jerkovic for Yugoslavia.

Russia 4, *Colombia* 4 (3–1)

Russia: Yachin; Tchokelli, Ostrovski; Netto, Maslenkin, Voronin; Chislenko, Ivanov, Ponedelnik, Kanevski, Meschki.
Colombia: Sanchez; Gonzalez, L., Lopez, Alzate, Etcheverri; Serrano, Coll; Aceros, Rada, Klinger, Gonzalez, C.
Scorers: Ivanov (2), Chislenko, Ponedelnik for Russia, Aceros, Coll, Rada, Klinger for Colombia.

Russia 2, *Uruguay* 1 (1–0)

Russia: Yachin; Tchokelli, Ostrovski; Netto, Maslenkin, Voronin; Chislenko, Ivanov, Ponedelnik, Mamikin, Hussainov.
Uruguay: Sosa; Troche, El. Alvarez, Em. Alvarez, Mendez; Goncalves, Cortes; Cubilla, Carera, Sasia, Perez.
Scorers: Mamikin, Ivanov for Russia, Sasia for Uruguay.

Yugoslavia 5, *Colombia* 0 (2–0)

Yugoslavia: Soskic; Durkovic, Yusufi; Radakovic, Markovic, Popovic; Ankovic, Sekularac, Jerkovic, Galic, Melic.
Colombia: Sanchez; Alzate, Gonzalez, O., Lopez, Etcheverri; Serrano, Coll; Aceros, Klinger, Rada, Gonzalez, C.
Scorers: Galic, Jerkovic (3), Melic for Yugoslavia.

GROUP II *Santiago*

Chile 3, *Switzerland* 1 (1–1)

Chile: Escuti; Eyzaguirre, Sanchez, R., Contreras, Navarro; Toro, Rojas; Ramirez, Landa, Fouilloux, Sanchez, L.
Switzerland: Elsener; Morf, Schneiter, Tacchella; Grobety, Weber; Allemann, Pottier, Eschmann, Wuthrich, Antenen
Scorers: Wuthrich for Switzerland, Sanchez, L. (2), Ramirez for Chile.

Germany 0, *Italy* 0 (0–0)

Germany: Fahrian; Novak, Schnellinger; Schulz, Erhardt, Szymaniak; Sturm, Haller, Seeler, Brulls, Schaefer.
Italy: Buffon; Losi, Robotti; Salvadore, Maldini, Radice; Ferrini, Rivera, Altafini, Sivori, Menichelli.

Chile 2, *Italy* 0 (0–0)

Chile: Escutti; Eyzaguirre, Contreras, Sanchez, R., Navarro; Toro, Rojas; Ramirez, Landa, Fouilloux, Sanchez, L.
Italy: Mattrel; David, Robotti; Salvadore, Janich, Tumburus; Mora, Maschio, Altafini, Ferrini, Menichelli.
Scorers: Ramirez, Toro for Chile.

Germany 2, *Switzerland* 1 (1–0)
Germany: Fahrian; Novak, Schnellinger; Schulz, Erhardt, Szymaniak; Koslowski, Haller, Seeler, Brulls, Schaefer.
Switzerland: Elsener; Schneiter, Tacchella, Groberty; Wuthrich, Weber; Antenen, Vonlanthen, Allemann, Eschmann, Durr.
Scorers: Brulls, Seeler for Germany, Schneiter for Switzerland.

Germany 2, *Chile* 0 (1–0)
Germany: Fahrian; Novak, Schnellinger; Schulz, Erhardt, Giesemann; Krauss, Szymaniak, Seeler, Schaefer, Brulls.
Chile: Escutti; Eyzaguirre, Contreras, Sanchez, R., Navarro; Tobar, Rojas; Moreno, Landa, Sanchez, L., Ramirez.
Scorers: Szymaniak (penalty), Seeler for Germany.

Italy 3, *Switzerland* 0 (1–0)
Italy: Buffon; Losi, Robotti; Salvadore, Maldini, Radice; Mora, Bulgarelli, Sormani, Sivori, Pascutti.
Switzerland: Elsener; Schneiter, Meier, Tacchella; Grobety, Weber; Antenen, Vonlanthen, Wuthrich, Allemann, Durr.
Scorers: Mora, Bulgarelli (2) for Italy.

GROUP III *Viña del Mar*

Brazil 2, *Mexico* 0 (0–0)
Brazil: Gilmar; Santos, D., Mauro, Zozimo, Santos, N.; Zito, Didi; Garrincha, Vavà, Pelé, Zagalo.
Mexico: Carbajal; Del Muro, Cardenas, Sepulveda, Villegas; Reyes, Najera; Del Aguila, Hernandez, Jasso, Diaz.
Scorers: Zagalo, Pelé for Brazil.

Czechoslovakia 1, *Spain* 0 (0–0)
Czechoslovakia: Schroiff; Lala, Novak; Pluskal, Popluhar, Masopust; Stibranyi, Scherer, Kvasniak, Adamec, Jelinek.

Spain: Carmelo; Rivilla, Reija; Segarra, Santamaria, Garay; Del Sol, Martinez, Puskas, Suarez, Gento.
Scorer: Stibranyi for Czechoslovakia.

Brazil 0, *Czechoslovakia* 0 (0–0)
Brazil: Gilmar; Santos, D., Mauro, Zozimo, Santos, N.; Zito, Didì; Garrincha, Vavà, Pelé, Zagalo.
Czechoslovakia: Schroiff; Lala, Novak; Pluskal, Popluhar, Masopust; Stibranyi, Scherer, Kvasniak, Adamec, Jelinek.

Spain 1, *Mexico* 0 (0–0)
Spain: Carmelo; Rodri, Garcia; Verges, Santamaria, Pachin; Del Sol, Pieró, Puskas, Suarez, Gento.
Mexico: Carbajal; Del Muro, Cardenas, Sepulveda, Jauregui; Reyes, Najera; Del Aguila, Hernandez, H., Jasso, Diaz.
Scorer: Peiró for Spain.

Brazil 2, *Spain* 1 (0–1)
Brazil: Gilmar; Santos, D., Mauro, Zozimo, Santos, N.; Zito, Didì; Garrincha, Vavà, Amarildo, Zagalo.
Spain: Araquistain; Rodri, Gracia; Verges, Echevarria, Pachin; Collar, Adelardo, Puskas, Peiró, Gento.
Scorers: Adelardo for Spain, Armarildo (2) for Brazil.

Mexico 3, *Czechoslovakia* 1 (2–1)
Mexico: Carbajal; Del Muro, Cardenas, Sepulveda, Jauregui; Reyes, Najera; Del Aguila, Hernandez, A., Hernandez, H., Diaz.
Czechoslovakia: Schroiff; Lala, Novak; Pluskal, Popluhar, Masopust; Stibranyi, Scherer, Kvasniak, Adamec, Masek.
Scorers: Masek for Czechoslovakia, Diaz, Del Aguila, Hernandez, H. (penalty) for Mexico.

GROUP IV *Rancagua*

Argentina 1, *Bulgaria* 0 (1–0)
Argentina: Roma; Navarro, Baez, Sainz, Marzolini; Sacchi, Rossi Facundo, Pagani, Sanfilippo, Belen.
Bulgaria: Naidenov; Rakarov, Kotov; Kostov, Dimitrov, Kovatchev Diev, Velitchkov, Iliev, Yakimov, Kolev.
Scorer: Facundo for Argentina.

Hungary 2, *England* 1 (1–0)
Hungary: Grosics; Matrai, Sarosi; Solymosi, Meszoly, Sipos; Sandc Rakosi, Albert, Tichy, Fenyvesi.
England: Springett; Armfield, Wilson; Moore, Norman, Flowei Douglas, Greaves, Hitchens, Haynes, Charlton.

Scorers: Tichy, Albert for Hungary, Flowers (penalty) for England.

England 3, *Argentina* 1 (2–0)
England: Springett; Armfield, Wilson; Moore, Norman, Flowers; Douglas, Greaves, Peacock, Haynes, Charlton.
Argentina: Roma; Capp, Baez, Navarro, Marzolini; Sacchi, Rattin; Oleniak, Sosa, Sanfilippo, Belen.
Scorers: Flowers (penalty), Charlton, Greaves for England, Sanfilippo for Argentina.

Hungary 6, *Bulgaria* 1 (4–0)
Hungary: Ilku; Matrai, Sarosi; Solymosi, Meszoly, Sipos; Sandor, Rakosi, Albert, Tichy, Fenyvesi.

Bulgaria: Naidenov; Rakarov, Kotov; Kostov, Dimitrov, Kovatchev; Sokolov, Velitchkov, Asparoukhov, Kolev, Dermendiev.
Scorers: Albert (3), Tichy (2), Solymosi for Hungary, Sokolov for Bulgaria.

Argentina 0, *Hungary* 0 (0–0)
Argentina: Dominguez; Capp, Sainz, Delgado, Marzolini; Sacchi, Pando; Facundo, Pagani, Oleniak, Gonzales.
Hungary: Grosics; Matra, Sarosi; Solymosi, Meszoly, Sipos; Kuharszki, Gorocs, Monostroi, Tichy, Rakosi.

England 0, *Bulgaria* 0 (0–0)
England: Springett; Armfield, Wilson; Moore, Norman, Flowers; Douglas, Greaves, Peacock, Haynes, Charlton.
Bulgaria: Naidenov; Rakarov, Jetchev; Kostov, D., Dimitrov, Kovatchev; Kostov, A., Velitchkov, Iliev, Kolev, Yakimov.

PLACINGS

GROUP I					Goals		
	P	W	D	L	F	A	Pts.
Russia	3	2	1	0	8	5	5
Yugoslavia	3	2	0	1	8	3	4
Uruguay	3	1	0	2	4	6	2
Colombia	3	0	1	2	5	11	1

GROUP II					Goals		
	P	W	D	L	F	A	Pts.
Germany	3	2	1	0	4	1	5
Chile	3	2	0	1	5	3	4
Italy	3	1	1	1	3	2	3
Switzerland	3	0	0	3	2	8	0

Group III	P	W	D	L	Goals F	A	Pts.
Brazil	3	2	1	0	4	1	5
Czechoslovakia	3	1	1	1	2	3	3
Mexico	3	1	0	2	3	4	2
Spain	3	1	0	2	2	3	2

Group IV	P	W	D	L	Goals F	A	Pts.
Hungary	3	2	1	0	8	2	5
England	3	1	1	1	4	3	3
Argentina	3	1	1	1	2	3	3
Bulgaria	3	0	1	2	1	7	1

QUARTER-FINALS

Yugoslavia 1, *Germany* 0 (0–0). *Santiago*
Yugoslavia: Soskic; Durkovic, Jusufi; Radakovic, Markovic, Popovic; Kovacevic, Sekularac, Jerkovic, Galic, Skoblar.
Germany: Fahrian; Novak, Schnellinger; Schulz, Erhardt, Giesemann; Haller, Szymaniak, Seeler, Brulls, Schaefer.
Scorer: Radakovic for Yugoslavia.

Brazil 3, *England* 1 (1–1). *Viña del Mar*
Brazil: Gilmar; Santos, D., Mauro, Zozimo, Santos, N.; Zito, Didì; Garrincha, Vavà, Amarildo, Zagalo.
England: Springett; Armfield, Wilson; Moore, Norman, Flowers; Douglas, Greaves, Hitchens, Haynes, Charlton.
Scorers: Garrincha (2), Vavà for Brazil, Hitchens for England.

Chile 2, *Russia* 1 (2–1). *Arica*
Chile: Escutti; Eyzaguirre, Contreras, Sanchez, R., Navarro; Toro, Rojas, Ramirez, Landa, Tobar, Sanchez, L.
Russia: Yachin; Tchokelli, Ostrovski; Voronin, Maslenkin, Netto; Chislenko, Ivanov, Ponedelnik, Mamikin, Meshki.
Scorers: Sanchez, L., Rojas for Chile, Chislenko for Russia.

Czechoslovakia 1, *Hungary* 0 (1–0). *Rancagua*
Czechoslovakia: Schroiff; Lala, Novak; Pluskal, Popluhar, Masopust; Pospichal, Scherer, Kvasniak, Kadraba, Jelinek.
Hungary: Grosics; Matrai, Sarosi; Solymosi, Meszoly, Sipos; Sandor, Rakosi, Albert, Tichy, Fenyvesi.
Scorer: Scherer for Czechoslovakia.

SEMI-FINALS

Brazil 4, *Chile* 2 (2–1). *Santiago*

Brazil: Gilmar; Santos, D., Mauro, Zozimo, Santos, N.; Zito, Didì; Garrincha, Vavà, Amarildo, Zagalo.
Chile: Escutti; Eyzaguirre, Contreras, Sanchez, R., Rodriguez; Toro, Rojas; Ramirez, Landa, Tobar, Sanchez, L.
Scorers: Garrincha (2), Vavà (2), for Brazil, Toro, Sanchez, L. (penalty) for Chile.

Czechoslovakia 3, *Yugoslavia* 1 (0–0). *Viña del Mar*
Czechoslovakia: Schroiff; Lala, Novak; Pluskal, Popluhar, Masopust; Pospichal, Scherer, Kvasniak, Kadraba, Jelinek.
Yugoslavia: Soskic; Durkovic, Jusufi; Radakovic, Markovic, Popovic; Sujakovic, Sekularac, Jerkovic, Galic, Skoblar.
Scorers: Kadraba, Scherer (2), for Czechoslovakia, Jerkovic for Yugoslavia.

THIRD PLACE MATCH *Santiago*

Chile 1, *Yugoslavia* 0 (0–0)
Chile: Godoy; Eyzaguirre, Cruz, Sanchez, R., Rodriguez; Toro, Rojas; Ramirez, Campos, Tobar, Sanchez, L.
Yugoslavia: Soskic; Durkovic, Svinjarevic; Radakovic, Markovic, Popovic; Kovacevic, Sekularac, Jerkovic, Galic, Skoblar.
Scorer: Rojas for Chile.

FINAL *Santiago*

Brazil 3, *Czechoslovakia* 1 (1–1)
Brazil: Gilmar; Santos, D., Mauro, Zozimo, Santos, N.; Zito, Didì; Garrincha, Vavà, Amarildo, Zagalo.
Czechoslovakia: Schroiff; Tichy, Novak; Pluskal, Popluhar, Masopust; Pospichal, Scherer, Kvasniak, Kadraba, Jelinek.
Scorers: Masopust for Czechoslovakia, Amarildo, Zito, Vavà for Brazil.
Leading Scorers: Albert (Hungary), Ivanov (Russia), Sanchez (Chile), Garrincha, Vavà (Brazil), Jerkovic (Yugoslavia) each 4.

WORLD CUP 1966 – ENGLAND

England, as Alf Ramsey had promised, won the World Cup. They won it, in the end, deservedly, with two fine performances in semi-final and final, won it without Jimmy Greaves, won it despite a brutal set-back, in the last minute of the Final itself.

Starting painfully and laboriously, their attack terribly unimpressive in the three qualifying games, the ill-tempered quarter-final against Argentina (when the Argentinians went virtually berserk in the tunnel, at the end) England "came good" when it was most necessary. Geoff Hurst, the West Ham United player, who had looked sadly out of form as recently as the tour match against Denmark, in Copenhagen, came back into the team against Argentina to become, perhaps, the decisive force in England's success. His three goals in the Final established a new record.

In general terms, it was a disappointing World Cup, with no team to match the Brazilians of 1958 and 1962, the Hungarians of 1954. England had a superb defence, but their 4–3–3 formation, generally without specialised wingers, was by no means as impressive in attack. What saved them was the eruption of Hurst, the sudden blossoming of Bobby Charlton, in semi-final and Final, the energy of Alan Ball against Portugal, followed by his astonishing, all-round performance against the West Germans.

Brazil were shown to be clearly in decline. This time, they and their manager, Feola, paid the penalty for an exaggerated reliance on old names, old faces. An injury to Pelé in the first game had an effect on them which it never had in Chile. Good young players had, it's true. been left behind, but obviously a period of retrenchment was needed.

The surprise of the tournament were the lively little North Koreans, who astonished and humiliated the listless Italians. Quick, intelligent, learning from game to game, wonderfully popular with the Middlesbrough crowd, they made one wonder just how good they'll be, with more international experience.

The Hungarians, with a novel tactical formation, played superbly against Brazil, but were betrayed by poor goalkeeping. Portugal, with Eusebio the leading scorer and perhaps the outstanding player of the whole tournament, might have done better still had their defence in any way matched their attack. As for the West Germans, the runners-up, their powerful, well-balanced side, though it never lived up to its opening flourish against Switzerland, was full of talent.

Fittingly, the tournament started with that epitome of modern World Cups, a goalless draw. Uruguay went out to stop England from scoring, massed eight and nine men in defence, and succeeded with little trouble. An ingenuously chosen England team, with Ball as a pseudo-winger and the essentially destructive Stiles at linking wing-half, played into their hands. The strikers and schemers alike were impotent against the tough, rhythmic, immensely professional Uruguayans, responding as always to the challenge of a World Cup.

It was Pelé, appropriately, who scored the first goal of the tournament next day – the player who, above all others, was expected to dominate the tournament. After 14 minutes of Brazil's match at Everton with Bulgaria, he smashed in a phenomenal right-footed free kick. In the second half, an equally remarkable free kick by Garrincha gave Brazil a second, but they were not over impressive. Pelé dazzlingly apart, the team often stuttered. He himself was ruthlessly marked by Zhechev, Yakimov followed him as the best player on the field. Ankle trouble blunted the edge of the much praised Bulgarian centre-forward, Asparoukhov. Brazil gave a first cap as a – largely destructive – midfield player to Edilson, taking the place of an injured Gerson.

At Sheffield, in Group II, the Germans annihilated a Swiss side which dropped two key men, Kuhn and Leimgruber, at the last moment, for breaking curfew. The Germans played splendidly powerful, intelligent football, Beckenbauer, Haller and Held, being especially good. No one but the bookmakers was surprised; they'd been widely favoured.

North Korea, the "mystery" side which had qualified by beating Australia twice in Cambodia, after the mass withdrawal of the Afro-Asian bloc, played bravely against a rough Soviet team at Middlesbrough, but still went down. They looked fit, but their finishing was poor, their small physique against them. The years they had spent monastically in barracks clearly weren't, on their own, enough.

On the Wednesday, in Group I, Mexico, after a lamentably unsuccessful tour of Europe, surprised a disappointing French side at Wembley. Both sides played 4–3–3, the fashionable pattern. Mexico took the lead through Borja, after he'd first miskicked, just after half-time. Hausser equalised. Guérin, the French manager, said his team was "paralysed by nervousness".

At Villa Park, in Group II, Argentina, inspired by Onega, beat Spain in an untidy game, with two goals by Artime, to one sandwiched in between, by Pirri. Spain's attack, though Suarez did some clever things, was most disappointing, especially on the wings.

At Sunderland, Italy won without glory against a Chilean team reduced for most of the second half to ten men; but at least there wasn't a second Battle of Santiago. Barison's fine, but late, second goal was one of the few features of a dullish match. Yet again, as many had feared, Italy, away from home, looked cautious. This, despite some splendid pre-tournament results . . . at home.

At Old Trafford, Hungary, with two bad goalkeeping errors, were rather unlucky to go down to Portugal. Their new tactics, with three link-men breaking frequently to support two strikers, were most effective. But Szentmihalyi let a corner escape him, for Augusto to score and, late in the game, he should have had either the centre from which Torres scored, or the actual header. Graça was in excellent form for Portugal, in midfield.

Three days later, Hungary confirmed their quality with a spectacular win against Brazil; Brazil's first defeat in the World Cup since they lost 4–2 in Berne in 1954: to Hungary. Played under steady rain, it was a game largely and brilliantly dominated by Hungary, for whom Bene scored a fine individual goal after three minutes. Brazil without Pelé severely felt the lack of him – and the burden of years carried by Djalma Santos, Bellini and Garrincha. They did equalise when Lima's free kick came out to Tostao, making his World Cup début. But with Florian Albert more irresistible by the minute, Alcindol limping, Hungary dominated the second half. Albert and Bene made a glorious goal for Farkas, then Meszoly scored from a penalty.

At Hillsborough, the Swiss, with eight changes, took the lead against Spain, who rallied in the second half to squeeze home by the odd goal. Uruguay, much more enterprising now, deservedly beat France at the White City, despite giving away an early penalty goal. North Korea fought bravely against a depleted Chilean side, to equalise with Pak

Seung Jin's 20-yard drive, three minutes from time. Chile had wasted their first-half dominance.

Saturday's surprise was the defeat of Italy by Russia, at Sunderland. Leaving out Rivera, off form against Chile, Fabbri surprisingly brought in a half-back, Leoncini. The team as a whole fell badly below its individual potential and a hard, uninspired Russian side won with a splendid goal by outside-right Chislenko, in the second half.

England, bringing in Paine and Peters (as a link-man) beat a nervous, ultra-defensive Mexico with difficulty. A superb right-footed shot by Bobby Charlton gave them the lead before half-time; Charlton's fine pass sent Greaves through near the end, for Hunt to put in the rebound. Moore was an impressive half-back, but the game was virtually a non-contest. Mexico barely tried to score.

Portugal, helped by defensive errors – an own goal, a silly pass-back – easily beat Bulgaria at Old Trafford. In Group 2, the most unpleasant match of the tournament so far saw Albrecht of Argentina sent off, both sides massing cautiously in defence. A great anti-climax after Germany's bright beginning.

So to the following Tuesday, the elimination of Brazil, the traumatic shock of North Korea beating Italy.

At Everton, Brazil made nine desperate changes, brought in seven men having their first World Cup game. But with Manga, Gilmar's deputy, unsafe in goal, Portugal quickly went two ahead, each a rather soft goal. After 14 minutes, Manga weakly punched out Eusebio's cross. Lively little Simoes, who'd started the move, headed in. Then Torres headed Coluna's free kick across for Eusebio to head another.

A brutal foul by Morais on the clearly half-fit Pelé then crippled him; and Brazil's last hope of recovery. Late in the game, Rildo came up to score a consolation goal, but when a right-wing corner was only half headed clear, the superb Eusebio whipped the ball in, to decide the match. Portugal, who played with Augusto as a deep inside-left, had always been the more impressive. An era had ended.

At Middlesbrough, Italy missed two good chances, lost Bulgarelli with an injury after 34 minutes, a goal (Pak Doo Ik) seven minutes later – and never recovered. Running fast and hard, the Koreans were worth their astonishing success against a flaccid, demoralised side.

In Group II, an unenterprising Argentina made heavy weather of beating Switzerland, while Uruguay, deplorably negative, allowed Mexico the initiative at Wembley. Still, their goalless draw was enough to qualify them.

Next day, England took the field to win a laboured 2–0 victory over France; reduced to ten fit men after Herbin's early injury. Roger Hunt scored a goal in each half, but the midfield build-up was again poor while the defence had two sustained bad periods.

Russia, with nine reserves, defended much of the game, but still beat Chile, after the injured Marcos had equalised. Bulgaria shocked Hungary with Asparoukhov's early goal (Gelei was stranded outside the penalty area) but Bulgaria's second own goal of the tournament helped

Hungary to come back, and join Portugal in the quarters.

In the quarter-finals, the four "first" teams in their groups knocked out the four "seconds". North Korea, playing wonderfully lively football, astonished Portugal with a goal in the first minute, followed by two more. Their attack in this period was mobile, inventive and incisive. Then Eusebio brilliantly took over, scoring twice before half-time – the second a penalty – two more (including another penalty) after the interval. A fifth goal from a corner, by Augusto, ended Korea's brave fight, but they had won the hearts of the Everton crowd.

At Wembley, England scraped through by 1–0 against a lamentably undisciplined Argentina. Rattin, the captain, was sent off shortly before half-time by the German referee, Herr Kreitlein; and wouldn't go. It took eight minutes' wrangling and a narrowly averted exodus by the whole Argentinian team before play re-started. Previously, Argentina's policy of cynical, deliberate fouling had led Kreitlein to put name after name in his notebook. Rattin's was one of them; soon afterwards, his angry protests led to his expulsion.

Geoff Hurst, brought in to replace the injured Greaves, beautifully headed the goal, 13 minutes from time, but England made awfully heavy weather of it against 10 men.

Gelei's feeble goalkeeping was largely responsible for Hungary going down to Russia, at Sunderland. Chislenko tapped in the first goal, after he fumbled a shot. Porkujan – kept in the side after his two mid-week goals – scored the second after he and Meszoly had failed to deal with a corner. If Rakosi had taken advantage of an open goal, all might have been different. As it was, there was only Bene's goal to console the Hungarians for the fact they'd lost, while playing much the better football.

At Sheffield, where Uruguay should have taken an early lead, Germany took it instead, Held's shot being deflected past the goalkeeper by Haller. Infuriated when they thought Schnellinger had handled with impunity on the line, some of the Uruguayans lost their heads. Troche went off for kicking Emmerich in the stomach, Silva for badly fouling Haller; and the Germans added three more goals.

Germany's semi-final with Russia, at Goodison, was a travesty of the game. Russia paid the penalty for their ruthless methods when, after only ten minutes, Sabo attempted to trip Beckenbauer, but succeeded only in injuring his ankle so badly that he was a passenger for the rest of the game.

In the early stages, only the astonishing goalkeeping of Yachin kept Germany from taking the lead. It was a minute from half-time when Schnellinger powerfully tackled – and lamed – Chislenko, sending Haller a perfect crossfield ball on to which he ran and scored spectacularly. When Chislenko limped back, he lost the ball at once to a fair tackle by Held, pursued him, kicked him, and was sent off by Lo Bello, the Italian referee.

Germany, then, should have overrun the nine fit Russians, in the second half. Instead, they played cautious, obvious, laborious football, which produced only one goal – a marvellous left-footed shot from outside the box, by Beckenbauer.

Russia fought bravely, with Khusainov and Voronin outstanding, Banichevski and Malafeev willingly chasing everything. A couple of minutes from time, they shamed the Germans with a goal, when Tilkowski dropped a cross from the left, under pressure, and Porkujan headed in. But, to the jeers of a disenchanted crowd, Germany held on, to reach their second Final.

Wembley's semi-final, by contrast, was a delight, one of the most attractive, and sporting, of the competition. England's defence, with Stiles capably looking after Eusebio, was as perfectly compact as ever, while for the first time, Bobby Charlton brilliantly struck his true form. Not only did he get both goals, he distributed the ball with an imaginative subtlety which should have gained a better response. Portugal's attack looked desperately for a way through the fine English defence, pressed for 15 minutes at the start of the second half, without making chances, and dominated the closing minutes, always at their most dangerous when the ball floated to Torres' head.

England led after 30 minutes when Wilson admirably put through Hunt, Pereira could only block the shot, and Charlton coolly scored. Eleven minutes from time, Hurst powerfully shook off a tackle near the right-hand post, and pulled the ball back for Charlton's right foot to strike the second.

Three minutes later, Torres headed in Simoes' centre, Jackie Charlton fisted it out, Eusebio scored handsomely from the penalty. In the last stages, Stiles' fine tackle thwarted Simoes, through alone, Banks, excellent throughout, turned over the bar a right-foot shot from the splendid Coluna. But sandwiched between these incidents was a fine left-footer from Bobby Charlton, which Pereira blocked but, again, couldn't hold. England were more than worth a famous victory.

The third place match was a dismal contrast; two disappointed teams playing jaded football. A ridiculous, quite unnecessary handling by Khurtsilava after 13 minutes, when jumping with Torres, allowed Eusebio to give Portugal the lead with yet another penalty. This made his personal total for the competition nine.

Two minutes from half-time, Pereira botched an uncomplicated shot from the lively Metreveli, allowing Malafeev to rush in the equaliser. Two minutes from the end, we were spared extra time when the two Russian centre-backs failed to head away a cross by Simoes from the right. Augusto nodded it down for Torres to score.

England won the Final, maintaining a 65-year unbeaten record against Germany, despite a contentious last-minute equaliser after Emmerich had sent a free kick of doubtful origin into the goalmouth. Weber scored, and the Final went into extra time for the first occasion since 1934.

It was a dramatic, unpredictable game, which produced a vast amount of incident. Germany led after 13 minutes, when Ray Wilson, most untypically, headed a cross weakly down to Haller – who scored.

England equalised six minutes later, when Hurst perfectly met Moore's free kick in the air, to head past Tilkowski.

There might well have been other goals. After a German corner, Banks made a double save from Overath, then Emmerich. Three minutes from half-time, Roger Hunt, who'd been preferred to a now fit Jimmy Greaves, should have converted Hurst's fine header. Instead, he shot straight at Tilkowski.

The second half woke up after 18 dull minutes, England being inspired by the splendid control, tireless running and subtle passing of the electrified Ball. Twelve and a half minutes from the end, Hurst's shot, after a half-cleared corner, bobbed up in the goalmouth from the German defence, for Peters to score from point blank range. England seemed to have the match won; but then came Weber's goal, and extra time. It was the more ironical as England, 3 minutes earlier, had wasted a marvellous chance, when Ball put through Hunt. With a three to one numerical advantage, Hunt passed so inaccurately, Bobby Charlton shot so quickly, that Germany escaped.

One hundred minutes had gone when Ball got away yet again, for a cross which Hurst thumped in off the underside of the bar. After a breathless hiatus, a conversation with his linesman, Herr Dienst allowed it. And in the closing seconds, Hurst ran through a stationary, demoralised German defence to get the fourth.

England's defence had again played splendidly, while Ball, Hurst and Bobby Charlton were the stars of the attack. For Germany, Schulz, the sweeper-up, Beckenbauer, in midfield, Uwe Seeler and the perpetually dangerous Held had been the most impressive.

There can have been no more dramatic World Cup Final.

GROUP I

London – Wembley, White City

England (0) 0, *Uruguay* (0) 0. *Wembley*
England: Banks (Leicester City); Cohen (Fulham), Wilson (Everton); Stiles (Manchester United), Charlton, J. (Leeds United), Moore (West Ham United); Ball (Blackpool), Greaves (Spurs), Charlton, R. (Manchester United), Hunt (Liverpool), Connelly (Manchester United).
Uruguay: Mazurkieviez; Troche, Ubinas; Gonçalves, Manicera, Caetano; Cortes, Viera, Silva, Rocha, Perez.

France (0) 1, *Mexico* (0) 1. *Wembley*
France: Aubour; Djorkaeff, Budzinski, Artelesa, De Michele; Bosquier, Herbin, Bonnel; Combin, Gondet, Hausser.
Mexico: Calderon; Chaires, Pena, Nunez, Hernandez; Diaz, Mercado, Reyes; Borja, Fragoso, Padilla.
Scorers: Borja for Mexico, Hausser for France.

Uruguay (2) 2, *France* (1) 1. *White City*
Uruguay: Mazurkieviez; Troche, Ubinas; Gonçalves, Manicera, Caetano; Viera, Cortes, Rocha, Sacia, Perez.
France: Aubour; Djorkaeff, Artelesa, Budzinski, Bosquier; Bonnel, Simon; Herbet, Gondet, De Bourgoing, Hausser.
Scorers: De Bourgoing (penalty) for France, Rocha, Cortes for Uruguay.

England (1) 2, *Mexico* (0) 0. *Wembley*
England: Banks (Leicester City); Cohen (Fulham), Wilson (Everton); Stiles (Manchester United), Charlton, J. (Leeds United), Moore (West Ham United); Paine (Southampton), Greaves (Spurs), Charlton, R. (Manchester United), Hunt (Liverpool), Peters (West Ham United).
Mexico: Calderon; Del Muro; Chaires, Pena, Nunez, Hernandez; Diaz, Jauregui, Reyes; Borja, Padilla.
Scorers: Charlton, R., Hunt for England.

Uruguay (0) 0, *Mexico* (0) 0. *Wembley*
Uruguay: Mazurkieviez; Troche; Ubinas, Gonçalves, Manicera, Caetano; Viera, Rocha, Cortes, Sacia, Perez.
Mexico: Carbajal; Chaires, Pena, Nunez, Hernandez; Diaz, Mercado; Reyes, Cisneros, Borja, Padilla.

England (1) 2, *France* (0) 0. *Wembley*
England: Banks (Leicester City); Cohen (Fulham), Wilson (Everton); Stiles (Manchester United), Charlton, J. (Leeds United), Moore (West Ham United); Callaghan (Liverpool), Greaves (Spurs), Charlton, R. (Manchester United), Hunt (Liverpool), Peters (West Ham United).
France: Aubour; Djorkaeff, Artelesa, Budzinski, Bosquier; Bonnel, Herbin, Simon; Herbet, Gondet, Hausser.
Scorer: Hunt 2 for England.

GROUP II

Birmingham, Sheffield

West Germany (3) 5, *Switzerland* (0) 0. *Sheffield*
West Germany: Tilkowski; Hottges, Schulz, Weber, Schnellinger; Beckenbauer, Haller; Brulls, Seeler, Overath, Held.
Switzerland: Elsener; Grobety, Schneiter; Tachella, Fuhrer, Bani; Durr, Odermatt, Kunzli, Hosp, Schindelholz.
Scorers: Held, Haller 2 (1 penalty), Beckenbauer 2 for West Germany.

Argentina (0) 2, *Spain* (0) 1. *Villa Park*
Argentina: Roma; Perfumo, Marzolini; Ferreiro, Rattin, Albrecht; Solari, Gonzalez, Artime, Onega, Mas.
Spain: Iribar; Sanchis, Eladio; Pirri, Gallego, Zoco; Ufarte, Del Sol, Peiro, Suarez, Gento.
Scorers: Artime 2 for Argentina, Pirri for Spain.

Spain (0) 2, *Switzerland* (1) 1. *Sheffield*
Spain: Iribar; Sanchis, Reija; Pirri, Gallego, Zoco; Amancio, Del Sol, Peiro, Suarez, Gento.
Switzerland: Elsener; Brodmann, Fuhrer; Leimgruber, Armbruster, Stierli; Bani, Kuhn, Gottardi, Hosp, Quentin.
Scorers: Quentin for Switzerland, Sanchis, Amancio for Spain.

Argentina (0) 0, *West Germany* (0) 0. *Villa Park*
Argentina: Roma; Perfumo, Marzolini; Ferreiro, Rattin, Albrecht; Solari, Gonzalez, Artime, Onega, Mas.
Germany: Tilkowski; Hottges, Schulz, Weber, Schnellinger; Beckenbauer, Haller; Brulls, Seeler, Overath, Held.

Argentina (0) 2, *Switzerland* (0) 0. *Villa Park*
Argentina: Roma; Perfumo, Marzolini; Ferreiro, Rattin, Calics; Solari, Gonzalez, Artime, Onega, Mas.
Switzerland: Eichmann; Fuhrer, Brodmann; Kuhn, Armbruster, Stierli; Bani, Kunzli, Gottardi, Hosp, Quentin.
Scorers: Artime, Onega for Argentina.

West Germany (1) 2, *Spain* (1) 1. *Villa Park*
West Germany: Tilkowski; Hottges, Schulz, Weber, Schnellinger; Beckenbauer, Overath; Kramer, Seeler, Held, Emmerich.
Spain: Iribar; Sanchis, Reija; Glaria, Gallego, Zoco; Amancio, Adelardo, Marcelino, Fuste, Lapetra.
Scorers: Fuste for Spain, Emmerich and Seeler for West Germany.

GROUP III

Liverpool, Manchester

Brazil (1) 2, *Bulgaria* (0) 0. *Everton*
Brazil: Gilmar; Djalma Santos, Bellini, Altair, Paolo Henrique; Edilson, Lima; Garrincha, Pelé, Alcindo, Jairzinho.
Bulgaria: Naidenov; Shalamanov, Vutzov, Ganganelov, Penev; Kitov, Zhechev, Yakimov; Dermendjiev, Asparoukhov, Kolev.
Scorers: Pelé, Garrincha for Brazil.

Portugal (1) 3, *Hungary* (0) 1. *Old Trafford*
Portugal: Carvalho; Morais, Baptista, Vicente, Hilario; Graça, Coluna; Augusto, Eusebio, Torres, Simoes.
Hungary: Szentmihalyi; Matrai, Kaposzta; Sovari, Meszoly, Sipos; Bene, Nagy, Albert, Farkas, Rakosi.
Scorers: Augusto 2, Torres for Portugal, Bene for Hungary.

Hungary (1) 3, *Brazil* (1) 1. *Everton*
Hungary: Gelei; Kaposzta, Matrai, Sipos, Szepesi; Mathesz, Meszoly; Bene, Albert, Farkas, Rakosi.
Brazil: Gilmar; Djalma Santos, Bellini, Altair, Paolo Henrique; Lima, Gerson; Garrincha, Alcindo, Tostao, Jairzinho.
Scorers: Bene, Farkas, Meszoly (penalty) for Hungary, Tostao for Brazil.

Portugal (2) 3, *Bulgaria* (0) 0. *Old Trafford*
Portugal: José Pereira; Festa, Germano, Vicente, Hilario; Graça, Coluna; Augusto, Eusebio, Torres, Simoes.
Bulgaria: Naidenov; Shalamanov, Vutzov, Gaganelov, Penev; Zhechev, Yakimov; Dermendjiev, Zhekov, Asparoukhov, Kostov.
Scorers: Vutzov (own goal), Eusebio, Torres for Portugal.

Portugal (2) 3, *Brazil* (0) 1. *Everton*
Portugal: José Pereira; Morais, Baptista, Vicente, Hilario; Graça, Coluna, Augusto; Eusebio, Torres, Simoes.
Brazil: Manga; Fidelis, Brito, Orlando, Rildo; Denilson, Lima; Jair, Silva, Pelé, Parana.
Scorers: Simoes, Eusebio 2 for Portugal, Rildo for Brazil.

Hungary (2) 3, *Bulgaria* (1) 1. *Old Trafford*
Hungary: Gelei; Kaposzta, Matrai, Meszoly, Sipos, Szepesi; Mathesz, Albert, Rakosi; Bene, Farkas.
Bulgaria: Simenov; Penev, Largov, Vutzov, Gaganelov; Zhechev, Davidov; Kotkov, Asparoukhov, Yakimov, Kolev.
Scorers: Asparoukhov for Bulgaria; Davidov (own goal), Meszoly, Bene for Hungary.

GROUP IV

Sunderland, Middlesbrough

Russia (2) 3, *North Korea* (0) 0. *Middlesbrough*
Russia: Kavazashvili; Ponomarev, Chesternjiev, Khurtsilava, Ostrovski; Sabo, Schinava; Chislenko, Malafeev, Banichevski, Khusainov.
North Korea: Li Chan Myung; Pak Li Sup, Shin Yung Kyoo, Lim Zoong Sun, Kang Bong Chil; Pak Seung Din, Im Seung Hwi; Han Bong Jin, Pak Doo Ik, Kang Ryong-Woon, Kim Seung II.
Scorers: Malafeev 2, Banichevski for Russia.

Italy (1) 2, *Chile* (0) 0. *Sunderland*
Italy: Albertosi; Burgnich, Facchetti; Rosato, Salvadore, Lodetti; Perani, Bulgarelli, Mazzola, Rivera, Barison.
Chile: Olivares; Eyzaguirre, Cruz, Figueroa, Villanueva; Prieto, Marcos; Araya, Tobar, Fouilloux, Sanchez.
Scorers: Barison, Mazzola for Italy.

Chile (1) 1, *North Korea* (0) 1. *Middlesbrough*
Chile: Olivares; Valentini, Cruz; Figueroa, Villanueva, Prieto; Marcos, Fouilloux, Landa, Araya, Sanchez.
North Korea: Li Chan Myung; Pak Li Sup, Shin Yung Kyoo, Kim Joon Sun, O Yoon Kyung; Pak Seung Jin, Im Sung Hwi; Han Bong Jin, Pak Doo Ik, Ri Dong Woon, Kim Seung II.
Scorers: Marcos (penalty) for Chile, Pak Seung Jin for North Korea.

Russia (0) 1, *Italy* (0) 0. *Sunderland*
Russia: Yachin; Ponomarev, Chesternjiev, Khurtsilava, Danilov; Sabo, Voronin; Chislenko, Malafeev, Banichevski, Khusainov.

Italy: Albertosi; Burgnich, Facchetti; Rosato, Salvadore, Leoncini; Meroni, Lodetti, Mazzola, Bulgarelli, Pascutti.
Scorer: Chislenko for Russia.

North Korea (1) 1, *Italy* (0) 0. *Middlesbrough*
North Korea: Li Chan Myung; Lim Zoong Sun, Shin Yung Kyoo; Ha Jung Won, O Yoon Kyung, Im Seun Hwi; Han Bong Jin, Pak Doo Ik, Pak Seung Zin, Kim Bong Hwan, Yan Sung Kook.
Italy: Albertosi; Landini, Facchetti; Guarneri, Janich, Fogli; Perani, Bulgarelli, Mazzola, Rivera, Barison.
Scorer: Pak Doo Ik for North Korea.

Russia (1) 2, *Chile* (1) 1. *Sunderland*
Russia: Kavazashvili; Getmanov, Chesternjiev, Afonin, Ostrovski; Voronin, Korneev; Metreveli, Serebrianikov, Markarov, Porkujan.
Chile: Olivares; Valentini, Cruz, Figueroa, Villanueva; Marcos, Prieto; Araya, Landa, Yavar, Sanchez.
Scorers: Porkujan 2 for Russia, Marcos for Chile.

PLACINGS

		Group I			Goals		
	P	W	D	L	F	A	Pts.
England	3	2	1	0	4	0	5
Uruguay	3	1	2	0	2	1	4
Mexico	3	0	2	1	1	3	2
France	3	0	1	2	2	5	1
		Group II					
	P	W	D	L	F	A	Pts.
W. Germany	3	2	1	0	7	1	5
Argentina	3	2	1	0	4	1	5
Spain	3	1	0	2	4	5	2
Switzerland	3	0	0	3	1	9	0
		Group III					
	P	W	D	L	F	A	Pts.
Portugal	3	3	0	0	9	2	6
Hungary	3	2	0	1	7	5	4
Brazil	3	1	0	2	4	6	2
Bulgaria	3	0	0	3	1	8	0
		Group IV					
	P	W	D	L	F	A	Pts.
Russia	3	3	0	0	6	1	6
N. Korea	3	1	1	1	2	4	3
Italy	3	1	0	2	2	2	2
Chile	3	0	1	2	2	5	1

QUARTER-FINALS

England (0) 1, *Argentina* (0) 0. *Wembley*
England: Banks (Leicester City); Cohen (Fulham), Wilson (Everton); Stiles (Manchester United), Charlton, J. (Leeds United), Moore (West Ham United); Ball (Blackpool), Hurst (West Ham United), Charlton, R. (Manchester United), Hunt (Liverpool), Peters (West Ham United).
Argentina: Roma; Ferreiro, Perfumo, Albrecht, Marzolini; Gonzalez, Rattin, Onega; Solari, Artime, Mas.
Scorer: Hurst for England.

West Germany (1) 4, *Uruguay* (0) 0. *Sheffield*
West Germany: Tilkowski; Hottges, Weber, Schulz, Schnellinger; Beckenbauer, Haller, Overath; Seeler, Held, Emmerich.
Uruguay: Mazurkieviez; Troche; Ubinas, Gonçalves, Manicera, Caetano; Salva, Rocha; Silva, Cortez, Perez.
Scorers: Held, Beckenbauer, Seeler, Haller for West Germany.

Portugal (2) 5, *North Korea* (3) 3. *Everton*
Portugal: José Pereira; Morais, Baptista, Vicente, Hilario; Graça, Coluna; Augusto, Eusebio, Torres, Simoes.
North Korea: Li Chan Myung; Rim Yung Sum, Shin Yung Kyoo, Ha Jung Won, O Yoon Kyung; Pak Seung Jin, Jon Seung Hwi; Han Bong Jin, Pak Doo Ik, Li Dong Woon, Yang Sung Kook.
Scorers: Pak Seung Jin, Yang Sung Kook, Li Dong Woon, for North Korea, Eusebio 4 (2 penalties), Augusto, for Portugal.

Russia (1) 2, *Hungary* (0) 1. *Sunderland*
Russia: Yachin; Ponomarev, Chesternjiev, Voronin, Danilov; Sabo, Khusainov; Chislenko, Banichevski, Malafeev, Porkujan.
Hungary: Gelei; Matrai; Kaposzta, Meszoly, Sipos, Szepesi; Nagy, Albert, Rakosi; Bene, Farkas.
Scorers: Chislenko, Porkujan for Russia, Bene for Hungary.

SEMI-FINALS

West Germany (1) 2, *Russia* (0) 1. *Everton*
West Germany: Tilkowski; Hottges, Weber, Schulz, Schnellinger; Beckenbauer, Haller, Overath; Seeler, Held, Emmerich.
Russia: Yachin; Ponomarev, Chesternjiev, Voronin, Danilov; Sabo, Khusainov; Chislenko, Banichevski, Malafeev, Porkujan.
Scorers: Haller, Beckenbauer for Germany, Porkujan for Russia.

England (1) 2, *Portugal* (0) 1. *Wembley*
England: Banks (Leicester City); Cohen (Fulham), Wilson (Everton); Stiles (Manchester United), Charlton, J. (Leeds United), Moore (West Ham United); Ball (Blackpool), Hurst (West Ham United), Charlton, R. (Manchester United), Hunt (Liverpool), Peters (West Ham United).

Portugal: José Pereira; Festa, Baptista, Carlos, Hilario; Graça, Coluna, Augusto; Eusebio, Torres, Simoes.
Scorers: Charlton, R. 2 for England, Eusebio (penalty) for Portugal.

THIRD PLACE MATCH

Portugal (1) 2, *Russia* (1) 1. *Wembley*
Portugal: José Pereira; Festa, Baptista, Carlos, Hilario; Graça, Coluna, Augusto; Eusebio, Torres, Simoes.
Russia: Yachin; Ponomarev, Khurtsilava, Korneev, Danilov; Voronin, Sichinava; Metreveli, Malafeev, Banichevski, Serebrianikov.
Scorers: Eusebio (penalty), Torres for Portugal, Malafeev for Russia.

FINAL *Wembley*

England 4, *W. Germany* 2 (1–1) (2–2) after extra time
England: Banks; Cohen, Wilson; Stiles, Charlton, J., Moore; Ball, Hurst, Hunt, Charlton, R., Peters.
West Germany: Tilkowski; Hottges, Schulz, Weber, Schnellinger; Haller, Beckenbauer, Overath; Seeler, Held, Emmerich.
Scorers: Hurst 3, Peters for England, Haller, Weber for Germany.

Chapter Sixteen

World Club Championship History

These matches began in 1960 – originally without the blessing of FIFA – between the winners of the European Cup and the winners of the more recently innovated South American Cup. They were to play one another at home and away, the championship to be decided not on goal average but on actual results. That is to say, were each team to win one match a play-off would be necessary, and that play-off would take place immediately, on the ground of the team playing at home in the second leg. Clearly this was monstrously unjust to the team playing away and, in view of the rules of the competition, the third match has twice been invoked. On each occasion, the team playing at home – a South American team – has duly won, by a goal.

In 1960 there was no need for such a play-off. Real Madrid, having drawn 0–0 in Montevideo on a day of pouring rain, easily crushed Penarol in Madrid – two full months later – though Penarol suffered from the lack of their brilliant linking half-back, Gonçalvez.

In 1961, Penarol had their revenge. Beaten 1–0 in Lisbon by Benfica, they thrashed the Portuguese club 5–0 in the return, although Benfica had to play without their two key men, Germano, centre-half and Aguas, centre-forward. For the third match, they flew out the 19-year-old coloured inside-forward, Eusebio. He scored a brilliant goal, but again Penarol prevailed.

In 1962, it was the turn of Santos. Once more, Benfica were the losers. There was nothing they could do against the astounding brilliance of Pelé who, if he was superb in the first leg in Brazil, reached supreme heights of virtuosity in Lisbon.

In 1963, Milan, who had already beaten Santos 4–0 earlier in the year in the Milan City Cup, beat them again 4–2 in the first leg, Amarildo, their new Brazilian star, playing superbly and scoring twice. But they fell badly to pieces in the return, after being two goals up, at the Maracana. Santos' recovery was all the more remarkable in that they lacked Zito and Pelé. Almir, who took Pelé's place, was their star.

The decider, a couple of days later, was bad tempered and violent. Two players were sent off, Maldini of Milan – who gave away the penalty that won the match – and Ismael of Santos. There could scarcely have been a better example of the competition's misbegotten rules.

In 1964, it was Inter who beat Independiente in a third match; played in Madrid.

In 1965, for the second year in succession, Internazionale defeated Independiente of Buenos Aires; but this time, there was no need for a third match. In Milan, Inter majestically overwhelmed an Independiente side foolishly committed to playing them at their own game, of defence and breakaway. Inter demonstrated that they knew how to attack, and express themselves, just as well as defend.

In Buenos Aires, by contrast, they rose above intimidation in the streets and on the field – Herrera and at least four players were struck by missiles – to cling to the draw they had come for.

In 1966, Penarol and Real Madrid met for the title, the Uruguayan club scoring two surprisingly decisive victories. Just as in their meeting seven years earlier, it rained heavily in Montevideo, but this time Penarol scored twice, each time through Spencer, their coloured centre-forward from Ecuador, to win. In the return, their fine defence and dazzling breakaways were too much for Real. With Leczano, of Paraguay, sweeping-up, the veteran Abbadie in midfield, Joya, from Peru, and Spencer brilliant strikers, they again won 2–0, the first goal coming from a penalty, Joya making the second with a clever backheel, for Spencer.

The finals of 1967 were a disgrace to the game. Violently provoked by the tactics of Racing Club of Buenos Aires, Glasgow Celtic eventually matched brutality with brutality, in the third game in Montevideo.

In Glasgow, they'd won a dull, bruising match through McNeill's header at a corner. Before the return, in Buenos Aires, could even begin, Ronnie Simpson, the goalkeeper, was hit by a stone on the back of the head, and had to leave the field. Cardenas scored the game's winning goal, three minutes after half-time.

In Montevideo, disgraceful scenes took place, involving culprits on both sides. Four Celtic and two Racing players were sent off. Celtic, on their return, fined each of their players £250. Racing gave theirs a new car. The only goal of the play-off was scored with a strong, high shot by Cardenas, in the second half.

The 1968 Finals were scarcely an improvement. Again, the disgraceful behaviour of an Argentinian team was at the root of it; this time, Estudiantes de la Plata. The first leg, in Buenos Aires, was preceded by an almost hysterical campaign against the little Manchester United and England half-back, Nobby Stiles. In the event, he was sent off for a mere gesture of disgust at a linesman who gave him wrongly offside, this, after he himself had been deliberately back-headed in the face, early in the game, cutting his eye, while Bobby Charlton had to have three stitches in his shin, after being brutally kicked by Pachamé. No wonder such famous forwards as Law and Best stood virtually apart from the proceedings; won 1–0 by Estudiantes through a goal headed from a corner-kick by Conigliaro.

The return, in Manchester, was predictably rough and ill tempered. A good goal headed by Veron, from a free kick, after only five minutes, virtually decided matters. Best and Medina were sent off for brawling; Morgan eventually though uselessly equalised.

1960 *Montevideo*, July 3

Penarol 0, *Real Madrid* 0 (0–0)
Penarol: Maidana; Martinez, Aguerre; Pino, Salvador, Gonçalvez; Cubilla, Linazza, Hohberg, Spencer, Borges.
Real Madrid: Dominguez; Marquitos, Pachin; Vidal, Santamaria, Zarraga; Canario, Del Sol, Di Stefano, Puskas, Bueno.

Madrid, September 4

Real Madrid 5, *Penarol* 1 (4–0)
Real Madrid: Dominguez; Marquitos, Pachin; Vidal, Santamaria, Zarraga; Herrera, Del Sol, Di Stefano, Puskas, Gento.
Penarol: Maidana; Pino, Mayewki, Martinez; Aguerre, Salvador; Cubilla, Linazza, Hohberg, Spencer, Borges.
Scorers: Puskas (2), Di Stefano, Herrera, Gento for Real, Borges for Penarol.

1961 *Lisbon*, September 4

Benfica 1, *Penarol* 0(0–0)
Benfica: Costa Pereira; Angelo, Joao; Netto, Saraiva, Cruz; Augusto, Santana, Aguas, Coluna, Cavem.
Penarol: Maidana; Gonzales, Martinez, Aguerre; Cano, Gonçalvez; Cubilla, Spencer, Cabrera, Sasia, Ledesma.
Scorer: Coluna for Benfica.

Montevideo, September 17

Penarol 5, *Benfica* 0 (4–0)
Penarol: Maidana; Gonzales, Martinez, Aguerre; Cano, Gonçalvez; Cubilla, Ledesma, Sasia, Spencer, Joya.
Benfica: Costa Pereira; Angelo, Joao; Netto, Saraiva, Cruz; Augusto, Santana, Mendes, Coluna, Cavem.
Scorers: Sasia penalty, Joya 2, Spencer 2 for Penarol.

Montevideo, September 19
Penarol 2, *Benfica* 1 (2–1)

Penarol: Maidana; Gonzales, Martinez, Aguerre; Cano, Gonçalvez; Cubilla, Ledesma, Sasia, Spencer, Joya.
Benfica: Costa Pereira; Angelo, Cruz; Netto, Humberto, Coluna; Augusto, Eusebio, Aguas, Cavem, Simoes.
Scorers: Sasia 2 (1 penalty), for Penarol, Eusebio for Benfica.

1962 *Rio*, September 19

Santos 3, *Benfica* 2 (1–0)
Santos: Gilmar; Lima, Calvet; Zito, Mauro, Dalmo; Dorval, Mengalvio, Coutinho, Pelé, Pepé.
Benfica: Costa Pereira; Jacinto, Raul, Humberto, Cruz; Cavem, Coluna; Augusto, Santana, Eusebio, Simoes.
Scorers: Pelé (2), Coutinho for Santos, Santana (2) for Benfica.

Lisbon, October 11

Benfica 2, *Santos* 5 (0–2)
Benfica: Costa Pereira; Jacinto, Raul, Humberto, Cruz; Cavem, Coluna; Augusto, Santana, Eusebio, Simoes.
Santos: Gilmar; Olavo, Calvet; Dalmo, Mauro, Lima; Dorval, Zito, Coutinho, Pelé, Pepé.
Scorers: Pelé (3), Coutinho, Pepé for Santos, Eusebio, Santana for Benfica.

1963 *Milan*, October 16

Milan 4, *Santos* 2 (2–0)
Milan: Ghezzi; David, Trebbi; Pelagalli, Maldini, Trapattoni; Mora, Lodetti, Altafini, Rivera, Amarildo.
Santos: Gilmar; Lima, Haroldo, Calvert, Geraldino; Zito, Mengalvio; Dorval, Coutinho, Pelé, Pepé.
Scorers: Trapattoni, Amarildo (2), Mora for Milan, Pelé 2 (1 penalty) for Santos.

Rio, November 14

Santos 4, *Milan* 2 (0–2)
Santos: Gilmar; Ismael, Dalmo, Mauro, Haroldo; Lima, Megalvio; Dorval, Coutinho, Almir, Pepé.

Milan Ghezzi; David, Trebbi; Pelagalli, Maldini, Trapattoni; Mora, Lodetti, Altafini, Rivera, Amarildo.
Scorers: Altafini, Mora for Milan, Pepé (2), Almir, Lima for Santos.

Rio, November 16

Santos 1, *Milan* 0 (1–0)

Santos: Gilmar; Ismael, Dalmo, Mauro, Haroldo; Lima, Mengalvio; Dorval, Coutinho, Almir, Pepé.
Milan: Balzarini (Barluzzi); Pelagalli, Trebbi; Benitez, Maldini, Trapattoni; Mora, Lodetti, Altafini, Amarildo, Fortunato.
Scorer: Dalmo (penalty) for Santos.

1964 *Buenos Aires*, September 9

Independiente 1, *Internazionale* 0 (0–0)

Independiente: Santoro; Ferreiro, Rolan; Acevedo, Guzman, Maldonado; Bernao, Mura, Prospitti, Rodriguez, Savoy.
Internazionale: Sarti; Burgnich, Facchetti; Tagnin, Guarneri, Picchi; Jair, Mazzola, Peirò, Suarez, Corso.
Scorer: Rodriguez for Independiente.

San Siro, September 23

Internazionale 2, *Independiente* 0 (2–0)

Internazionale: Sarti; Burgnich, Facchetti; Malatrasi, Guarneri, Picchi; Jair, Mazzola, Milani, Suarez, Corso.
Independiente: Santoro; Acevedo, Decaria; Maldonado, Ferreiro, Paflik; Suarez, Mura, Prospitti, Rodriguez, Savoy.
Scorers: Mazzola, Corso for Inter.

Madrid, September 26

Internazionale 1, *Independiente* 0 (0–0)
(*After extra time*)

Internazionale: Sarti; Maletrasi, Facchetti; Tagnin, Guarneri, Picchi; Domenghini, Peirò, Milani, Suarez, Corso.
Independiente: Santoro; Guzman, Decaria; Acevedo, Paflik, Maldonado; Bernao, Prospitti, Suarez, Rodrigues, Savoy.
Scorer: Corso for Inter.

1965 *Milan*, September 8

Internazionale 3, *Independiente* 0 (2–0)

Internazionale: Sarti; Burgnich, Facchetti; Bedin, Guarneri, Picchi; Jair, Mazzola, Peirò, Suarez, Corso.
Independiente: Santoro; Pavoni, Navorro; Acevedo, Guzman, Ferreiro; Bernao, De La Mata, Avallay, Rodriguez, Savoy.
Scorers: Peirò, Mazzola (2) for Internazionale.

Buenos Aires, September 15
Independiente 0, *Internazionale* 0 (0–0)
Independiente: Santoro; Navarro, Pavoni; Rolan, Guzman, Ferreiro; Bernao, Mura, Avallay, Mori, Savoy.
Internazionale: Sarti; Burgnich, Facchetti; Bedin, Guarneri, Picchi; Jair, Mazzola, Peirò, Suarez, Corso.

1966 *Montevideo*, October 12
Penarol 2, *Real Madrid* 0 (1–0)
Penarol: Mazurkiewicz; Forlan, Gonzales; Gonçalves, Lezcano, Varela; Abbadie, Cortes, Spencer, Rocha, Joya.
Real Madrid: Betancort; Pachin, Sanchis; Ruiz, De Felipe, Zoco; Serena, Amancio, Pirri, Velasquez, Bueno.
Scorer: Spencer (2) for Penarol.

Madrid, October 26
Real Madrid 0, *Penarol* 2 (0–2)
Real Madrid: Betancort; Calpe, Sanchis; Pirri, Del Felipe, Zoco; Serena, Amancio, Grosso, Velasquez, Gento.
Penarol: Mazurkiewicz; Gonzales, Caetano; Gonçalves, Lezcano, Varela; Abbadie, Cortes, Spencer, Rocha, Joya.
Scorers: Rocha (pen), Spencer for Penarol.

1967 *Glasgow*, October 18

Celtic (0) 1	*Racing Club* (0) 0
McNeill	

Celtic: Simpson; Craig, Gemmell; Murdoch, McNeill, Clark; Johnstone, Lennox, Wallace, Auld, Hughes.
Racing: Cejas; Perfumo, Diaz; Martin, Mori, Basile; Raffo, Rulli, Cardenas, Rodrigues, Maschio.

Buenos Aires, November 1

Racing Club (1) 2	*Celtic* (1) 1
Raffo, Cardenas	Gemmell (penalty)

Racing: Cejas; Perfumo, Chabay; Martin, Rulli, Basile; Raffo, Cardoso, Cardenas, Rodrigues, Maschio.
Celtic: Fallon; Craig, Gemmell; Murdoch, McNeill, Clark; Johnstone, Wallace, Chalmers, O'Neill, Lennox.

Montevideo, November 4

Racing Club (0) 1	*Celtic* (0) 0
Cardenas	

Racing: Cejas; Perfumo, Chabay; Martin, Rulli, Basile; Raffo, Cardoso, Cardenas, Rodrigues, Maschio.
Celtic: Fallon: Craig, Gemmell; Murdoch, McNeill, Clark; Johnstone, Lennox, Wallace, Auld, Hughes.

1968 *Buenos Aires*, September 25

Estudiantes (1) 1 — *Manchester United* (0) 0

Estudiantes: Poletti; Malbernat, Suarez, Madero, Medina; Bilardo, Pachamè, Togneri; Ribaudo, Conigliaro, Veron.
Manchester United: Stepney; Dunne, Burns; Crerand, Foulkes, Stiles; Morgan, Sadler, Law, Charlton, Best.

Manchester, October 16

Manchester United (0) 1 — *Estudiantes* (1) 1
Morgan — Veron

Manchester United: Stepney; Dunne, Brennan; Crerand, Foulkes, Sadler; Morgan, Kidd, Charlton, Law (Sartori), Best.
Estudiantes: Poletti; Malbernat, Suarez, Madero, Medina; Bilardo, Pachame, Togneri; Ribaudo, Conigliaro, Veron (Echecopar).

Chapter Seventeen

The European Nations Cup History

THIS was initiated as a home and away knock-out tournament, with the semi-finals and Final to be played on neutral soil, in 1958, and dragged on till 1960 and a somewhat anti-climactic finish in Paris. Russia won it, but they had been favoured by the withdrawal of Spain, whom they were due to meet in the quarter-final. No British country competed. The final rounds were notable for the superb form of Russia's goalkeeper, Lev Yachin.

EUROPEAN NATIONS CUP 1958–60

Preliminary Round

Eire 2, *Czechoslovakia* 0
Czechoslovakia 4, *Eire* 0

First Round

France 7, *Greece* 1
Greece 1, *France* 1
Russia 3, *Hungary* 1
Hungary 0, *Russia* 1
Rumania 3, *Turkey* 0
Turkey 2, *Rumania* 0
Norway 0, *Austria* 1
Austria 5, *Norway* 2

Yugoslavia 2, *Bulgaria* 0
Bulgaria 1, *Yugoslavia* 1
Portugal 2, *East Germany* 0
East Germany 2, *Portugal* 3
Denmark 2, *Czechoslovakia* 2
Czechoslovakia 5, *Denmark* 1
Poland 2, *Spain* 4
Spain 3, *Poland* 0

Quarter-finals

Portugal 2, *Yugoslavia* 1
Yugoslavia 5, *Portugal* 1
France 5, *Austria* 2
Austria 2, *France* 4
Rumania 0, *Czechoslovakia* 2
Czechoslovakia 3, *Rumania* 0
Russia beat Spain who withdrew

Semi-finals

Yugoslavia 5, *France* 4 in Paris
Russia 3, *Czechoslovakia* 0 in Marseilles

Final *Paris, July* 10, 1960

Russia 2, *Yugoslavia* 1 after extra time
Russia: Yachin; Tchekeli, Kroutikov; Voinov, Maslenkin, Netto; Metreveli, Ivanov, Ponedelnik, Bubukin, Meshki.
Yugoslavia: Vidinic; Durkovic, Jusufi; Zanetic, Miladinovic, Perusic; Sekularac, Jerkovic, Galic, Matus, Kostic.
Scorers: Metreveli, Ponedelnik for Russia, Netto (own goal) for Yugoslavia.

EUROPEAN NATIONS CUP 1962–4

This time, England, Ireland and Wales competed, but Scotland inexcusably and inexplicably stayed out. England's performance was far from glorious. After struggling to draw with France in Sheffield, they played the return during the bitter winter of 1963, took a floundering team to Paris, poorly selected (no scheming inside-forward) and with a goalkeeper out of practice and form, to lose 5–2.

Ireland did better, playing gallantly to beat Poland, and exceedingly well to hold Spain to a draw, away. For the return, however, Spain recalled their Italian-based stars, Del Sol and Suarez, and just squeezed through, in Belfast. The Welsh, meanwhile, had already gone out to Hungary. Spain did not need Del Sol and Suarez to put out Eire, which they did with ease, while Hungary surprised France in Paris; a revitalised team.

The closing rounds, played in Spain, not surprisingly saw the home team prevail, though not without infinite trouble. After narrowly prevailing against Hungary, Spain ran up against a packed Russian defence, scored in five minutes, let in an eighth-minute equaliser, then inspired by Suarez, had enough of the play for Marcellino to give them the game with a brilliant opportunist goal. The Russians used Kornaev as an extra defender. Hungary took third place with a laborious win over Denmark.

Preliminary Round

Spain 6, *Rumania* 0
Rumania 3, *Spain* 1
Poland 0, *Northern Ireland* 2
Northern Ireland 2, *Poland* 0
Denmark 6, *Malta* 1
Malta 1, *Denmark* 3
Greece withdrew against Albania
East Germany 2, *Czechoslovakia* 1
Czechoslovakia 1, *East Germany* 1
Hungary 3, *Wales* 1
Wales 1, *Hungary* 1
Italy 6, *Turkey* 0
Turkey 0, *Italy* 1
Holland 3, *Switzerland* 1
Switzerland 1, *Holland* 1
Norway 0, *Sweden* 2
Sweden 1, *Norway* 1
Yugoslavia 3, *Belgium* 2
Belgium 0, *Yugoslavia* 1
Bulgaria 3, *Portugal* 1
Portugal 3, *Bulgaria* 1
Bulgaria 1, *Portugal* 0
England 1, *France* 1
France 5, *England* 2

Second Round

Spain 1, *Northern Ireland* 1
Northern Ireland 0, *Spain* 1
Denmark 4, *Albania* 0
Albania 1, *Denmark* 0
Austria 0, *Eire* 0
Eire 3, *Austria* 2
East Germany 1, *Hungary* 2
Hungary 3, *East Germany* 3
Russia 2, *Italy* 0
Italy 1, *Russia* 1
Holland 1, *Luxemburg* 1

Luxemburg 2, *Holland* 1
Yugoslavia 0, *Sweden* 0
Sweden 3, *Yugoslavia* 2
Bulgaria 1, *France* 0
France 3, *Bulgaria* 1

Quarter-finals

Luxemburg 3, *Denmark* 3
Denmark 2, *Luxemburg* 2
Denmark 1, *Luxemburg* 0
Spain 5, *Eire* 1
Eire 0, *Spain* 2
France 1, *Hungary* 3
Hungary 2, *France* 1
Sweden 1, *Russia* 1
Russia 3 *Sweden* 1

Semi-finals

Russia 3, *Denmark* 0 in Barcelona
Spain 2, *Hungary* 1 in Madrid

Third Place match:
Hungary 3, *Denmark* 1 after extra time

Final *Madrid, June* 21, 1964

Spain 2, *Russia* 1 (1–1)
Spain: Iribar; Rivilla, Calleja; Fuste, Olivella, Zocco; Amancio, Pereda, Marcellino, Suarez, Lapetra.
Russia: Yachin; Chustikov, Mudrik; Voronin, Chesternijev, Anitchkine; Chislenko, Ivanov, Ponedelnik, Kornaev, Khusainov.
Scorers: Pereda, Marcellino for Spain, Khusainov for Russia.

EUROPEAN NATIONS CUP 1966–8

Italy won a most unsatisfactory final series, on their own soil. In the semi-finals, they drew with Russia after extra time at Naples and won the toss: a competition rule which properly met with bitter criticism. In the final, a late goal from a free kick gave them a lucky draw against the superior Yugoslav side. The replay, two days later, found Yugoslavia exhausted, Italy reinforced by capable reserves, and the Italians won with some ease. Previously, in a brutally hard match, Yugoslavia had put out England in Florence through a late goal by Dzajic.

England had qualified for the quarter finals by winning the home international championship. Beaten at Wembley by Scotland, they drew the vital match at Hampden in February, 1968. The Scots threw away points against weaker opposition. England went on to eliminate Spain in the quarter-finals, playing specially well in Madrid.

The competition was this time divided into eight qualifying groups, in which the results were as follows:

Group I

Eire 0, *Spain* 0
Eire 2, *Turkey* 1
Spain 2, *Eire* 0
Turkey 0, *Spain* 0
Turkey 2, *Eire* 1
Eire 0, *Czechoslovakia* 2
Spain 2, *Turkey* 0
Czechoslovakia 1, *Spain* 0
Spain 2, *Czechoslovakia* 1
Czechoslovakia 4, *Turkey* 0
Turkey 0, *Czechoslovakia* 0
Czechoslovakia 1, *Eire* 2

Group II

Norway 0, *Bulgaria* 2
Portugal 1, *Sweden* 2
Bulgaria 4, *Norway* 2
Sweden 1, *Portugal* 1
Norway 1, *Portugal* 2
Sweden 0, *Bulgaria* 2
Norway 3, *Sweden* 1
Sweden 5, *Norway* 2
Bulgaria 3, *Sweden* 0
Portugal 2, *Norway* 1
Bulgaria 1, *Portugal* 0
Portugal 0, *Bulgaria* 0

Group III

Finland 0, *Austria* 0
Greece 2, *Finland* 1
Finland 1, *Greece* 1
Russia 4, *Austria* 3
Russia 2, *Finland* 0
Finland 2, *Russia* 5
Austria 2, *Finland* 1
Greece 4, *Austria* 0
Austria 1, *Russia* 0
Greece 0, *Russia* 1
Austria 1, *Greece* 1
Russia 4, *Greece* 1

Group IV

Albania 0, *Yugoslavia* 2
West Germany 6, *Albania* 0
Yugoslavia 1, *West Germany* 0
West Germany 3, *Yugoslavia* 1
Yugoslavia 4, *Albania* 0
Albania 0, *West Germany* 0

Group V

Holland 2, *Hungary* 2
Hungary 6, *Denmark* 0
Holland 2, *Denmark* 0
East Germany 4, *Holland* 3
Hungary 2, *Holland* 1
Denmark 0, *Hungary* 2
Denmark 1, *East Germany* 1
Holland 1, *East Germany* 0
Hungary 3, *East Germany* 1
Denmark 3, *Holland* 2
East Germany 3, *Denmark* 2
East Germany 1, *Hungary* 0

Group VI

Cyprus 1, *Rumania* 5
Rumania 4, *Switzerland* 2
Italy 3, *Rumania* 1
Cyprus 0, *Italy* 2
Rumania 7, *Cyprus* 0
Switzerland 7, *Rumania* 1
Italy 5, *Cyprus* 0
Switzerland 5, *Cyprus* 0
Switzerland 2, *Italy* 2
Italy 4, *Switzerland* 0
Cyprus 2, *Switzerland* 1
Rumania 0, *Italy* 1

Group VII

Poland 4, *Luxemburg* 0
France 2, *Poland* 1
Luxemburg 0, *France* 3
Luxemburg 0, *Belgium* 5
Luxemburg 0, *Poland* 0
Poland 3, *Belgium* 1
Belgium 2, *France* 1

Poland 1, *France* 4
Belgium 2, *Poland* 4
France 1, *Belgium* 1
Belgium 3, *Luxemburg* 0
France 3, *Luxemburg* 1

Group VIII

Ireland 0, *England* 2
Wales 1, *Scotland* 1
England 5, *Wales* 1
Scotland 2, *Ireland* 1
Ireland 0, *Wales* 0
England 2, *Scotland* 3
Wales 0, *England* 3
Ireland 1, *Scotland* 0
England 2, *Ireland* 0
Scotland 3, *Wales* 2
Scotland 1, *England* 1
Wales 2, *Ireland* 0

Quarter-finals

England 1, *Spain* 0
Spain 1, *England* 2
Bulgaria 3, *Italy* 2
Italy 2, *Bulgaria* 0
France 1, *Yugoslavia* 1
Yugoslavia 5, *France* 1
Hungary 2, *Russia* 0
Russia 3, *Hungary* 0

Semi-finals (*Italy*)

Yugoslavia 1, *England* 0
Italy 0, *Russia* 0 *Italy won toss*

Third-place match (*Rome*)

England 2, *Russia* 0

Final (*Rome*)

Italy 1, *Yugoslavia* 1

Replayed Final *Rome, June* 10, 1968

Italy (2) 2, *Yugoslavia* (0) 0
Italy: Zoff; Burgnich, Facchetti; Rosato, Guarneri, Salvadore; Domenghini, Mazzola, Anastasi, De Sisti, Riva.

Yugoslavia: Pantelic; Fazlagic, Damjanovic; Pavlovic, Paunovic, Holcer; Hosic, Acimovic, Musemic, Trivic, Dzajic.
Scorers: Riva, Anastasi for Italy.

Chapter Eighteen

The European Cup History

THE European Cup was the brainchild of the veteran French journalist, selector and international player, Gabriel Hanot, and his Parisian newspaper, *L'Equipe*. Confined to clubs which have won their national League championship (though the holders' country may enter a second team), matches preceding the final are decided on a home and away, goal aggregate basis.

Though Scotland entered at once when the tournament began in 1955, England did not. The Football League refused Chelsea, then the English champions, permission to take part, and the following season advised Manchester United not to enter. Fortunately United would have no truck with such negative counsel, and duly took part, but in 1958, when the organisers generously invited them to take part again, as a token of sympathy for the Munich air crash disaster, they were meanly frustrated. The League forbade them to enter, maintaining that this was a competition for national champions, and United had not won the League title (thus claiming to make EUFA's rules for them). United appealed successfully to the Football Association but the League, in turn, were upheld in their decision by a joint F.A.-F.L. body. It was a thoroughly shabby episode.

The feature of the first five European Cups was the extraordinary dominance of Real Madrid. Off the field, the credit belonged to their vigorous President, Santiago Bernabeu; but on it, to the great Argentinian centre-forward, Alfredo Di Stefano. Long before the coming of Puskas, Di Stefano had inspired his team to bestride Europe. Not until 1960–1 did Barcelona at last become the first team to knock Real out of the European Cup.

EUROPEAN CUP 1955–6

With no entry from England, Hibernian of Edinburgh were the sole representatives of Britain and they reached the semi-finals with an excellent team which included Tommy Younger in goal, and a forward-line of Gordon Smith, Combe, Reilly, Turnbull and Ormond. A brilliant 4–0 away win against Rot Weiss Essen took them through the first round; Djurgarden of Sweden were twice beaten on Scottish soil in the second, but Reims proved too strong for them in the semi-final. The return match, at Easter Road, was a brilliant one, with Kopa and Bob Jonquet in splendid form for Reims, but Hibernian having most of the play – and failing to score.

The Final, in Paris, provided a splendid match between Reims and Real, in which Di Stefano and Kopa reached great heights of technique and organisation. Leblond and Templin gave Reims a 2–0 lead in the first ten minutes, it was 2–2 at half-time, Hidalgo restored the lead for Reims, but a remarkable individual goal by the Real centre-half Marquitos equalised, and Rial, the Argentinian-born inside-left, scored the winner, 11 minutes from time.

First Round

Sporting Club Lisbon 3, *Partizan Belgrade* 3
Partizan Belgrade 5, *Sporting Club* 2
Voros Logobo 6, *Anderlecht* 3
Anderlecht 1, *Voros Logobo* 4
Servette Geneva 0, *Real Madrid* 2
Real Madrid 5, *Servette* 0
Rot Weiss Essen 0, *Hibernian* 4
Hibernian 1, *Rot Weiss Essen* 1
Aarhus 0, *Reims* 2
Reims 2, *Aarhus* 2
Rapid Vienna 6, *Eindhoven* 1
Eindhoven 1, *Rapid* 0
Djurgarden 0, *Gwardia Warsaw* 0
Gwardia 1, *Djurgarden* 4
Milan 3, *Saarbrücken* 4
Saarbrücken 1, *Milan* 4

Quarter-finals

Hibernian 3, *Djurgarden* 1
Djurgarden 0, *Hibernian* 1 (Edinburgh)
Reims 4, *Voros Logobo* 2
Voros Logobo 4, *Reims* 4
Real Madrid 4, *Partizan Belgrade* 0
Partizan Belgrade 3, *Real Madrid* 0
Rapid Vienna 1, *Milan* 1
Milan 7, *Rapid Vienna* 2

Semi-finals

Reims 2, *Hibernian* 0
Hibernian 0, *Reims* 1
Real Madrid 4, *Milan* 2
Milan 2, *Real Madrid* 1

Final *Paris, June* 13, 1956

Real Madrid 4 (2), *Reims* 3 (2)
Real: Alsonso; Atienza, Lesmes; Munoz, Marquitos, Zarraga; Joseito; Marchal, Di Stefano, Rial, Gento.
Reims: Jacquet; Zimny, Giraudo; Leblond, Jonquet, Siatka; Hidalgo, Glovacki, Kopa, Bliard, Templin.
Scorers: Leblond, Templin, Hidalgo for Reims, Di Stefano, Rial (2), Marquitos for Real Madrid.

EUROPEAN CUP 1956–7

Manchester United now entered the lists for England, and put up an excellent performance, reaching the semi-finals with a dazzling young team among whose stars were Roger Byrne, Duncan Edwards and Tommy Taylor – all to die at Munich. Their ten-goal win over Anderlecht, at Maine Road, was a remarkable one. Denis Viollet, their inside-left, scored four of the goals. The third round, in Bilbao, saw United beaten 5–3 on a very heavy pitch, but they recovered for a splendid 3–0 victory in the return, and went through to the semi-finals, where the power of Real was just too much for them.

Rangers, Scotland's entry, went out ingloriously to Nice.

In the Final, Italy's gifted Fiorentina side, which had splendid South American forwards in Julinho and Montuori, succumbed to Real, on Real's own ground.

First Round (*Preliminary*)

Dortmund Borussia 4, *Spora Luxemburg* 3
Spora Luxemburg 2, *Dortmund Borussia* 1
Dortmund Borussia 7, *Spora Luxemburg* 0
Dynamo Bucharest 3, *Galatassaray* 1
Galatassaray 2, *Dynamo Bucharest* 1
Slovan Bratislava 4, *CWKS Warsaw* 0
CWKS Warsaw 2, *Slovan Bratislava* 0
Anderlecht 0, *Manchester United* 2
Manchester United 10, *Anderlecht* 0
Aarhus 1, *Nice* 1
Nice 5, *Aarhus* 1
Porto 1, *Atletico Bilbao* 2
Atletico Bilbao 3, *Porto* 2

First Round Proper

Manchester United 3, *Dortmund Borussia* 2
Dortmund Borussia 0, *Manchester United* 0
CDNA Sofia 8, *Dynamo Bucharest* 1
Dynamo Bucharest 3, *CDNA Sofia* 2
Slovan Bratislava 1, *Grasshopper* 0
Grasshopper 2, *Slovan Bratislava* 0

Rangers 2, *Nice* 1
Nice 2, *Rangers* 1
Rangers 1, *Nice* 3
Real Madrid 4, *Rapid Vienna* 2
Rapid Vienna 3, *Real Madrid* 1
Real Madrid 2, *Rapid Vienna* 0
Rapid Juliana 3, *Red Star Sofia* 4
Red Star Sofia 2, *Rapid Juliana* 0
Fiorentina 1, *Norrköping* 1
Norrköping 0, *Fiorentina* 1
Atletico Bilbao 3, *Honved* 2
Honved 3, *Atletico Bilbao* 3

Quarter-finals

Atletico Bilbao 5, *Manchester United* 3
Manchester United 3, *Atletico Bilbao* 0
Fiorentina 3, *Grasshoppers* 1
Grasshoppers 2, *Fiorentina* 2
Red Star 3, *CDNA Sofia* 1
CDNA Sofia 2, *Red Star* 1
Real Madrid 3, *Nice* 0
Nice 2, *Real Madrid* 3

Semi-finals

Red Star 0, *Fiorentina* 1
Fiorentina 0, *Red Star* 0
Real Madrid 3, *Manchester United* 1
Manchester United 2, *Real Madrid* 2

Final *Madrid, May* 30, 1957

Real Madrid 2, *Fiorentina* 0 (0–0)
Real: Alonso; Torres, Lesmes; Munoz, Marquitos, Zarraga; Kopa, Mateos, Di Stefano, Rial, Gento.

Fiorentina: Sarti; Magnini, Cervato; Scaramucci, Orzan, Segato; Julinho, Gratton, Virgili, Montuori, Bizzarri.
Scorers: Di Stefano (penalty), Gento for Real Madrid.

EUROPEAN CUP 1957–8

For British football, this was the European Cup which was cruelly overshadowed by the Munich disaster, when the Elizabethan carrying Manchester United back from their match in Belgrade crashed on take-off, killing seven players. United had already qualified for the semi-finals, and their patched-up team made a brave show against Milan, winning the first leg in Manchester 2–1, Ernie Taylor getting the winner from a penalty, but losing the return 4–0. Rangers, who knocked out

St. Etienne, had been comfortably despatched by Milan in the eighth-finals.

Real, who now had Santamaria at centre-half, were lucky to get the better of Milan in a really thrilling final. Real survived when a shot by Cucchiaroni hit the bar, to go on and win in extra time with a 107th-minute goal by Gento. It was a fine day for the Milan inside-forwards, Nils Liedholm and Argentina's Ernesto Grillo.

Preliminary Round

Rangers 3, *St. Etienne* 1
St. Etienne 2, *Rangers* 1
CDNA Sofia 2, *Vasas* 1
Vasas 6, *CDNA Sofia* 1
Red Star 5, *Stade Dudelange* 0
Stade Dudelange 1, *Red Star* 9
Aarhus 0, *Glenavon* 0
Glenavon 0, *Aarhus* 3
Gwardia Warsaw 3, *Wismut Karl-Marx-Stadt* 1
Wismut Karl-Marx-Stadt 2, *Gwardia Warsaw* 0
Wismut Karl-Marx-Stadt 1, *Gwardia Warsaw* 1 (Wismut won the toss)
Seville 3, *Benfica* 1
Benfica 0, *Seville* 0
Shamrock Rovers 0, *Manchester United* 6
Manchester United 3, *Shamrock Rovers* 2
Milan 4, *Rapid Vienna* 1
Rapid Vienna 5, *Milan* 2
Milan 4, *Rapid Vienna* 2
Antwerp 1, *Real Madrid* 2
Real Madrid 6, *Antwerp* 0

First Round Proper

Norrköping 2, *Red Star* 2
Red Star 2, *Norrköping* 1
Wismut Karl-Marx-Stadt 1, *Ajax Amsterdam* 3
Ajax Amsterdam 1, *Wismut Karl-Marx-Stadt* 0
Manchester United 3, *Dukla Prague* 0
Dukla Prague 1, *Manchester United* 0
Young Boys Berne 1, *Vasas* 1
Vasas 2, *Young Boys Berne* 1
Rangers 1, *Milan* 4
Milan 2, *Rangers* 0
Seville 4, *Aarhus* 0
Aarhus 2, *Seville* 0
Dortmund Borussia 4, *CCA Bucharest* 2
CCA Bucharest 3, *Dortmund Borussia* 1
Dortmund Borussia 3, *CCA Bucharest* 1

Quarter-finals

Manchester United 2, *Red Star* 1
Red Star 3, *Manchester United* 3
Real Madrid 8, *Seville* 0
Seville 2, *Real Madrid* 2
Ajax Amsterdam 2, *Vasas* 2
Vasas 4, *Ajax Amsterdam* 0
Dortmund Borussia 1, *Milan* 1
Milan 4, *Dortmund Borussia* 1

Semi-finals

Real Madrid 4, *Vasas Budapest* 0
Vasas 2, *Real Madrid* 0
Manchester United 2, *Milan* 1
Milan 4, *Manchester United* 0

Final *Brussels, May* 28, 1958

Real Madrid 3, *Milan* 2 (0–0) (2–2) *after extra time*
Real Madrid: Alonso; Atienza, Lesmes; Santisteban, Santamaria, Zarraga; Kopa, Joseito, Di Stefano, Rial, Gento.

Milan: Soldan; Fontana, Beraldo; Bergamaschi, Maldini, Radice: Danova, Liedholm, Schiaffino, Grillo, Cucchiaroni.

Scorers: Schiaffino, Grillo for Milan, Di Stefano, Rial, Gento for Real Madrid.

EUROPEAN CUP 1958–9

After the champagne of Manchester United, the rather flat beer of the Wolves, who were put out, somewhat obscurely, by Schalke 04 in their first time. As for Hearts, the coloured Liège centre-forward, quaintly named Bonga-Bonga, tore their defence to shreds. Real proved more majestic than ever, especially in the crushing of Wiener Sportklub. But the all-Madrid semi-final with Atletico turned out to be a frighteningly close affair, in which Atletico (led by Brazil's Vavà) fought with magnificent spirit, forcing a third match. The final, against Reims, was anti-climax; a dull match in which Real won despite an injury to Kopa, playing against his old club.

Preliminary Round

Boldklub Copenhagen 3, *Schalke 04* 0
Schalke 04 5, *Boldklub Copenhagen* 2
Schalke 04 3, *Boldklub Copenhagen* 1
Standard Liège 5, *Hearts* 1
Hearts 2, *Standard Liège* 1
Dynamo Zagreb 2, *Dukla Prague* 2

Dukla Prague 2, *Dynamo Zagreb* 1
Esch 1, *Gothenburg* 2
Gothenburg 0, *Esch* 1
Gothenburg 5, *Esch* 1
Wismut Karl-Marx-Stadt 4, *Petrolul Ploesti* 2
Petrolul Ploesti 2, *Wismut Karl-Marx-Stadt* 0
Wismut Karl-Marx-Stadt 4, *Petrolul Ploesti* 0
Polonia Bytom 0, *MTK Budapest* 3
MTK Budapest 3, *Polonia Bytom* 0
Atletico Madrid 8, *Drumcondra* 0
Drumcondra 1, *Atletico Madrid* 5
DOS Utrecht 3, *Sporting Lisbon* 4
Sporting Lisbon 2, *DSO Utrecht* 1
Ards 1, *Reims* 4
Reims 6, *Ards* 2
Juventus 3, *Wiener SK* 1
Wiener SK 7, *Juventus* 0

First Round Proper

Sporting Lisbon 2, *Standard Liège* 3
Standard Liège 3, *Sporting Lisbon* 0
MTK 1, *Young Boys Berne* 2
Young Boys Berne 4, *MTK* 1
Wiener SK 3, *Dukla Prague* 1
Dukla Prague 1, *Wiener SK* 0
Atletico Madrid 2, *CDNA* 1
CDNA 1, *Atletico Madrid* 0
Atletico Madrid 3, *CDNA* 1 after extra time
Gothenburg 2, *Wismut Karl-Marx-Stadt* 2
Wismut Karl-Marx-Stadt 4, *Gothenburg* 0
Wolverhampton Wanderers 2, *Schalke 04* 2
Schalke 04 2, *Wolverhampton Wanderers* 1
Real Madrid 2, *Besiktas Istanbul* 0
Besiktas Istanbul 1, *Real Madrid* 1
Reims 4, *Helsinging Palloseura* 0
Reims 3, *Helsinging Palloseura* 0

Quarter-finals

Standard Liège 2, *Reims* 0
Reims 3, *Standard Liège* 0
Atletico Madrid 3, *Schalke 04* 0
Schalke 04 1, *Atletico Madrid* 1
Wiener SK 0, *Real Madrid* 0
Real Madrid 7, *Wiener SK* 1
Young Boys Berne 2, *Wismut Karl-Marx-Stadt* 2
Wismut Karl-Marx-Stadt 0, *Young Boys Berne* 0
Young Boys Berne 2, *Wismut Karl-Marx-Stadt* 1

Semi-finals

Young Boys Berne 1, *Reims* 0
Reims 3, *Young Boys Berne* 0
Real Madrid 2, *Atletico Madrid* 1
Atletico Madrid 1, *Real Madrid* 0
Real Madrid 2, *Atletico Madrid* 1

Final *Stuttgart, June* 2, 1959

Real Madrid 2, *Reims* 0 (1–0)
Real Madrid: Dominguez; Marquitos, Zarraga; Santisteban, Santamaria, Ruiz; Kopa, Mateos, Di Stefano, Rial, Gento.
Reims: Colonna; Rodzik, Giraudo; Penverne, Jonquet, Leblond; Lamartine, Bliard, Fontaine, Piantoni, Vincent.
Scorers: Mateos, Di Stefano for Real Madrid.

EUROPEAN CUP 1959–60

The year 1960 produced one of the greatest and most spectacular Finals, a match in which Real – who now had the great Puskas in the side, with tireless Del Sol at inside right – easily rode an early goal by Eintracht, to crush them 7–3. The immense Hampden crowd gave them a memorable ovation after the match. Di Stefano and Puskas were peerlessly brilliant, Puskas getting four of the goals, his left foot as ferocious as ever, with Di Stefano, tirelessly inventive, scoring the other three.

But Eintracht must not be written off; their progress to the Final was splendid, not least their contemptuous home and away thrashing of Rangers. Their veteran inside-left, Pfaff, was a major star.

Nor must one forget the virtuosity of Barcelona and their polyglot team, under the flamboyant Herrera – who was attacked by fans and sacked, after the elimination by Real in two awe-inspiring matches. Previously, they had killed the legend that Continentals cannot play in thick mud by humiliating Wolves on just such a pitch at Molineux. Of all the European Cups played, this was so far the most exciting and glittering.

Preliminary Round

Nice 3, *Shamrock Rovers* 2
Shamrock Rovers 1, *Nice* 1
CDNA Sofia 2, *Barcelona* 2
Barcelona 6, *CDNA Sofia* 2
Linfield 2, *IFK Gothenburgh* 1
IFK Gothenburgh 6, *Linfield* 1
Esch-sur-Alzetta 5, *Lodz* 1
Lodz 2, *Esch-sur Alzetta* 1
Wiener SK 0, *Petrolul Ploesti* 0
Petrolul Ploesti 1, *Wiener SK* 2

Olympiakos 2, *Milan* 2
Milan 3, *Olympiakos* 1
Fenerbachce 1, *Csepel* 1
Fenerbachce 2, *Csepel* 3
Rangers 5, *Anderlecht* 2
Anderlecht 0, *Rangers* 2
Red Star 2, *Porto* 1
Porto 0, *Red Star* 2
Vorwärts Berlin 2, *Wolverhampton Wanderers* 1
Wolverhampton Wanderers 2, *Vorwärts Berlin* 0

First Round

Real Madrid 7, *Esch* 0
Esch 2, *Real Madrid* 5
BK Odense 0, *Wiener SK* 3
Wiener SK 2, *BK Odense* 2
Sparta Rotterdam 3, *IFK Gothenburg* 1
IFK Gothenburg 3, *Sparta Rotterdam* 1
Sparta Rotterdam 3, *IFK Gothenburg* 1
Milan 0, *Barcelona* 2
Barcelona 5, *Milan* 1
Young Boys Berne 1, *Eintracht Frankfurt* 4
Eintracht Frankfurt 1, *Young Boys Berne* 1
Red Star 1, *Wolverhampton Wanderers* 1
Wolverhampton Wanderers 3, *Red Star* 0
Rangers 4, *Red Star Bratislava* 3
Red Star Bratislava 1, *Rangers* 1
Fenerbachce 2, *Nice* 1
Nice 2, *Fenerbachce* 1
Nice 5, *Fenerbachce* 1

Quarter-finals

Nice 3, *Real Madrid* 2
Real Madrid 4, *Nice* 0
Barcelona 4, *Wolverhampton Wanderers* 0
Wolverhampton Wanderers 2, *Barcelona* 5
Eintracht 2, *Wiener SK* 1
Wiener SK 1, *Eintracht* 1
Rangers 3, *Sparta* 2
Sparta 1, *Rangers* 0
Rangers 3, *Sparta* 2

Semi-finals

Eintracht 6, *Rangers* 1
Rangers 3, *Eintracht* 6
Real Madrid 3, *Barcelona* 1
Barcelona 1, *Real Madrid* 3

Final *Glasgow, May* 18, 1960

Real Madrid 7, *Eintracht Frankfurt* 3 (3–1)

Real Madrid: Dominguez; Marquitos, Pachin; Vidal, Santamaria, Zarraga; Canario, Del Sol, Di Stefano, Puskas, Gento.

Eintracht: Loy; Lutz, Hoefer; Wellbaecher, Eigenbrodt, Stinka; Kress, Lindner, Stein, Pfaff, Meier.

Scorers: Di Stefano (3) Puskas (4) for Real, Kress, Stein (2) for Eintracht.

EUROPEAN CUP 1960–1

At long last, the reign of Real Madrid was brought to an end. But the team that eliminated them – Barcelona, taking revenge for the previous year – did not win the Cup. Instead, it went, against all expectation, to Benfica, the Portuguese club, managed with immense shrewdness by the veteran Hungarian, Bela Guttmann. Benfica may have had a little luck in the Final, when the sun dazzled Ramallets, and he let in a couple of simple goals, but they undoubtedly had a splendid team. Germano, the centre-half, was the best and most mobile in Europe, Coluna a superb midfield player, and Aguas a mature centre-forward.

Burnley, England's representatives, played skilful football, but failed badly against Hamburg in their return quarter-final, when they had enough of the play to have won. Hearts were unfortunate enough to meet Benfica in the first round.

Preliminary Round

Frederikstadt 4, *Ajax Amsterdam* 3
Ajax Amsterdam 0, *Frederikstadt* 0
Limerick 0, *Young Boys* 6
Young Boys 4, *Limerick* 2
Kamraterna 1, *IFK Malmö* 3
IFK Malmö 2, *Kamraterna* 1
Reims 6, *Esch* 1
Esch 0, *Reims* 5
Rapid Vienna 4, *Besiktas Istanbul* 0
Besiktas Istanbul 1, *Rapid Vienna* 0
Juventus 2, *CDNA Sofia* 0
CDNA Sofia 4, *Juventus* 1
Aarhus GF 3, *Legia Warsaw* 0
Legia Warsaw 1, *Aarhus GF* 0
Red Star Belgrade 1, *Ujpest* 2
Ujpest 3, *Red Star Belgrade* 0
Barcelona 2, *Lierse SK* 0
Lierse SK 0, *Barcelona* 3
Hearts 1, *Benfica* 2

Benfica 3, *Hearts* 0
Forfeited: Glenavon and CCA Bucharest.

First Round

Aarhus GF 3, *Frederikstadt* 0
Frederikstadt 0, *Aarhus GF* 1
IFK Malmö 1, *CDNA Sofia* 0
CDNA Sofia 1, *IFK Malmö* 1
Young Boys Berne 0, *SV Hamburg* 5
SV Hamburg 3, *Young Boys Berne* 3
Spartak Kralove 1, *Panathanaikos* 0
Panathanaikos 0, *Spartak Kralove* 0
Benfica 6, *Ujpest* 2
Ujpest 2, *Benfica* 1
Real Madrid 2, *Barcelona* 2
Barcelona 2, *Real Madrid* 1
Rapid Vienna 3, *Wismut Karl-Marx-Stadt* 1
Wismut Karl-Marx-Stadt 2, *Rapid Vienna* 0
Rapid Vienna 1, *Wismut Karl-Marx-Stadt* 0
Burnley 2, *Reims* 0
Reims 3, *Burnley* 2

Quarter-finals

Burnley 3, *Hamburg* 1
Hamburg 4, *Burnley* 1
Barcelona 4, *Spartak Kralove* 0
Spartak Kralove 1, *Barcelona* 1
Benfica 3, *Aarhus* 1
Aarhus 2, *Benfica* 4
Rapid Vienna 2, *IFK Malmö* 0
IFK Malmö 0, *Rapid Vienna* 2

Semi-finals

Barcelona 1, *Hamburg* 0
Hamburg 2, *Barcelona* 1
Barcelona 1, *Hamburg* 0
Benfica 3, *Rapid Vienna* 0
Rapid Vienna 1, *Benfica* 1

Final *Berne, March* 31, 1961

Benfica 3, *Barcelona* 2 (2–1)
Benfica: Costa Pereira; Joao, Angelo; Netto, Germano, Cruz; Augusto, Santana, Aguas, Coluna, Cavem.
Barcelona: Ramallets; Foncho, Gracia; Verges, Garay, Gensana; Kubala, Koscis, Evaristo, Suarez, Czibor.
Scorers: Aguas, Ramallets (own goal), Coluna for Benfica, Koscis, Czibor for Barcelona.

EUROPEAN CUP 1961–2

It was now the turn of the brilliant Spurs team to represent England. They played some memorable matches, not least the one in which they crushed Gornik of Poland 8 1 in a frenzied atmosphere of partisan passion, after losing the first leg. But over-emphasis on defence in Lisbon, mistakes by the backs, and a little bad luck in a frenetic return, against Benfica, cost them the semi-finals. Benfica went on to win a marvellous Final against Real, in Amsterdam, proving that their success the season before had been no fluke. They survived a fine early goal worked out by Di Stefano and Puskas, and the shooting in this match from Puskas, Coluna, Eusebio, Cavem, really had to be seen to be believed.

Rangers, once again representing Scotland, had a creditable passage, but failed sadly and surprisingly in Liège against Standard.

Preliminary Round

Nuremberg 5, *Drumcondra* 0
Drumcondra 1, *Nuremberg* 4
Vorwärts 3, *Linfield* 0
(Linfield gave Vorwärts a walkover in the second leg when the East Germans were refused visas.)
Spora Luxemburg 0, *Odense* 6
Odense 9, *Spora Luxemburg* 2
Monaco 2, *Rangers* 3
Rangers 3, *Monaco* 2
Vasas 0, *Real Madrid* 2
Real Madrid 3, *Vasas* 1
CDNA Sofia 4, *Dukla* 4
Dukla 2, *CDNA Sofia* 1
Standard Liège 2, *Frederikstadt* 1
Frederikstadt 0, *Standard Liège* 2
IFK Gothenburg 0, *Feyenoord* 3
Feyenoord 8, *IFK Gothenburg* 2
Servette 5, *Valetta* 0
Valetta 1, *Servette* 2
Gornik 4, *Tottenham Hotspur* 2
Tottenham Hotspur 8, *Gornik* 1
Sporting Lisbon 1, *Partizan Belgrade* 1
Partizan Belgrade 2, *Sporting Lisbon* 0
Panathanaikos 1, *Juventus* 1
Juventus 2, *Panathanaikos* 1
Bucharest 0, *FK Austria* 0
FK Austria 2, *Bucharest* 0

First Round

Odense 0, *Real Madrid* 3
Real Madrid 9, *Odense* 0

Fenerbachce 1, *Nuremberg* 2
Nuremberg 1, *Fenerbachce* 0
Standard Liège 5, *Valkeakosken* 1
Valkeakosken 0, *Standard Liège* 2
FK Austria 1, *Benfica* 1
Benfica 5, *FK Austria* 1
Servette 4, *Dukla* 3
Dukla 2, *Servette* 0
Feyenoord 1, *Tottenham Hotspur* 3
Tottenham Hotspur 1, *Feyenoord* 1
Partizan 1, *Juventus* 2
Juventus 5, *Partizan* 1
Vorwärts Berlin 1, *Rangers* 2
Rangers 4, *Vorwärts Berlin* 1

Quarter-finals

Nuremberg 3, *Benfica* 1
Benfica 6, *Nuremberg* 0
Standard Liège 4, *Rangers* 1
Rangers 2, *Standard Liège* 0
Dukla 1, *Tottenham Hotspur* 0
Tottenham Hotspur 4, *Dukla* 1
Juventus 0, *Real Madrid* 1
Real Madrid 0, *Juventus* 1
Real Madrid 3, *Juventus* 1

Semi-finals

Benfica 3, *Tottenham Hotspur* 1
Tottenham Hotspur 2, *Benfica* 1
Real Madrid 4, *Standard Liège* 0
Standard Liège 0, *Real Madrid* 2

Final *Amsterdam, May* 2, 1962

Benfica 5, *Real Madrid* 3 (2–3)
Benfica: Costa Pereira; Joao, Angelo; Cavem, Germano, Cruz; Augusto, Eusebio, Aguas, Coluna, Simoes.
Real Madrid: Araquistain; Cassado, Miera; Felo, Santamaria, Pachin; Tejada, Del Sol, Di Stefano, Puskas, Gento.
Scorers: Puskas (3) for Real Madrid, Aguas, Cavem, Coluna, Eusebio (2) for Benfica.

EUROPEAN CUP 1962–3

For the third successive time, Benfica reached the Final, but this one was to end in their defeat. Milan beat them at Wembley in a slightly disappointing game. Managed now by the Chilean, Riera, instead of

Guttmann, Benfica had gone over to 4–2–4 and a more defensive outlook, partly dictated by the loss of Germano through injury, Aguas through form. Milan, well generalled by the precocious young Rivera, hit back with two goals by Brazil's Altafini (the second of which looked offside) after Eusebio had put Benfica ahead. But an injury to Coluna, who had to go off in the second half, badly affected them.

Ipswich, England's representatives, and Dundee both went out to Milan. Ipswich floundered in heavy rain in Milan, played more briskly in the return – and won – but Dundee were a revelation. Clever breakaway tactics and a defence splendidly marshalled by Ian Ure enabled them to become the dark horse of the tournament. For Real, knocked out in Belgium by a goal from Jef Jurion, this was a season of relative twilight.

Preliminary Round

Linfield 1, *Esbjerg* 2
Esbjerg 0, *Linfield* 0
Real Madrid 3, *Anderlecht* 3
Anderlecht 1, *Real Madrid* 0
Floriana Malta 1, *Ipswich Town* 4
Ipswich Town 10, *Floriana Malta* 0
Dundee 8, *Cologne* 1
Cologne 4, *Dundee* 0
Shelbourne 0, *Sporting Lisbon* 2
Sporting Lisbon 5, *Shelbourne* 1
Vorwärts 0, *Dukla* 3
Dukla 1, *Vortwärts* 0
Norrköping 9, *Partizan Tirana* 2
Partizan Tirana 1, *Norrköping* 1
Dynamo Bucharest 1, *Galatassaray* 1
Galatassaray 3, *Dynamo Bucharest* 0
Polonia 2, *Panathanaikos* 1
Panathanaikos 1, *Polonia* 4
Frederikstadt 1, *Vasas* 4
Vasas 7, *Frederikstadt* 0
FK Austria 5, *Kamraterna* 3
Kamraterna 0, *FK Austria* 2
CDNA Sofia 2, *Partizan Belgrade* 1
Partizan Belgrade 1, *CDNA Sofia* 4
Milan 8, *US Luxemburg* 0
US Luxemburg 0, *Milan* 6

First Round

FK Austria 3, *Reims* 2
Reims 5, *FK Austria* 0
Sporting Lisbon 1, *Dundee* 0
Dundee 4, *Sporting Lisbon* 1

Norrköping 1, *Benfica* 1
Benfica 5, *Norrköping* 1
Galatassaray 4, *Polonia Bytom* 1
Polonia Bytom 1, *Galatassaray* 0
Esbjerg 0, *Dukla* 0
Dukla 5, *Esbjerg* 0
Feyenoord 1, *Vasas* 1
Vasas 2, *Feyenoord* 2
Feyenoord 1, *Vasas* 0
Milan 3, *Ipswich Town* 0
Ipswich Town 2, *Milan* 1

Quarter-finals

Anderlecht 1, *Dundee* 4
Dundee 2, *Anderlecht* 1
Galatassaray 1, *Milan* 3
Milan 5, *Galatassaray* 0
Benfica 2, *Dukla* 1
Dukla 0, *Benfica* 0
Reims 0, *Feyenoord* 1
Feyenoord 1, *Reims* 1

Semi-finals

Milan 5, *Dundee* 1
Dundee 1, *Milan* 0
Benfica 3, *Feyenoord* 1
Feyenoord 0, *Benfica* 0

Final *Wembley Stadium, May* 22, 1963

Milan 2, *Benfica* 1 (0–1)
Milan: Ghezzi; David, Trebbi; Benitez, Maldini, Trapattoni; Pivatelli, Sani, Altafini, Rivera, Mora.

Benfica: Costa Pereira; Cavem, Cruz; Humberto, Raul, Coluna; Augusto, Santana, Torres, Eusebio, Simoes.
Scorers: Eusebio for Benfica, Altafini (2) for Milan.

EUROPEAN CUP 1963–4

Britain's challenge disappeared with depressing speed. Rangers, somewhat unlucky to lose to a late goal by Puskas, at Ibrox, in a breakaway, were torn apart in Madrid, where Puskas showed much of his old form. It must be said in Rangers' defence that they lacked several experienced forwards. Everton were baffled by the reinforced Inter defence, at Goodison, though many feel they did breach it, when a goal by Vernon was narrowly judged offside. In Milan, they themselves employed massive defence, and it was only a freak goal from near the by-line, scored by Jair, which beat them.

Benfica, lacking Costa Pereira and Eusebio, were thrashed in their return match with Borussia Dortmund who went on to eliminate Dukla. A superb display in Madrid enabled Real to eliminate Milan, while Inter's massive defence and breakaway attacks accounted for Monaco, Partizan and Borussia. In the Final, Inter left out their extra defender, Szymaniak, gambled on a genuine leader in Milani, blotted out Real's attack, and exploited the mistakes of their defence. Mazzola scored from long range just before half-time. Poor goalkeeping gave Milani a second, Felo headed in from a corner, but an incredible blunder by Santamaria presented Mazzola with the third.

Preliminary Round

Galatassaray 4, *Ferencvaros* 0
Ferencvaros 2, *Galatassaray* 0
Partizan Belgrade 3, *Anorthosis* 0
Anorthosis 1, *Partizan Belgrade* 3
Dundalk 0, *FC Zürich* 3
FC Zürich 1, *Dundalk* 2
Lyn Oslo 2, *Borussia Dortmund* 4
Borussia Dortmund 3, *Lyn Oslo* 1
Dukla 6, *Valetta* 0
Valetta 0, *Dukla* 2
Everton 0, *Internazionale* 0
Internazionale 1, *Everton* 0
Gornik 1, *FK Austria* 0
FK Austria 1, *Gornik* 0
Gornik 2, *FK Austria* 1
Monaco 7, *AEK Athens* 2
AEK Athens 1, *Monaco* 1
Dynamo Bucharest 2, *Motor Jena* 0
Motor Jena 0, *Dynamo Bucharest* 1
Valkae Kosken 4, *Jeunesse Esch* 1
Jeunesse Esch 4, *Valkea Kosken* 0
Standard Liège 1, *Norrköpping* 0
Norrköpping 2, *Standard Liège* 0
Tirania 1, *Spartak Plovdiv* 0
Spartak Plovdiv 3, *Tirania* 1
Eindhoven 7, *Esbjerg* 1
Esbjerg 3, *Eindhoven* 4
Distillery 3, *Benfica* 3
Benfica 5, *Distillery* 0
Rangers 0, *Real Madrid* 1
Real Madrid 6, *Rangers* 0

First Round

Benfica 2, *Dortmund Borussia* 1
Dortmund Borussia 5, *Benfica* 0
Internazionale 1, *Monaco* 0
Monaco 0, *Internazionale* 3
Norrköpping 1, *Milan* 1
Milan 5, *Norrköpping* 2
FC Zürich 3, *Galatassaray* 0
Galatassaray 2, *FC Zürich* 0
Gornik 2, *Dukla* 0
Dukla 4, *Gornik* 1
Jaunesse Esch 2, *Partizan Belgrade* 1
Partizan Belgrade 6, *Jeunesse Esch* 2
Spartak Plovdiv 0, *Eindhoven* 1
Eindhoven 0, *Spartak Plovdiv* 0
Dynamo Bucharest 1, *Real Madrid* 3
Real Madrid 5, *Dynamo Bucharest* 3

Quarter-finals

Real Madrid 4, *Milan* 1
Milan 2, *Real Madrid* 0
Partizan Belgrade 0, *Internazionale* 3
Internazionale 2, *Partizan Belgrade* 1
Eindhoven 1, *FC Zürich* 0
FC Zürich 3, *Eindhoven* 1
Dukla 0, *Borussia Dortmund* 4
Borussia Dortmund 1, *Dukla* 3

Semi-finals

Borussia Dortmund 2, *Internazionale* 2
Internazionale 2, *Borussia Dortmund* 0
FC Zürich 1, *Real Madrid* 2
Real Madrid 6, *FC Zürich* 0

Final *Vienna, May* 27, 1964.

Internazionale 3, *Real Madrid* 1
Internazionale: Sarti; Burgnich, Facchetti; Tagnin, Guarneri, Picchi; Jair, Mazzola, Milani, Suarez, Corso.
Real Madrid: Vicente; Isidro, Pachin; Muller, Santamaria, Zocco; Amancio, Felo, Di Stefano, Puskas, Gento.
Scorers: Mazzola (2), Milani for Internazionale, Felo for Real Madrid.

EUROPEAN CUP 1964–5

Once again, Inter won the tournament, though not without considerable difficulty on the way. Much of this was gallantly provided by Liverpool who, three days after a bruising Cup Final, involving extra time, and playing without two key men, brilliantly defeated them, at Anfield. Inter, however, recovered to win in Milan, though Peiró's goal, after a challenge on the goalkeeper, Lawrence, is still a subject of dispute. Previously, Liverpool had had a notable success against an Anderlecht team till then in splendid form. A clever tactical plan, using Smith as a second centre-half, was their chief weapon, but they were very lucky indeed to win the toss in Rotterdam against a brave 10-man Cologne team, which fought back from 0–2.

Rangers also did well, and might have done better still, had not Jim Baxter broken a leg, while helping materially to get them through, in Vienna.

In the Final, Inter won laboriously and unconvincingly against a brave Benfica side, naturally reluctant to play it on Inter's own ground. Benfica lost Costa Pereira, their goalkeeper, half-an-hour from time, but the score remained unchanged. And the goal, by Jair, was really owed to the appalling, rainy conditions; a shot which slipped under Costa Pereira's body.

Preliminary Round

Anderlecht 1, *Bologna* 0
Bologna 2, *Anderlecht* 1
Anderlecht 0, *Bologna* 0 (in Barcelona)
Anderlecht won toss
Rangers 3, *Red Star* 1
Red Star 4, *Rangers* 2
Rangers 3, *Red Star* 1 (Highbury)
Chemie Leipzig 0, *Vasas Gyoer* 2
Vasas Gyoer 4, *Chemie Leipzig* 2
Dukla 4, *Gornik* 1
Gornik 3, *Dukla* 0
Gornik 0, *Dukla* 0 (Duisburg)
Dukla won toss
Reipas 2, *Lyn* 1
Lyn 3, *Reipas* 0
Tirana 0, *Cologne* 0
Cologne 2, *Tirana* 0
St. Etienne 2, *Chaux de Fonds* 2
Chaux de Fonds 2, *St. Etienne* 1
Glentoran 2, *Panathanaikos* 2
Panathanaikos 3, *Glentoran* 2
Odense 2, *Real Madrid* 5
Real Madrid 4, *Odense* 0
Aris 1, *Benfica* 5
Benfica 5, *Aris* 1
DWS Amsterdam 3, *Fenerbachce* 0
Fenerbachce 0, *DWS Amsterdam* 1
Rapid Vienna 3, *Shamrock Rovers* 0

Shamrock Rovers 0, *Rapid Vienna* 2
Lokomotiv Sofia 8, *Malmö* 3
Malmö 2, *Lokomotiv Sofia* 0
Reykjavic 0, *Liverpool* 5
Liverpool 6, *Reykjavic* 1
Dinamo Bucharest 5, *Sliema Wanderers* 0
Sliema Wanderers 0, *Dinamo Bucharest* 2

First Round
Panathanaikos 1, *Cologne* 1
Cologne 2, *Panathanaikos* 1
Internazionale 6, *Dinamo Bucharest* 0
Dinamo Bucharest 0, *Internazionale* 1
Vasas Gyoer 5, *Lokomotiv Sofia* 3
Lokomotiv Sofia 4, *Vasas Gyoer* 3
Rangers 1, *Rapid Vienna* 0
Rapid Vienna 0, *Rangers* 2
Real Madrid 4, *Dukla* 0
Dukla 2, *Real Madrid* 2
Liverpool 3, *Anderlecht* 0
Anderlecht 0, *Liverpool* 1
DWS Amsterdam 5, *Lyn* 0
Lyn 1, *DWS Amsterdam* 3
Chaux de Fonds 1, *Benfica* 1
Benfica 5, *Chaux de Fonds* 0

Quarter-finals
Cologne 0, *Liverpool* 0
Liverpool 0, *Cologne* 0
Liverpool 2, *Cologne* 2 (*Rotterdam*)
Liverpool won toss
Internazionale 3, *Rangers* 1
Rangers 1, *Internazionale* 0
Benfica 5, *Real Madrid* 1
Real Madrid 2, *Benfica* 1
DWS Amsterdam 1, *Vasas Gyoer* 1
Vasas Gyoer 1, *DWS Amsterdam* 0

Semi-finals
Vasas Gyoer 0, *Benfica* 1
Benfica 4, *Vasas Gyoer* 0
Liverpool 3, *Internazionale* 1
Internazionale 3, *Liverpool* 0

Final *Milan, May* 27, 1965
Internazionale 1, *Benfica* 0 (1–0)
Internazionale: Sarti; Burgnich, Facchetti; Bedin, Guarneri, Picchi; Jair, Mazzola, Peiró, Suarez, Corso.

Benfica: Costa Pereira; Cavem, Cruz; Netto, Germano, Paul; Augusto, Eusebio, Torres, Coluna, Simoes.
Scorer: Jair for Inter.

EUROPEAN CUP 1965–6

Once again, Manchester United reached the semi-finals – and folded up. Once again Real Madrid, for the sixth time in their history, took the Cup. The virtual Final was composed by their two matches against Inter, the holders and favourites, who made the mistake of fielding a defensive formation against them in the first leg of the semi-finals, in Madrid. Real got through by the only goal and, at San Siro, virtually settled matters when they took the lead through Amancio. Inter equalised; but never seemed likely to win.

In the Final, Real, a young, vigorous side with none of the high quality of the Di Stefano days, duly beat Partizan, the Belgrade dark horses, despite falling behind to a goal by Vasovic, 10 minutes after half-time.

Previously, Partizan had beaten a sloppy Manchester United side in Belgrade, and held them to a single, rather lucky, goal by Stiles, at Old Trafford, where United were without Best, Partizan without their midfield schemer, Kovacevic – and without Galic, doing his military service but recalled for the Final, in Brussels. United had the consolation of putting up perhaps the finest display of the competition, when they brilliantly thrashed Benfica in Lisbon, in the return leg of the quarter finals. George Best, irresistible, scored the two opening goals in the first 12 minutes.

Preliminary Round

Lyn 5, *Derry City* 3
Derry City 5, *Lyn* 1
Feyenoord 2, *Real Madrid* 1
Real Madrid 5, *Feyenoord* 0
Kevflavik 1, *Ferencvaros* 4
Ferencvaros 9, *Kevflavik* 1
Fenerbachce 0, *Anderlecht* 0
Anderlecht 5, *Fenerbachce* 1
Tirania 0, *Kilmarnock* 0
Kilmarnock 1, *Tirania* 0
Djurgarden 2, *Levski* 1
Levski 6, *Djurgarden* 0
Drumcondra 1, *Vorwärts* 0
Vorwärts 3, *Drumcondra* 0
Linz 1, *Gornik* 3
Gornik 2, *Linz* 1
Partizan 2, *Nantes* 0
Nantes 2, *Partizan* 2

HIK 2, *Manchester United* 3
Manchester United 6, *HIK* 0
Lausanne 0, *Sparta Prague* 0
Sparta Prague 4, *Lausanne* 0
Dudelange 0, *Benfica* 8
Benfica 10, *Dundelange* 0
Panathanaikos 4, *Sliema* 1
Sliema 1, *Panathanaikos* 0
Hapoel Nicosia 0, *Werder Bremen* 5 (*Bremen*)
Werder Bremen 5, *Hopoel Nicosia* 0
Dynamo Bucharest 4, *Odense* 0
Odense 2, *Dynamo Bucharest* 3

First Round

Partizan 3, *Werder Bremen* 0
Werder Bremen 1, *Partizan* 0
Levski 2, *Benfica* 2
Benfica 3, *Levski* 2
Ferencvaros 0, *Panathanaikos* 0
Panathanaikos 1, *Ferencvaros* 3
Kilmarnock 2, *Real Madrid* 2
Real Madrid 5, *Kilmarnock* 1
Vorwärts 0, *Manchester United* 2
Manchester United 3, *Vorwärts* 1
Sparta 3, *Gornik* 0
Gornik 1, *Sparta* 2
Dynamo Bucharest 2, *Internazionale* 1
Internazionale 2, *Dynamo Bucharest* 0
Anderlecht 9, *Derry City* 0 (no return match)

Second Round

Manchester United 3, *Benfica* 2
Benfica 1, *Manchester United* 5
Anderlecht 1, *Real Madrid* 0
Real Madrid 4, *Anderlecht* 2
Sparta 4, *Partizan* 1
Partizan 5, *Sparta* 0
Internazionale 4, *Ferencvaros* 0
Ferencvaros 1, *Internazionale* 1

Semi-finals

Partizan 2, *Manchester United* 0
Manchester United 1, *Partizan* 0
Real Madrid 1, *Internazionale* 0
Internazionale 1, *Real Madrid* 1

Final *Brussels, May* 11, 1966

Real Madrid 2, *Partizan* 1 (0–0)
Real Madrid: Araquistain; Pachin, Sanchis; Pirri, De Felipe, Zoco; Serena, Amancio, Grosso, Velazquez, Gento.

Partizan: Soskic; Jusufi, Mihailovic; Becejac, Rasovic, Vasovic; Bajic, Kovacevic, Hasanagic, Galic, Primajer.
Scorers: Amancio and Serena for Real, Vasovic for Partizan.

EUROPEAN CUP 1966–7

To the general surprise, and delight, the Cup was won by a Celtic team competing in it for the first time; one, moreover, which overwhelmed a weary and pathetically negative Inter in the Final, at Lisbon. Shrewdly and forcefully managed by their old centre-half, Jock Stein, Celtic's football was (with the exception of a cautious holding action away to Dukla) fast, muscular and attacking. Gemmell overlapped powerfully at left-back, scoring a magnificent, half-volleyed goal in the Final, Auld was a fine midfield player, little Johnstone a superb outside-right.

Inter reached their zenith in the quarter-finals, when they took an ample revenge on Real Madrid for the previous year's elimination. Cappellini, then, looked an impressive new centre-forward. Then the bubble burst, and they made pitifully heavy weather disposing, in three matches, of the honest, modest CSK Sofia, previously much troubled by Linfield.

Liverpool were thrashed by a splendid Ajax forward-line, in Amsterdam; finely led by Cruyff; but Dukla knew too much for Ajax. Torpedo, Russia's first entrants, put up a sturdy fight against Inter, in Milan, but went out by the only goal – Voronin's own goal – of the tie.

In the Final, Inter, without their midfield general, Suarez, and with Mazzola not fully fit, took the lead from a penalty when, in the eighth minute, Craig tripped Cappellini, then bolted back into defence, to be besieged for the rest of the game. Gemmell equalised after 63 minutes, and Chalmers got the winner five minutes from time.

Extra Preliminary Round

Sliema Wanderers 1, *CSK Sofia* 2
CSK Sofia 4, *Sliema Wanderers* 0
Waterford 1, *Vorwärts Berlin* 6
Vorwärts Berlin 6, *Waterford* 0

First Round

Reykjavik 2, *Nantes* 3
Nantes 5, *Reykjavik* 2

Aris Bonnevoie 3, *Linfield* 3
Linfield 6, *Aris Bonnevoie* 1
Admira 0, *Vojvodina* 1
Vojvodina 0, *Admira* 0
Anderlecht 10, *Valkeakovski* 1
Valkeakovski 0, *Anderlecht* 2 (*Brussels*)
Munich 1860 8, *Nicosia* 0
Nicosia 1, *Munich 1860* 2 (*Munich*)
Liverpool 2, *Petrolul Ploesti* 0
Petrolul Ploesti 3, *Liverpool* 1
Liverpool 2, *Petrolul Ploesti* 0 (*Brussels*)
Celtic 2, *Zurich* 0
Zurich 0, *Celtic* 3
Malmö 0, *Atletico Madrid* 2
Atletico Madrid 3, *Malmö* 1
Ejsberg 0, *Dukla Prague* 2
Dukla Prague 4, *Ejsberg* 0
Ajax Amsterdam 2, *Besiktas* 0
Besiktas 1, *Ajax Amsterdam* 2
Vasas 5, *Sporting Lisbon* 0
Sporting Lisbon 0, *Vasas* 2
CSK 3, *Olimpiakos Piraeus* 1
Olimpiakos Piraeus 1, *CSK* 0
Gornik 2, *Vorwärts* 1
Vorwärts 2, *Gornik* 1
Gornik 3, *Vorwärts* 1 (*Budapest*)
Internazionale 1, *Torpedo* 0
Torpedo 0, *Internazionale* 0

Second Round

Valerengen Oslo 1, *Linfield* 4
Linfield 1, *Valerengen Oslo* 1
Inter 2, *Vasas* 1
Vasas 0, *Inter* 2
Dukla 4, *Anderlecht* 1
Anderlecht 1, *Dukla* 2
Munich 1860 1, *Real Madrid* 0
Real Madrid 3, *Munich 1860* 1
CSK 4, *Gornik* 0
Gornik 3, *CSK* 0
Vojvodina 3, *Atletico Madrid* 1
Atletico Madrid 2, *Vojvodina* 0
Atletico Madrid 2, *Vojvodina* 3 (*Madrid*)
Nantes 1, *Celtic* 3
Celtic 3, *Nantes* 1
Ajax 5, *Liverpool* 1
Liverpool 2, *Ajax* 2

Quarter-Finals

Inter 1, *Real Madrid* 0
Real Madrid 0, *Inter* 2
Linfield 2, *CSK* 2
CSK 1, *Linfield* 0
Ajax 1, *Dukla* 1
Dukla 2, *Ajax* 1
Vojvodina 1, *Celtic* 0
Celtic 2, *Vojvodina* 0

Semi-Finals

Celtic 3, *Dukla* 1
Dukla 0, *Celtic* 0
Inter 1, *CSK* 1
CSK 1, *Inter* 1
Inter 1, *CSK* 0 (*Bologna*)

Final *Lisbon, May* 25, 1967

Celtic 2, *Internazionale* 1 (0–1)
Celtic: Simpson; Craig, Gemmell; Murdoch, McNeill, Clark; Johnstone, Wallace, Chalmers, Auld, Lennox.
Inter: Sarti; Burgnich, Facchetti; Bedin, Guarneri, Picchi,; Bicicli, Mazzola, Cappellini, Corso, Domenghini.
Scorers: Gemmell, Chalmers for Celtic, Mazzola (penalty) for Inter.

EUROPEAN CUP 1967–8

For the first time, the European Cup was won by an English club; most fittingly, Manchester United, who had been semi-finalists on three previous occasions. The final, at Wembley, was remarkable. United dominated the first half, but couldn't turn their advantage into goals, flagged badly late in the second half, when Benfica equalised Charlton's goal, and were ultimately galvanised by a superb goal, early in extra time, scored by George Best. The young forwards, Aston and Kidd, made an unexpectedly large contribution to their success. The injured Law didn't play.

Previously, they'd had little trouble with the Maltese – though they surprisingly drew 0–0 in Malta – had overcome a rough, determined Sarajevo, and beaten Real Madrid after an astonishing revival at Bernabeu Stadium, Foulkes, centre-half, getting the equaliser. There was also a memorable quarter final versus Gornik, when brilliant goalkeeping defied them at Old Trafford, and they kept the score down to 1–0 on an impossibly Arctic pitch, in Poland.

Celtic, the holders, surprisingly went out to Dynamo Kiev in the first round. Bychevetz was their destroyer in Glasgow, but they were rather unlucky in the return, when Murdoch was sent off, and fighting broke out late in the game. Glentoran, the Irish champions, gave Benfica a terrible fright in the same round, going out only on the newly and dubiously introduced rule whereby away goals, in case of equality, count double. Benfica did not really find form, and recover from their manager's, Riera, resignation, till the semi-finals, when Vasas were overcome. At Wembley, they lost many friends with their rough treatment of Best.

This was the first European Cup to be seeded.

First Round

Glentoran 1, *Benfica* 1
Benfica 0, *Glentoran* 0
Besiktas 0, *Rapid Vienna* 1

Rapid Vienna 3, *Besiktas* 0
Celtic 1, *Dynamo Kiev* 2
Dynamo Kiev 1, *Celtic* 1
Olimpiakos 0, *Juventus* 0
Juventus 2, *Olimpiakos* 0
Dundalk 0, *Vasas* 1
Vasas 8, *Dundalk* 1
Manchester United 4, *Hibernian* (*Malta*) 0
Hibernian 0, *Manchester United* 0
St. Etienne 2, *Kuopio* 0
Kuopio 3, *St. Etienne* 0
Karl-Marx-Stadt 1, *Anderlecht* 3
Anderlecht 2, *Karl-Marx-Stadt* 1
Basel 1, *Hvidovre* 2
Hvidovre 3, *Basel* 3
Skeid Oslo 0, *Sparta Prague* 1
Sparta Prague 1, *Skeid Oslo* 1
Olimpiakos Nicosia 2, *Sarajevo* 2
Sarajevo 3, *Olimpiakos Nicosia* 1
Ajax 1, *Real Madrid* 1
Real Madrid 2, *Ajax* 1
Valur 1, *Jeunesse Esch* 1
Jeunesse Esch 3, *Valur* 3
Gornik 3, *Djurgarden* 0
Djurgarden 0, *Gornik* 1
Plovdiv Traka 2, *Rapid Bucharest* 0
Rapid Bucharest 3, *Plovdiv Traka* 0
Eintracht bye, Tirania scr.

Second Round

Sarajevo 0, *Manchester United* 0
Manchester United 2, *Sarajevo* 1
Hvidovre 2, *Real Madrid* 2
Real Madrid 4, *Hvidovre* 1

Rapid Vienna 1, *Eintracht Brunswick* 0
Eintracht Brunswick 2, *Rapid Vienna* 0
Benfica 2, *St. Etienne* 0
St. Etienne 1, *Benfica* 0
Vasas 6, *Reykjavik* 0
Reykjavik 1, *Vasas* 5
Dynamo Kiev 1, *Gornik* 2
Gornik 1, *Dynamo Kiev* 1
Juventus 1, *Rapid Bucharest* 0
Rapid Bucharest 0, *Juventus* 0
Sparta Prague 3, *Anderlecht* 2
Anderlecht 3, *Sparta Prague* 3

Quarter-finals

Eintracht Brunswick 3, *Juventus* 2
Juventus 1, *Eintracht Brunswick* 0
Juventus 1, *Eintracht Brunswick* 0 (*play-off*)
Manchester United 2, *Gornik* 0
Gornik 1, *Manchester United* 0
Real Madrid 3, *Sparta Prague* 0
Sparta Prague 2, *Real Madrid* 1
Vasas 0, *Benfica* 0
Benfica 3, *Vasas* 0

Semi-finals

Manchester United 1, *Real Madrid* 1
Real Madrid 3, *Manchester United* 3
Benfica 2, *Juventus* 0
Juventus 0, *Benfica* 1

Final *Wembley Stadium, May* 29, 1968

Manchester United (0) (1) 4, *Benfica* (0) (1) 1 (after extra time).
Manchester United: Stepney; Brennan, Dunne; Crerand, Foulkes, Stiles; Best, Kidd, Charlton, Sadler, Aston.
Benfica: Henrique; Adolfo, Humberto, Jacinto, Cruz; Graça, Coluna; Augusto, Eusebio, Torres, Simoes.
Scorers: Charlton 2, Best, Kidd for Manchester United. Graça for Benfica.

EUROPEAN CUP 1968-9

Milan won their second European Cup, gathering strength and momentum as the competition progressed, knocking out both Celtic and Manchester United, finally overwhelming Ajax in a one-sided final. Pierino Prati established himself as one of the game's most dangerous finishers, ruthlessly exploiting a slip by McNeill, at a throw-in, to put out Celtic, in Glasgow, scoring three times, with much help from Gianni Rivera, in the Final, in Madrid.

Mistaken selection and sloppy defensive play helped to put out Manchester United, after they had comfortably accounted for Rapid – Best showing superb form. Surprisingly, in the first leg of the quarter-final in Milan, they chose the veteran Foulkes for centre-half; Sormani was thus allowed his best game for months. The inexperienced Rimmer played in goal. United lost 2–0, and though they won an ill-tempered return in Manchester – during which Cudicini was felled by a missile from the notorious Stretford End – they properly went out; once again gifted but maddening.

Ajax, with Cruyff a dazzling centre-forward, were first astonished by Benfica, before astonishing them in their turn. A poor first game by Spartak Trnava's goalkeeper assisted their passage into the Final, but there, they were simply outclassed.

All the Iron Curtain teams but the Czech withdrew in protest against a decision to re-draw the First Round.

First Round

St. Etienne 2, *Celtic* 0
Celtic 4, *St. Etienne* 0
Waterford 1, *Manchester United* 3
Manchester United 7, *Waterford* 1
Manchester City 0, *Fenerbahce* 0
Fenerbahce 2, *Manchester City* 1
Anderlecht 3, *Glentoran* 0
Glentoran 2, *Anderlecht* 2
AEK 3, *Jeunesse Esch* 0
Jeunesse Esch 3, *AEK* 2
Nuremberg 1, *Ajax* 1
Ajax 4, *Nuremberg* 0
Malmo 2, *Milan* 1
Milan 4, *Malmo* 1
Steaua 3, *Spartak Trnava* 1
Spartak Trnava 4, *Steaua* 0
Zurich 1, *AB Copenhagen* 3
AB Copenhagen 1, *Zurich* 2
Trondheim 1, *Rapid Vienna* 3
Rapid Vienna 3, *Trondheim* 3
Valetta 1, *Reipas Lahti* 1
Reipas Lahti 2, *Valetta* 0
Real Madrid 6, *Limassol* 0
Real Madrid 6, *Limassol* 0 (played in Madrid)
Valur Reykjavik 0, *Benfica* 0
Benfica 8, *Valur Reykjavik* 0

Second Round

Manchester United 3, *Anderlecht* 0
Anderlecht 3, *Manchester United* 1
Celtic 5, *Red Star* 1
Red Star 1, *Celtic* 1
Rapid Vienna 1, *Real Madrid* 0
Real Madrid 2, *Rapid Vienna* 1
Reipas Lahti 1, *Spartak Trnava* 9
Spartak Trnava 7, *Reipas Lahti* 1
AEK Athens 0, *AB Copenhagen* 0
AB Copenhagen 0, *AEK Athens* 2
Ajax 2, *Fenerbahce* 0
Fenerbahce 0, *Ajax* 2

Quarter-finals

Ajax 1, *Benfica* 3
Benfica 1, *Ajax* 3
Ajax 3, *Benfica* 0
Milan 0, *Celtic* 0
Celtic 0, *Milan* 1
Manchester United 3, *Rapid Vienna* 0
Rapid Vienna 0, *Manchester United* 0
Spartak Trnava 2, *AEK* 1
AEK 1, *Spartak Trnava* 1

Semi-finals

Milan 2, *Manchester United* 0
Manchester United 1, *Milan* 0
Ajax 3, *Spartak Trnava* 0
Spartak Trnava 2, *Ajax* 0

Final *Madrid, May* 28, 1969

Milan 4, *Ajax Amsterdam* 1 (2–0)
Milan: Cudicini; Anquilletti, Schnellinger; Maldera, Rosato, Trapattoni; Hamrin, Lodetti, Sormani, Rivera, Prati.
Ajax: Blas; Suurbier (Nuninga), Vasovic, Van Duivenbode, Hulshoff; Pronk, Groot; Swart, Cruyff, Danielsson, Keizer.
Scorers: Prati 3, Sormani for Milan. Vasovic (penalty) for Ajax.

Chapter Nineteen
The European Cup Winners' Cup History

This Cup is something of a poor relation to the European Cup, if only because relatively few countries have a *bona fide* Cup competition. Italy, who play theirs off obscurely in midweek, are a notable instance. On the other hand, the decisive matches have drawn mammoth crowds and evinced huge enthusiasm, while Tottenham's performance in winning the 1963 tournament was of high quality.

CUP WINNERS' CUP 1960–1

This was really Glasgow Rangers' finest hour to date in a European competition. Their appetite whetted by the European Cup, their fans took wholeheartedly to the new tournament, and virtually invaded Wolverhampton, on the occasion of the floodlit tie there.

In the Final, however, Fiorentina were a little too well balanced and experienced. Above all, they had in Kurt Hamrin, their Swedish international outside-right, one of the greatest match winners in Europe.

Qualifying Round

Vorwärts 2, *Red Star Brno* 1
Red Star Brno 2, *Vorwärts* 0
Rangers 4, *Ferencvaros* 2
Ferencvaros 2, *Rangers* 1

Quarter-finals

Red Star Brno 0, *Dynamo Zagreb* 0
Dynamo Zagreb 2, *Red Star Brno* 0
FK Austria 2, *Wolverhampton Wanderers* 0
Wolverhampton Wanderers 5, *FK Austria* 0
Borussia Dusseldorf 0, *Rangers* 3
Rangers 8, *Borussia Dusseldorf* 0
Lucerne 0, *Fiorentina* 3
Fiorentina 6, *Lucerne* 2

Semi-finals

Fiorentina 3, *Dynamo Zagreb* 0
Dynamo Zagreb 2, *Fiorentina* 1
Rangers 2, *Wolverhampton Wanderers* 0
Wolverhampton Wanderers 1, *Rangers* 1

Final

1st Leg. *Glasgow, May* 17, 1961
Rangers 0, *Fiorentina* 2 (0–1)
Rangers: Ritchie; Shearer, Caldow; Davis, Paterson, Baxter; Wilson, McMillan, Scott, Brand, Hume.
Fiorentina: Albertosi; Robotti, Castelletti; Gonfiantini, Orzan, Rimbaldo; Hamrin, Micheli, Da Costa, Milan, Petris.
Scorer: Milan (2) for Fiorentina.

2nd Leg. *Florence, May* 27, 1961
Fiorentina 2, *Rangers* 1 (1–1)
Fiorentina: Albertosi; Robotti, Castelletti; Gonfiantini, Orzan, Rimbaldo; Hamrin, Micheli, Da Costa, Milan, Petris.
Rangers: Ritchie; Shearer, Caldow; Davis, Paterson, Baxter; Scott, McMillan, Millar, Brand, Wilson.
Scorers: Milan, Hamrin for Fiorentina, Scott for Rangers.

CUP WINNERS' CUP 1961–2

Leicester City took the place of Spurs, who had beaten them in the Final but, having also won the League, were committed to the European Cup. Spain, entering for the first time in the imposing shape of Atletico Madrid, won the tournament, beating Leicester on the way, and ultimately defeating Fiorentina in a replayed Final – no longer a two-legged affair.

Preliminary Round

Glenavon 1, *Leicester City* 4
Leicester City 3, *Glenavon* 1
Dunfermline 4, *St. Patrick's* 1
St. Patrick's 0, *Dunfermline* 4
Swansea Town 2, *Motor Jena* 2
Motor Jena 5, *Swansea Town* 1
Chaux de Fonds 6, *Leixoes* 2
Leixoes 5, *Chaux de Fonds* 0
Sedan 2, *Atletico Madrid* 3
Atletico Madrid 4, *Sedan* 1
Rapid Vienna 0, *Spartak Varna* 0
Spartak Varna 2, *Rapid Vienna* 5
Floriana 2, *Ujpest* 5
Ujpest 10, *Floriana* 2

First Round

Fiorentina 3, *Rapid Vienna* 1
Rapid Vienna 2, *Fiorentina* 6

Leicester City 1, *Atletico Madrid* 1
Atletico Madrid 2, *Leicester City* 0
Dunfermline 5, *Vardar* 2
Vardar 2, *Dunfermline* 0
Werder Bremen 2, *Aarhus* 0
Aarhus 2, *Werder Bremen* 3
Ajax 2, *Ujpest* 1
Ujpest 3, *Ajax* 1
Olympiakos 2, *Dynamo Zilina* (*Czech.*) 3
Dynamo Zilina 1, *Olympiakos* 0
Leixoes (*Portugal*) 1, *Progresul* 1
Progresul 0, *Leixoes* 1
Motor Jena 7, *Alliance* 0
Alliance 2, *Motor Jena* 2

Quarter-finals

Atletico Madrid 3, *Werder Bremen* 1
Werder Bremen 1, *Atletico Madrid* 1
Ujpest 4, *Dunfermline* 3
Dunfermline 0, *Ujpest* 1
Fiorentina 2, *Dynamo Zilina* 3
Dynamo Zilino 0, *Fiorentina* 2
Motor Jena 1, *Leixoes* 1
Leixoes 1, *Motor Jena* 3

Semi-finals

Fiorentina 2, *Ujpest* 0
Ujpest 0, *Fiorentina* 1
Atletico Madrid 1, *Motor Jena* 0
Motor Jena 0, *Atletico Madrid* 4

Final *Glasgow, May* 10, 1962

Fiorentina 1, *Atletico Madrid* 1 (1–1)
Scorers: Peirò for Atletico Madrid, Hamrin for Fiorentina.

Replay *Stuttgart, September* 5, 1962

Atletico Madrid 3, *Fiorentina* 0 (2–0)

Atletico Madrid: Madinabeytia; Rivilla, Calleja; Ramirez, Griffa, Glaria; Jones, Adelardo, Mendonça, Peirò, Collar.

Fiorentina: Albertosi; Robotti, Castelletti; Malatrasi, Orzan, Marchesi; Hamrin, Ferretti, Milani, Dell'Angelo, Petris.
Scorers: Jones, Mendonça, Peirò for Atletico Madrid.

CUP WINNERS' CUP 1962–3

This was most impressively won by the Spurs. Invincible at home, they played brilliant football to humiliate Rangers, and recovered impressively after a poor performance in Bratislava. OFK, after losing in Belgrade, never had much of a chance of survival. In the Final, though robbed at the last moment of the dynamic Mackay with a stomach injury, the Spurs played some magnificent football to defeat Atletico Madrid, dominated the first half, survived a sticky patch at the beginning of the second, and at last turned the game with a surprising long-range goal by outside-left Terry Dyson.

One must not leave this Cup without recording the brave achievement of the little Welsh non-League club, Bangor City, who actually beat the expensive Naples team and forced them to a third, decisive, game.

Preliminary Round

Lausanne 3, *Sparta* 0
Sparta 4, *Lausanne* 2
St. Etienne 1, *Vitoria* 1
Vitoria 0, *St. Etienne* 3
Alliance 1, *Odense* 1
Odense 8, *Alliance* 1
Rangers 4, *Seville* 0
Seville 2, *Rangers* 0
OFK Belgrade 2, *Chemie* 0
Chemie 3, *OFK Belgrade* 3
Steaua 3, *Botev* 2
Botev 5, *Steaua* 1
Ujpest 5, *Zaglebie* 0
Zaglebie 0, *Ujpest* 0
Bangor City 2, *Naples* 0
Naples 3, *Bangor City* 1
Naples 2, *Bangor City* 1 (*at Highbury*)

First Round

St. Etienne 0, *Nuremburg* 0
Nuremburg 3, *St. Etienne* 0
Atletico Madrid 4, *Hibernian Malta* 0
Hibernian Malta 0, *Atletico Madrid* 1
Botev 4, *Shamrock Rovers* 0
Shamrock Rovers 0, *Botev* 1
Graz 1, *Odense* 1
Odense 5, *Graz* 3
Tottenham Hotspur 5, *Rangers* 2
Rangers 2, *Tottenham Hotspur* 3
OFK Belgrade 5, *Portadown* 1

Portadown 3, *OFK Belgrade* 2
Lausanne 1, *Slovan Bratislava* 1
Slovan Bratislava 1, *Lausanne* 0
Ujpest 1, *Naples* 1
Naples 1, *Ujpest* 1
Naples 3, *Ujpest* 1

Quarter-finals

Slovan 2, *Tottenham Hotspur* 0
Tottenham Hotspur 6, *Slovan* 0
Odense 0, *Nuremberg* 1
Nuremberg 6, *Odense* 0
Botev 1, *Atletico Madrid* 1
Atletico Madrid 6, *Botev* 0
OFK Belgrade 2, *Naples* 0
Naples 3, *OFK Belgrade* 1
Play off: OFK Belgrade 3, *Naples* 1

Semi-finals

OFK Belgrade 1, *Tottenham Hotspur* 2
Tottenham Hotspur 3, *OFK Belgrade* 1
Nuremberg 2, *Atletico Madrid* 1
Atletico Madrid 2, *Nuremberg* 0

Final

Rotterdam, May 15, 1963
Tottenham Hotspur 5, *Atletico Madrid* 1 (2–0)
Spurs: Brown; Baker, Henry; Blanchflower, Norman, Marchi; Jones, White, Smith, Greaves, Dyson.
Atletico Madrid: Madinabeytia; Rivilla, Rodrigues; Ramiro, Griffa, Glaria; Jones, Adelardo, Chuzo, Mendonça, Collar.
Scorers: Greaves (2), White, Dyson (2) for Spurs, Collar (penalty) for Atletico Madrid.

CUP WINNERS' CUP 1963–4

Tottenham's success in 1963 meant that England were able to enter two teams, and as luck would have it, Spurs and Manchester United were quickly drawn together. A dour first leg at Tottenham saw Spurs get through with great difficulty, 2–0. But in the return the unhappy Mackay fractured a leg, and Manchester United took the game 4–1 and qualified. It was the first time the holders had been eliminated before the final. United, who should have had a bigger lead in their first leg against Sporting, lost the return in Lisbon a few days after an exhausting F.A. Cup Semi-final. Glasgow Celtic were the splendid surprise of the tournament. Qualified only because Rangers, the

Scottish Cupholders, were in the European Cup, they sailed through Europe, before falling to MTK in the semi-final. Celtic put up a brave fight, but were overwhelmed in the reply when MTK got their international stars, Sandor and Nagy, back. Sporting won a tremendously tight semi-final series in a third, deciding match; Lyon had a man sent off in the second half. In the Final, the opportunism of Sandor enabled MTK to hold their own in Vienna, but the better-balanced Sporting team defeated them in Antwerp. The winning goal was scored by Morais, direct from a corner, in the twentieth minute.

Preliminary Round

Fenebachce, 4, *Petrolul* 1
Petrolul 1, *Fenerbachce* 0
Basel 1, *Celtic* 5
Celtic 5, *Basel* 0
Tilburg Holland 1, *Manchester United* 1
Manchester United 6, *Tilburg* 1
SV Hamburg 4, *US Luxemburg* 0
US Luxemburg 2, *SV Hamburg* 3
Olympiakos 2, *Zaglebie* 1
Zaglebie 1, *Olympiakos* 0
Olympiakos 2, *Zaglebie* 0
Shelbourne 0, *Barcelona* 2
Barcelona 3, *Shelbourne* 1
Lyon 3, *Odense* 1
Odense 1, *Lyon* 3
MTK Budapest 1, *Slavia* 0
Slavia 1, *MTK Budapest* 1
Linz 1, *Dynamo Zagreb* 0
Dynamo Zagreb 1, *Linz* 0
Dynamo Zagreb 1, *Linz* 1
(Linz lost the toss, Dynamo Zagreb w.o.)
Sliema Wanderers 0, *Borough United* 0
Borough United 2, *Sliema Wanderers* 0
Atalanta 2, *Sporting Lisbon* 0
Sporting Lisbon 3, *Atalanta* 1
Sporting Lisbon 3, *Atalanta* 1
Apoel (*Cyprus*) 6, *Gjoevik* (*Norway*) 0
Gjoevik 1, *Apoel* 0
Hellsingin Palloseura 1, *Slovan Bratislava* 4
Slovan Bratislava 8, *Hellsingin Palloseura* 1

First Round

Tottenham Hotspur 2, *Manchester United* 0
Manchester United 4, *Tottenham Hotspur* 1
Fenerbachce 4, *Linfield* 1
Linfield 2, *Fenerbachce* 0

Barcelona 4, *SV Hamburg* 4
SV Hamburg 0, *Barcelona* 0
SV Hamburg 3, *Barcelona* 2
Sporting Lisbon 16, *Apoel* 1
Apoel 0, *Sporting Lisbon* 2
Lyon 4, *Olympiakos* 1
Olympiakos 2, *Lyon* 1
Motor Zwickau 1, *MTK Budapest* 0
MTK Budapest 2, *Motor Zwickau* 0
Celtic 3, *Dynamo Zagreb* 0
Dynamo Zagreb 2, *Celtic* 1
Borough United 0, *Slovan Bratislava* 1
Slovan Bratislava 3, *Borough United* 0

Quarter-finals

Manchester United 4, *Sporting Lisbon* 1
Sporting Lisbon 5, *Manchester United* 0
SV Hamburg 1, *Lyon* 1
Lyon 2, *SV Hamburg* 0
Celtic 1, *Slovan Bratislava* 0
Slovan Bratislava 0, *Celtic* 1
Fenerbachce 3, *MTK Budapest* 1
MTK Budapest 1, *Fenerbachce* 0

Semi-finals

Celtic 3, *MTK Budapest* 0
MTK Budapest 4, *Celtic* 0
Lyon 0, *Sporting Lisbon* 0
Sporting Lisbon 1, *Lyon* 1
Lyon 0, *Sporting Lisbon* 1

Final *Brussels, May* 13, 1964

MTK Budapest 3, *Sporting Lisbon* 3 after extra time (full-time 3–3)
MTK Budapest: Kovalik; Keszei, Dansky; Jenei, Nagy, Kovaks; Sandor, Vasas, Kuti, Bodor, Halapi.
Sporting Lisbon: Carvalho; Gomez, Peridis; Battista, Carlos, Geo; Mendes, Oswaldo, Mascarenhas, Figueiredo, Morais.
Scorers: Sandor (2), Kuti for MTK Budapest, Figueiredo (2), Dansky (own goal) for Sporting Lisbon.

Replay *Antwerp, May,* 15 1964
MTK Budapest 0, *Sporting Lisbon* 1
Scorer: Morais for Sporting Lisbon.

EUROPEAN CUPWINNERS' CUP 1964–5

For the second time in three years, a London team was the winner, and West Ham's splendid performance at Wembley, in an exciting Final, was a memorable one. Hammers' achievement was the more impressive as they lost Johnny Byrne, their outstanding forward, injured while playing for England against Scotland. This caused him to miss the second leg of the semi-final, in Saragossa, and the Final itself. Saragossa were probably the second best team in the competition, with outstanding forwards in Lapetra, on the left wing, and the centre-forward, Marcelino. Mention must also be made of the astonishing achievement of Cardiff City, a Second Division club, in knocking out the holders, Sporting Lisbon. They did almost as well by pulling back two goals to draw in Saragossa, but a defensive slip cost them the return match.

Munich 1860 were a physically strong, direct, intelligent side, thwarted in the Final by Standen's splendid goalkeeping. Late in the game, after a rash of missed chances, Alan Sealey scored twice for West Ham, to settle the match.

Preliminary Round

Admira Vienna 1, *Legia Warsaw* 3
Legia Warsaw 1, *Admira Vienna* 0
Lausanne 2, *Honved* 0
Honved 1, *Lausanne* 0
US Luxemburg 0, *Munich 1860* 4
Munich 1860 6, *US Luxemburg* 0
Valetta 0, *Saragossa* 3
Saragossa 5, *Valetta* 1
AEK Athens 2, *Dynamo Zagreb* 0
Dynamo Zagreb 3, *AEK Athens* 0
Dinamo Bucharest 3, *Derry City* 0
Derry City 0, *Dinamo Bucharest* 2
Magdeburg 1, *Galatassaray* 1
Galatassaray 1, *Magdeburg* 1
Magdeburg 1, *Galatassaray* 1 (*Vienna*)
Galatassaray won toss
Esbjerg 0, *Cardiff City* 0
Cardiff City 1, *Esbjerg* 0
Skeid Oslo 1, *Haka Finland* 0
Haka Finland 2, *Skeid Oslo* 0
Porto 3, *Lyon* 0
Lyon 0, *Porto* 1
Sparta Prague 10, *St. Anorthosis* (*Cyprus*) 0
St. Anorthosis 0, *Sparta* 6
La Gantoise 0, *West Ham United* 1
West Ham United 1, *La Gantoise* 1
Torino 3, *Fortuna Geelen* 1
Fortuna Geelen 2, *Torino* 2

Slavia Sofia 1, *Cork Celtic* 1
Cork Celtic 0, *Slavia Sofia* 2

First Round
Dundee 2, *Saragossa* 2
Saragossa 2, *Dundee* 1
Slavia 1, *Lausanne* 0
Lausanne 2, *Slavia* 1
Lausanne 3, *Slavia* 2 (*Rome*)
Legia 2, *Galatassaray* 1
Galatassaray 2, *Legia* 1
Legia 2, *Galatassaray* 1
West Ham United 2, *Sparta* 0
Sparta 2, *West Ham United* 1
Porto 0, *Munich 1860* 1
Munich 1860 1, *Porto* 1
Dinamo Bucharest 1, *Dynamo Zagreb* 1
Dynamo Zagreb 2, *Dinamo Bucharest* 0
Sporting Lisbon 1, *Cardiff City* 2
Cardiff City 0, *Sporting Lisbon* 0
Torino 5, *Haka* 0
Haka 0, *Torino* 1

Quarter-finals
Saragossa 2, *Cardiff City* 2
Cardiff City 0, *Saragossa* 1
Legia 0, *Munich 1860* 4
Munich 1860 0, *Legia* 0
Torino 1, *Dynamo Zagreb* 1
Dynamo Zagreb 1, *Torino* 2
Lausanne 1, *West Ham United* 2
West Ham United 4, *Lausanne* 3

Semi-finals
West Ham United 2, *Saragossa* 1
Saragossa 1, *West Ham United* 1
Torino 2, *Munich 1860* 0
Munich 1860 3, *Torino* 1
Munich 1860 2, *Torino* 0 (*Zurich*)

Final *Wembley Stadium*, *May* 19, 1965
West Ham United 2, *Munich 1860* 0 (0–0)
West Ham United: Standen; Kirkup, Burkett; Peters, Brown, Moore; Sealey, Boyce, Hurst, Dear, Sissons.

Munich 1860: Radenkovic; Wagner, Kohlars; Bena, Reich, Luttrop; Heiss, Kuppers, Brunnenmeier, Grosser, Rebele.
Scorer: Sealey (2) for West Ham United.

EUROPEAN CUPWINNERS' CUP 1965–6

Despite getting three of their four entrants into the semi-finals, Britain failed to retain the Cup, which went to Borussia and Germany—on merit. The Dortmund team, astoundingly fit and very incisive, broke wonderfully well from defence, despite the fact that they used Paul as sweeper-up behind four backs. Sigi Held, later to play so well in the World Cup, was a splendid striker, powerfully abetted by the Bundesliga's top scorer, Lothar Emmerich, the nominal left-winger.

Defending powerfully and breaking rapidly, Borussia surprisingly took all West Ham, the holders, could hurl at them, at Upton Park, and won on a couple of counterattacks. In the Final, they deserved to beat a disappointing Liverpool team, terribly vulnerable through the middle and lucky to equalise when the ball had so clearly crossed the goal line. Celtic, beaten by Liverpool in the semi-final, had an excellent run, and showed how their manager and former centre-half, Jock Stein, had tempered them for major competition.

First Round

Reykjavik 1, *Rosenberg Trondheim* 3
Rosenberg Trondheim 3, *Reykjavik* 1
Wiener Neustadt 0, *Stintza Cluj* 1
Stintza Cluj 2, *Wiener Neustadt* 0
Reipas Lahti 2, *Honved* 10
Honved 6, *Riepas Lahti* 0
Coleraine 1, *Dynamo Kiev* 6
Dynamo Kiev 4, *Coleraine* 0
Sion 5, *Galatassaray* 1
Galatassaray 2, *Sion* 1
Atletico Madrid 4, *Dynamo Zagreb* 0
Dynamo Zagreb 0, *Atletico Madrid* 1
Dukla 2, *Rennes* 0
Rennes 0, *Dukla* 0
SC Magdeburg 1, *Spora* 0
Spora 0, *SC Magdeburg* 2
Go Ahead Deventer 0, *Celtic* 6
Celtic 1, *Go Ahead Deventer* 0
Juventus 1, *Liverpool* 0
Liverpool 2, *Juventus* 0
Limerick 1, *CSKA Sofia*, 2
CSKA Sofia 2, *Limerick* 0
Floriana 1, *Borussia Dortmund* 5
Borussia Dortmund 8, *Floriana* 0
Omonia Nicosia 0, *Olympiakos* 1
Olympiakos 1, *Omonia Nicosia* 1
Aarhus 2, *Vitoria Setubal* 1
Vitoria Setubal 1, *Aarhus* 2

Cardiff City 1, *Standard Liège* 2
Standard Liège 1, *Cardiff City* 0

Second Round

Dukla 2, *Honved* 3
Honved 1, *Dukla* 2
Honved won on away goals rule
Borussia Dortmund 3, *CSKA* 0
CSKA 4, *Borussia Dortmund* 2
SC Magdeburg 8, *Sion* 1
Sion 2, *SC Magdeburg* 2
Stintza Cluj 0, *Atletico Madrid* 2
Atletico Madrid 4, *Stintza Cluj* 0
Aarhus 0, *Celtic* 1
Celtic 2, *Aarhus* 0
West Ham United 4, *Olympiakos* 0
Olympiakos 2, *West Ham United* 2
Liverpool 3, *Standard Liège* 1
Standard Liège 1, *Liverpool* 2
Rosenberg 1, *Dynamo Kiev* 4
Dynamo Kiev 2, *Rosenberg* 0

Quarter-finals

Celtic 3, *Dynamo Kiev* 0
Dynamo Kiev 1, *Celtic* 1
Atletico Madrid 1, *Borussia Dortmund* 1
Borussia Dortmund 1, *Atletico Madrid* 0
Honved 0, *Liverpool* 0
Liverpool 2, *Honved* 0
West Ham United 1, *SC Magdeburg* 0
SC Magdeburg 1, *West Ham United* 1

Semi-finals

West Ham United 1, *Borussia Dortmund* 2
Borussia Dortmund 3, *West Ham United* 1
Celtic 1, *Liverpool* 0
Liverpool 2, *Celtic* 0

Final *Glasgow, May* 5, 1966

Borussia Dortmund 2, *Liverpool* 1 (0–0)
Borussia: Tilkowski; Cyliax, Redder; Kurrat, Paul, Assauer; Libuda, Schmidt, Held, Sturm, Emmerich.

Liverpool: Lawrence; Lawler, Byrne; Milne, Yeats, Stevenson; Callaghan, Hunt, St. John, Smith, Thompson.
Scorers: Held, Yeats (own goal) for Borussia, Hunt for Liverpool.

EUROPEAN CUPWINNERS' CUP 1966–7

After a fine passage to their second Cupwinners' Cup Final, Rangers found the luck of the (German) venue and Bayern's all-round accomplishment just too much for them.

The competition was played under the highly suspect dispensation of away goals counting double, in the event of two teams finishing level on aggregate. Rangers put out the holders, Borussia Dortmund, beating them in Glasgow more easily than the score suggests, and holding them in Munich, despite an injury to Watson. But they were lucky to get through against Saragossa, on the toss of a coin. Bayern scraped through against a brave Shamrock Rovers, and recovered from defeat in Vienna to beat Rapid in a rough second leg, to take the other semi-final. Muller, their young centre-forward, scored the winner in extra time.

In the Final, played at Nuremberg, Rangers dominated the first half, Bayern the second. Beckenbauer missed a penalty, and extra time was again needed. It produced the decisive goal, by Roth.

Preliminary Round

Valur Reykjavik 1, *Standard Liège* 1
Standard Liège 8, *Valur Reykjavik* 1

First Round

Skeid Oslo 3, *Saragossa* 2
Saragossa 3, *Skeid Oslo* 1
Rapid Vienna 4, *Galatassaray* 0
Galatassaray 3, *Rapid Vienna* 5
Servette 1, *Kamraterna Turku* 1
Kamraterna Turku 1, *Servette* 2
Glentoran 1, *Rangers* 1
Rangers 4, *Glentoran* 0
Swansea Town 1, *Slavia Sofia* 1
Slavia Sofia 4, *Swansea Town* 0
Tatan Presov 1, *Bayern Munich* 1
Bayern Munich 3, *Tatan Presov* 2
AEK Athens 0, *Braga (Portugal)* 1
Braga 3, *AEK Athens* 2
Shamrock Rovers 4, *Spora Luxemburg* 0
Spora 1, *Shamrock Rovers* 4
Aalborg 0, *Everton* 0
Everton 2, *Aalborg* 1
OFK Belgrade 1, *Spartak Moscow* 3
Spartak Moscow 3, *OFK Belgrade* 0
Fiorentina 1, *Vasas Gyoer* 0
Vasas Gyoer 4, *Fiorentina* 2
Chemie Leipzig 3, *Legia Warsaw* 0

Legia Warsaw 2, *Chemie Leipzig* 2
Strasbourg 1, *Steaua Bucharest* 0
Steaua Bucharest 1, *Strasbourg* 1
Floriana Valetta 1, *Sparta Rotterdam* 1
Sparta Rotterdam 6, *Floriana Valletta* 0
Standard Liège 5, *Limassol* 1
Limassol 0, *Standard Liège* 1

Second Round

Saragossa 2, *Everton* 0
Everton 1, *Saragossa* 0
Shamrock Rovers 1, *Bayern Munich* 1
Bayern Munich 3, *Shamrock Rovers* 2
Vasas Gyoer 3, *Sporting Braga* 0
Sporting Braga 2, *Vasas Gyoer* 0
Spartak Moscow 1, *Rapid Vienna* 1
Rapid Vienna 1, *Spartak Moscow* 0
Servette 2, *Sparta Rotterdam* 0
Sparta Rotterdam 1, *Servette* 0
Rangers 2, *Borussia Dortmund* 1
Borussia Dortmund 0, *Rangers* 0
Strasbourg 1, *Slavia Sofia* 0
Slavia Sofia 2, *Strasbourg* 0
Chemie Leipzig 2, *Standard Liège* 1
Standard Liège 1, *Chemie Liepzig* 0

Quarter-finals

Rapid Vienna 1, *Bayern Munich* 0
Bayern Munich 2, *Rapid Vienna* 0
Rangers 2, *Saragossa* 0
Saragossa 2, *Rangers* 0
Vasas Gyoer 2, *Standard Liège* 1
Standard Liège 2, *Vasas Gyoer* 0
Servette 1, *Salvia Sofia* 0
Slavia Sofia 3, *Servette* 0

Semi-finals

Bayern Munich 2, *Standard Liège* 0
Standard Liège 1, *Bayern Munich* 3
Slavia Sofia 0, *Rangers* 1
Rangers 1, *Slavia Sofia* 0

Final *Nuremberg, May* 31

Bayern Munich (0) 1, *Rangers* 0 (0)
Scorer: Roth *After Extra Time*
Bayern: Maier; Nowak, Kupferschmidt; Roth, Beckenbauer, Olk; Nafziger, Ohlhauser, Muller, Koulmann, Brenninger.

Rangers: Martin; Johansen, Provan; Jardine, McKinnon, Greig; Henderson, Smith, A., Hynd, Smith, D., Johnston.

EUROPEAN CUP WINNERS' CUP 1967–8

Milan, who in the meantime were comfortably carrying off the Italian Championship, added to it the European Cupwinners' Cup, on their first appearance in the tournament. Their victory over Hamburg in the Final, at Rotterdam, was a mere canter. Both goals were scored by the veteran Swedish right-winger, Kurt Hamrin, the second a brilliant individual affair. It was far easier for Milan than their painfully hard qualifications against Vasas Gyoer and Standard Liège.

Cardiff City were Britain's most impressive competitors, doing wonderfully well. Shamrock Rovers and Breda were no great problem, and in the quarter finals, they belied recent poor League form by knocking out Torpedo, Moscow. They won at home with a fine, late headed goal by Barrie Jones, went down 1–0 in Tashkent then, with five reserves, won the play-off, in Augsburg, 1–0, Toshack heading down for Dean to score. In the semi-finals, still fighting relegation in the League, they held Hamburg (without Seeler and Schulz) to a draw, away, then lost unluckily at home.

Spurs went out feebly to Lyon, after a brawl in the away match, and some dismal defence at home. Aberdeen went down to Liège, though they played well at home in the return leg. Liège went on to draw twice with Milan, but lost the play-off, while Milan then knocked out the holders, Bayern, in the semi-finals.

First Round

FK Austria 0, *Steaua Bucharest* 2
Steaua Bucharest 2, *FK Austria* 1
Hamburg 5, *Randers Freja* 3
Randers Freja 0, *Hamburg* 2
Milan 5, *Levski* 1
Levski 1, *Milan* 1
Hajduk 0, *Tottenham Hotspur* 2
Tottenham Hotspur 4, *Hajduk* 3
Shamrock Rovers 1, *Cardiff City* 1
Cardiff City 2, *Shamrock Rovers* 0
Lausanne Sports 3, *Spartak Trnava* 2
Spartak Trnava 2,*Lausanne* 0
Aberdeen 10, *Reykjavik* 0
Reykjavik 1, *Aberdeen* 4
Valencia 4, *Crusaders* 0
Crusaders 2, *Valencia* 4
Torpedo Moscow 0, *Motor Zwickau* 0
Motor Zwickau 0, *Torpedo Moscow* 1
Izmir 2, *Standard Liège* 3
Standard Liège 0, *Izmir* 0

Aris Bonnevoie 0, *Lyon* 3
Lyon 2, *Aris Bonnevoie* 1
Fredrikstadt 1, *Setubal* 5
Setubal 2, *Frederikstadt* 1
Vasas Gyoer 5, *Apollon Limassol* 0
Apollon Limassol 0, *Vasas Gyoer* 4
Bayern Munich 5, *Panathanaikos* 0
Panathanaikos 1, *Bayern Munich* 2
JHK Helsinki 1, *Wislaw Cracow* 4
Wislaw Cracow 4, *JHK Helsinki* 0
FlorianaMalta 1, *NAC Breda* 2
NAC Breda 1, *Floriana Malta* 0

Second Round

Bayern Munich 6, *Vittoria Setubal* 2
Vittoria Setubal 1, *Bayern Munich* 1
Wislaw 0, *Hamburg* 1
Hamburg 4, *Wislaw* 0
NAC Breda 1, *Cardiff City* 1
Cardiff City 4, *NAC Breda* 1
Vasas Gyoer 2, *Milan* 2
Milan 1, *Vasas Gyoer* 1
Lyon 1, *Tottenham Hotspur* 0
Tottenham Hotspur 4, *Lyon* 3
Standard Liège 3, *Aberdeen* 0
Aberdeen 2, *Standard Liège* 0
Torpedo Moscow 3, *Spartak Trnava* 1
Spartak Trnava 1, *Torpedo Moscow* 3
Steaua Bucharest 1, *Valencia* 0
Valencia 3, *Steaua Bucharest* 0

Quarter-finals

SV Hamburg 2, *Lyon* 0
Lyon 2, *SV Hamburg* 0
SV Hamburg 2, *Lyon* 0
Standard Liège 1, *Milan* 1
Milan 1, *Standard Liège* 1
Milan 2, *Standard Liège* 0
Cardiff City 1, *Torpedo Moscow* 0
Torpedo Moscow 1, *Cardiff City* 0
Cardiff City 1, *Torpedo Moscow* 0
Valencia 1, *Bayern Munich* 1
Bayern Munich, 1 *Valencia* 0

Semi-finals

SV Hamburg 1, *Cardiff City* 1
Cardiff City 2, *SV Hamburg* 3

Milan 2, *Bayern Munich* 0
Bayern Munich 0 *Milan* 0

Final *Rotterdam, May* 23, 1968
Milan (2) 2, *SV Hamburg* (0) 0
Milan: Cudicini; Anquilletti, Schnellinger; Trappatoni, Rosato, Scala; Hamrin, Lodetti, Sormani, Rivera, Prati.
SV Hamburg: Ozcan; Sondemann, Kurbjohn; Dieckemann, Horst, Schulz, H.; Dorfel II, Kramer, Seeler, Hornig, Dorfel I.
Scorer: Hamrin (2) for Milan.

EUROPEAN CUPWINNERS' CUP 1968–9

For the first time, one of the two major European club competitions was won by an Iron Curtain country; more precisely by the Czech team, Slovan Bratislava. It was, in a way, especially appropriate, given that the other Iron Curtain clubs had withdrawn in protest against the decision to "zone" the first round, so many West European clubs having refused to play Iron Curtain teams in protest against the invasion of Czechoslovakia the previous summer.

Dunfermline, cleverly managed by the old Blackpool goalkeeper, George Farm, did best of the British entry, surviving until the semi-final. After a rough second leg, in which they had a player sent off, they protested at the way they were treated in Bratislava.

West Bromwich Albion, the F.A. Cup holders, were surprisingly among Dunfermline's victims. After conceding a draw at home, Dunfermline adjusted better to the icy circumstances at The Hawthorns, and won by Gardner's headed goal scored after only 90 seconds.

Barcelona, if anybody, looked favourites for the Final, especially after their fine 4–1 victory over Cologne, in the second leg of the semi-finals. But for the second time they lost a European final on Swiss soil. Cvetler, Slovan's clever winger, put them ahead in the second minute, and by half time discomfited Barcelona was 3–1 behind. Though Rexach proceeded to score straight from a corner kick, the Czechs held on to win.

Cardiff, veteran of so many brave battles in this tournament, alas went out at the first hurdle.

First Round

Bruges 3, *West Bromwich Albion* 1
West Bromwich Albion 2, *Bruges* 0
Dunfermline 10, *Apoel Nicosia* 1
Apoel Nicosia 0, *Dunfermline* 2
Crusaders 2, *Norrköpping* 2
Norrköpping 4, *Crusaders* 1
Cardiff City 2, *Porto* 2
Porto 2, *Cardiff City* 1

Bordeaux 2, *Cologne* 1
Cologne 3, *Bordeaux* 0
Slovan Bratislava 3, *Bor* 0
Bor 2, *Slovan Bratislava* 0
Partizan Tirana 1, *Torino* 0
Torino 3, *Partizan Tirana* 1
Rumelange 2, *Sliema Malta* 1
Sliema Malta 1, *Rumelange* 0
Izmir 3,*Lyn Oslo* 1
Lyn Oslo 4, *Izmir* 1
Freja 1, *Shamrock Rovers* 0
Shamrock Rovers 1, *Freja* 2
Lugano 0, *Barcelona* 1
Barcelona 3,*Lugano* 0
Olimpiakos 2, *Frem Reykjavik* 0
Frem Reykjavik 0, *Olimpiakos* 2
ADO 4, *Graz* 1
Graz 0, *ADO* 2

Second Round

Dinamo Bucharest 1, *West Bromwich Albion* 1
West Bromwich Albion 4, *Dinamo Bucharest* 0
Dunfermline 4, *Olimpiakos* 0
Olimpiakos 3, *Dunfermline* 0
Porto 1, *Slovan Bratislava* 0
Slovan Bratislava 4, *Porto* 0
Randers Freja 6, *Sliema Malta* 0
Sliema Malta 0, *Randers Freja* 2
ADO 0, *Cologne* 1
Cologne 3, *ADO* 0

Quarter-finals

Barcelona 3, *Lyn Oslo* 2
Barcelona 2, *Lyn Oslo* 2 (played in Barcelona)
Cologne 2, *Randers Freja* 1
Randers Freja 0, *Cologne* 3
Torino 0, *Slovan Bratislava* 1
Slovan Bratislava 2, *Torino* 1
Dunfermline 0, *West Bromwich Albion* 0
West Bromwich Albion 0, *Dunfermline* 1

Semi-finals

Dunfermline 1, *Slovan Bratislava* 1
Slovan Bratislava 1, *Dunfermline* 0
Cologne 2,*Barcelona* 2
Barcelona 4, *Cologne* 1

Final *Basel, May* 21, 1969
Slovan Bratislava (3) 3, *Barcelona* (1) 2
Slovan: Vencel; Filo, Hrivnak; Jan Zlocha, Horvarth, Hrdlicka; Cvetler, Moder, Josef Capkovic, Jokl, Jan Capkovic.
Barcelona: Sadurni; Franch, Eladio; Rife, Olivella, Zabalza; Pelicer, Castro, Zaldua, Fuste, Rexach, subs: Pereda, Mendonca.
Scorers: Cvetler, Hrivnak, Jan Capkovic for Slovan; Zaldua, Rexach for Barcelona.

Chapter Twenty

The European Inter-Cities Fairs Cup History

This competition, which made a creaking start, taking an unconscionable time a-playing, has since gathered prestige and popularity. It is nominally open to cities which put on trade fairs, and initially, London entered a representative team, later falling into line and putting out club sides. Home and away aggregate decides.

1955-8

London eliminated Basel, Frankfurt and Lausanne, but lost in the Final to Barcelona. Birmingham City knocked out Inter and Zagreb, but lost (4–3, 0–1, 1–2 at Basel) to Barcelona.
London 2, *Barcelona* 2 (*Chelsea*)
Barcelona 6, *London* 2

1958-60

Chelsea, representing London, went out in the second round (1–0, 1–4) to Belgrade. Birmingham eliminated Cologne (2–2, 2–0), Zagreb (2–0, 3–3) and Union St. Gilloise (4–2, 4–2) but lost to Barcelona in the Final.
Birmingham 1, *Barcelona* 1
Barcelona 4, *Birmingham* 1

1960-1

By now the competition had been properly stabilised, and played off within one season. Hibernian, representing Scotland, put out Barcelona in the second round. The match at Edinburgh which decided produced violent scenes, as the Barcelona players ran riot. Hibernian, having drawn 4–4 in Barcelona, won this 3–2.

Birmingham City eliminated BK Copenhagen (4–4, 5–0), having previously put out Ujpest of Hungary, while Hibernian had a walkover against Lausanne.

In the semi-finals, Birmingham maintained their fine record in this contest by defeating Inter 2–1 both at home and away. But Hibernian, having drawn 2–2 and 3–3 with Roma, crashed 6–0 in the play-off.

In the Final, Roma beat Birmingham.

Birmingham City 2, *Roma* 2
Roma 2, *Birmingham City* 0

1961-2

The Spaniards now succeeded in getting the entry temporarily increased to three clubs per country; and one of their own clubs, Valencia, was successful.

Of the British clubs, Sheffield Wednesday knocked out Lyon and Roma, but were eliminated by Barcelona, on 4–3 aggregate, in the quarter-finals. Valencia crushed Nottingham Forest on 7–1 aggregrate in the first round, but Hearts eliminated Union St. Gilloise (5–1 aggregate). In the next round, however, Inter put them out, 5–0 on aggregate.

In the Final, Valencia, having accounted for Inter in the quarter-finals, won an all-Spanish clash with Barcelona, most convincingly.

Valencia 6, *Barcelona* 2
Barcelona 1, *Valencia* 1

1962-3

Valencia, their teeth now well into this trophy, won it again. Everton, coming in for the first time, were surprisingly knocked out (1–0 and 0–2) by the compact Dunfermline side. Hibernian had another excellent run, eliminating Staevnet, Copenhagen, 4–0 and 3–2, Utrecht of Holland 1–0 and 2–1, and finally going out, 0–5, 2–1, to Valencia who had beaten Dunfermline in a third match decider in the second round. Dunfermline lost away, 4–0, but won gallantly at home, 6–2.

Dynamo Zagreb 1, *Valencia* 2
Valencia 2, *Dynamo Zagreb* 0

1963-4

In an all-Spanish final at Barcelona, Saragossa narrowly got home against Valencia.

First Round

(Results of British Teams only)
Copenhagen 1, *Arsenal* 7
Arsenal 2, *Copenhagen* 3
Utrecht 1, *Sheffield Wednesday* 4
Sheffield Wednesday 4, *Utrecht* 1
Glentoran 1, *Partick Thistle* 4
Partick Thistle 3, *Glentoran* 0
Lausanne 2, *Hearts* 2
Hearts 2, *Lausanne* 2
Lausanne 3, *Hearts* 2

Second Round

Cologne 3, *Sheffield Wednesday* 2
Sheffield Wednesday 1, *Cologne* 2
Arsenal 1, *Royal Liegois* 1
Royal Liegois 3, *Arsenal* 1
Partick Thistle 3, *Spartak Brno* 2
Spartak Brno 4, *Partick Thistle* 0
Lausanne 1, *Saragossa* 2
Saragossa 3, *Lausanne* 0
Juventus 1, *Atletico Madrid* 0
Atletico Madrid 1, *Juventus* 2
Roma 2, *Belenenses* 1
Belenenses 0, *Roma* 1
Valencia 0, *Rapid Vienna* 0
Rapid Vienna 2, *Valencia* 3

Quarter-finals

Roma 3, *Cologne* 1
Cologne 4, *Roma* 0
Saragossa 3, *Juventus* 2
Juventus 0, *Saragossa* 0
Royal Liegois 2, *Spartak Brno* 0
Spartak Brno 2, *Royal Liegois* 0
Royal Liegois 1, *Spartak Brno* 0
Valencia 5, *Ujpest* 2
Ujpest 3, *Valencia* 1

Semi-finals

Valencia 4, *Cologne* 1
Cologne 2, *Valencia* 0
Royal Liegois 1, *Saragossa* 0
Saragossa 2, *Royal Liegois* 0

Final

Saragossa 2, *Valencia* 1

EUROPEAN INTER-CITIES FAIRS CUP 1964–5

A tournament surprisingly and meritoriously won by Ferencvaros of Budapest; very much the outsiders from the semi-finals onward, despite a forward-line which included the internationals Albert, Rakosi and Fenyvesi, whose goal beat Juventus in the Final. Manchester United, England's hopes, who had won an all-English clash with Everton on the way, slipped badly in the semi-finals, confirming the fears of those who believed their organisation hardly matched their talent. The first of their two matches in Budapest, won by Ferencvaros with a disputed penalty, was bad tempered and unpleasant; a man from each side was sent off. Juventus, after making a very laborious way to the semi-final, suddenly found some form, to recover against Atletico Madrid, but in the end went down at home to Ferencvaros—and Dr. Fenyvesi.

Preliminary Round

Eintracht 3, *Kilmarnock* 0
Kilmarnock 5, *Eintracht* 1
Wiener Sportklub 2, *S.C. Leipzig* 1
S.C. Leipzig 0, *Wiener Sportklub* 1
Strasbourg 2, *Milan* 0
Milan 1, *Strasbourg* 0
Basel 2, *Spora Luxemburg* 0
Spora Luxemburg 0, *Basel* 1
Bilbao 2, *OFK Belgrade* 2
OFK Belgrade 0, *Bilbao* 2
Ferencvaros 2, *Spartak Brno* 0
Spartak Brno 1, *Ferencvaros* 0
Goztep Smyrna 0, *Petrolul Ploesti* 1
Petrolul Ploesti 2, *Goztep Smyrna* 1
Odense 1, *VfB Stuttgart* 3
VfB Stuttgart 1, *Odense* 0
Betis Seville 1, *Stade Francais* 1
Stade Francais 2, *Betis Seville* 0
Dynamo Zagreb 3, *Grazer A.K.* 2
Grazer A.K. 0, *Dynamo Zagreb* 6
Borussia Dortmund 4, *Bordeaux* 1
Bordeaux 2, *Borussia Dortmund* 0
Union St. Gilloise 0, *Juventus* 1
Juventus 1, *Union St. Gilloise* 0
Valencia 1, *Liège* 1
Liège 3, *Valencia* 1
Vojvodina 1, *Lokomotiv* 1
Lokomotiv 1, *Vojvodina* 1
Lokomotiv 2, *Vojvodina* 1 (*Sofia*)
Djurgaarden 1, *Manchester United* 1
Manchester United 6, *Djurgaarden* 1
Valerenger 2, *Everton* 5
Everton 4, *Valerenger* 2
Leixoes 1, *Celtic* 1
Celtic 3, *Leixoes* 0
Barcelona 0, *Fiorentina* 1
Fiorentina 0, *Barcelona* 2
Aris 0, *Roma* 0
Roma 3, *Aris* 0
Belenenses 1, *Shelbourne* 1
Shelbourne 0, *Belenenses* 0
Shelbourne 2, *Belenenses* 1 (*Dublin*)

Dunfermline 4, *Oergryte* 2
Oergryte 0, *Dunfermline* 0
Hertha Berlin 2, *Antwerp* 1
Antwerp 2, *Hertha Berlin* 0
BK Copenhagen 3, *DOS Utrecht* 4
DOS 2, *BK Copenhagen* 1
Servette 2, *Atletico Madrid* 2
Atletico Madrid 6, *Servette* 1

First Round

Dynamo Zagreb 1, *Roma* 1
Roma 1, *Dynamo Zagreb* 0
Stade Francais 0, *Juventus* 0
Juventus 1, *Stade Francais* 0
Basel 0, *Strasbourg* 1
Strasbourg 5, *Basel* 2
Kilmarnock 0, *Everton* 2
Everton 4, *Kilmarnock* 1
Petrolul 1, *Lokomotiv Plovdiv* 0
Lokomotiv Plovdiv 2, *Petrolul* 0
Borussia Dortmund 1, *Manchester United* 6
Manchester United 4, *Borussia Dortmund* 0
Dunfermline 1, *VfB Stuttgart* 0
VfB Stuttgart 0, *Dunfermline* 0
Bilbao 2, *Antwerp* 0
Antwerp 0, *Bilbao* 1
Barcelona 3, *Celtic* 1
Celtic 0, *Barcelona* 0
Utrecht 0, *Liège* 2
Liège 2, *Utrecht* 0
Ferencvaros 1, *Wiener S.K.* 0
Wiener S.K. 0, *Ferencvaros* 0
Shelbourne 0, *Atletico Madrid* 1
Atletico Madrid 1, *Shelbourne* 0

Second Round

Torino 1, *Dynamo Zagreb* 1
Dynamo Zagreb 1, *Torino* 2
Strasbourg 0, *Barcelona* 0
Barcelona 2, *Strasbourg* 2
Barcelona 0, *Strasbourg* 0 (*Barcelona*)
Strasbourg won toss
Manchester United 1, *Everton* 1
Everton 1, *Manchester United* 2
Juventus 1, *Lokomotiv* 1
Lokomotiv 1, *Juventus* 1
Juventus 2, *Lokomotiv* 1 (*Turin*)

Bilbao 1, *Dunfermline* 0
Dunfermline 1, *Bilbao* 0
Bilbao 2, *Dunfermline* 1 (*Bilbao*)
Roma 1, *Ferencvaros* 2
Ferencvaros 1, *Roma* 0
Liège 1, *Atletico Madrid* 0
Atletico Madrid 2, *Liège* 0

Quarter-finals

Ferencvaros 1, *Bilbao* 0
Bilbao 1, *Ferencvaros* 0
Ferencvaros 3, *Bilbao* 0 (*Budapest*)
Strasbourg 0, *Manchester United* 5
Manchester United 0, *Strasbourg* 0

Semi-finals

Manchester United 3, *Ferencvaros* 2
Ferencvaros 1, *Manchester United* 0
Ferencvaros 2, *Manchester United* 1 (*Budapest*)
Atletico Madrid 3, *Juventus* 1
Juventus 3, *Atletico Madrid* 1
Juventus 3, *Atletico Madrid* 1 (*Turin*)

Final *Turin*

Juventus (0) 0, *Ferencvaros* (0) 1; Fenyvesi, M.

EUROPEAN INTER-CITIES FAIRS CUP 1965–6

A tournament which produced a rash of violent matches ended in anticlimax, the two Spanish finalists being ordered by their Federation to postpone the two-legged Final till the following season. When it was at last played, it turned out thoroughly dramatic; winning on Barcelona's ground, Saragossa proceeded to lose on their own, three of Barcelona's goals being scored by a young newcomer to the attack, Pujol.

Chelsea's young team did well, none better than the brilliant young forward, Peter Osgood. Their three ties with Milan were memorable, above all the game at Stamford Bridge, when Schnellinger gave a performance for Milan which was matchlessly combative. Memorable for more sinister reasons was the previous round's game in Rome, where the players were bombarded with missiles. Leeds' home game against Valencia gave rise to a disgraceful brawl. But it was Saragossa who eventually eliminated them, with surprising ease, in a decider played at Leeds.

First Round

Union Luxembourg 0, *Cologne* 4
Cologne 13, *Union Luxembourg* 0
Hibernian 2, *Valencia* 0
Valencia 2, *Hibernian* 0
Valencia 3, *Hibernian* 0
F.C. Liège 1, *Zagreb* 0
Zagreb 2, *F.C. Liège* 0
Red Star 0, *Fiorentina* 4
Fiorentina 3, *Red Star* 1
Stade Francais 0, *Porto* 0
Porto 1, *Stade Francais* 0
Malmö 0, *Munich 1860* 3
Munich 1860 4, *Malmö* 0
Bordeaux 0, *Sporting Lisbon* 4
Sporting Lisbon 6, *Bordeaux* 1
Milan 1, *Strasbourg* 0
Strasbourg 2, *Milan* 1
Milan 1, *Strasbourg* 1
(Milan won toss)
Chelsea 4, *Roma* 1
Roma 0, *Chelsea* 0
Spartak Brno 2, *Lokomotiv Plovdiv* 0
Lokomotiv Plovdiv 1, *Spartak Brno* 0
Nuremberg 1, *Everton* 1
Everton 1, *Nuremberg* 0
Antwerp 1, *Glentoran* 0
Glentoran 3, *Antwerp* 3
Wiener S.K. 6, *PAOK Salonika* 0
PAOK Salonika 2, *Wiener S.K.* 1
Leeds United 2, *Torino* 1
Torino 0, *Leeds United* 0
DSO Utrecht 0, *Barcelona* 0
Barcelona 7, *DSO Utrecht* 1
Valerengen 1, *Hearts* 3
Hearts 1, *Valerengen* 0

Second Round

Aris 2, *Cologne* 1
Cologne 2, *Aris* 0
Goztepe Izmir 2, *Munich 1860* 1
Munich 1860 9, *Goztepe Izmir* 1
Ujpest 3, *Everton* 0
Everton 2, *Ujpset* 1
Dunfermline 5, *BK Copenhagen* 0
BK Copenhagen 2, *Dunfermline* 4

Hanover 96 5, *Porto* 0
Porto 2, *Hanover 96* 1
Sporting Lisbon 2, *Espanol Barcelona* 1
Espanol Barcelona 4, *Sporting Lisbon* 3
Espanol Barcelona 2, *Sporting Lisbon* 1
Zagreb 2, *Red Star Brasov* 2
Red Star Brasov 1, *Zagreb* 0
Antwerp 2, *Barcelona* 1
Barcelona 2, *Antwerp* 0
Shamrock Rovers 1, *Saragossa* 1
Saragossa 2, *Shamrock Rovers* 1
Wiener S.K. 1, *Chelsea* 0
Chelsea 2, *Wiener S.K.* 0
Leipzig 1, *Leeds United* 2
Leeds United 0, *Leipzig* 0
C.U.F. Setubal 2, *Milan* 0
Milan 2, *C.U.F. Setubal* 0
Milan 1, *C.U.F. Setubal* 0
Basel 1, *Valencia* 3
Valencia 5, *Basel* 1
Fiorentina 2, *Spartak Brno* 0
Spartak Brno 4, *Fiorentina* 0

Third Round

Hearts 3, *Saragossa* 3
Saragossa 2, *Hearts* 2
Saragossa 1, *Hearts* 0
Leeds United 1, *Valencia* 1
Valencia 0, *Leeds United* 1
Hanover 96 2, *Barcelona* 1
Barcelona 1, *Hanover 96* 0
Hanover 96 1, *Barcelona* 1
(Barcelona won toss)
Cologne 3, *Ujpest* 2
Ujpest 4, *Cologne* 0
Dunfermline 2, *Spartak Brno* 0
Spartak Brno 0, *Dunfermline* 0
Espanol 3, *Red Star Brasov* 1
Red Star Brasov 4, *Espanol* 2
Espanol 1, *Red Star Brasov* 0
Milan 2, *Chelsea* 1
Chelsea 2, *Milan* 1
Milan 1, *Chelsea* 1
(Chelsea won toss)

Fourth Round

Leeds United 4, *Ujpest* 1
Ujpest 1, *Leeds United* 1

Munich 1860 2, *Chelsea* 2
Chelsea 1, *Munich 1860* 0
Dunfermline 1, *Saragossa* 0
Saragossa 4, *Dunfermline* 2

Semi-finals

Saragossa 1, *Leeds United* 0
Leeds United 2, *Saragossa* 1
Leeds United 1, *Saragossa* 3
Barcelona 2, *Chelsea* 0
Chelsea 2, *Barcelona* 0
Barcelona 5, *Chelsea* 0

Final

Barcelona 0, *Saragossa* 1
Saragossa 2, *Barcelona* 4

EUROPEAN INTER-CITIES FAIRS CUP 1966-7

Postponed for the second time until the following season, the final of the 1966-7 competition was ultimately won by Dynamo Zagreb, at the expense of Leeds United. In Zagreb, they deservedly won, both goals being scored by their 18-year-old outside-right, Cercer. At Elland Road, their defence, with Skoric excellent in goal, massed to keep out the Leeds attack. Two other well-known internationals, Belin, the right-half, and Zambata, the striker, also increased their reputations.

Barcelona, the holders, had gone out only a matter of weeks after winning the postponed 1966 Final, to Dundee United, who shocked them by beating them on their own ground, Seemann and Perssonn, their Scandinavian wingers, playing splendidly. Juventus, however, were too strong for them in the Third Round, even though they won the return, in Dundee.

Burnley had a very good run, beating VfB Stuttgart, Lausanne and Naples—where, in the return match, they had to survive a short and vicious riot, involving Naples players and spectators.

Burnley's own robust tactics provoked a brawl late in the home game against Eintracht, which they surprisingly lost—thus going out of the competition.

Leeds United did very well to beat Valencia away from home, got through against Bologna on the toss of a coin, and competently disposed of Kilmarnock, on their way to the Final. But Benfica, on their first appearance in the tournament, surprisingly went out to Leipzig in the Third Round. Dynamo Zagreb had a splendid 3–0 home win to put out Juventus in the quarter finals, then turned a 3–0 deficit into a 4–3 aggregate win over Eintracht, in the semis.

First Round

VfB Stuttgart 1, *Burnley* 1
Burnley 2, *VfB Stuttgart* 0
Frigg Oslo 1, *Dunfermline Ath.* 3
Dunfermline Ath. 3, *Frigg Oslo* 1
Red Star 5, *Bilbao* 0
Bilbao 2, *Red Star* 0
Valencia 2, *Nuremberg* 1
Nuremberg 0, *Valencia* 2
Drumcondra 0, *Eintracht* 2
Eintracht 5, *Drumcondra* 1
Naples 3, *Wiener S.K.* 1
Wiener S.K. 1, *Naples* 2
Porto 2, *Bordeaux* 1
Bordeaux 2, *Porto* 1
(Bordeaux won toss)
Nice 2, *Oergryte* 2
Oergryte 2, *Nice* 1
Djurgaarden 1, *Lokomotiv Leipzig* 3
Lokomotiv Leipzig 2, *Djurgaarden* 1
Dynamo Pitesti 2, *Seville* 0
Seville 2, *Dynamo Pitesti* 2
Spartak Brno 2, *Dynamo Zagreb* 0
Dynamo Zagreb 2, *Spartak Brno* 0
(Dynamo won toss)
U.S. Luxemburg 0, *Antwerp* 1
Antwerp 4, *U.S. Luxemburg* 0
Bologna 3, *Goeztepe* 1
Goeztepe 1, *Bologna* 2
DWS 1, *Leeds United* 3
Leeds United 5, *DWS* 1

Second Round

Lokomotiv Leipzig 0, *Liège* 0
Liège 1, *Lokomotiv Leipzig* 2
Lausanne 1, *Burnley* 3
Burnley 5, *Lausanne* 0
La Gantoise 1, *Bordeaux* 0
Bordeaux 0, *La Gantoise* 0
Oergryte 0, *Ferencvaros* 0
Ferencvaros 7, *Oergryte* 1
Toulouse 3, *Dynamo Pitesti* 0
Dynamo Pitesti 5, *Toulouse* 1
Dunfermline 4, *Dynamo Zagreb* 2
Dynamo Zagreb 2, *Dunfermline* 0
Barcelona 1, *Dundee United* 2
Dundee United 2, *Barcelona* 0

Odense b. 1909 1, *Naples* 4
Naples 2, *Odense b. 1909* 1
Antwerp 0, *Kilmarnock* 1
Kilmarnock 7, *Antwerp* 2
Valencia 1, *Red Star* 0
Red Star 1, *Valencia* 2
Sparta Prague 2, *Bologna* 2
Bologna 2, *Sparta Prague* 1
Spartak Plovdiv 1, *Benfica* 1
Benfica 3, *Spartak Plovdiv* 0
DOS Utrecht 1, *West Bromwich Albion* 1
West Bromwich Albion 5, *DOS Utrecht* 2
Juventus 3, *Setubal* 1
Setubal 0, *Juventus* 2
Eintracht 5, *BK Copenhagen* 1
BK Copenhagen 2, *Eintracht* 2

Third Round

Lokomotiv Leipzig 3, *Benfica* 1
Benfica 2, *Lokomotiv Leipzig* 1
Kilmarnock 1, *La Gantoise* 0
La Gantoise 1, *Kilmarnock* 2
Burnley 3, *Naples* 0
Naples 0, *Burnley* 0
Leeds United 1, *Valencia* 1
Valencia 0, *Leeds United* 2
Bologna 3, *West Bromwich Albion* 0
West Bromwich Albion 1, *Bologna* 3
Juventus 3, *Dundee United* 0
Dundee United 1, *Juventus* 0
Dynamo Zagreb 1, *Dynamo Pitesti* 0
Dynamo Pitesti 0, *Dynamo Zagreb* 0
Eintracht 4, *Ferencvaros* 1
Ferencvaros 2, *Eintracht* 1

Quarter-finals

Bologna 1, *Leeds United* 0
Leeds United 1, *Bologna* 0
(Leeds won toss)
Juventus 2, *Dynamo Zagreb* 2
Dynamo Zagreb 3, *Juventus* 0
Eintracht 1, *Burnley* 1
Burnley 1, *Eintracht* 2
Lokomotiv Leipzig 1, *Kilmarnock* 0
Kilmarnock 2, *Lokomotiv Leipzig* 0

Semi-finals

Leeds United 4, *Kilmarnock* 2
Kilmarnock 0, *Leeds United* 0
Eintracht 3, *Dynamo Zagreb* 0
Dynamo Zagreb 4, *Eintracht* 0

Final

August 30, 1967	*Dynamo Zagreb* (1) 2 Cercer 2	*Leeds United* (0) 0
September 6, 1967	*Leeds United* (0) 0	*Dynamo Zagreb* (0) 0

EUROPEAN INTER-CITIES FAIRS CUP 1967-8

This time, Leeds United, in another postponed final—or finals—consoled themselves for the previous year's disappointment by defeating Ferencvaros, to win. They were two hard games, each on the same pattern; an away team clamming up in defence and allowing the home team to come at them. Leeds won the first game and scored the only goal of the finals in controversial circumstances; Jackie Charlton standing on the goal line at a corner and blocking the goalkeeper's path, Jones thumping the ball home.

On their way to the Final, Leeds had tough opposition from Partizan of Belgrade and Hibernian—who had rallied superbly in their return match with Naples, winning 5–0 after losing 4–1 away—but didn't concede a goal against Rangers.

Ferencvaros, winners of the trophy in 1965, played beautiful football at Liverpool, where Munich had crashed—and were cheered off the field by the Kop. Bologna, in the semi-finals, pushed them very hard.

Dundee had a splendid run into the semi-finals, but Leeds, again, were too good for them, defeating a Scottish side for the third time in the competition. They won the return, at Elland Road, nine minutes from time through a goal by Gray, during an accumulation of postponed matches.

First Round

Spora Luxemburg 0, *Leeds United* 9
Leeds United 7, *Spora Luxemburg* 0
PAOK Salonika 0, *Liège* 2
Liège 3, *PAOK Salonika* 2
Wiener S.K. 0, *Atletico Madrid* 5
Atletico Madrid 2, *Wiener S.K.* 1
St. Patrick's 1, *Bordeaux* 3
Bordeaux 6, *St. Patrick's* 3
Utrecht 3, *Saragossa* 2
Saragossa 3, *Utrecht* 1
Naples 4, *Hanover* 0
Hanover 1, *Naples* 1

Bologna 2, *Lyn Oslo* 0
Lyn Oslo 0, *Bologna* 0
Nice 0, *Fiorentina* 1
Fiorentina 4, *Nice* 0
Dresden Dynamo 1, *Rangers* 1
Rangers 2, *Dresden Dynamo* 1
Argesul Pitesti 3, *Ferencvaros* 1
Ferencvaros 4, *Argesul Pitesti* 0
Malmö 0, *Liverpool* 2
Liverpool 2, *Malmö* 1
Hibernian 3, *Porto* 0
Porto 3, *Hibernian* 1
Eintracht 0, *Nottingham Forest* 1
Nottingham Forest 4, *Eintracht* 0
Dynamo Zagreb 5, *Petrolul Ploesti* 0
Petrolul Ploesti 2, *Dynamo Zagreb* 0
Atletico Bilbao 1, *Frem* 0
Frem 0, *Atletico Bilbao* 1
Bruges 0, *Sporting Lisbon* 0
Sporting Lisbon 2, *Bruges* 1
Frem 0 *Atletico Bilbao* 1
Atletico Bilbao 3, *Frem* 2
Zurich 3, *Barcelona* 1
Barcelona 1, *Zurich* 0
Lokomotiv Leipzig 5, *Linfield* 1
Linfield 1, *Lokomotiv Leipzig* 0
DWS Amsterdam 2, *Dundee* 1
Dundee 3, *DWS Amsterdam* 0
Partizan 5, *Lokomotiv Plovdiv* 1
Lokomotiv Plovdiv 1, *Partizan* 1
Vojvodina 1, *CUF* 0
CUF 1, *Vojvodina* 3
Cologne 2, *Slavia Prague* 0
Slavia Prague 2, *Cologne* 2
Royal Antwerp 1, *Goeztepe Izmir* 2
Goeztepe Izmir 0, *Royal Antwerp* 0

Second Round
Nottingham Forest 2, *Zurich* 1
Zurich 1, *Nottingham Forest* 2
Bordeaux 1, *Atletico Bilbao* 3
Atletico Bilbao 1, *Bordeaux* 0
Dundee 3, *Liège* 1
Liège 1, *Dundee* 4
Vojvodina 0, *Lokomotiv Leipzig* 0
Lokomotiv Leipzig 0, *Vojvodina* 2
Saragossa 2, *Ferencvaros* 1
Ferencvaros 3, *Saragossa* 0

Liverpool 8, *Munich 1860* 0
Munich 1860 2, *Liverpool* 1
Rangers 3, *Cologne* 0
Cologne 3, *Rangers* 1
Bologna 0, *Dynamo Zagreb* 0
Dynamo Zagreb 1, *Bologna* 2
Naples 4, *Hibernian* 1
Hibernian 5, *Naples* 0
Partizan 1, *Leeds United* 2
Leeds United 1, *Partizan* 1
Fiorentina 1, *Sporting Lisbon* 1
Sporting Lisbon 2, *Fiorentina* 1

Third Round

Ferencvaros 1, *Liverpool* 0
Liverpool 0, *Ferencvaros* 1
Leeds United 1, *Hibernian* 0
Hibernian 1, *Leeds United* 1
Vojvodina 1, *Goeztepe Izmir* 0
Goeztepe Izmir 0, *Vojvodina* 1
Zurich 3, *Sporting Lisbon* 0
Sporting Lisbon 1, *Zurich* 0

Quarter Finals

Ferencvaros 2, *Bilbao* 1
Bilbao 1, *Ferencvaros* 2
Rangers 0, *Leeds United* 0
Leeds United 2, *Rangers* 0
Dundee 1, *F.C. Zurich* 0
F.C. Zurich 0, *Dundee* 1
Bologna 0, *Vojvodina* 0
Vojvodina 0, *Bologna* 2

Semi-finals

Dundee 1, *Leeds United* 1
Leeds United 1, *Dundee* 0
Ferencvaros 3, *Bologna* 2
Bologna 2, *Ferencvaros* 2

Final

Leeds United 1 (*Jones*), *Ferencvaros* 0
Ferencvaros 0, *Leeds United* 0

EUROPEAN INTER-CITIES FAIRS CUP 1968–9

For the second successive year, an English club won the Fairs Cup; surprisingly and laudably, Newcastle United, on their first entry into European competition. After a somewhat erratic beginning, in which they played irresistibly at home, indifferently away, they reached a brilliant crescendo in the two-legged Final against Ujpest – conquerors of the holders, Leeds United.

Having soundly beaten them at Gallowgate, thanks to two goals by their normally defensive half-back, Bobby Moncur, they rode a two-goal deficit in Budapest to win dramatically, 3–2.

Leeds might have done rather better had they not become so intensely engaged with the League Championship. They put out Standard Liege, were lucky to eliminate Naples on the iniquitous toss of a coin (Naples must be getting used to it; a similar expedient decided the 1960 Olympic semi-final and the 1968 European Nations semi-final, at Fuorigrotta), annihilated Hanover, but were well beaten, home and away, by Ujpest.

Newcastle overcame Feyenoord, Sporting Lisbon, Saragossa, Vitoria Setubal, then Rangers. "Away goals" allowed them to scrape through against the Spanish team, but Rangers couldn't score a goal against them. Their failure provoked a barbaric invasion of the Newcastle pitch by Rangers' fans, and a prolonged stoppage of the game.

Thus to the Final, in which Moncur got yet another fine goal in Budapest, and young Foggon, coming on as substitute, raced splendidly through alone to score the winner.

First round
Chelsea 5, *Morton* 0
Morton 3, *Chelsea* 4
Newcastle United 4, *Feyenoord* 0
Feyenoord 2, *Newcastle United* 0
Slavia Sofia 0, *Aberdeen* 0
Aberdeen 2, *Slavia Sofia* 0
Atletico Bilbao 2, *Liverpool* 1
Liverpool 2, *Atletico Bilbao* 1
Rangers 2, *Vojvodina* 0
Vojvondina 1, *Rangers* 0
Ljubljana 0, *Hibernian* 3
Hibernian 2, *Ljubljana* 1
OFK Belgrade 6, *Rapid Bucharest* 1
Rapid Bucharest 3, *OFK Belgrade* 1
Wiener Sportklub 1, *Slavia Prague* 0
Slavia Prague 5, *Wiener Sportklub* 0
Skied Oslo 1, *AIK Stockholm* 1
AIK Stockholm 2, *Skied Oslo* 1
Trakia Plovdiv 3, *Real Saragossa* 1
Real Saragossa 2, *Trakia Plovdiv* 0
Dynamo Zagreb 1, *Fiorentina* 1
Fiorentina 2, *Dynamo Zagreb* 1
Legia Warsaw 6, *Munich 1860* 0
Munich 1860 2, *Legia Warsaw* 3
Daring Brussels 2, *Panathanaikos* 1
Panathanaikos 2, *Daring Brussels* 0

Wacker Innsbruck 2, *Eintracht Frankfurt* 2
Eintracht Frankfurt 3, *Wacker Innsbruck* 0
Sporting Lisbon 4, *Valencia* 0
Valencia 4, *Sporting Lisbon* 1
Bologna 4, *Basel* 1
Basel 1, *Bologna* 2
Aris Salonika 1, *Hibernian Malta* 0
Hibernian Malta 0, *Aris Salonika* 6
DOS Utrecht 1, *Dundalk* 1
Dundalk 2, *DOS Utrecht* 1
Atletico Madrid 2, *Waregem* 1
Waregem 1, *Atletico Madrid* 0
Goztepe Izmir 2, *Marseilles* 0
Marseilles 2, *Goztepe Izmir* 0
Metz 1, *Hamburg S.V.* 4
Hamburg S.V. 3, *Metz* 2
Lyon 1, *Academica Coimbra* 0
Academica Coimbra 1, *Lyon* 0
Lausanne 0, *Juventus* 2
Juventus 2, *Lausanne* 0
Beerschot 1, *DWS Amsterdam* 1
DWS Amsterdam 2, *Beerschot* 1
BK Odense 1, *Hanover 96* 3
Hanover 96 1, *BK Odense* 0
Vitoria Setubal 3, *Linfield* 0
Linfield 1, *Vitoria Setubal* 3
Standard Liège 0, *Leeds United* 0
Leeds United 3, *Standard Liège* 2
Naples 3, *Grasshoppers* 1
Grasshoppers 1, *Naples* 0

Second Round
Hibernian 3, *Lokomotiv Leipzig* 1
Lokomotiv 0, *Hibernian* 1
Leeds United 2, *Naples* 0
Naples 2, *Leeds United* 0
Rangers 6, *Dundalk* 1
Dundalk 0, *Rangers* 3
Aberdeen 2, *Real Saragossa* 1
Real Saragossa 3, *Aberdeen* 0
Chelsea 0, *DWS Amsterdam* 0
DWS Amsterdam 0, *Chelsea* 0
Sporting Lisbon 1, *Newcastle United* 1
Newcastle United 1, *Sporting Lisbon* 0
Vitoria Setubal 5, *Lyon* 0
Lyon 1, *Vitoria Setubal* 2
Goztepe Izmir 3, *Argesul Pitesti* 0
Argesul Pitesti 3, *Goztepe Izmir* 2

Hansa Rostock 3, *Fiorentina* 2
Fiorentina 2, *Hansa Rostock* 1
Hamburg SV 4, *Slavia Prague* 1
Slavia Prague 3, *Hamburg SV* 1
Panathanaikos 0, *Bilbao* 0
Bilbao 1, *Panathanaikos* 0
OFK Belgrade 1, *Bologna* 0
Bologna 1, *OFK Belgrade* 1
Aris Salonika 1, *Ujpest* 2
Ujpest 9, *Aris Salonika* 1
AIK Stockholm 4, *Hanover 96* 2
Hanover 96 5, *AIK Stockholm* 2

Third Round

Leeds United 5, *Hanover* 96 1
Hanover 96 1, *Leeds United* 2
Hamburg S.V. 1, *Hibernian* 0
Hibernian 2, *Hamburg S.V.* 1
Legia Warsaw 0, *Ujpest* 1
Ujpest 2, *Legia Warsaw* 2
Real Saragossa 3, *Newcastle United* 2
Newcastle United 2, *Real Saragossa* 1
OFK Belgrade 3, *Goztepe Izmir* 1
Goztepe Izmir 2, *OFK Belgrade* 0
Eintracht Frankfurt 1, *Atletico Bilbao* 1
Atletico Bilbao 1, *Eintracht Frankfurt* 0
DWS Amsterdam 0, *Rangers* 2
Rangers 2, *DWS Amsterdam* 1
Vitoria Setubal 3, *Fiorentina* 0
Fiorentina 2, *Vitoria Setubal* 1

Quarter-finals

Newcastle United 5, *Vitoria Setubal* 1
Vitoria Setubal 3, *Newcastle United* 1
Rangers 4, *Atletico Bilbao* 1
Atletico Bilbao 2, *Rangers* 0
Leeds United 0, *Ujpest* 1
Ujpest 2, *Leeds United* 0
Goztepe Izmir v. *S.V. Hamburg. Hamburg scr.*

Semi-finals

Goztepe Izmir 1, *Ujpest* 4
Ujpest 4, *Goztepe Izmir* 0
Rangers 0, *Newcastle United* 0
Newcastle United 2, *Rangers* 0

Final

Newcastle United (0) 3	*Ujpest* (0) 0
Moncur 2, Scott	
Ujpest (2) 2	*Newcastle United* (0) 3
Bene, Gorocs	Moncur, Arentoft, Foggon

Newcastle United's team in both matches: McFaul; Craig, Clark; Gibb, Burton, Moncur; Scott, Robson, Davies, Arentoft, Sinclair. Substitute in each match: Foggon.

Chapter Twenty-one

South American Championship History

		Winners	Runners-up
1917	Montevideo	Uruguay	Argentina
1919	Rio	Brazil	Uruguay
1920	Valparaiso	Uruguay	Argentina
1921	Buenos Aires	Argentina	Brazil
1922	Rio	Brazil	Paraguay
1923	Montevideo	Uruguay	Argentina
1924	Montevideo	Uruguay	Argentina
1925	Buenos Aires	Argentina	Brazil
1926	Santiago	Uruguay	Argentina
1927	Lima	Argentina	Paraguay
1929	Buenos Aires	Argentina	Uruguay
1937	Buenos Aires	Argentina	Paraguay
1939	Lima	Peru	Brazil
1942	Montevideo	Uruguay	Argentina
1947	Guayaquil	Argentina	Paraguay
1949	Rio	Brazil	Paraguay
1953	Lima	Paraguay	Brazil
1955	Santiago	Argentina	Chile
1957	Lima	Argentina	Brazil
1959	Buenos Aires	Argentina	Brazil
1963	La Paz	Bolivia	Paraguay
1967	Montevideo	Uruguay	Argentina

Chapter Twenty-two

South American Cup History

THE South American Cup, or Copa de Los Libertadores, was founded in 1960 to provide a South American team to play the winners of the European Cup, for the unofficial championship of the world. It was initially confined, like the European Cup, to champions of various countries – Brazil organised a new cup tournament to find one – but when, in the later 60s, it was enlarged to include two teams per country, Brazilian and Argentinian clubs objected and, on various occasions, withdrew. Thus, no Brazilian clubs competed in 1965, or 1969, a year in which Argentina were represented only by the South American Cup-holders and world champions, Estudiantes. The clubs now qualify in "mini-league" groups, in two stages, for a final played at home and away, with goal average irrelevant.

1960

Penarol 1, *Olimpia Paraguay* 0
Olimpia Paraguay 1, *Penarol* 1

1961

Penarol 1, *Palmeiras* 0 (*Sao Paulo*)
Palmeiras 1, *Penarol* 1

1962

Santos 2, *Penarol* 1
Penarol 3, *Santos* 2
Santos 3, *Penarol* 0

1963

Santos 3, *Boca Juniors* 2
Boca Juniors 1, *Santos* 2

1964

Nacional 0, *Independiente* 0
Independiente 1, *Nacional* 0

1965

Independiente 1, *Penarol* 0
Penarol 3, *Independiente* 1
Independiente 4, *Penarol* 1

1966

Penarol 2, *River Plate* 0
River Plate 3, *Penarol* 2
Penarol 4, *River Plate* 2

1967

Racing Club 0, *Nacional* 0
Nacional 0, *Racing Club* 0
Racing Club 2, *Nacional* 1

1968

Estudiantes 3, *Palmeiras* 1
Palmeiras 3, *Estudiantes* 1
Estudiantes 2, *Palmeiras* 0

1969

Nacional 0, *Estudiantes* 1
Estudiantes 2, *Nacional* 0

Chapter Twenty-three

Olympic Football

The Olympic Games football tournament, a knock-out affair, goes back to the London Olympics of 1908, and has been held at every subsequent Olympiad except Los Angeles, in 1932. Beyond doubt, its most brilliant and notable winners were the Uruguayan teams of 1924 and 1928, at a time when Uruguayan football was quite new to Europe. Indeed, it remained unknown to Britain for another twenty-five years. Even then, the thin, sometimes non-existent, line between amateurism and professionalism flawed the tournament, and in 1924 Britain withdrew over the question of "broken time" payments, not to return until 1936.

Though frequently interesting, this blemish has made the competition increasingly unsatisfactory, as the amateur footballer – at high level – became more and more a figure of the past. Several members of the alleged "student" team with which Italy won in Berlin, in 1936, went straight into the full national side. Indeed, the full-backs, Foni and Rava, were the World Cup Final pair two years later.

In the 1960 Olympic football tournament, no player who had taken part in the 1958 World Cup was allowed to be chosen, a rule which still exists, with dubious effect. On that occasion it led to the elimination of Russia (who had reached the 1958 Finals and could not field their full international team) and by Bulgaria, who could. Italy got round the problem, and still do, by deciding that, since their players could not *officially* be professional till 21, they must in the meantime be amateurs. Thus they were able to field a brilliant young side, almost every member of which has since been fully capped.

The 1908 tournament was won by a very powerful United Kingdom side, including the Rev. K. F. G. Hunt, of Wolves, and the brilliant Spurs and England inside-forward, Vivian Woodward. France entered two teams in a knock-out tournament, each of which was annihilated, but the Swedes, Dutch and, above all, the Danes, greatly impressed. Denmark, in fact, lost only by 2–0 to the United Kingdom in the Final, and had more of the play.

In 1912, at Stockholm, the United Kingdom again beat Denmark in the Final 4–2, but the Danes were reduced to ten men by injury.

In 1920, in Antwerp, Britain surprisingly went out 3–1 to Norway in the first round. The Belgians won the tournament, after the Czechs walked off the field in the Final, in protest against the sending off of one of their players. Thus, second position was awarded to the rising Spanish team, who had beaten Denmark.

The year 1924 saw the first triumph of Uruguay, bringing such brilliant forwards to Paris as Petrone and Scarone. A crowd of 60,000 watched Uruguay beat Switzerland in the Final. Four years later, in Amsterdam, Argentina entered for the first time, losing 2–1 to Uruguay in a replayed Final.

In 1936, a less powerful field, in Berlin, saw the victory of the Italians. Britain, with Bernard Joy at centre-half, beat China 2–0 then lost 4–5 to Poland. The Italians won the Final, 2–1, against Austria, coached by Jimmy Hogan.

The 1948 tournament, again held in London, was a fine one. The Swedish, Danish and Yugoslav teams were among the strongest of the day, while the British amateur side put up a very fine display. After beating the powerful Dutch team in a gruelling match at Highbury, they knocked out France 1–0 at Fulham, with a goal by Bob Hardisty; lost in the semi-final to the powerful Yugoslavs; and again – with honour – in the third match with Denmark.

The Swedes, who beat Yugoslavia 3–1 at Wembley in the Final, included all three famous Nordahl brothers, and had Nils Leidholm, Gunnar Gren and Garvis Carlsson in attack.

The year 1952 saw the entry into the lists of a still greater team – Puskas and his Hungarians. Britain were ingloriously knocked out 4–5 in the first match, by little Luxemburg. Russia competed, coming out of splendid isolation, and fought out a remarkable 5–5 draw with Yugoslavia, after being four behind, but lost the replay 3–1. In the Helsinki Final, Hungary beat the Slavs 2–0, but not without hard labour.

In 1956 it was Russia's turn. Britain, though knocked out in the eliminators, were invited to Australia to make up the complement, but, without their regular goalkeeper, were thrashed by Bulgaria. The

Russians (who had to replay to beat the Indonesians) plodded to an unsatisfying success, against the Yugoslavs. India were the surprise, taking fourth place.

In 1960, the Yugoslavs at last had their victory, in Rome, but it was a lucky one; they won their Naples semi-final against Italy on the toss of a coin. A fine Danish team, having knocked out Hungary, played wearily in the final and went down 3–1, even though the Slav forward, Galic, was sent off.

In 1964 Britain, after eliminating Iceland, were defeated by Greece, 5–3 on aggregate, thus failing to qualify for Tokyo. Hungary, with Bene superb, beat the Czechs 2–1 in a splendid final.

OLYMPIC FOOTBALL

The Mexican tournament, in 1968, was convincingly won by Hungary, even though the over-rigorous officiating of Diego De Leo, the referee, reduced the Final to farce, three Bulgarians and a Hungarian being sent off. By and large, the sea level teams adapted themselves very well to the high altitude; three of them, France, Bulgaria and Japan, in fact defeated Mexico. The Japanese, their attack superbly led by Kamamoto, were the revelation of the tournament.

OLYMPIC WINNERS

1908 London: United Kingdom, 2 Denmark 0

1912 Stockholm: United Kingdom 4, Denmark 2: 3rd, Holland

1920 Antwerp: Belgium 2, Czechoslovakia 0 (match abandoned) 2nd place awarded to Spain

1924 Paris: Uruguay 3, Switzerland 0: 3rd, Sweden

1928 Amsterdam: Uruguay 2, Argentina 1 (after 1–1 draw): 3rd, Italy

1936 Berlin: Italy 2, Austria 1: 3rd, Norway

1948 London: Sweden 3, Yugoslavia 1: 3rd Denmark

1952 Helsinki: Hungary 2, Yugoslavia 0: 3rd, Sweden

1956 Melbourne: Russia 1, Yugoslavia 0: 3rd, Bulgaria

1960 Rome: Yugoslavia 3, Denmark 1: 3rd, Hungary

1964 Tokyo: Hungary 2, Czechoslovakia 1: 3rd, E. Germany

1968 Mexico City: Hungary 4, Bulgaria 1: 3rd, Japan

Chapter Twenty-four

England and Great Britain against the Rest

October 26, 1938. *Arsenal Stadium*
England 3, *Rest of Europe* 0 (2–0)
England: Woodley (Chelsea); Sproston (Spurs), Hapgood (Arsenal); Willingham (Huddersfield Town), Cullis (Wolves), Copping (Arsenal); Matthews (Stoke), Hall (Spurs), Lawton (Everton), Goulden (West Ham), Boyes (Everton.)
Europe: Olvieri; Foni, Rava (Italy); Kupfer (Germany), Andreolo (Italy), Kitzinger (Germany); Aston (France), Braine (Belgium), Piola (Italy), Szengeller (Hungary), Brustad (Norway).
Scorers: Hall, Goulden, Lawton for England.

May 10, 1947. *Hampden Park, Glasgow*
Great Britain 6, *Rest of Europe* 1 (4–1)
Britain: Swift (England); Hardwick (England), Hughes (Wales); Macaulay (Scotland), Vernon (Ireland), Burgess (Wales); Matthews (England), Mannion (England), Lawton (England), Steel (Scotland), Liddell (Scotland).
Europe: Da Rui (France); Petersen (Denmark), Steffen (Switzerland); Carey (Ireland), Parola (Italy), Ludl (Czechoslovakia); Lambrecht (Belgium), Gren (Sweden), Nordahl (Sweden), Wilkes (Holland), Praest (Denmark).
Scorers: Mannion (2), Lawton (2), Steel, Parola (own goal) for Britain, Nordahl for Europe.

October 21, 1953. *Wembley*
England 4, *Rest of Europe* (*FIFA*) 4 (2–3)
England: Merrick (Birmingham); Ramsey (Spurs), Eckersley (Blackburn R.); Wright (Wolves), Ufton (Charlton Athletic), Dickinson (Portsmouth); Matthews (Blackpool), Mortensen (Blackpool), Lofthouse (Bolton Wanderers), Quixall (Sheffield Wednesday), Mullen (Wolves).
Fifa: Zeman (Austria) [Beara (Yugoslovia)], Navarro (Spain), Hanappi (Austria); Cjaicowski (Yugoslavia), Posipal (Germany), Ocwirk (Austria); Boniperti (Italy), Kubala (Spain), Nordahl (Sweden), Vukas, Zebec (Yugoslovia).
Scorers: Mullen (2), Mortensen, Ramsey (penalty) for England, Boniperti (2), Kubala (2) (1 penalty) for FIFA.

August 15, 1955. *Belfast*
Great Britain 1, *Rest of Europe* 4 (1–1)
Britain: Kelsey (Wales); Sillett, P. (England), MacDonald (Scotland); Blanchflower (Ireland), Charles (Wales), Peacock (Ireland); Matthews (England), Johnstone (Scotland), Bentley (England), McIlroy (Ireland), Liddell (Scotland).
Europe: Buffon (Italy); Gustavsson (Sweden), Van Brandt (Belgium); Ocwirk (Austria), Jonquet (France), Boskov (Yugoslavia); Soerensen, (Denmark), Vukas (Yugoslavia), Kopa (France), Travassos (Portugal), Vincent (France).
Scorers: Johnstone for Britain, Vincent, Vukas (3) for Europe.

October 23, 1963. *Wembley*. Centenary International
England 2, *Rest of the World* 1 (0–0)
England: Banks (Leicester City); Armfield (Blackpool), Wilson (Huddersfield Town); Milne (Liverpool), Norman (Spurs), Moore (West Ham United); Paine (Southampton), Greaves (Spurs), Smith, R. (Spurs), Eastham (Arsenal), Charlton (Manchester United).
Fifa: Yachin (Russia) [Soskic (Yugoslavia)]; Santos, D. (Brazil) [Eyzaguirre (Chile)]; Schnellinger (Germany); Pluskal, Popluhar (Czechoslovakia), Masopust (Czechoslovakia) [Baxter (Scotland)]; Kopa (France) [Seeler (Germany)], Law (Scotland), Di Stefano (Spain), Eusebio (Portugal) [Puskas (Spain)], Gento (Spain).
Scorers: Paine, Greaves for England, Law for FIFA.

FINAL LEAGUE TABLES

DIVISION I

	P	W	D	L	F	A	Pts
Everton	42	29	8	5	72	34	66
Leeds	42	21	15	6	84	49	57
Chelsea	42	21	13	8	70	50	55
Derby County	42	22	9	11	64	37	53
Liverpool	42	20	11	11	65	42	51
Coventry City	42	19	11	12	58	48	49
Newcastle U.	42	17	13	12	57	35	47
Manchester U.	42	14	17	11	66	61	45
Stoke City	42	15	15	12	56	52	45
Manchester C.	42	16	11	15	55	48	43
Tottenham ...	42	17	9	16	54	55	43
Arsenal	42	12	18	12	51	49	42
Wolves	42	12	16	14	55	57	40
Burnley	42	12	15	15	56	61	39
Nottm. Forest..	42	10	18	14	50	71	38
West Brom. A.	42	14	9	19	58	66	37
West Ham Utd.	42	12	12	18	51	60	36
Ipswich Town	42	10	11	21	40	63	31
Southampton .	42	6	17	19	46	67	29
Crystal Palace.	42	6	15	21	34	68	27
Sunderland ...	42	6	14	22	30	68	26
Sheffield Wed.	42	8	9	25	40	71	25

DIVISION II

	P	W	D	L	F	A	Pts
Huddersfield T.	42	24	12	6	68	37	60
Blackpool	42	20	13	9	56	45	53
Leicester City .	42	19	13	10	64	50	51
Middlesbrough	42	20	10	12	55	45	50
Swindon Town	42	17	16	9	51	47	50
Sheffield Utd. .	42	22	5	15	73	38	49
Cardiff City ..	42	17	13	11	59	40	47
Blackburn R...	42	20	7	15	54	40	47
Q.P.R.	42	17	11	14	66	57	45
Millwall	42	15	14	13	56	56	44
Norwich City .	42	16	11	15	49	46	43
Carlisle Utd. .	42	14	13	15	58	56	41
Hull City	42	15	11	16	72	70	41
Oxford Utd. ...	42	12	15	15	35	42	39
Bristol City....	42	13	13	16	54	50	39
Bolton Wan. ..	42	12	12	18	54	61	36
Portsmouth ..	42	13	9	20	66	80	35
Birmingham C.	42	11	11	20	51	78	33
Watford	42	9	13	20	44	57	31
Charlton Ath. .	42	7	17	18	35	76	31
Aston Villa ...	42	8	13	21	36	62	29
Preston N.E. ..	42	8	12	22	43	63	28

DIVISION III

	P	W	D	L	F	A	Pts
Orient	46	25	12	9	67	36	62
Luton Town ..	46	23	14	9	77	43	60
Bristol Rovers.	46	20	16	10	80	59	56
Fulham	46	20	15	11	81	55	55
Brighton H. A..	46	23	9	14	57	43	55
Mansfield T. ..	46	21	11	14	70	49	53
Barnsley	46	19	15	12	68	59	53
Reading	46	21	11	14	87	77	53
Rochdale	46	18	10	18	69	60	46
Bradford City..	46	17	12	17	57	50	46
Doncaster R...	46	17	12	17	52	54	46
Walsall	46	17	12	17	54	67	46
Torquay U.....	46	14	17	15	62	59	45
Rotherham U. .	46	15	14	17	62	54	44
Shrewsbury T.	46	13	18	15	62	63	44
Tranmere R. ..	46	14	16	16	56	72	44
Plymouth Arg.	46	16	11	19	56	64	43
Halifax Town..	46	14	15	17	47	63	43
Bury	46	15	11	20	74	80	41
Gillingham ...	46	13	13	20	52	64	39
Bournemouth .	46	12	15	19	48	71	39
Southport	46	14	10	22	48	66	38
Barrow	46	8	14	24	46	81	30
Stockport C. ..	46	6	11	29	27	71	23

DIVISION IV

	P	W	D	L	F	A	Pts
Chesterfield ..	46	27	10	9	77	32	64
Wrexham	46	26	9	11	84	49	61
Swansea City .	46	21	18	7	66	45	60
Port Vale	46	20	19	7	61	33	59
Brentford	46	20	16	10	58	39	56
Aldershot	46	20	13	13	78	65	53
Notts. County .	46	22	8	16	73	62	52
Lincoln City ..	46	17	16	13	66	52	50
Peterbro' Utd.	46	17	14	15	77	69	48
Colchester U. .	46	17	14	15	64	63	48
Chester.......	46	21	6	19	58	66	48
Scunthorpe U.	46	18	10	18	67	65	46
York City	46	16	14	16	55	62	46
Northampton..	46	16	12	18	64	55	44
Crewe Alex....	46	16	12	18	51	51	44
Grimsby Town	46	14	15	17	54	58	43
Southend Utd.	46	15	10	21	59	85	40
Exeter City	46	14	11	21	57	59	39
Oldham.......	46	13	13	20	60	65	39
Workington ..	46	12	14	20	46	64	38
Newport C.....	46	13	11	22	53	74	37
Darlington ...	46	13	10	23	53	73	36
Hartlepool	46	10	10	26	42	82	30
Bradford	46	6	11	29	41	96	23

SCOTTISH

DIVISION I

	P	W	D	L	F	A	Pts
Celtic.........	34	27	3	4	96	33	57
Rangers	34	19	7	8	67	40	45
Hibernian	34	19	6	9	65	40	44
Hearts	34	13	12	9	50	36	38
Dundee United	34	16	6	12	62	64	38
Dundee.......	34	15	6	13	49	44	36
Kilmarnock ...	34	13	10	11	62	57	36
Aberdeen.....	34	14	7	13	55	45	35
Dunfermline ..	34	15	5	14	45	45	35
Morton	34	13	9	12	52	52	35
Motherwell....	34	11	10	13	49	51	32
Airdrie	34	12	8	14	59	64	32
St. Johnstone.	34	11	9	14	50	62	31
Ayr United ...	34	12	6	16	37	52	30
St. Mirren	34	8	9	17	39	54	25
Clyde	34	9	7	18	34	56	25
Raith Rovers ..	34	5	11	18	32	67	21
Partick Thistle	34	5	7	22	41	82	17

DIVISION II

	P	W	D	L	F	A	Pts
Falkirk	36	25	6	5	94	34	56
Cowdenbeath .	36	24	7	5	81	35	55
Q. of the South	36	22	6	8	72	49	50
Stirling Albion	36	18	10	8	70	40	46
Arbroath	36	20	4	12	76	39	44
Alloa Athletic.	36	19	5	12	62	41	43
Dumbarton ...	36	17	6	13	55	46	40
Montrose	36	15	7	14	57	55	37
Berwick.......	36	15	5	16	67	55	35
East Fife	36	15	6	17	59	63	36
Albion Rovers.	36	14	5	17	53	64	33
East Stirling...	36	14	5	17	58	75	33
Clydebank	36	10	10	16	47	65	30
Brechin City ..	36	11	6	19	47	74	28
Queen's Park .	36	10	6	20	38	62	26
Stenhousemuir	36	10	6	20	47	89	26
Stranraer	36	9	7	20	56	75	25
Forfar Athletic	36	11	1	24	55	83	23
Hamilton	36	8	4	24	42	92	20

EUROPEAN CUP

PRELIMINARY ROUND. – Bulgaria League champions v. Austria Vienna.

FIRST ROUND. – Spartak Moscow v. F.C. Basle; Fenerbance v. Carl Zeiss Jena; Standard Liège v. Rosenborg; Sporting Lisbon v. Floriana (Malta); Slovan Bratislava v. B.K. 1903 Copenhagen; E.P.A. (Cyprus) v. Borussia Munchengladback; Feyenoord v. Rumanian League champions; Everton v. Keflavik (Iceland); Nendori Tirana (Albania) v. Ajax Amsterdam; Kamraterna Goteborg v. Legia Warsaw; Bulgaria champions or Austria Vienna v. Atletico Madrid; Ujpest Dozsa v. Red Star Belgrade; Cagliari v. St. Etienne; Celtic v. K.P.V. Kokkola (Finland); Panathinaikos Athens v. La Jeunesse d'Esch; Glentoran v. Waterford.

CUP WINNERS' CUP

PRELIMINARY ROUND. – First match. – Atvidabergs (Sweden) v. FC. Partizani (Albania): Second match. – Bohemians (Republic of Ireland) v. Gottwaldov (Czechoslovakia).

FIRST ROUND – Aris Salonica v. Chelsea; Iba Akureyi (Iceland) v. Zurich; Cardiff City v. Pol Larnaca; West Germany Representatives v. Royal F. C. Brugeois; Hibernian (Malta) v. Real Madrid; F. C. Vorwaerts (East Germany) v. Bologna; Russia Representatives v. Rumania Representatives; Bulgaria Representatives v. Valkeakosken Haka (Finland); Aberdeen v. Honved, Budapest; Stromsgodset (Norway) v. Nantes; Aalborg (Denmark) v. Poland Representatives; Goeztepe Izmir v. U.S. Luxembourg; Benfica v. Olympia Ljubljana; Wacker Innsbruck v. Atvidabergs or Partizani, Albania; Manchester City v. Linfield; Bohemians or Gottwaldov v. Eindhoven.

First round ties to be played on September 16 and 30.

HOW TO PLAY WINNING TENNIS 7/-

Rod Laver

Here is the complete book on tennis instruction, for the beginner and the seasoned player alike. Rod Laver describes how each shot is played, and weaves his own story through the book—all the way from the time when he played his first game, aged eight, in the balmy north Queensland town of Rockhampton, to the gruelling Grand Slam victories in all the major tennis tournaments in the world.
Learn how to deliver: the hoodoo shot, the smash, the lob as well as the chop, spin, dinks, stop volleys and drop shots.

A MAYFLOWER HANDBOOK
ILLUSTRATED

HAVING BEEN A SOLDIER
6/-

Lieutenant-Colonel Colin Mitchell

The controversial autobiography everyone has been waiting for!

A career which began in the uniform of the Home Guard at the age of fifteen reached its climax in the bomb-and-bullet-scored alleys of seething Crater a quarter of a century later.
A few months after one of the most successful military operations since the end of World War Two—the reoccupation of Crater in Aden which had fallen into the hands of Arab terrorists—the First Battalion of the Argyll and Sutherland Highlanders, led by Lieutenant-Colonel Colin Mitchell, was disbanded. There was a public outcry and Mitchell became a national hero.
Now Colin Mitchell has written the story of his army life in full. It reveals him as a man of strong principles and ambitions, peerless courage and intellectual accomplishment.
Above all it is an honest self-appraisal—the enthralling story of an officer who led the Jocks into action from Italy in 1945 to Palestine, Korea, Cyprus, Borneo and Aden. The reader's involvement is total.

"An impressive and disconcerting story"
The Listener

"One vivid chapter after another"
Sunday Times

ALL QUIET ON THE WESTERN FRONT 5/-

Erich Maria Remarque

Erich Maria Remarque belongs to a family of French extraction that emigrated into Germany at the time of the French Revolution and settled in the Rhineland. In 1914 at the age of 18 he went straight from school into the army and was sent to the Western Front. During the course of the war his mother died and all his friends were killed. At the end of the war he found himself alone in the world. He wrote his book, without taking previous thought, about his own and his friends' experiences in the war. It arose out of the consideration that so many men of his generation, who were yet still young, nevertheless lived a friendless, embittered, resigned life without knowing why.

All Quiet on the Western Front
sets out to describe three things: the war, the fate of a generation and true comradeship.

FOUR MILLION FOOTSTEPS 5/-

Bruce Tulloh

This is Bruce Tulloh's own story—the story of his amazing battle with a continent—the marathon run across the United States, all the way until he came jogging into New York in June 1969 after a long-distance epic of endurance lasting 2,876 miles and 65 days.
Here Bruce tells the whole story of how he set up the new world record—the months of solid training, the long-distance journey through towns and cities and countryside, the hardships and the triumph.
And he answers the tantalising questions:
What was the value in all this effort?
Why did he do it?
How did he last out?